MEDIEVAL MARRIAGE

Medieval Marriage

Symbolism and Society

D. L. d'AVRAY

OXFORD

UNIVERSITY PRESS

OXFORD
UNIVERSITY PRESS

Great Clarendon Street, Oxford OX2 6DP

Oxford University Press is a department of the University of Oxford.
It furthers the University's objective of excellence in research, scholarship,
and education by publishing worldwide in

Oxford   New York

Auckland Bangkok Buenos Aires Cape Town Chennai
Dar es Salaam Delhi Hong Kong Istanbul Karachi Kolkata
Kuala Lumpur Madrid Melbourne Mexico City Mumbai Nairobi
São Paulo Shanghai Taipei Tokyo Toronto

Oxford is a registered trade mark of Oxford University Press
in the UK and in certain other countries

Published in the United States
by Oxford University Press Inc., New York

First published 2005

British Library Cataloguing in Publication Data

Data available

Library of Congress Cataloging in Publication Data

Data available

ISBN 0–19–820821–9

1 3 5 7 9 10 8 6 4 2

Typeset by John Waś, Oxford
Printed in Great Britain
on acid-free paper by
Biddles Ltd., King's Lynn, Norfolk

UXORI CARISSIMAE

Acknowledgements

The following are among those who have earned my gratitude. The Archivio Segreto Vaticano Prefect and staff, Louis-Jacques Bataillon, Nicole Bériou, John Blair, Paul Brand, Paul Brennan, Martin Brett, the British Academy for a Research Readership to work on this project and for microfilm, Christopher Brooke, Jim Brundage, Peter Clarke, Stephen Davies, Trevor Dean, Sally Dixon-Smith, Gero Dolezalek, Charles Donahue, Jenifer Dye, Barbara Harvey, Julian Hoppit, Olwen Hufton, Robert Lerner, my Love and Marriage Special Subject classes, in which some brilliant students have taught me a lot, David Luscombe, Patrick Nold, the officials of the Penitenzieria Apostolica for permission to use their archive, Catherine Rider, Kirsi Salonen, Ludwig Schmugge, Rüdiger Schnell, Julia Walworth (both as *uxor carissima* and as Merton Fellow Librarian), John Waś, Chris Wickham, and Anders Winroth.

D.L.D'A.

December 2004

Contents

Note on Transcriptions   xii

Abbreviations   xii

Introduction   1

1. Mass Communication   19
   (a) Preliminaries   19
   (b) The Early Middle Ages   20
   (c) Mass Communication in the Age of the Friars   37
   (d) The Message about Marriage   58

2. Indissolubility   74
   (a) From the Roman Empire to the Carolingian Empire   74
   (b) c.800–c.1200   82
   (c) The Age of Innocent III   99
   (d) Indissolubility in Practice   108

3. Bigamy   131
   (a) Bigamy and Becoming a Priest   131
   (b) The Marriage Ceremony   141
   (c) Clerics in Minor Orders   157

4. Consummation   168
   (a) Consummation and the Medieval Church's Idea of
       Sex   168
   (b) The Dissolution of the Unconsummated Marriage:
       From Hincmar to Alexander III   176
   (c) The Social Effects of Alexander III's Decision   180
   (d) Long-Term Developments   188

Conclusion   200

DOCUMENTS

Chapter 1
1. 1. Marriage symbolism in the Bavarian Homiliary   208
1. 2. Homily on the text 'Nuptiae factae sunt' (John 2: 1) in
      the Bavarian Homiliary   211
1. 3. Marriage symbolism in the Beaune Homiliary   214
1. 4. Nonconformist variants in Hugues de Saint-Cher   217
1. 5. Nonconformist variants in Jean de la Rochelle   217
1. 6. Nonconformist variants in Pierre de Saint-Benoît   218
1. 7. Nonconformist variants in Gérard de Mailly   218
1. 8. Nonconformist variants in Guibert de Tournai   219
1. 9. A sermon on marriage by Jean Halgrin d'Abbeville   219
1. 10. A sermon on marriage by Konrad Holtnicker   223
1. 11. A sermon on marriage by Servasanto da Faenza   226
1. 12. A sermon on marriage by Aldobrandino da Toscanella
       (Schneyer no. 404)   232
1. 13. A sermon on marriage by Aldobrandino da Toscanella
       (Schneyer no. 48)   238

Chapter 2
2. 1. Proof in 'forbidden degrees' cases: Hostiensis attacks
      laxity   242
2. 2. Proof in 'forbidden degrees' cases: the rigorism of
      Hostiensis   246

Chapter 3
3. 1. Johannes de Deo, *De dispensationibus*, on bigamy   249
3. 2. Innocent IV (Sinibaldo dei Fieschi) on Decretals of
      Gregory IX, X. 5. 9. 1: bigamy and loss of clerical
      status   250
3. 3. Innocent IV (Sinibaldo dei Fieschi) on Decretals of
      Gregory IX, X. 1. 21. 5: the symbolic understanding
      of bigamy   251
3. 4. Bull of Pope Alexander IV to the prelates of France   253
3. 5. Bull of Pope Gregory X to King Philip III of France   254
3. 6. Bull of Pope John XXII to King Philip V of France   254
3. 7. Bull of Pope John XXII to King Charles IV of France   255
3. 8. Questions on marriage in MS London, BL Royal
      11. A. XIV   256

Contents

3. 9. Passage on bigamy in the *Pupilla oculi* of Johannes de Burgo   262

3. 10. A 'bigamy' case from the gaol delivery rolls (6 June 1320)   265

3. 11. The case of Five-Wife Francis, from the archive of the Apostolic Penitentiary   267

3. 12. The case of Petrus Martorel, from the archive of the Apostolic Penitentiary   269

Chapter 4

4. 1. Consummation and its consequences in a canon-law commentary: a link to late medieval papal dissolutions of *ratum non consummatum* marriages   270

4. 2. Ricardus de Mediavilla: marriage and entry into a religious order before consummation   273

4. 3. Ricardus de Mediavilla on the marriage of Mary and Joseph   275

4. 4. A consummation case in the papal registers (John XXII)   276

4. 5. Consummation and indissolubility in the *Oculus sacerdotis* of William of Pagula   282

4. 6. Johannes de Burgo on the marriage of Mary and Joseph   283

4. 7. A case from the archive of the Apostolic Penitentiary: Constance of Padilla   285

4. 8. Another non-consummation case from the archive of the Apostolic Penitentiary   286

Bibliography   288

Index of Manuscripts   310

General Index   312

Note on Transcriptions

My transcription conventions are explained in detail in previous books (*The Preaching of the Friars: Sermons Diffused from Paris before 1300* (Oxford, 1985), xi; *Death and the Prince: Memorial Preaching before 1350* (Oxford, 1994), 7–8; *Medieval Marriage Sermons: Mass Communication in a Culture without Print* (Oxford, 2001), 43). An asterisk before a word indicates the presence of an error too trivial to deserve specifying. In the present volume I normalize 'd' to 't' in 'sicut', and 't' to 'd' in 'sed'; and 'n' to 'm' in words like 'comprobatum', 'imprecatur', 'immo', and 'tempore'. The problem arises because the letter is often swallowed up in an abbreviation and there is no standard classical or medieval orthography. I have normalized in these cases even where, as occasionally happens, the other form is written in full: e.g. *sicud* or *inprecatur*.

Abbreviations

BAV	Bibliotheca Apostolica Vaticana
BL	British Library
BN	Bibliothèque Nationale de France
Migne, *PL*	J.-P. Migne, *Patrologia Latina*
MS/*ms.*	Manuscript
X.	Decretals of Gregory IX (X. 2. 20. 47 = book 2, titulus 20, chapter 47 of the Decretals)

Introduction

How the modern intellectual sees medieval marriage

For centuries in Europe, formal marriage was a private contract between landed families, designed to insure that property remained within a particular lineage. In the upper classes, families essentially married other families, forging political alliances and social obligations among relatives and kin. It was during the Reformation, with the emergence of the early Protestant idea of 'companionate marriage,' that the emotional bond between husband and wife came to be seen as an end in itself. As the social historian Lawrence Stone noted, this was a marked departure from the Catholic idea of chastity, which considered earthly marriage a more or less unfortunate necessity meant to accommodate human weakness; 'It is better to marry than to burn,' St. Paul had said, but he made it sound like a close call. So when the Puritans wrote of husbands and wives as mutually respectful and affectionate partners they were moving towards a new understanding of marriage as a kind of spiritual friendship.[1]

It is too easy for scholars to forget what the non-specialist intelligentsia thinks about their field, and the *New Yorker* is a good place to find out. Such a caricature in such a high-quality magazine reminds one of the time lag between research and general educated awareness. Not everything is wrong. Marriages were a mechanism for linking families and family fortunes in the Middle Ages[2] as in subsequent ages up until and including the nineteenth century. Still, most of the rest is wrong. It was not always the family that had power. In some periods and regions lords controlled marriages of those who held land from them.[3] Free choice by individuals was an

---

[1] A. Haslett, 'A Critic at Large', *New Yorker* (31 May 2004), 76–80 at 76.

[2] See e.g. R. Bartlett, *England under the Norman and Angevin Kings 1075–1225* (Oxford, 2000), 549–51; A. Molho, *Marriage Alliance in Late Medieval Florence* (Cambridge, Mass., etc., 1994), *passim*.

[3] See e.g. Bartlett, *England under the Norman and Angevin Kings 1075–1225*, 547–9; R. Boutruche, *Seigneurie et féodalité: l'apogée (XIᵉ–XIIIᵉ siècles)* (Paris, 1970), 229–30; G. Duby, *Medieval Marriage: Two Models from Twelfth-Century France*, trans. E. Forster (Baltimore etc., 1978), 97–8 (there was no published French edition); J. B. Freed, *Noble Bondsmen: Ministerial Marriages in the Archdiocese of Salzburg, 1100–1343* (Ithaca, NY, etc., 1995); S. L. Waugh, *The Lordship of England:*

important factor in the later Middle Ages, with backing from the Church.[4] Marital affection was a social reality[5] (as common sense would suggest), and it was strongly encouraged by influential texts.[6] None of this is at all new, though clearly a reminder is not super-fluous. This book aims to bring out a different dimension of the social history of medieval marriage, correcting from another angle the idea that it was driven mainly by the landed ambitions of fami-lies. Social and legal practice was infused with marriage symbolism. Symbolism gave meaning to practice and affected it, not least by helping to create a combination of monogamy and indissolubility probably unique in the history of literate societies.

Marriage symbolism in religions

The theme, then, is marriage symbolism's effect on social practice. Symbolism was crucial in the theory of marriage first, and even before the Middle Ages began. Central to the meaning of marriage, symbolism eventually became part of marriage law and changed behaviour through law, the decades around 1200 marking a turning point.

I shall start with a rapid glance at the comparative religious his-tory of the topic. Then I shall briefly indicate the kind of work that has already been done on medieval Western marriage sym-bolism. That will be balanced by the most rapid *tour d'horizon* of recent work on the social history of medieval marriage, since I aim to bring it together with the history of marriage symbol-ism.

Like food, love and marriage are the basis of strong religious symbolism. In the study of comparative religion there is a keyword for it: 'sacred marriage' or *hieros gamos*.[7] An important variety is parallelism between the marriage of two gods and the marriage of

---

Royal Wardships and Marriages in English Society and Politics 1217–1327 (Princeton etc., 1988).

[4] See below, pp. 124–9.

[5] F. M. Powicke, *King Henry III and the Lord Edward: The Community of the Realm in the Thirteenth Century* (2 vols.; Oxford, 1947), i. 157 n. 1.

[6] See below, pp. 69, 129; also A. MacFarlane, *Marriage and Love in England, 1300–1840: Modes of Reproduction* (Oxford, 1986), 182–3, to show that a non-medievalist can get it right. Scholars have known all this for a long time: see e.g. H. A. Kelly, *Love and Marriage in the Age of Chaucer* (Ithaca, NY, 1975).

[7] K. W. Bolle, 'Hieros Gamos', in M. Eliade (ed.), *The Encyclopedia of Religion*, vi (New York etc., 1987), 317–21.

ordinary men and women. It can be found in ancient Mesopotamia,[8] and it has been studied quite recently as living religion in a south Indian temple. In the second case we know a lot about it. The marriage ritual between the two gods is represented by statues in the temple. If the gods do not consummate the marriage regularly, the female becomes a dangerous force and a general threat.[9]

This temple ritual belongs to one of the main types of marriage symbolism in the world history of religions: the union of a male and a female god, mirroring the union of man and woman in marriage. There are a number of such marriages or sexual relationships in the Hindu pantheon: notably Rama and Sita, Vishnu and Laksmi, Siva and Parvati, Krishna and Radha.[10] With the last two pairs at least the female partner can be presented as human or quasi-human, as we shall see. However, the motif of the marriage of two unambiguously divine beings has in itself only a loose relation to the argument of this book. Analogy between the marriage of two gods and marriage of human to human is not the same as analogy between human union with God and marriage of human to human.

Non-Christian cases of this second sort of symbolism are harder to find. Some promising possibilities turn out on inspection to be very different from the symbolism with which we are concerned. There is a scholarly literature on what looks at first like the same kind of thing in ancient Mesopotamia: a mythical human hero, represented by a king, who wins the love of a goddess. The story has even been connected with the Song of Songs, subject of St Bernard's famous sermons, which would bring it even closer to our theme.[11] However, the stories or putative rituals may have had another meaning—say the celebration of the king's prowess in love as in everything else—and the whole subject is too fraught with controversy to be drawn into our argument.[12]

---

[8] G. Leick, *Sex and Eroticism in Mesopotamian Literature* (London etc., 1994), ch. 12.

[9] C. J. Fuller, 'The Divine Couple's Relationship in a South Indian Temple: Minaksi and Sundareśvara at Madurai', *History of Religions*, 19 (1980), 321–48.

[10] For an interesting analysis of different types of relationship see F. A. Marglin, 'Types of Sexual Union and their Implicit Meanings', in J. S. Hawley and D. M. Wulff (eds.), *The Divine Consort: Radha and the Goddesses of India* (Berkeley, 1982), 298–315.

[11] S. N. Kramer, *The Sacred Marriage Rite: Aspects of Faith, Myth, and Ritual in Ancient Sumer* (Bloomington, Ind., etc., 1969), esp. ch. 5.

[12] Leick, *Sex and Eroticism in Mesopotamian Literature*, ch. 11, on '"Words of Seduction": Courtly Love Poetry', argues against 'the neo-primitive "fertility rite"

Introduction

The ancient Greek stories in which gods and humans mate do
not on the whole look like symbols of non-sexual love betweeen
the divine and the human.[13] A possible exception is the marriage
of the god Dionysus to the 'Basilinna', the wife of the Archon
Basileus ('ruler-king', literally, the member of the panel of rulers at
Athens most especially responsible for sacred affairs). In this case
a marriage ritual may stand for the union of human and divine.[14]
In Hindu India at least marriage can represent the union of
human and divine. There is even a specific name for this kind
of passionate devotion to a god: 'Bhakti'. The love of Radha and
the god Krishna is particularly relevant. Radha would stand for
the human side. There is a problem: Radha herself has a 'claim
to divinity'.[15] Still, at least sometimes the idea of Radha seems
to gather up in it the idea of a devout person's union with the
divine. As one historian of religion has commented: 'As the feminine
worldward side of the masculine–feminine Radha–Krishna she is
the tie between deity and all souls, since she is one with the *gopis*
[milkmaids or cowgirls, co-lovers with Radha of Krishna] and thus
with those whom the *gopis* represent, namely all humankind.'[16] The

notion that the construct of Sacred Marriage implies' (129; on the king's prowess,
109–10). If she is right, one cannot use without reservation the conclusions of
Kramer. For further references on the debate about 'sacred marriage' in ancient
Mesopotamia see A. Kuhrt, 'Babylon', in E. J. Bakker, I. J. F. De Jong, and H.
van Wees (eds.), *Brill's Companion to Herodotus* (Leiden etc., 2002), 475–96 at 492
n. 37. In the foregoing (not only on Mesopotamia) I have been helped by Kuhrt's
clear distinction between two kinds of sacred marriage: 'one is the marriage of two
gods, represented by their statues; the other a ceremony during which the goddess
of erotic love, Inanna/Ishtar (represented by a priestess?), and the king in the guise
of her mythical lover, Dumuzi, had intercourse'. It is the second kind which is the
subject of dispute.

[13] On the whole subject see A. Avagianou, *Sacred Marriage in the Rituals of Greek
Religion* (Europäische Hochschulschriften, ser. 15, 54; Berne etc., 1991).
[14] 'We could explain this strange and unique ritual in Greek religion as the legitimized σύμμειξις of divine and human via marriage' (Avagianou, *Sacred Marriage
in the Rituals of Greek Religion*, 200).
[15] Cf. Hawley, 'A Vernacular Portrait: Radha in the *Sur Sagar*', in Hawley and
Wulff, *The Divine Consort*, 42–56 at 56.
[16] N. Hein, 'Comments: Radha and Erotic Community', in Hawley and Wulff,
The Divine Consort, 116–24 at 120, commenting on Hawley's paper. Max Weber
has some good remarks on the love of Krishna, and his parallel with Pietism is helpful: 'Was der alten klassischen Bhagavata-Religiosität zunächst noch fehlte oder
jedenfalls—wenn es in ihr schon existierte—von der vornehmen Literatenschicht
nicht rezipiert wurde, war die brünstige Heilandsminne der späteren Krischna-
Religiosität. Ähnlich wie etwa die lutherische Orthodoxie die psychologisch gleich-
artige pietistische Christus-Liebe (Zinzendorf) als unklassische Neuerung ablehnte'

role of these *gopi*s accentuates the human side.

There are other problems. The love of Krishna and Radha (not to mention the other *gopi*s) is sensual in the extreme—too much so for a divine message? Perhaps not. Look at the following passage from Mechtild of Magdeburg, a thirteenth-century female mystic in the spiritual tradition of Bernard of Clairvaux.[17]

> 'Stay, Lady Soul.'
> 'What do you bid me, Lord?'
> 'Take off your clothes.'
> 'Lord, what will happen to me then?'
> 'Lady Soul, you are so utterly formed to my nature
> That not the slightest thing can be between you and me.'
> . . .
> Then a blessed stillness
> That both desire comes over them.
> He surrenders himself to her,
> And she surrenders herself to him.
> What happens to her then—she knows—
> And that is fine with me.
> But this cannot last long.
> When two lovers meet secretly,
> They must often part from one another inseparably.[18]

At least since St Bernard a surface sensuality has been part of the discourse of Christian mysticism.

It might be objected that the love affair of Krishna and Radha is extra-marital. Then again, she is one of many lovers of Krishna. Does his polygyny nullify the analogy with the medieval West?

(*Die Wirschaftsethik der Weltreligionen: Hinduismus und Buddhismus* (1916–20), repr. in *Gesammelte Aufsätze zur Religionssoziologie*, ii. *Hinduismus und Buddhismus* (Tübingen, 1988), 198). Weber also mentions the 'brünstige kultische Minne zu persönlichen Nothelfern, welche als Fleischwerdung großer erbarmender Götter galten' (ibid. 202) of the popular 'orgiastic' religion rejected by Brahman intellectuals.

[17] There is a large literature on Mechtild. See e.g. A. Hollywood, *The Soul as Virgin Wife: Mechtild of Magdeburg, Marguerite Porete, and Meister Eckhart* (Studies in Spirituality and Theology, 1; Notre Dame etc., 1995), 1–2, and chs. 3 and 7; H. E. Keller, *My Secret is Mine: Studies on Religion and Eros in the German Middle Ages* (Leuven, 2000), 107–10, with further bibliographical references. Mechtild's *Flowering Light of Godhead*, from which the passage quoted comes, was probably composed in or near the third quarter of the thirteenth century (ibid. 108).

[18] Mechtild of Magdeburg, *The Flowing Light of the Godhead*, trans. and intro. F. Tobin (New York etc., 1998), 62; cf. B. Newman, *From Virile Woman to Woman-Christ: Studies in Medieval Religion and Literature* (Philadelphia, 1995), 150.

These objections fade on closer inspection even if they do not entirely disappear. The passion of Krishna and Radha may be extra-
marital or even adulterous in some versions, but one line strongly
represented in Hindu theology is that they were in reality married.[19]
The other passionate cowgirls can be understood as different forms
of Radha herself.[20] Anyway, one must not be too literal-minded
with this sort of religious language. The Western image of God
as the bridegroom of enormous numbers of soul-brides could be
understood as polygamy, but this would be clumsy. Medieval Western marriage sermons sometimes built their symbolism around an
Old Testament story: Esther's triumphant displacement of Vashti
as wife of the Persian king.[21] In context this is clearly not an endorsement of divorce. With any symbol the analogy breaks down
somewhere, and the trick is to know when to stop pressing the
comparison (a principle very relevant to gendered imagery).

The union of the the male god Siva with his wife Parvati can also
symbolize the union of human and divine. As a standard reference
work puts it, 'Their marriage is a model of male dominance with
Parvati docilely serving her husband, though this is also a model
of the way a mortal should serve the god.'[22] It is true that Parvati
is also a goddess, but a goddess close to humanity. Thus humans,
women at least, can assimilate their religious experience to Parvati's loving devotion to her husband. 'Parvati, the daughter of the
mountain Himalaya, is an ambiguous semi-divinity . . . Although
poetic metaphors accorded her divine status, she is the quintessence
of the lowly mortal woman worshipping the lofty male god.'[23]

It is true that this description cannot be simply applied to Christian marriage symbolism. There may indeed be a tendency in Christian mysticism towards gender specialization—human woman as

---

[19] Hawley, 'A Vernacular Portrait', 53; D. M. Wulff, 'Radha: Consort and Conqueror of Krishna', in J. S. Hawley and D. M. Wulff (eds.), *Devi: Goddesses of India*
(Berkeley etc., 1996), 109–34 at 133 n. 30.

[20] S. Goswami, 'Radha: The Play; and Perfection of *Rasa*', in Hawley and Wulff,
The Divine Consort, 72–88 at 81: 'the many *gopis* are but manifestations of the body
of Radha'. (This represents the point of view of a modern devotee.).

[21] D. L. d'Avray, *Medieval Marriage Sermons: Mass Communication in a Culture
without Print* (Oxford, 2001), index, s.v. 'Assuerus'.

[22] Article on 'Pārvatī', in J. Bowker (ed.), *The Oxford Dictionary of World Religion*
(Oxford, 1997), 737.

[23] W. D. O'Flaherty, 'The Shifting Balance of Power in the Marriage of Siva and
Parvati', in Hawley and Wulff, *The Divine Consort*, 129–43 at 135. (The comment
relates to a specific set of sources.).

bride, notably[24]—but either sex can take the female role in the symbolic register, as is evident from Bernard of Clairvaux's sermons on the Song of Songs, where the monks are the bride.[25] Nevertheless, the following simple and powerful idea is shared by Christianity and Hinduism: that union between humans and the divine is like a marriage.

Hinduism also shares with Catholic Christianity a strong doctrine of the indissolubility of marriage. The correlation with the similar approach to marriage symbolism is significant and should be borne in mind by readers following the argument of this book. There is no sociological entailment here, no necessity, but the ideal type of a relation between the social rule of unbreakable marriage and highly developed marriage symbolism makes sense.

In Christian spirituality it is the 'soul–God=bride–bridegroom' imagery which comes closest to Hinduism. Another variant of marriage symbolism, the image of the Church as bride of Christ, is further away from Hindu analogues. This is because of its collective or corporate community character, the idea of 'the Church' and even the human race as in some sense a unity, capable of being collectively infected by original sin and collectively redeemed by Christ. So far as one can generalize, Hinduism does indeed emphasize the character of the whole universe as a collective whole, but much less so the human race, or the collective identity of a society within it. In Hinduism there is the self (*atman*), there are status groups (castes) through which the self passes on the journey of reincarnations towards final release, and there is the All, but the idea of a society as an organic body with a collective role in the drama of History is alien. The medieval Church saw itself as just such a society, whose relation to God could be called a marriage.

To this symbolism the closest parallel is in ancient Israel, where the Jewish people are themselves, collectively, the bride of God. It has been pointed out that according to Deuteronomy 24: 1–4 'a divorced woman who has remarried can never be reconciled with her former husband. Because God is anxious to bring back Israel as his beloved spouse, he must never have divorced her.'[26]

[24] Keller argues that 'the roles of bride and bridegroom become fixed with regard to gender', suggesting that there was a 'gradual narrowing of the role of the bride to (primarily religious) women on the one hand' and a 'successive masculinization of the divine bridegroom on the other hand' (*My Secret is Mine*, 8).
[25] See, however, below, n. 36.
[26] C. Stuhlmueller, ch. 22 on 'Deutero-Isaiah', in *The Jerome Biblical Commen-*

The Song of Songs may or may not be about the love of God
and his people, but in any case this religious interpretation of these
songs is the 'oldest interpretation, in both Christian and Jewish
tradition'.[27] Hebrew ideas about God's marriage to or love of his
chosen people are not only a parallel to but also a crucial source for
Christian marriage symbolism. The reading of the Song of Songs
adopted by the third-century Christian theologian Origen owed
much to Jewish tradition, and Origen is a decisive influence on the
whole subsequent tradition of Christian marriage symbolism (on
the 'Church as bride of Christ' as well as on the 'Soul as bride of
Christ' themes).[28]

Thus the Bernardine tradition of bridal mysticism has parallels in
Hinduism, and the image of Christ's marriage to the Church draws
on Old Testament Judaism. What may be harder to find in other
religious traditions is the sober rationality with which medieval
scholastic writers and canon lawyers integrated marriage symbolism into their systematic and coherent religious frameworks. The
Supplement to the *Summa theologica* of Thomas Aquinas succinctly
integrates the different levels into a coherent structure. Marriage
is formed by signs of consent, usually verbal, not necessarily in a
religious ceremony. These external signs represent a further level:
the binding of man and woman. If the couple are Christians, this
signifies and also brings about a spiritual union. This is the 'sacrament' in the more technical theological sense, worked out by the
time of Aquinas, of a sign of grace that brought about what it represented. Beyond that, there is another layer still. The spiritual
union of man and woman represents, but does not bring about, the
union of Christ and the Church.[29] This dense symbolism from the

tary, ed. R. E. Brown, J. A. Fitzmyer, and R. E. Murphy, i (London, 1968), 366–86
at 377, on Isa. 50, with reference to Isa. 54: 6–8 and 61: 4–5.

[27] R. E. Murphy, ch. 30, 'Canticle of Canticles', ibid. 506–10 at 507.

[28] 'For Christian readings of the Song of Songs, especially as popularized by
Origen, this assumption [that the "Old Testament" is reflected in the "New Testament"] automatically suggested the scope of prior meanings; that is, the poems read
by Jews as the love between God and Israel naturally find their "true" sense as the
love between Christ and the Church' (E. A. Matter, *The Voice of my Beloved: The
Song of Songs in Western Medieval Christianity* (Philadelphia, c.1990), 51).

[29] *Supplementum*, 42. 1, 'Ad quartum' and 'Ad quintum', 42. 2, 'Respondeo',
and 42–3, 'Respondeo' and 'Ad secundum': see *Sancti Thomae Aquinatis . . . opera
omnia, iussu . . . Leonis XIII P.M. edita*, xii (Rome, 1906), 81–2. For the *Supplement*,
put together after the death of Aquinas on the basis of his commentary on the
Sentences of Peter the Lombard, see J. Weisheipl, *Friar Thomas d'Aquino: His Life,*

Introduction   9

world of rational speculative scholastic theology is a far cry from
the emotional outpourings of the Bernardine tradition.
The parallelism between symbolic and literal can take one by
surprise. The *Summa theologica Supplement* raises this objection:
Sacraments have efficacy from the passion of Christ.[30] But a person
does not become conformed to the passion through marriage, which
is accompanied by delight.[31] The answer is that marriage is conformed to the passion not through pain but through the love which
Christ showed the Church by suffering to unite her to himself as
his bride.[32]

State of research

Aquinas is one writer among many powerful minds who created a
tradition of rationally analysing marriage symbolism. This tradition has been well studied, above all in a little-known but (for our

Thought and Works (Oxford, 1974), 362. In his view the compilation 'was, no doubt,
the work of Thomas's earliest editors working under the direction of Reginald of
Piperno'. These passages are taken from Aquinas's commentary on the *Sentences*
of Peter Lombard at dist. 26, qu. 2, arts. 1–3 (see the concordance of *Supplement*
and commentary in *Sancti Thomae Aquinatis . . . opera omnia*, vol. xii, p. xxv, and
*S. Tommaso d'Aquino: Commento alle Sentenze di Pietro Lombardo e testo integrale
di Pietro Lombardo. Libro quarto. Distinzioni 24–42. L'Ordine, il Matrimonio*, trans.
and ed. by 'Redazione delle Edizioni Studio Domenicano' (Bologna, 2001), 196–
206. For Aquinas on marriage as a symbol of the union of Christ and the Church
see R. J. Lawrence, *The Sacramental Interpretation of Ephesians 5: 32 from Peter
Lombard to the Council of Trent* (The Catholic University of America Studies in
Sacred Theology, Second Series, 145; Washington, 1963), 67–72. The whole of this
work is relevant for the theological background it provides to the social history
which is the main focus of this book. For another scholastic theologian's marriage
symbolism see Pierre de Tarantaise, commenting on Peter Lombard, *Sentences*,
4, dist. 26, qu. 3: 'Coniunctio exterius apparens per signa aliqua est sacramentum
tantum: coniunctio animorum interior sacramentum et res: effectus gratiae quae ibi
confertur, res non sacramentum: res inquantum primo significata, res vero significata
secundario coniunctio Christi et Ecclesiae' (*Innocentii Quinti Pontificis Maximi . . .
In IV. librum Sententiarum commentaria*, iv (Toulouse, 1651), 287).

[30] Cf. *Summa theologica*, 3. 62. 5 for the theology presupposed.

[31] *Supplementum*, 42. 1, obj. 3.

[32] Ibid., 'ad tertium' (objection and response are taken from Aquinas's commentary on the *Sentences* of Peter Lombard: see *Commento alle Sentenze di Pietro
Lombardo . . .*, trans. and ed. 'Redazione delle Edizioni Studio Domenicano', dist. 26,
qu. 2, a. 1, pp. 196, 198). Cf. Pierre de Tarantaise: 'Ad 4 de Passione. Resp. Christus
est passus afflictionem carnis ex charitate spirituali quam habebat ad Ecclesiam.
Quoad primum, matrimonium non significabat passum, sed quoad secundum' (*Innocentii Quinti . . . commentaria*, iv. 287). For the similar thinking in Ricardus de
Mediavilla see T. Rincón, *El matrimonio, misterio y signo: siglos IX al XIII* (Pamplona, 1971), 319–20.

topic) fundamental book, Rincón's *El matrimonio, mistero y signo*.[33] A main function of the present volume is to demonstrate the relevance of Rincón's findings to legal practice and social history. Rincón prefers the word 'Significacíon' to symbolism. He wants to emphasize that the connection between human marriage and Christ's union with the Church goes far beyond subjective 'spiritual sense'-type parallelism.[34] Though 'symbolism' will be used loosely to cover both kinds of meaning here, the distinction is worth bearing in mind: it reminds us that in theological texts marriage is linked to the union of Christ and the Church by a tight web of close logical reasoning. The same is true of canon-law commentaries, which Rincón studies alongside the strictly theological texts.

It is rash but important to generalize about world history: if the generalization is misleading, someone will point it out, but otherwise no one will know either way. I would suggest, then, that there is nothing in the world history of religions much like the developments Rincón describes. If Rincón has made an exemplary analysis of the theological and canon legal texts, marriage symbolism in literary and mystical texts has been the object of studies distinguished by literary sensitivity[35] and a preoccupation with the paradoxes of a gendered symbolism which both men and women could in principle use for their relation to God.[36] The bridal mysticism of Bernard of

---

[33] See n. 32 ad fin. I have not found this book in the British Library, Bodleian Library, or Cambridge University Library. There are copies in the Birmingham University Library, the Bibliothèque Nationale de France, in several German libraries, and of course in Spain. More recently, see T. Rincón-Pérez [the same author, I take it], *El matrimonio cristiano: sacramento de la Creación y de la Redención. Claves de un debate teológico-canónico* (Estudios Canónicos, 1; Pamplona, 1997), chs. 1–3. For marriage symbolism in connection with sacramentality see also Lawrence, *The Sacramental Interpretation of Ephesians 5: 32*, which should in turn be bracketed with S. P. Heaney, *The Development of the Sacramentality of Marriage from Anselm of Laon to Thomas Aquinas* (The Catholic University of America Studies in Sacred Theology, Second Series, 134; Washington, 1963).

[34] 'Creemos fundamental distinguir entre simbolismo o paralelismo simbólico y significación come tal. Lo primero, en términos gramaticales, equivale a una simple yuxtaposición del sentido místico y el sentido literal. Mientras que en la en la significación come tal existe un subordinación o dependencia profunda del signo en relación con la cosa significada' (Rincón, *El matrimonio, misterio y signo*, 270 n. 48).

[35] Thus N. Cartlidge, *Medieval Marriage: Literary Approaches, 1100–1300* (Cambridge etc., 1997), develops a persuasive argument that despite the exaltation of virginity over marriage in some of the texts he studies they still make marriage symbolize a 'true drama of feeling' and stand as 'a paradigm of emotional commitment'; 'the *sponsa Christi*-motif is much more than a rhetorical metaphor for spiritual union: it is used to evoke a psychological process' (159).

[36] e.g. Newman, *From Virile Woman to WomanChrist*: 'If monks wished to play

Clairvaux has also been thoroughly examined.[37] Perhaps a majority of the writers on all these topics have a background in literature
or religious studies (defined to include theology and canon law).
That is no defect: it has doubtless sharpened their perception of
religious subtleties and nuances. The present study has a somewhat
different and complementary aspect because it comes from a historian formed in an age when the social history of marriage was the
hottest of historiographical topics. Before the 1970s not much of the history of marriage was written from history departments. Excellent work was done by church
lawyers: catholics like Esmein[38] and Dauvillier,[39] but also Protestants like Sohm[40] and Friedberg,[41] engaged in a controversy about
the introduction of civil marriage into Prussia, whose resonances
seem faint today. (The contribution of German Protestants to medi-

the starring role in this love story, they had to adopt a feminine persona—as many
did—to pursue a heterosexual love affair with their God. It might be assumed that
when women began to compose their own mystical texts, they could more easily
have followed the path already laid out by men. But . . . some women forged a . . .
less stereotypical way that allowed them a wider emotional range', adopting the
discourse of *fin amour* which 'could encourage women writers to experiment with
gender roles just as monks did within the Song of Songs tradition' (138). (C. W.
Bynum is almost certainly an inspiration behind this kind of analysis: see e.g. her
' "And Woman his Humanity": Female Imagery in the Religious Writings of the
Later Middle Ages', in *Fragmentation and Redemption: Essays on Gender and the
Human Body in Medieval Religion* (New York, 1991), 151–79 at 176–9.) Or again
Keller, *My Secret is Mine*: 'Bernard of Clairvaux's efforts to re-establish the bridal
metaphor in the monastic life of both sexes mark precisely the beginning of the
definitive exclusion of monks from the concept' (35); 'Precisely the history of the
motif of the bride of God itself, both its gender-specific fixing of the role of the bride
of God and its attempts to force open such narrowings make clear that the human
world of the sexes and its historically-determined mechanisms push their way into
spiritual eroticism by the back door' (263). Keller's bibliography is a good guide
to recent literature on marriage/bridal symbolism. For an exemplary analysis of
gender in marriage symbolism see A. Volfing, *John the Evangelist and Medieval
German Writing: Imitating the Inimitable* (Oxford, 2001), 138–60.

   [37] J. Leclercq, *Le Mariage vu par les moines au XIIᵉ siècle* (Paris, 1983), ch. 7, is an
especially important study. See too his *Monks and Love in Twelfth-Century France:
Psycho-Historical Essays* (Oxford, 1979).
   [38] A. Esmein, *Le Mariage en droit canonique* ed. R. Génestal and J. Dauvillier, 2nd
edn. (2 vols.; Paris, 1929–35).
   [39] J. Dauvillier, *Le Mariage dans le droit classique de l'église depuis le Décret de
Gratien (1140) jusqu'à la mort de Clément V (1314)* (Paris, 1933).
   [40] R. Sohm, *Das Recht der Eheschließung aus dem deutschen und kanonischen Recht
geschichtlich entwickelt: Eine Antwort auf die Frage nach dem Verhältniss der kirchlichen Trauung zur Civilehe* (Weimar, 1875).
   [41] E. Friedberg, *Verlobung und Trauung, zugleich als Kritik von Sohm: Das Recht
der Eheschließung* (Leipzig, 1876).

eval canon-law history would be an interesting topic.) The great Gabriel Le Bras[42] defies classification: he was somewhere between law, theology and sociology: a great historian by nature but not by formal training. Joyce, a theologian, wrote a fine synthesis,[43] and the German school of Catholic medieval historical theology, notably Müller,[44] Brandl,[45] and Ziegler,[46] also made contributions which have lost little of their value today. Still, they were not writing primarily for a community of historians and, perhaps more important, they wrote at a time when social history had not attained the dominance it enjoyed in the last decades of the twentieth century.

Non-historians have continued to contribute even in those decades. Goody, who raised with great intelligence even if he did not solve the historical problem of the 'forbidden degrees',[47] came from anthropology; Gaudemet,[48] Weigand,[49] Helmholz,[50] and Donahue[51] were again from law; Jean Leclercq,[52] though clearly a historian in his attitudes and approach and with his finger on the

[42] See especially his article on 'Mariage. III. La doctrine du mariage chez les théologiens et canonistes depuis l'an mille', in *Dictionnaire de théologie catholique* (15 vols. excluding indexes; Paris, 1899–1950), ix (1926), 2123–223.

[43] G. H. Joyce, *Christian Marriage: An Historical and Doctrinal Study* (London etc., 1933).

[44] M. Müller, *Die Lehre des hl. Augustinus von der Paradiesesehe und ihre Auswirkung in der Sexualethik des 12. und 13. Jahrhunderts bis Thomas von Aquin: Eine moralgeschichtliche Untersuchung* (Studien zur Geschichte der katholischen Moraltheologie, 1; Regensburg, 1954).

[45] L. Brandl, *Die Sexualethik des heiligen Albertus Magnus* (Regensburg, 1955).

[46] J. G. Ziegler, *Die Ehelehre der Pönitentialsummen von 1200–1350: Eine Untersuchung zur Geschichte der Moral- und Pastoraltheologie* (Regensburg, 1956).

[47] J. Goody, *The Development of the Family and Marriage in Europe* (Cambridge, 1983). This has received a fair amount of criticism though there has been a general appreciation too of the way the book has opened up the subject. For my own critiques see 'Peter Damian, Consanguinity and Church Property', in L. Smith and B. Ward (eds.), *Intellectual Life in the Middle Ages: Essays Presented to Margaret Gibson* (London, 1992), 71–80 at 76–7, and 'Lay Kinship Solidarity and Papal Law', in P. Stafford, J. L. Nelson, and J. Martindale (eds.), *Law, Laity and Solidarities: Essays in Honour of Susan Reynolds* (Manchester, 2001), 188–99.

[48] J. Gaudemet, *Le Mariage en Occident: les mœurs et le droit* (Paris, 1987), to name only one of his contributions.

[49] R. Weigand, *Liebe und Ehe im Mittelalter* (Bibliotheca Eruditorum, 7; Goldbach, 1993).

[50] R. H. Helmholz, *Marriage Litigation in Medieval England* (Cambridge, 1974).

[51] C. Donahue, Jr., 'The Monastic Judge: Social Practice, Formal Rule, and the Medieval Canon Law of Incest', in P. Landau, with M. Petzolt (eds.), *De iure canonico medii aevi: Festschrift für Rudolf Weigand* (Studia Gratiana, 27; Rome, 1996), 49–69; (with Norma Adams), *Select Cases from the Ecclesiastical Courts of the Province of Canterbury, c. 1200–1301* (Selden Society, 95; London, 1981).

[52] See above, n. 37.

pulse of his time's historiography, was writing from a monastery
rather than a history department. Hubertus Lutterbach comes from
theology.[53] Students of vernacular literature like Schumacher[54] and
Burch[55] have done thought-provoking work. Cartlidge's study,
mentioned above under the rubric of symbolic marriage, talks
about perceptions of real human marriage as well. Perhaps the
most important recent historian of medieval marriage and sexu-
ality, Rüdiger Schnell holds his chair in a department of Germanistik, though he has mastered the bibliography in all medieval
fields on these topics to an astonishing degree.[56] Only the historian
Brundage, on whom below, can come near him as a guide to this
practically endless sea of secondary scholarship.[57]

Brundage is one of a substantial number of historians employed
in history departments who have added to this tower of scholarship
recently, holding their own with colleagues from other sectors of
academe. They are not necessarily more impartial—indeed, in this
field historians tend to make their ideological affiliations as evident
as historians of monasticism used to before the First World War.
Moreover, some have continued to use the same types of evidence as
scholars from other disciplines: Payer's *The Bridling of Desire*[58] is
in the tradition of historical theology and Brundage's *opus magnum*
is based above all on penitentials and canon-law commentaries so
far as primary sources are concerned, although, as just noted, he
is remarkably successful in getting a grip on the enormous mass

[53] H. Lutterbach, *Sexualität im Mittelalter: Eine Kulturstudie anhand von Bußbüchern des 6. bis 12. Jahrhunderts* (Cologne etc., 1999). Although the style is detached,
there are signs that he is himself fighting a battle within the world of Catholic
theology.

[54] M. Schumacher, *Die Auffassung der Ehe in den Dichtungen Wolframs von Eschenbach* (Germanische Bibliothek, 2. Abt., Untersuchungen und Texte, 3. Reihe,
Untersuchungen und Einzeldarstellungen; Heidelberg, 1967).

[55] S. L. Burch, 'A Study of Some Aspects of Marriage as Presented in Selected
Octosyllabic French Romances of the 12th and 13th Centuries' (unpublished Ph.D.
thesis, University College London, 1982).

[56] See above all R. Schnell, *Sexualität und Emotionalität in der vormodernen Ehe*
(Cologne etc., 2002).

[57] The *opus magnum* is J. A. Brundage, *Law, Sex, and Christian Society in Medieval
Europe* (Chicago etc., 1987). Brundage's publications on medieval marriage and sex
are too numerous to list here, but special mention must be made of his 'The Merry
Widow's Serious Sister: Remarriage in Classical Canon Law', in R. R. Edward and
V. Ziegler (eds.), *Matrons and Marginal Women in Medieval Society* (Woodbridge,
1995), 33–48, which is directly relevant to Chapter 3.

[58] P. J. Payer, *The Bridling of Desire: Views of Sex in the Later Middle Ages*
(Toronto etc., 1993).

of secondary scholarship about medieval marriage in three or four academic languages. Conversely, the analyses of actual court records by Weigand and Helmholz take us firmly beyond the world of 'book texts', if one may so put it. By and large, however, the professional historians have helped to root the subject more firmly in social history—converging with some of the lawyers in this respect.

Christopher Brooke was very early in the field, including sections on marriage in a general survey,[59] a historian somewhat ahead of his time. In a series of subsequent publications, he brought to bear on the history of marriage a knowledge of central medieval social history that owed much to his involvement with the Oxford Medieval Texts editorial project.[60] The present study takes up a question that he put more clearly than any of the other historians who made up the wave of writing on medieval marriage: namely, what was different about the Christian marriage of the Middle Ages? The Christianization of marriage in the twelfth century has been a central thread. Georges Duby used his remarkable architectonic literary gifts to develop an elegant and still broadly valid schema: an aristocratic model, favouring legitimate marriage but allowing easy divorce, and tolerating the marriage of close relatives, opposed to a clerical model emphasizing indissoluble monogamous marriage—exogamy.[61] The endogamy/exogamy part of the thesis requires further commentary out of place in this argument, but the notion that the two models grew closer together in the early thirteenth century is broadly right. The lay nobility came to accept indissolubility, and the Church reduced the circle of forbidden degrees of relationship, allowing closer relatives to marry. All this needs to be put in the context of a rationality perhaps not fully understood by Duby. It should also be noted that he was able to draw on some crucial discoveries made earlier by John Baldwin about the thinking behind the changes in marriage law effected by the Fourth Lateran Council in 1215.[62] In general Duby's work tends to leave the impression that the medieval Church took a nega-

[59] C. N. L. Brooke, *Europe in the Central Middle Ages 962–1154* (London, 1964; 3rd edn. Harlow, 2000): in first edition 245–7 and index s.v. 'Marriage'.

[60] His results were drawn together in *The Medieval Idea of Marriage* (Oxford, 1989), still probably the best way into the subject.

[61] Duby, *Medieval Marriage*; id., *Le Chevalier, la femme et le prêtre: le mariage dans la France féodale* (Paris, 1981).

[62] J. W. Baldwin, *Masters, Princes, and Merchants: The Social Views of Peter the Chanter and his Circle* (2 vols.; Princeton, 1970), i. 332–7, ii. 222–7 (classic pages).

tive view of marriage, a view corrected in friendly fashion by Jean Leclercq (and as we shall see quite contrary to copious evidence of which he was unaware). Dyan Elliott's study of 'Spiritual Marriage' (understood not in the usual sense of symbolic marriage but as marriage without sex) used saints' lives alongside theological and canon-law texts, and tried to reconstruct actual practices.[63] David Herlihy traced the change from an early medieval society where the rich and powerful had more than their fair share of women to a society where the husband-and-wife couple was the norm at all levels of society: the slimness of his *Medieval Households* is in inverse proportion to its achievement.[64] Michael Borgolte has set the medieval Church's efforts to enforce monogamy and indissolubility in a comparative framework by showing how its sphere of influence was ringed with an outer sphere of polygyny, among the Muslims and Jews outside the borders of Latin Europe but also among Christians who came in contact with them or who maintained a polygynous subculture.[65]

The general trend of most recent work has been to emphasize the growing though always limited influence of the Church's models on the social history of marriage (indeed, Borgolte emphasizes it too).[66] This is particularly but not exclusively true of the work by scholars in history departments.[67] This study will draw heavily on their results, especially the findings of scholars who have studied ecclesiastical court evidence.

The argument

The specific aim of the present study is to draw together the social history of marriage and the history of marriage symbolism. I am not quite the first historian to have seen the connection, for

[63] D. Elliott, *Spiritual Marriage: Sexual Abstinence in Medieval Wedlock* (Princeton, 1993). Her use of 'spiritual marriage' to mean marriage without sex is perhaps confusing since the phrase often means marriage as metaphor, but there is a pedigree behind her terminology: see P. de Labriolle, 'Le "mariage spirituel" dans l'antiquité chrétienne', *Revue historique*, 137 (1921), 204–25.

[64] D. Herlihy, *Medieval Households* (Cambridge, Mass., etc., 1985).

[65] M. Borgolte, 'Kulturelle Einheit und religiöse Differenz: Zur Verbreitung der Polygynie im mittelalterlichen Europa', *Zeitschrift für historische Forschung*, 31 (2004), 1–36; for aristocratic polygyny in regions or cultures within Christian Europe see ibid. 7 n. 23 from p. 6 (referring to the work of Jan Rüdiger).

[66] Ibid. 11, 13.

[67] As an example see the able survey by D. O. Hughes, 'Il matrimonio nell'Italia medievale', in M. De Giorgio and C. Klapisch-Zuber (eds.), *Storia del matrimonio* (Rome etc., 1996), 5–61, notably 18–24, 44–9.

I think that Marcel Pacaut caught the essence of it in a few percep-
tive lines.[68] Most of the actual links of causation need to be traced.
This enterprise is related to the skilful elucidations by canon-law
historians of marriage symbolism's influence on the idea of the
episcopal office,[69] to Dye's important study of Marian marriage

[68] In a brief article that anticipates more than any other study the general approach
of this book, Pacaut develops with respect to the twelfth century an argument that
works even better for the mid-thirteenth century and after. To do justice to his
priority a full quotation is required:

le renvoi du couple Christ-Église . . . tend aussi à exposer que le Christ et l'Église
— et de même le Christ et l'âme — sont uns comme le sont l'époux et l'épouse
dans leur union charnelle, ainsi que le suggère Pierre Lombard, ce qui se rapporte
à une image claire et simple selon laquelle l'union des corps est d'autant plus
parfaite qu'elle repose sur l'amour et ce qui revient à rapprocher un modèle (pour
l'âme) et une réalité difficile à saisir (pour l'Église) d'un autre modèle facilement
concevable, presque "visualisé" et non utopique, car il existait certainement. C'est
là aussi le sens profond de la métaphore reprise dans les sermons sur le *Cantique
des Cantiques*, qui ne peuvent exclure l'appel à la réalité charnelle, et dont on peut
tirer parfois, à l'inverse, qu'il serait souhaitable que les époux soient unis comme
le Christ l'est avec son Église.

Ces propos ressortissent en fait à une méditation mystique et sont en même
temps le reflet de la pastorale diffusée par le clergé. Celle-ci insiste sur la valeur
de l'amour conjugal et sur sa nécessité pour accomplir le mariage par le moyen de
l'union des corps. Elle souligne que le consentement, qui fait que l'union charnelle
n'est pas honteuse, oriente les vies vers l'amour. Elle atteste donc aussi de ce qu'un
effort s'accomplit alors afin que la réussite amoureuse, physique et sentimentale,
soit facilitée par l'engagement consensuel reconnu, à l'époque où le droit cherche,
sur une autre voie, à normaliser cet engagement, sans lequel la prédication et
la réflexion spirituelle ne reposeraient, dans leur élaboration, sur aucun support
solide. ('Sur quelques données du droit matrimonial dans la seconde moitié du
XIIe siècle', in *Histoire et société: mélanges offerts à Georges Duby. Textes réunis
par les médiévistes de l'Université de Provence* (2 vols.; Aix-en-Provence, 1992), i.
31–41 at 40)

Keller, *My Secret is Mine*, especially chapter 2, also explores the interplay between symbolism and social practice. Her findings are very different (without being necessarily incompatible), because she concentrates on social practices which
are 'Firmly rooted in the tradition of Germanic Law' (p. 69)—*Muntehe* etc.—
rather than the social structure created in the high and late Middle Ages by canon
law. I. Persson, *Ehe und Zeichen: Studien zu Eheschließung und Ehepraxis anhand
der frühmittelhochdeutschen religiösen Lehrdichtungen 'Vom Rechte', 'Hochzeit' und
'Schopf von dem lône'* (Göppinger Arbeiten zur Germanistik, 617; Göppingen, 1995),
takes a close look at the relation between the details of marriage in poetic allegory and
legal notions of marriage: see notably pp. 127–8. I am in sympathy with the approach
but the contrast she draws between the Germanic and the canon-law attitudes to
consummation may be overstated: see below, ch. 4 n. 16.

[69] S. Kuttner, 'Pope Lucius III and the Bigamous Archbishop of Palermo' (1961),
repr. in id., *The History of Ideas and Doctrines of Canon Law in the Middle Ages*
(London, 1980), no. VII; R. L. Benson, *The Bishop Elect: A Study in Medieval
Ecclesiastical Office* (Princeton, 1968), 122–9, 136–49; J. Gaudemet, 'Le symbolisme
du mariage entre l'évêque et son église et ses consequences juridiques' (1985), repr.

symbolism,[70] and to Gabriella Zarri's remarkable account of marriage symbolism in rituals and iconography.[71] It is nevertheless a quite distinct line of enquiry.

There will be a lot of thick description of the symbolic forms of thought underlying marriage law and practice, but the book has preoccupations which are rather played down in anthropology *à la* Clifford Geertz (which sees the study of society as more like interpreting a poem than causal analysis): force (not necessarily in a negative sense) and timing. In a nutshell, I shall try to establish how, when, and why marriage symbolism became a force in the lay world. Stated baldly, the line of interpretation goes like this. Marriage is a powerful symbol of the union of the human and the divine. Most relationships are superficial compared with marriage. Marriage is one of the strongest experiences in many people's lives. Comparison with marriage is a way of conveying the strength of the bond between God and humanity. Marriage has many dimensions which can be explored to bring out by analogy aspects of union with God. A symbol or metaphor is capable of generating new ideas about the relationship it describes, whether that relationship is real or imaginary. It can also affect social policy and structures.[72] Marriage is a 'generative' metaphor, vivid, full of unexpected possibilities, potentially a powerful influence on thought and action. (Not all metaphors are like this. Many have limited use and quickly become desiccated, like the 'man is a wolf' formula beloved of philosophers who discuss metaphor.) Other powerful generative metaphors are the meal as a symbol of community, the body as a symbol of the state, or the 'conduit' metaphor for communication.[73]

in id., *Droit de l'Église et vie sociale au Moyen Âge* (Northampton, 1989), no. IX, 110–23.

[70] J. M. Dye, 'The Virgin as *Sponsa c.*1100–*c.*1400' (unpublished Ph.D. dissertation, University College London, 2001).

[71] G. Zarri, *Recinti: donne, clausura e matrimonio nella prima età moderna* ([Bologna], 2000), ch. 4. It deals (to quote a summary earlier in the same book) especially with the 'pratica medievale di matrimoni simbolici, che aveva lo scopo, tra l'altro, di confermare la sacralità del matrimonio cristiano, in assenza di una ritualità religiosa pubblica nel matrimonio della coppia celebrato prevalentemente tra le mura domestiche' (26). I share Zarri's preoccupation with the connections between symbolism and social practices.

[72] D. A. Schön, ''Generative Metaphor: A Perspective on Problem-Setting in Social Policy', in A. Ortony (ed.), *Metaphor and Thought* (Cambridge, 1979), 254–83.

[73] M. J. Reddy, 'The Conduit Metaphor: A Case of Frame Conflict in our Language about Language', in Ortony (ed.), *Metaphor and Thought*, 284–324.

It will be argued that marriage symbolism had a quite limited causal impact for much of the Middle Ages: up until the long century around the year 1200. Therefore the explanations advanced in this book will often take the form of elucidating 'neutralizing causes', forces that neutralize a causal process which might otherwise be expected. I shall attempt to explain what prevented marriage symbolism for so long from becoming a force in the lay world. From the thirteenth century on it was indeed a force and changed social patterns.

I

Mass Communication

(a) Preliminaries

The bulk of this book deals with the effect of marriage symbolism outside the texts that transmitted it. Much of the discussion is about the changes it brought about through law in social practice, but a natural starting point is its power over the minds of the laity through the cumulative force of mass communication. The argument of the present chapter makes the assumption that the cumulative repetition of much the same message by a powerful mass medium does have an effect on the thoughts of the people at the receiving end. It is an assumption. Some feel that the mass media do not really change people's thinking at all. They may be right with regard to short-term propaganda. Brief intense political campaigns or revivalist preaching may well have a transitory impact and no lasting effect on attitudes. Can the same be true of ideas repeated over years and decades? Ideas propagated over a long period of time by modern newspapers (for instance) surely leave some mark on the minds of readers, as a dripping tap leaves a stain in a sink. As with modern newspapers, there is little hard empirical evidence at the reception end. Could one establish with absolute certainty the effect of newspapers on a single reader? Paradoxically, one can be more confident about aggregate effects.[1] Ideas repeated to great masses of people over many decades will have impinged in some way on the minds of a significant portion of the audience: this much is taken for granted. The whole argument of this chapter is vulnerable to extreme scepticism on this point, but such scepticism flies in the face of common sense. The question then becomes one of timing and scale: when did marriage symbolism become such a regular part of preaching that laypeople who went to sermons could hardly escape it? It will be answered as follows:

[1] D. L. d'Avray, *Medieval Marriage Sermons: Mass Communication in a Culture without Print* (Oxford, 2001), 14.

- Marriage symbolism was not preached to a mass public in the early Middle Ages. The influential collections containing marriage symbolism were not intended for popular preaching, the many surviving sermons intended for popular preaching contain relatively little marriage symbolism, and the impact of marriage symbolism would have been limited by extra-textual factors (late development of the parish system, incapacity of many priests to use Latin models effectively).
- Preaching was a system of mass communication in the age of the friars. The large number of surviving manuscripts of model sermons represents a tiny proportion of the number that once existed, and each model sermon could be preached again and again.
- Marriage symbolism is highly developed in late medieval preaching and rested securely on a literal-sense idea of marriage as good and holy. The symbolism of marriage and the praise of ordinary human marriage were complementary and are found together in the sermons that transmitted marriage symbolism to the masses.

The middle section on preaching as mass communication and the long discussion of the loss rate of preaching manuscripts and of how so many could have been produced in the first place is the key to the argument that in the age of the Franciscans and Dominicans marriage symbolism was propagated so insistently and repeatedly to so many people that it must have been a social force. Some of the people could have ignored it all of the time and all of the people surely ignored it much of the time, but all of the people could not have ignored it all of the time.

(b) The Early Middle Ages

Bernard of Clairvaux and Haymo of Auxerre

Marriage symbolism in preaching is associated with the sermons on the Song of Songs by Bernard of Clairvaux, but in fact it can be found long before, though in a more sober idiom. A ninth-century homily by Haymo of Auxerre[2] has, at least embryonically, the main features of the genre of sermons on the second Sunday

---

[2] On Haymo/Haimo see B. Gansweidt, 'Haimo. 1. Haimo v. Auxerre', in *Lexikon des Mittelalters*, iv (Munich etc., 1989), 1863; on the homily see D. L. d'Avray, 'Sym-

after Epiphany (mostly sermons on the text *Nuptiae factae sunt,* John 2: 1) that would be the principal vehicle for marriage preaching in future centuries. Marriage is good. Christ's presence at a wedding refutes heretics who condemn marriage. (He mentions Tatian and Marcion: later preachers would have the Cathars in mind.) Genesis proves that God created man male and female, and said that for the love of her husband a woman should leave father and mother and be one flesh with her husband. In Matthew Christ told the apostles that a husband must not leave his wife. Teachings of St Paul take their turn: husband and wife must pay the marriage 'debt' (make love at the other's request). Husbands should love their wives as Christ loved his Church. In fact Haymo makes a good florilegium of biblical texts which are positive about marriage—ordinary human marriage. Then he goes on to the marriage of Christ and the Church, again presented through scriptural authorities. This combination of literal and spiritual (i.e. symbolic) marriage within the same framework is characteristic of the later 'Marriage feast of Cana' genre of sermons on the second Sunday after Epiphany. (From here on this genre will also be called the *Nuptiae factae sunt* genre, the Latin for the first words of the reading 'There was a marriage . . .'.) The question remains, did this kind of marriage symbolism get through to the laity via popular preaching in the early Middle Ages? It is a hard question to answer. That will be apparent from the oscillations in the presentation of the data below. On balance, however, and in the current state of the evidence, it looks as though marriage symbolism in sermons could not have had a major impact on the laity before the thirteenth century.

The debate about early medieval popular preaching

It is much disputed whether popular preaching happened at all in this period (defined roughly as from the late sixth to the late twelfth century). A relatively recent article argues for a minimalist position: hardly any preaching.[3] That rather extreme position seems hard to maintain in the light of work by Thomas Amos, who seems to have shown that there was a good deal of popu-

bolism and Medieval Religious Thought', in P. Linehan and J. L. Nelson (eds.), *The Medieval World* (London etc., 2003), 267–78 at 268–9.

[3] R. E. McLaughlin, 'The Word Eclipsed: Preaching in the Early Middle Ages', *Traditio*, 46 (1991), 77–122.

lar preaching. (He concentrates on the Carolingian period, but
casts an eye back to earlier preaching.) His doctoral thesis on early
medieval preaching unfortunately remains unpublished,[4] but some
of the findings have appeared in print as articles. He has identified 'over nine hundred sermons written or adapted by Carolingian authors as sources of popular preaching in the period
750–950'.[5] One collection has been properly edited in a modern
edition: I shall refer to this by the name of its editor, Mercier.[6]
Three more are in Migne's *Patrologia Latina* and easy to consult. Other popular Carolingian homiliaries have been studied in
articles by three specialists whose work has changed our understanding of homiliaries: Barré, Bouhot, and Étaix.[7] Yet another
article argues that the homilies on the Gospels of Gregory the
Great were widely used for popular preaching in the early Middle
Ages.[8]

Marriage symbolism in early medieval popular preaching: a significant absence

This is not sufficient to show that marriage symbolism reached the
people via the pulpit. We still need to ask how regularly marriage
symbolism appeared in these sermons, and how many ordinary
priests actually used the sermons Amos has studied. Even assuming that a non-trivial number of priests had reasonable Latin and
a homiliary of the right level for their needs, a problem to which
we must return, how much about marriage and marriage symbolism would it contain? My provisional verdict is that there was
relatively little preaching about marriage symbolism in the Carolingian period. This is based mainly on a search for sermons on
the Gospel reading of the marriage feast of Cana, which would

---

[4] 'The Origin and Nature of the Carolingian Sermon' (unpublished Ph.D. dissertation, Michigan State University, 1983). I have used this important thesis extensively: it led me to most of those sermons/homiliaries discussed below which Amos
does not discuss in print.

[5] T. L. Amos, 'Preaching and the Sermon in the Carolingian World', in T. L.
Amos, E. A. Green, and B. M. Kienzle (eds.), *De ore Domini: Preacher and Word in
the Middle Ages* (Kalamazoo, 1989), 41–60 at 47.

[6] *XIV homélies du IXe siècle de l'Italie du Nord*, ed. P. Mercier (Sources chrétiennes, 161; Paris, 1970).

[7] Amos, 'Preaching and the Sermon in the Carolingian World', 57 n. 31, for
bibliography.

[8] P. A. DeLeeuw, 'Gregory the Great's "Homilies on the Gospels" in the Early
Middle Ages', *Studi medievali*, 3rd ser., 26 (1985), 855–69.

be a powerful vehicle for the popularization of marriage symbolism from the thirteenth century on. In the last three medieval
centuries sermons on this reading or 'pericope' would combine
a real appreciation of marriage as a human institution with well-
developed symbolism. Arguably, it was this complementarity of
literal and symbolic levels that gave the symbolism its force. It is
conceivable that early medieval marriage symbolism was expressed
through some other preaching genre—say sermons on a different
pericope—but it is unlikely. I have probably missed a few marriage
feast of Cana sermons, but perhaps not a significant number of
those that survive.⁹ There are few early medieval sermons on the
marriage feast of Cana pericope, but when one looks at them one
by one it becomes clear that most contain little marriage symbolism, or were probably not intended primarily for popular preaching.

Caesarius of Arles (d. 542) wrote two sermons on this pericope.¹⁰
Moreover, he was an influential popular preacher both in his own
time and afterwards, through copies of his homilies.¹¹ One of the
series of Carolingian popular sermons analysed by Amos in fact
includes one of the two sermons in question.¹² However, on closer
inspection the relevance of the two sermons fades away—there is
too little marriage symbolism of any significance in them. In each
case it amounts to only a few lines.¹³ Incidentally, the sermons are
written in a Latin which would probably have proved challeng-

⁹ I have followed up most of the relevant footnotes to texts in Amos's very thoroughly documented 'The Origin and Nature of the Carolingian Sermon', and also
made searches in the CD-ROM of Migne's *PL*.

¹⁰ *Sancti Caesarii Arelatensis sermones*, pt. 2, ed. G. Morin (Corpus Christianorum Series Latina, 104; Turnhout, 1953), sermon 167, pp. 682–87, and sermon 168,
pp. 688–91.

¹¹ Amos, 'The Origin and Nature of the Carolingian Sermon', emphasizes Caesarius' importance: he preached himself and encouraged parish priests to preach from
collections of sermons (31–2); after his death his sermons circulated in Merovingian
Gaul (56); his influence continued in the Carolingian period (213, 215 ('a sermon
modelled closely after the works of Caesarius'), 393).

¹² Ibid. 393: Caesarius, sermon 167 = no. 15 on Amos's list.

¹³ Caesarius, sermon 167: 'Dies ergo erat nuptialis et festa, quia advenienti sponso
redempta iungebatur ecclesia: illi, inquam, sponso, quem omnia ab initio mundi
saecula spoponderunt; qui descendit ad terras, ut dilectam suam ad celsitudinis suae
thalamos invitaret, dans ei in praesenti arram sanguinis sui, ⟨daturus postmodum
dotem regni sui⟩'; sermo 168: 'Itaque TAMQUAM SPONSUS PROCEDENS DE THALAMO
SUO descendit ad terras, ecclesiae ex gentibus congregandae suscepta incarnatione
iungendus. Cui quidem ecclesiae, quae utique sumus nos, et arras et dotem dedit:
arras dedit, quando nobis est ex lege promissus; dotem dedit, quando pro nobis est

ing to the average member of the lower clergy in Merovingian or
Carolingian Francia.

Moving forward from the dying Roman Empire to Anglo-Saxon
England in the age of Bede (d. 735), we find a sermon on the
marriage feast of Cana reading in the latter's homiliary,[14] but no
evidence that the homily was meant for a lay audience. It is worth
hearing Andries Van der Walt, the scholar who has studied it most
intensively:[15] 'There is little doubt among modern scholars that
Bede's homilies were primarily intended to be delivered to his
fellow monks. . . . There is ample evidence in the homilies that
Bede was indeed talking to monks' (ibid. 52).[16] Among a good
deal of other evidence, Van Der Walt quotes the following words
from Bede's Homily 1. 13: 'we who have left behind carnal af-
fections and earthly possessions, who, out of love for the angelic
way of life, have declined to marry and produce children after
the flesh'—and comments that this 'seems to be a fairly accurate
description of Bede's usual audience' (ibid. 56). A note of cau-
tion is added: 'there is no evidence in the homilies to support
the belief that he preached either outside the monastery or to a
purely secular audience. A few homilies, however, do suggest that a
larger audience than usual were present when they were delivered'
(ibid. 56–7). Van Der Walt discusses a few passages which may
suggest that 'lay people from the vicinity came to the monastery
church either to attend the last week of Easter celebrations or to
receive baptism' (ibid. 57). Thus 'it . . . cannot be ruled out altogether that on occasions such as Easter and Pentecost Bede had
a number of lay people among his audience. But in all these instances the tone of the homilies remains distinctly monastic' (ibid.
58). The Sunday with the marriage-feast reading was in any case

inmolatus. Et alio modo potest accipi: ut arras praesentem gratiam, dotem intellega-
mus vitam aeternam' (pp. 682–3, 688 Morin).

[14] *Bedae venerabilis Homeliarum libri II*, in *Bedae venerabilis opera, pars III: opera
homiletica, pars IV: opera rhythmica*, ed. D. Hurst (Corpus Christianorum Series
Latina, 122; Turnout, 1955), 95–104: homilia 14 post Epiphaniam. Hurst believes
that the homilies in this collection were written towards the end of Bede's life
(ibid. vii).

[15] A. G. P. Van Der Walt, 'The Homiliary of the Venerable Bede and Early Medieval Preaching' (unpublished thesis, University of London, 1981). The early death
of this meticulous scholar (my first doctoral student) precluded publication of more
than a tiny fraction of his thesis.

[16] The evidence is set out on pp. 52–8.

probably not important enough to warrant an exceptional audience.

Conceivably, the homilies were later adapted to a non-monastic audience. In the mid-eighth century (747–51) the English missionary Boniface asked Egbert, Archbishop of York to send him Bede's book of homilies for the year 'because it would be a very handy and useful manual for us in our preaching'.[17] Presumably Boniface did not know what the homilies were like when he wrote, so this does not prove that he actually found them usable for popular preaching. (Or again, perhaps Boniface had preaching to the clergy in mind.) One cannot rule out the possibility that the marriage symbolism in the Cana homily reached some laypeople in the course of the homiliary's reception history, but to assume a major impact on lay society would not be remotely justified by the evidence.

The next natural stopping place in this brief survey is the Carolingian period. Here material becomes plentiful. The ensuing discussion will need to work laboriously through it, in order to demonstrate the broadly negative conclusion, viz. that not much marriage symbolism got through to the laity in the early Middle Ages. Perhaps this finding should be put more cautiously: that sermon evidence for transmission of marriage symbolism to the people through preaching is slight. It is fair to the reader to say that only scholars specially interested in early medieval preaching need read through the collection-by-collection analysis which follows.

The homiliaries of the 'School of Auxerre' might seem to offer evidence of the diffusion of marriage symbolism to a mass audience, but in fact it is unlikely that they did so. The homily by Haymo discussed above deserves close attention here. There is also a homily on the Gospel reading of the marriage feast of Cana by Heiric of Auxerre.[18] The question is: were these homilies used for popular preaching? The great specialist on the homilies of the Auxerre school believed that they were for private devotion, at least

---

[17] *The Anglo-Saxon Missionaries in Germany, Being the Lives of SS. Willibrord, Boniface, Sturm, Leoba and Lebuin, together with the* Hodoeporicon *of St. Willibald and a Selection from the Correspondence of St. Boniface*, ed. and trans. C. H. Talbot (London etc., 1954), 138.

[18] *Heirici Autissiodorensis homiliae per circulum anni*, ed. R. Quadri (Corpus Christianorum Continuatio Mediaevalis, 116; Turnhout, 1992), homily 1. 20, pp. 160–8. The homilies of Remigius of Auxerre printed in Migne, *PL* 131. 865–932, do not include a sermon on the marriage feast of Cana pericope.

at first.[19] Heiric's scholarly editor echoed his sentiments.[20] Jean Leclercq too believed that the homiliaries of the School of Auxerre 'were used, except in exceptional cases, neither for the [monastic] office, nor for the mass, but for devotion'[21]—i.e. private devotion, not popular preaching. It would be rash to exclude the possibility of the redeployment of these works for popular preaching. Still, if that was not the original intention, and if Europe was not exactly full of parish priests whose Latin was good enough to adapt homiliaries with ease from Latin into the vernacular and for the needs of a lay audience, one must wonder how large a lay public the marriage feast of Cana sermons in these compilations ever reached.

Similar considerations apply to the homiliary of Paul the Deacon. This was commissioned by Charlemagne, who approved it and ordered its publication.[22] However, he probably did not see it as a tool for popular preaching. His idea in commissioning the work was to make available 'a series of readings from the works of the Fathers for use at the night office of the church' (Smetana, loc. cit.): an essentially clerical liturgical ritual.

So collections which look like obvious starting points for a history of the impact of marriage symbolism on the lay world turn out not to have been intended for the laity at all, at least by those who brought them into being. It is worth quoting here the comment of Thomas Amos, especially since he is in general a 'maximalist' about preaching in the Carolingian world as well as the scholar who has examined the whole problem most thoroughly: 'The collection of Paul the Deacon and the works of the Auxerre masters were not

[19] 'Ils sont d'abord destinés à l'usage privé' (H. Barré, *Les Homéliaires carolingiens de l'école d'Auxerre: authenticité, inventaire, tableaux comparatifs, initia* (Studi e testi, 225; Vatican City, 1962), 140.

[20] 'Dopo la prima generazione di omeliari cosidetti "patristici" come quelli de Alano di Farfa o di Paolo Diacono, si arriva, passando da Smaragdo di St. Mihiel, Rabano Mauro e le composizioni bavaresi a una nuova generazione di raccolte omiletiche non più direttamente destinate alla predicazione, ma piuttosto e in primo luogo alla lettura privata. . . . È in questo nuovo genere dove i due celebri scolastici di S. Germano di Auxerre, Aimone ed Eirico, faranno valere tutta la loro tecnica esegetica' (*Heirici . . . homiliae*, ed. Quadri, x–xi).

[21] J. Leclercq, 'Préface' to R. Grégoire, *Les Homéliaires du Moyen Âge: inventaire et analyse des manuscrits* (Rerum Ecclesiarum Documenta, series maior, Fontes, 6; Rome, 1966), vi.

[22] C. L. Smetana, 'Paul the Deacon's Patristic Anthology', in P. E. Szarmach and B. F. Huppé (eds.), *The Old English Homily and its Backgrounds* (Albany, NY, 1978), 75–97 at 76.

intended for popular audiences. The first of those was liturgical in nature, designed for the use of cathedral clergy during the offices, while the last was monastic in nature, intended for private or group study and meditation.'[23]

The homiliary of Smaragdus of St Mihiel (d. after 825) does contain a homily on our marriage feast pericope;[24] according to Amos it was written for 'private meditation'.[25] He adds that it 'came from and was intended for a monastic milieu' (ibid. 199). This opinion carries much weight.

A set of 'Catéchèses celtiques' discovered by André Wilmart in MS Vatican Library Reg. Lat. 49 does contain a homiletic commentary on the marriage feast of Cana.[26] At first sight this looks promising. On closer examination the quantity of marriage symbolism turns out to be fairly exiguous.[27]

I have also drawn a blank with the following sets of homilies or sermons, in that they they seem *not* to deal with the marriage feast of Cana, the natural locus for marriage symbolism in a sermon collection:

---

[23] Amos, 'The Origin and Nature of the Carolingian Sermon', 12 n. 6.

[24] Migne, *PL* 102. 84–90.

[25] Amos, 'The Origin and Nature of the Carolingian Sermon', 198–9.

[26] *Analecta reginensia: extraits des manuscrits latins de la Reine Christine conservés au Vatican*, ed. A. Wilmart (Studi e testi, 59; Vatican City, 1933), 'III Catéchèses celtiques', 29–112. Wilmart's extract VII from this manuscript is a commentary on 2 John: 1–11, the marriage feast of Cana narrative.

[27] The passages are so short that they may be quoted (I run Wilmart's paragraphs together): 'DIE TERTIO: dies tertius legem tertiam sig(nificat), in qua Christus et aeclesia copulati sunt, quando ad illam uenit post tribulationem fidei trinitatis. NUPTIAE FACTAE SUNT: idest copulatio Christi est et aecclesiae, de qua sal(uator) dixit: OSCULETUR ME AB OSCULO ORIS SUI. IN CA(NAM) GAL(ILAEAE), id est in aeclesia in mundo constituta. Chanan enim domus epularum interpretatur, quod significat aeclesiam, in qua aepulae Christi per orationem Sanctorum praeparantur, ut ipse dicit: DOMUS MEA DOMUS ORATIONIS VOCABITUR . . .' (74). There follows the interpretation of the Hebrew names 'Chanan' and 'Galilea'. Here the connection with marriage symbolism is rather exiguous and insubstantial. Then: 'ET ERAT IBI MATER IHESU. Rogatus autem et Ihesus uenire ad nuptias cum discipulis suis ad nuptias uenit, idest ad copula(tionem) sibi aeclesiae catholicae quae erat sponsa eius, quia demancipatum diaboli eruens dedit ei dotem. Nam tribuit ei pignus, idest spiritum sanctum, nec gratis eam eruit, sed pretio sancti sanguinis sui redimit' (75). There is a little more further on: 'Sponsus autem in postremo afferens uinum optimum significat Christum praedicantem euangelium post legem et profe(tas), qui est sponsus aecclesiae catholicae, cuius filii sunt omnes fideles. Item architriclinus figura est eorum omnium qui prius nesciunt uerbi dei uinum et postea bibunt, ut Paulus fuit' (78). That is about all the marriage symbolism there is in the passage printed by Wilmart.

- a homily *sermo de conscientia* printed by Roger Reynolds;²⁸
- the homilies in *XIV homélies*, ed. Mercier;²⁹
- the pseudo-Bede collection of homilies (to judge from the manuscript I used);³⁰
- the thirty-three sermons surviving in MS Cracow, Capitular Library 43 (to judge by the thorough sermon-by-sermon analysis of them by Pierre David);³¹
- the homilies attributed to Eligius;³²
- the homilies attibuted to Boniface;³³
- the homilies written by Rhabanus Maurus for Bishop Haistulf of Metz;³⁴
- the 'Bouhot–Folliet' Carolingian sermon collection;³⁵
- the 'Saint Père de Chartres' homiliary;³⁶
- The 'Newberry Library Homiliary';³⁷

²⁸ R. E. Reynolds, 'The Pseudo-Augustinian "Sermo de Conscientia" and the Related Canonical "Dicta sancti Gregorii papae"', *Revue bénédictine*, 81 (1971), 310–17 at 316–17.
²⁹ *XIV homélies du IXᵉ siècle d'un auteur inconnu de l'Italie du nord* , ed. P. Mercier (Paris, 1970).
³⁰ On the pseudo-Bede collection see Amos, 'The Origin and Nature of the Carolingian Sermon', 212, 231–2 n. 63. To check this collection I used MS Oxford, Bodleian Library Laud. Misc. 427.
³¹ P. David, 'Un recueil de conférences monastiques irlandaises du viiiᵉ siècle: notes sur le manuscrit de la bibliothèque du chapitre de Cracovie', *Revue bénédictine*, 49 (1937), 62–89; cf. Amos, 'The Origin and Nature of the Carolingian Sermon', 210–11.
³² Migne, *PL* 87. 593–654. On this collection see Amos, 'The Origin and Nature of the Carolingian Sermon', 208–9, 230 n. 48.
³³ Migne, *PL* 89. 843–72; see Amos, 'The Origin and Nature of the Carolingian Sermon', 207–8, 229 nn. 40–4.
³⁴ Migne, *PL* 110. 9–134; see Amos, 'The Origin and Nature of the Carolingian Sermon', 203, 227–8 nn. 26–7.
³⁵ See J.-P. Bouhot, 'Un sermonnaire carolingien', *Revue d'histoire des textes*, 4 (1974), 181–223; G. Folliet, 'Deux nouveaux témoins du Sermonnaire carolingien récemment reconstitué', *Revue des études augustiniennes*, 23 (1977), 155–98 at 181–98; Amos, 'The Origin and Nature of the Carolingian Sermon', 211, 231 n. 59; Migne, *PL*, suppl. 2. 1234–5.
³⁶ There is no sermon on the 'Nuptiae' pericope for Epiphany, to judge from Barré's analysis in *Les Homéliaires*, 17–24 and table of incipits; on this homiliary see also Amos, 'The Origin and Nature of the Carolingian Sermon', 213, 232 n. 64.
³⁷ To judge by the list of incipits in M. P. Cunningham, 'Contents of the Newberry Library Homiliarium', *Sacris erudiri*, 7 (1955), 267–301 at 298–300; on this homiliary see also Amos, 'The Origin and Nature of the Carolingian Sermon', 213, 232 n. 66.

- the sermon for Epiphany found by Étaix in a homiliary written in Luxeuil script;[38]
- the sermons on the Christian life from MSS Verdun 64 and Munich, Clm. 12612 edited by Morin in 1905[39] (though there is interesting material on marriage in the literal sense in these);[40]
- a homily on tithes and fasting (in other respects rather significant);[41]
- a lengthy sermon by Agobard of Lyons (apart from a short passage);[42]
- Atto of Vercelli's sermons edited in Migne;[43]
- the florilegium in MS Montpellier H308, put together by Florus of Lyons;[44]
- the sermon on St Judocus by Abbot Lupus of Ferrières;[45]

[38] R. Étaix, 'Sermon pour l'Épiphanie tiré d'un homiliaire en Écriture de Luxeuil', *Revue bénédictine*, 81 (1971), 7–13.
[39] D. G. Morin, 'Textes inédits relatifs au symbole et à la vie chrétienne', *Revue bénédictine*, 22 (1905), 505–24 at 515–19 and 519–23.
[40] Notably, from the Verdun manuscript sermon: 'Nullus homo praesumat cumcupinam habere: quia quamdiu cumcupinam habet homo, deum contra se iratum habet, quia deus uxorem dixit habere, non cumcupinam. Nullus homo se praesumat cum comatre sua aut parente propinqua aut filiastra aut nouerca aut cognata aut deo sacrata ad uxorem sociatam: quia propter ista mala opera uenit ira dei super uos . . . Ille homo qui uxorem suam dimiserat propter fornicationis causam et aliam sociauerat, dimittat illam uxorem quam postea priserat, et agat paenitentiam propter peccata sua: quia si hoc non fecerit, non potest penitentiam fructuosam agere. Uxores uestras in Christi amore diligite: quia qui uxorem habuit, et dimiserat illam propter se ipsam, si despecta fuerit, damnatus erit in die iudicii: quia talem uxorem te uoluit deus dare, talem tibi dedit. Et uos, feminae, diligite maritos uestros, et amate illos in Christi amore' (ibid. 516–17). Note the idea that marriages are made in heaven.
[41] Migne, *PL* 129. 1261–2; see Amos, 'The Origin and Nature of the Carolingian Sermon', 217, 234 n. 86.
[42] Migne, *PL* 104. 267–88; see Amos, 'The Origin and Nature of the Carolingian Sermon', 204, 228 n. 31; the few lines of marriage symbolism in this long sermon are as follows: 'Ostendit etiam caput exaltatum ad quantam sublimitatem elevat corpus suum, et unitatem capitis et corporis, sponsi videlicet et sponsae. Unde dicitur: *Induit me vestimentis salutis, et indumento justitiae circumdedit me quasi sponsum decoratum corona, et quasi sponsam ornatam monilibus suis.* Se enim dixit sponsum, se sponsam. Haec tanta unitas est illud inaestimabile et ineffabile bonum, quod nec oculus vidit, nec auris audivit, nec in cor hominis ascendit, quod praeparavit Deus diligentibus se; cum Agnus ille est sponsus gregis sui, pastor ovium suarum; et qui est agnus in passione, leo in resurrectione . . .' (Migne, *PL* 104. 273). [43] Migne, *PL* 134. 833–60.
[44] The florilegium is analysed in C. Charlier, 'Une œuvre inconnue de Florus de Lyon: la collection "de fide" de Montpellier', *Traditio*, 8 (1952). 81–109 at 81–5; cf. Amos, 'The Origin and Nature of the Carolingian Sermon', 204, 228 n. 32.
[45] See Amos, 'The Origin and Nature of the Carolingian Sermon', 205, 228 n. 34,

- the homilies of Gregory the Great (much used for preaching in the early Middle Ages).[46]

One may probably add MS Laon, Bibliothèque Municipale 265. I have not seen this directly but there is a fairly full analysis in a study of Laon Cathedral School by John Contreni, which does not suggest that it contains marriage symbolism, apart perhaps from a few lines which are not enough to affect the argument being developed here.[47] Of the 'Mondsee Homiliary' (of Abbot Lantperhtus of St Michael of Mondsee) only the summer portion has survived[48] (the marriage feast of Cana reading comes in the winter).

One cannot exclude the possibility that these collections contain some marriage symbolism in other places. I have mostly worked from beginnings of sermons (incipits) in compiling the list in the preceding paragraph, and it is always conceivable that pockets of marriage symbolism lurk in the body of the sermons or homilies, without the incipit giving a clue, as is the case with the fifteen lines or so of spousal symbolism in the last of the 'five sermons of Abbo' of St-Germain printed in Migne,[49] or with paragraphs 4 and 5 of MS Munich, Bayerische Staatsbibliothek, Clm. 3883, transcribed below as Document 1. 1. We may also note that a Wolfenbüttel collection analysed by Reginald Grégoire contains a sermon by Augustine, again not on the Cana reading, where marriage symbolism is an important part of the structure.[50] Even so, it is hard to ima-

---

citing W. Levison, 'Eine Predigt des Lupus von Ferrieres', in id., *Aus rheinischer und fränkischer Frühzeit* (Düsseldorf, 1947), 561–4 (not seen, but I have read the sermon in MS BL Royal 8. B. XIV, fos. 131ᵛ–133ᵛ).

[46] DeLeeuw, 'Gregory the Great's "Homilies on the Gospels" in the Early Middle Ages'. Marriage symbolism is only rather slightly represented, to judge by the old but full index: see Migne, *PL* 76. 1414.

[47] Analysis of the manuscript in J. J. Contreni, *The Cathedral School of Laon from 850 to 930: Its Manuscripts and Masters* (Munich, 1978), 130–3. In his list of the contents of this composite manuscript he includes (131) 'texts on matrimony and baptism, an excerpt from Isidore of Seville's *De ecclesiasticis officiis*'. Contreni does not give a reference, but this work by Isidore does have a section on marriage at 2. 20, and this includes short passages of marriage symbolism, for which see Migne, *PL* 83. 810, 812–13.

[48] Amos, 'The Origin and Nature of the Carolingian Sermon', 203–4.

[49] For the five sermons, see Amos, 'The Origin and Nature of the Carolingian Sermon', 206, 229 nn. 36–7, and Migne, *PL* 132. 761–78. The passage in question is at 775. 9–24.

[50] Augustine, sermon 238, Migne, *PL* 38. 1125–6: see R. Grégoire, 'La collection

gine that this would substantially affect the shape of our imaginary graph charting the prominence of marriage as metaphor.

Marriage symbolism in early 'marriage feast of Cana' homilies: some exceptional examples

A few surviving homiliaries do have sermons on the marriage feast of Cana pericope containing some marriage symbolism. Two of them are transcribed below, as Documents **1. 2** and **1. 3.** There are some good passages of marriage symbolism, which are short enough to be quoted. We may begin with the following from the 'Bavarian Homiliary' (Document **1. 1**)—not, however, from the pericope of the marriage feast of Cana, which would be the usual venue for marriage doctrine and symbolism in sermons of the last three medieval centuries. It is especially interesting for the way it combines commentary on marriage in the literal sense with the symbolic meaning of marriage:

Therefore, although a virgin is ranked at one hundred, and a married woman at thirty,[51] nevertheless a chaste [married] woman is better than a proud virgin. For that chaste woman, serving her husband, has a rank of thirty: for the proud virgin no rank at all will be left. In her is fulfilled the words of the Psalmist (Ps. 17: 28): 'You will save the humble people, and you will bring down the eyes of the proud.' And since St Paul calls the whole catholic Church a virgin, seeing in her not only the virgins in body, but [also] wanting the minds of all to be free from corruption: when he says this: 'I have [52]prepared you for one husband, to present you as a chaste virgin', the souls not only of holy nuns, but also of all men and women, if they have had the will to keep, with chastity of body, virginity in those aforesaid five senses, should not doubt that they are brides of Christ. For Christ is to be understood as the bridegroom not of bodies but of souls. And therefore, dearest brethren: both men and women, both boys and girls, if they keep their virginity until they are married, and do not corrupt their souls through these five senses, that is, sight, hearing, taste, smell, or touch, while they use them well, on the day of judgement, when the gates are opened, will be worthy to enter into the eternal marriage chamber of the bridegroom. But those who both corrupt their bodies before marriage by some adulterous union, and afterwards do not cease to wound their souls

homilétique du Ms. Wolfenbüttel 4096', *Studi medievali*, 3rd ser., 14 (1973), 259–86 at 276 no. 41, and Amos, 'The Origin and Nature of the Carolingian Sermon', 214 at nn. 71–2.

[51] Cf. Mark 4: 20.

[52] prepared] espoused *in Vulgate, but it may not be a scribal error*

by living evilly throughout their lives, by hearing evilly, by speaking evilly, if a fruitful and worthy penance does not provide a cure, will shout out without justification after the gates have been closed: 'Lord, Lord, open for us' (Mt. 25: 11; cf. Luke 13: 25).—'Amen I tell you, I know you not whence you are' (Mt. 25: 12; Luke 13: 25). (Document **1. 1. 4**)

There may be other such passages in early medieval homiliaries, since (as already noted) I have concentrated my search on Cana pericope homiliaries (influenced by the late medieval pattern), but I would be surprised if they are very plentiful. The Cana pericope of the same 'Bavarian Homiliary' does include a couple of relevant passages. Near the beginning of the sermon we find:

It says: 'There was a marriage in Cana of Galilee and the mother of Jesus was there. Jesus and his disciples were invited to the marriage.' It is great humility in our Lord that he deigned to come to a human marriage. But yet, in that same place he produced a great mystery.

Therefore, there came to a marriage celebrated in the carnal way on earth our Lord and Saviour, who descended from heaven to earth to join the Church to himself by a spiritual love. His marriage bed, indeed, was the womb of the uncorrupted Virgin, in which God was joined to human nature, and from which, when he was born, he came out to join the Church of the faithful to himself. But he had always from the beginning of the world been invited to this marriage by holy and just men, who begged him with all their might to carry out the redemption of the human race that he had promised. (Document **1. 2. 1–2**)

The remainder of the sermon concentrates on other parts of the Gospel reading: the transformation of the water into wine, the conversation between Jesus and his mother and its meaning, and the six water jars which provide a vehicle for surveying the six ages of world history.

Some more quotable and relevant passages can be found in the homily on the Cana reading in the 'Beaune Homiliary'. It starts with marriage symbolism:

Dearest brethren, we have heard when the holy Gospel was read that on the third day there was a marriage in Cana of Galilee. What is that marriage, if not our winning?[53] What are those celebrations but the joys of our salvation? They are done on the third day, because in the third period of the world the delight of this celebration occurred. For there was one period of nature, and the other of the grace of heaven, in which Christ,

---

[53] Probably in the sense of 'Christ's winning of us', rather than 'our gain'.

invited to the marriage, revealed himself by the power of his works as God hidden in man, and from the unstable history of the heathen united to himself a permanent wife. But among the music provided by the prophets to celebrate the wedding, the wine of grace was lacking. This the mother raised reproachfully with her son. (Document 1. 3. 1)

Marriage symbolism reappears a little later as the theme of the six ages of the world is introduced—an interesting combination of two motifs with no necessary connection:

Those six water jars, however, signify the six ages, and these ages continue to stay like empty vessels, unless filled by Christ. In each and every one of them there were not lacking prophecies of the bride and bridegroom, and these, made clear in Christ, aimed at the salvation of all the nations.

In the first water jar, who is symbolized by Adam and Eve, if not Christ and the Church? And who is shown in the second, in which Noah commanded the mystical ark, if not the same Christ on the wood of the cross, joining to himself as bride the Church from all the nations? (Document 1. 3. 3–4)

After a rapid survey of the ages of the world, there is another passage of marriage symbolism, this time launched by the remark in the Gospel reading that the water jars held 'two or three measures apiece':

To Christ, indeed, and his intervention on behalf of the nations, pertained the prophecies of the six water jars, each of which held twofold or threefold measures, and are signified in the foreskin and circumcision, or in the three divisions of the world, since Christ the bridegroom came to choose for himself a single bride out of every people and every kind of men, and for her he mixed the wine of grace, a wine which is pronounced good by the wine steward, that is, the chorus of holy doctors, and preferred to all the pleasures of the previous age . . . (Document 1. 3. 5)

These are nice passages, but they are not enough to change the general impression of a meagre crop, especially compared to the last three medieval centuries, where there are extremely large numbers of sermons on the marriage feast of Cana pericope, a high proportion of them with much to say both about human marriage proper and about what it symbolizes.

England: a special case

The biggest exception to our generalization about the early Middle Ages is England, where homilies were produced in the vernacular.

This may have been because the Latin of the English clergy was even worse on average than elsewhere—a plausible position though hard to prove. Whatever the reason, vernacular homilies would surely have been much more accessible to the lower clergy. They are easily accessible to the historian too, since the content of the corpus has been thoroughly indexed.[54]

Perhaps the earliest relevant passage is from the Blickling Homilies. (These are one of two collections of vernacular Anglo-Saxon homilies whose date, setting in life, and audience all seem uncertain.[55]) In a sermon for the Annunciation we find the following: 'the Heavenly King shall prepare thy womb as a bridal chamber for his son, and also great joy in the bride-chamber . . .'[56] And again, 'Let us rejoice then in the union of God and men, and in the union of the bridegroom and the bride, that is Christ and holy church.'[57] This is marriage symbolism, but there is apparently not much more of it in vernacular collections other than Ælfric's. Ælfric uses marriage symbolism in several places,[58] one of them his homily on the marriage feast of Cana Gospel reading.[59]

Pastoral delivery systems in the early Middle Ages

The vernacular tradition in England raises a question about the Continent and indeed about the impact of Latin texts in England itself. Were most laypeople near enough to a church to have even the possibility of hearing regular sermons? Would the mass of the clergy have been capable, sufficiently Latin-literate, to use Latin

[54] R. DiNapoli, *An Index of Theme and Image to the Homilies of the Anglo-Saxon Church, Comprising the Homilies of Ælfric, Wulfstan, and the Blickling and Vercelli Codices* (Hockwold cum Wilton, 1995): for marriage, see pp. 62–3.

[55] C. D. Wright, 'Vercelli Homilies XI–XIII and the Anglo-Saxon Benedictine Reform: Tailored Sources and Implied Audiences', in C. Muessig (ed.), *Preacher, Sermon and Audience in the Middle Ages* (Leiden etc., 2002), 203–27 at 205–6. See also especially M. Clayton, *The Cult of the Virgin Mary in Anglo-Saxon England* (Cambridge, 1990): 'we have no unambiguous proof that the anonymous works do belong to the pre-reform period, rather than to a date closer to the dates of compilation of the manuscripts in which they are found' (264); she cautions against assigning the anonymous homilies to the pre-reform period (264–6).

[56] *The Blickling Homilies of the Tenth Century, from the Marquis of Lothian's Unique MS. A.D. 971*, ed. and trans. R. Morris (London, 1880), 8.

[57] Ibid. 10.

[58] See DiNapoli, *Index of Theme and Image*, 63, under 'the Church is Christ's bride'.

[59] For a commentary on this homily with analysis of its sources see M. Godden, *Ælfric's Catholic Homilies: Introduction, Commentary and Glossary*, ed. M. Godden (Early English Text Society, SS 18; Oxford, 2000), 370–80.

sermons intended for popular preaching? Now pastoral provision in the early Middle Ages is a low-certainty area. The map of the spread of the parish system has not yet been definitively drawn, and there was almost certainly significant regional variation.[60] Scholars can provide respectable reasons for almost diametrically opposite positions: one can believe in massive pastoral provision and one can doubt if there was much, outside the radius of a small number of centres. There has been a tendency recently to take a 'maximalist' view.[61] On this view, substantial 'mother churches' in one way or another provided pastoral services to large areas, and did so quite efficiently. The communities of clergy in these mother churches may have been quite well educated.

The tendency to show that there could have been a lot of pastoral provision before the parish has done good by stopping scholars from taking the contrary for granted, but the question remains: how efficient was the delivery system for turning written Latin sermons into vernacular popular preaching? Here one should remember a famous passage of Bede about the need for everyone to know the Lord's Prayer and the Apostles' Creed.[62] He tells Archbishop Egbert to

[m]ake the ignorant people—that is, those who are acquainted with no language but their own—say them in their own language and repeat them assiduously. This ought to be done, not only in the case of laymen, that is, those still leading a secular life, but also of those clerics or monks who are ignorant of the Latin language. . . . On this account I have myself often given to many ignorant priests both of these, the Creed and the Lord's Prayer, translated into the English language.[63]

Many priests whose Latin was so bad that they could not translate the Lord's Prayer? The implications are considerable. Only the very simplest model sermons or homilies would have been helpful to the average priest, and for some of these ill-educated priests the Latin of even the simplest model sermon would have been challenging. So how much got through to the laity?

---

[60] Cf. W. Davies, *Small Worlds: The Village Community in Early Medieval Brittany* (London, 1988), 25 and n. 44.

[61] See notably, for the British Isles, J. Blair and R. Sharpe (eds.), *Pastoral Care before the Parish* (Leicester etc., 1992).

[62] John Blair reminded me of this passage.

[63] Letter of Bede to Archbishop Egbert, translated in *English Historical Documents c. 500–1042*, ed. D. Whitelock (London, 1955), no. 170, pp. 735–45 at 737–8.

It is worth listing the possibilities in ascending order of improbability. That some Latin sermons written for popular preaching were actually preached from monasteries or pre-parish pastoral centres is almost certain. That such texts were available in most pre-parish centres is much less certain. That there was a critical mass of Latin educated priests in most pre-parish centres is about equally unlikely, though not impossible. That most pre-parish pastoral centres had both a critical mass of Latin educated priests and model popular sermons in Latin for them to use is less likely still. That they prepared sermons from these Latin texts every Sunday and took them out to the surrounding villages is even less likely, and we may note that the Sunday on which the marriage feast of Cana reading occurred was not a major feast. Add to this accumulation of improbabilities the earlier finding, that little of the surviving corpus of popular early medieval sermons is about marriage symbolism, and the probability of such symbolism being preached to large numbers of laypeople in the early medieval centuries looks remote.

'Maximalists' about pastoral care and preaching in the early Middle Ages should not regard this as an attack on their position. The point at issue is the impact of one particular theme, marriage symbolism. It may very well be that many quasi-monastic centres reached out to large areas of the countryside surrounding them, and evangelized energetically.[64]

The England of Ælfric apart, however, it is far from clear that there was much marriage preaching accessible to laypeople until the end of the twelfth century. That century is a great age of preaching, but it was predominantly directed towards clerics, notably monks and canons.[65] No doubt a careful search for popular sermons such as Amos conducted for the Carolingian era would yield a significant number of Latin texts designed to serve as models for popular preaching. Whether many of them would contain a lot of marriage symbolism is much more doubtful. The natural place to look for such symbolism is preaching on the text 'There was a marriage in Cana of Galilee': *Nuptiae factae sunt in Chana Galileae*. Migne's *Patrologia Latina* contains relatively few sermons on this text, no-

---

[64] In a personal communication John Blair has raised the possibility of lively 'charismatic' vernacular preaching, not too much tied to Latin sources, in pre-Viking England.

[65] M. de Reu, *La Parole du Seigneur: moines et chanoines médiévaux prêchant l'Ascension et le Royaume des Cieux* (Brussels etc., 1996), 228–9.

tably few from the twelfth century. The homily on the marriage feast of Cana Gospel reading by Bruno of Segni (d. 1123)[66] does not contain a great deal of marriage symbolism, but concentrates mainly on the symbolism of the water jars that figure in the Cana reading.[67] To recapitulate: in the early medieval centuries and up until *c.*1200, there was no mass communication of marriage symbolism, or at least, no significant evidence of anything like that has come to light so far. With the thirteenth century everything changes, even before mendicant preachers made their mark.

(c) Mass Communication in the Age of the Friars

Model sermons and oral preaching

Any given model sermon could be preached 'live' again and again to different audiences, so that the model sermons written on parchment are the tip of an 'oral' iceberg: this is one half of the proposition that preaching was a form of mass communication, the less controversial half. The more controversial half is that surviving sermon manuscripts are the tip of an iceberg of lost codices and quires.

This chapter is in a sense a remote sequel to a 1985 study which tried among other things to show how model sermons worked.[68] Synthesizing and reinforcing a scholarly consensus,[69] it argued that

---

[66] The audience and 'setting in life' of Bruno's homilies have been cautiously characterized by his historian: 'Les morceaux qui ne se trouvent pas dans les commentaires sont de la main de Bruno, semble-t-il. Cet ensemble offre donc un certain intérêt: il prouve qu'un commentaire exégétique était jugé apte à une utilisation pastorale, bien qu'il soit très probable que cet homéliaire de Bruno n'était pas destiné à une célébration liturgique, mais plutôt à une lecture publique ou privée' (R. Grégoire, *Bruno de Segni, exégète médiévale et théologien monastique* (Centro Italiano di Studi sull'alto medioevo, 3; Spoleto, 1965), 87; and de Reu, *La Parole*, 228).

[67] 'S. Brunonis Episcopi Signiensis Homilia XVIII, Dominica II post Epiphaniam', in Migne, *PL* 165. 767 and 461–6.

[68] D. L. d'Avray, *The Preaching of the Friars: Sermons Diffused from Paris before 1300* (Oxford, 1985), chs. 2 and 3, and *passim*.

[69] A particularly important influence on the field in general was L.-J. Bataillon, 'Approaches to the Study of Medieval Sermons', *Leeds Studies in English*, NS 11 (1980), 19–35, repr. in id., *La Prédication au XIIIᵉ siècle en France et Italie: études et documents* (Aldershot, 1993), no. 1 (most of the other articles in the same collection of reprints are relevant in one way or another). See now N. Bériou, 'Les sermons latins après 1200', in B. M. Kienzle (ed.), *The Sermon* (Typologie des sources du Moyen Âge Occidental, 81–3; Turnhout, 2000), 363–447, esp. 405–9. The same author's magisterial *L'Avènement des maîtres de la Parole: la prédication à Paris au XIIIᵉ siècle* (2 vols.; Collection des Études Augustiniennes, Série Moyen Âge et

model sermons were readily available to Franciscans, Dominicans, and similar preachers in manuscript books and quires. These books were often very small and portable and can be called pocket books or vade-mecum books.[70] The number of such portable books to have survived is noteworthy, expecially in view of the huge loss rate of manuscripts, above all the sort friars were likely to carry around with them (on this see the following section). These model sermons could be preached again and again by the same or different preachers. The Latin of the model could be turned into any vernacular, so a book of model sermons could be used in any part of Europe.

Most of this holds good in principle for popular model sermons of the earlier Middle Ages. Yet it is a different world. The respectable list of early medieval popular sermons put together by Thomas Amos and others pales into total insignificance when one looks at the nine volumes (excluding indexes) of J. B. Schneyer's *Repertorium*. Each volume lists only the beginnings and ends of sermons and the call numbers of manuscripts, but requires hundreds of pages—sometimes around a thousand—to convey that basic information: and this just for sermons between 1150 and 1350. We have seen that few popular sermons on the marriage feast of Cana Gospel reading survive from the early Middle Ages, whereas the index of the *Repertorium* lists some 280 for these two centuries alone. Furthermore, there were almost certainly many more preachers with the education to get good use out of model sermons. Richard Southern calculated that there were around 28,000 Franciscans and 12,000 Dominicans in the early fourteenth century, and a great many of these would have been preachers.[71]

Since model sermons were meant to be reused, and there was no prejudice against derivative preaching except to an élite congregation, one may infer that many oral events corresponded to each written sermon. Preachers would not have to follow the model ex-

---

Temps Modernes, 31; Paris, 1998) concentrates on sermons actually preached and transmitted by *reportatio*.

[70] D. L. d'Avray (with A. C. de la Mare), 'Portable *Vademecum* Books Containing Franciscan and Dominican Texts', in A. C. de la Mare and B. C. Barker-Benfield (eds.), *Manuscripts at Oxford: An Exhibition in Memory of Richard William Hunt . . . on Themes Selected and Described by Some of his Friends* (Exhibition catalogue, Bodleian Library; Oxford, 1980), 60–4.

[71] R. W. Southern, *Western Society and the Church in the Middle Ages* (Harmondsworth, 1970), 285.

actly, and almost certainly mixed and matched their contents with
material from other preaching aids like exemplum collections and
collections of saints' lives. Yet even if one cannot assume a precise correlation between any one model sermon and any one live
preaching event, there was probably a fair correspondence between
the aggregate content of widely diffused model sermon collections
and the aggregate content of live preaching. It is the same with
newspapers today. It would be hard to know the effect of any one
tabloid topos on any one reader, but one can be fairly sure that the
aggregate of newspaper articles on, say, immigration has an effect
on the aggregate of attitudes in large sectors of the population, so
that newspapers may be regarded as a social force. So too with
model sermons in the Middle Ages.

The ultimate audience would usually be lay. Not invariably. Some
friars or other priests might simply read a book of sermons for pleasure or edification.[72] When the sermons were by a famous man like
Bonaventure, that might even be the normal usage. But with the
general run of workaday sermon collections one can hardly see usage stopping with reading. On that hypothesis the instructions for
preachers in sermons are hard to explain.[73] When we do have prefaces, they make it clear that the sermon collections could indeed
be designed to serve as models and tools for preaching: and this
really settles the issue.[74] Furthermore, however, many model sermons were not much more than divisions and scriptural authorities.
These were definitely not just for reading. But if they were tools
for preachers, there is no reason to doubt that the fuller sermons
were too. Again, there are other genres of preaching aid: exempla,
distinction collections, etc.[75] Why should actual sermons not serve
as a preaching aid? They provide structures to hold materials from
other preaching aids together.

Another proviso: model sermons might be used from time to time
to preach not to lay but to clerical audiences in circumstances where

[72] As Robert Lerner wisely pointed out to me in a personal communication.
[73] D'Avray, *Preaching of the Friars*, 106–8.
[74] Ibid. 108–10; see now N. Bériou, 'Les prologues de recueils de sermons latins
du xiiᵉ au xvᵉ siècle', in J. Hamesse (ed.), *Les Prologues médiévaux: actes du colloque
international organisé par l'Academia Belgica et l'École Française de Rome avec le
concours de la F.I.D.E.M. (Rome, 26–28 mars 1998)* (Textes et études du Moyen
Âge, 15; Turnhout, 2000) 395–426 at 414–16.
[75] Bériou, 'Les prologues', sect. II.i; R. H. Rouse and M. A. Rouse, *Preachers, Florilegia and Sermons: Studies on the Manipulus florum of Thomas of Ireland*
(Studies and Texts, Pontifical Institute of Mediaeval Studies, 47; Toronto, 1979).

the listeners were unlikely to care about intellectual property.[76] However, it would be natural for a preacher to think twice about using for (say) fellow Franciscans a sermon which members of his audience might have in a book of their own. *Grosso modo*, one may assume that the content of model sermons tells us about the content of preaching to the laity. We cannot tell which sentences of any given model sermon were used on any given occasion, but we can be fairly sure that themes and structures of thought which recur again and again in model sermons reached large numbers of laypeople at some time or another. Similarly, we cannot know what any one lay listener made of a sermon, but we can make very educated guesses about aggregate impact, or at least about whether a given idea was likely to be familiar to large numbers of people.

Lost sermon manuscripts

The present volume is the sequel to a 2001 study seeking among other things to demonstrate that marriage preaching belonged to a system of mass communication.[77] The sermons edited there would have circulated in large numbers of manuscripts now lost (quite apart from the fact that any written version could be preached again and again to different audiences). The number of lost manuscripts would seem to have been unconsciously but grossly underestimated. There are two connected theses: first, that the loss rate of manuscripts of this genre at least was a lot higher than most medievalists tend to suspect; and second, that not only professional scribes, but also Franciscans and Dominicans, copied sermon manuscripts to professional standards—so that they were available to confrères and were not just personal books. Thus we have a fact: that the number of written model sermons was greater than the large number surviving to an extent that has not been appreciated; and an explanation of how it was possible to put so many manuscripts into circulation before the invention of printing.

The evidence is cumulative: recent discoveries about a massive destruction of 'useless' manuscripts to provide pieces of parchment for binders, whose business was expanding through the ceiling; the almost total disappearance of books from Franciscan and

---

[76] Academics in particular could in some circumstances think a great deal about intellectual property: B. Smalley, *English Friars and Antiquity in the Early Fourteenth Century* (Oxford, 1960), 308.

[77] D'Avray, *Medieval Marriage Sermons*.

Dominican libraries that must once have been very large; the utilitarian attitude to books; the book rules of the friars, quite different from the conventions governing the libraries of Benedictine and Cistercian houses—rules that made attrition inevitable; the use of *quaterni*, unbound quires; and, finally, technical textual arguments that also point to large-scale losses. These arguments each have considerable force on their own, but they also converge towards the same conclusion—massive losses of sermon manuscripts. The convergence strengthens each individual argument, as is normal with evidence of the historical type.[78]

It should be noted that the argument has implications that go beyond the history of preaching. Model sermons were not the only books produced and then lost in enormous numbers. The arguments developed below relativize the whole notion of the print revolution (while showing that the pressure it put on binders led to destruction of manuscripts and a misleading impression today about the difference between the number of manuscripts and of printed books). However, these implications for other genres are

[78] Here I return to the case argued in *Medieval Marriage Sermons*, 15–30, in order to answer the arguments set out in Robert Lerner's courteous but critical review in *Speculum*, 79 (2004), 163–5. First a clarification. I did not mean to say that only practising preachers would have made 'nonconformist' changes and that formal hands point to the existence of an industry. My point about nonconformist changes (see below) was that they show that there was a skilled and confident amateur labour force copying manuscripts—for the use of others as well as themselves—in addition to the production by commercial scribes. My aim at this point was *not* to demonstrate a massive loss rate (my arguments for that are quite different) but to explain how it had been possible for so many manuscripts to be produced. So Lerner's evidence that *independent* scribal variation can be found in all sorts of texts (not just sermons) is no objection to my argument, and indeed I made a similar point myself in *Medieval Marriage Sermons*, 23 n. 62. My argument about formal hands, too briefly made, was that confident variation was not confined to personal notebooks which would never be copied and which only one person could use: see *Medieval Marriage Sermons*, 25, 'not the end of the line'. Since Lerner's reading of my book will have reached more readers than the book itself, I must stress that his version of it contains misunderstandings, for which my over-compression is probably responsible. I further develop the arguments about mass communication in 'Printing, Mass Communication and Religious Reformation: The Middle Ages and After', in J. Crick and A. Walsham (eds.), *The Uses of Script and Print, 1300–1700* (Cambridge, 2004), 50–70. Note that there I analyse the arguments of Uwe Neddermeyer's very important *Von der Handschrift zum gedruckten Buch: Schriftlichkeit und Leseinteresse im Mittelalter und in der frühen Neuzeit. Quantitative und qualitative Aspekte* (2 vols.; Buchwissenschaftliche Beiträge aus dem Deutschen Bucharchiv München, 61; Wiesbaden, 1998). I do not repeat this analysis here but it is important for the present argument: Neddermeyer has arguments for a lower loss rate which are ingenious but do not take into account the difference between the ways in which the friars and the older orders used books.

not the principal concern: and of course most other genres would not be further diffused by the oral 'multiplier' effect that has just been discussed.

Binding and the great book massacre

One of the stranger phenomena of book history is the great destruction of books around 1500. Destruction of books in the Reformation need not surprise us, but this elimination of a large part of the book stock had nothing to do with religious differences. The phenomenon was uncovered by Gerhardt Powitz in an essay that no historian of the transition from script to print can afford to ignore. Its implications for the present argument are considerable, and in fact they ought to affect the whole way we look at the impact of printing: hence the liberal quotations from a paper that could easily escape the attention of non-specialist readers.[79]

Old manuscript books were broken up to provide parchment to help bind more favoured books, according to Powitz, for parchment was in demand for binding, used for pastedowns, flyleaves, and in the structure of the spine. Thus, for instance:

> The Dominican house at Frankfurt possessed the *Summa dictaminis* of Guido Faba in a manuscript of the thirteenth century. Even towards the end of the fifteenth century the the librarian of the convent . . . gave the volume the call number *N 4* and the ex-libris 'fratrum predicatorum in Franckfordia' [Dominicans in Frankfurt]. Not long after (around 1500) the manuscript was cut up; remains of it can still be found in the bindings of incunables which belonged to the convent, among them the sheet with the call number and the ex-libris. (Powitz, '*Libri inutiles*', 300)

Or again:

> new books in a modern form were appearing in an abundance hitherto unimaginable; in view of this, it was inevitable that a replacement of the textual foundations within genres, a change of repertoire, should take place. *The sermon collections of Pierre de Reims and Jacques de Lausanne*, neither of which got into print in the fifteenth century, were in the possession of the Frankfurt Dominican house in manuscripts of the thirteenth and fourteenth centuries. Around 1500 these preaching texts were recycled—

---

[79] G. Powitz, '*Libri inutiles* in mittelalterlichen Bibliotheken: Bemerkungen über Alienatio, Palimpsestierung und Makulierung', *Scriptorium*, 50 (1996), 288–304. The key word is 'Makulierung', which I translate as 'recycling'. I am very grateful to Marc-Aeilko Aris for drawing my attention to this article.

perhaps because of a preference for building up a collection of some of the printed preaching collections by other authors that were just coming on the market? (Powitz, '*Libri inutiles*', 301–2, emphasis added)[80]

Unfashionable books were sacrificed in a frenetic period of book-binding. Powitz writes of a

> great wave of recycling, which in the fifteenth century, and to be precise in the decades around 1500, burst over ecclesiastical libraries. It is a process of unprecedented intensity and one with highly influential consequences for the history of libraries: a very large proportion of the medieval manuscripts that had been successfully passed down to that point was destroyed within a few decades, at a stroke, just like that. (Powitz, '*Libri inutiles*', 299)

Powitz calls this the 'great work of destruction [große Zerstörungswerk]', the 'book massacre [Büchersterben]' of the period around 1500 (ibid.).

Why?[81] The principal answer is that the invention of printing produced a flood of books that needed to be bound.[82] However, this is not the sole explanation. For some reason, the period around 1500 also saw the rebinding of many old manuscripts. So other old manuscripts were cannibalized to provide parchment for pastedowns etc.[83]

Demand for recycled manuscripts went through the ceiling, both in the in-house binderies of religious houses and also in the com-

---

[80] Together with ibid. n. 40: 'Frankfurt a.M. StUB Fragm.lat. VIII 53 (Petrus Remensis); III 72 (Jacobus de Lausanna); vgl. auch Fragm.lat. X 27'.

[81] 'Die Kernfrage, die sich stellt, lautet: Wie konnte es in der Zeit um 1500 zu einer Makulierungswelle diesen Ausmaßes kommen?' (ibid. 300).

[82] 'Als eine bestimmende Triebkraft ist ohne Zweifel die Einführung des Buchdrucks in Rechnung zu stellen, der große Medienwandel, dessen tiefgreifender, epochaler Charakter den Zeitgenossen seit etwa 1470/80 zunehmend bewußt geworden sein muß. . . . Nicht selten wird der Erwerb von Drucken mit dem Ausscheiden von Handschriften gleichen Inhalts Hand in Hand gegangen sein. Ein Beispiel: Für den Lateinunterricht der Klosterschule erwarben die Frankfurter Dominikaner zwischen 1485 und 1500 mindestens 20 gedruckte Exemplare des Doctrinale, der Versgrammatik des Alexander de Villa Dei. Vollständige Handschriften dieses Textes aus dem Frankfurter Kloster sind bezeichnenderweise nicht nachweisbar, wohl aber 10 Codices discissi . . . Dies könnten die Reste von Handschriften sein, die man bis zum Erwerb der Drucke benutzt hatte' (ibid. 301).

[83] 'Zu der gleichen Zeit, als die in Mengen auf den Markt drängenden ältesten Drucke und die zunächst weiterhin entstehenden Handschriften ihren ersten Einband erhielten, machten Klöster und Stifte sich daran, Tausende von älteren Büchern (also Handschriften) umzubinden' (ibid. 302).

mercial city binderies.[84] 'The "looting" . . . was universal, wherever parchment was available' (ibid. 303).

Powitz's revolutionary findings were anticipated in a very restricted domain by Neil Ker in his study of Oxford pastedowns, a study with such an antiquarian air that its implications for the history of the book were not properly realized.[85] This too is a study of the recycling of manuscripts, revealing large-scale destruction of manuscripts, and making it clear that the pastedowns that survive must be a modest proportion of the number binders actually used:

> We can seldom collect together as much as the twentieth part of a complete book; often no more than a hundredth part, or even less. There is no reason to doubt that the binders used the whole of these books and many others now entirely lost. They will have used many thousands of leaves as wrappers of ephemeral notebooks, account books, and light-weight printed books and many thousands as pastedowns in bindings which no longer exist. (Ker, *Fragments of Medieval Manuscripts*, xii)

Ker also points out (p. xi) that not one of the 265 philosophical books in the Merton College distribution for borrowing by the fellows of 1519 is extant, at least in the college library—the implication being that recycling for the benefit of binders has much to do with this.

These borrowable philosophical books were only one sector of Merton's magnificent library, and other sectors have survived very well. The same cannot be said for the libraries of the Franciscans and Dominicans in England. Their history shows that the modern distribution of manuscripts is an utterly unreliable guide to the medieval state of affairs. It is possible to speak with some confidence thanks to the researches of Ker, Watson, Humphreys, Mynors, and of Richard and Mary Rouse.[86] It is in fact astonishing

---

[84] 'Der auf diesen Voraussetzungen basierende Aufschwung des Buchbindewesens hat den Bedarf an Handschriftenmakulatur in die Höhe schnellen lassen, und dies nicht nur im Bereich der klösterlichen und kirchlichen Hausbuchbindereien, sondern ebenso in den Buchbinderwerkstätten des städtischen Gewerbes' (ibid.).

[85] N. R. Ker, *Fragments of Medieval Manuscripts Used as Pastedowns in Oxford Bindings, with a Survey of Oxford Binding c. 1515–1620* (Oxford Bibliographical Society Publications, NS 5; Oxford, 1954).

[86] N. R. Ker, *Medieval Libraries of Great Britain: A List of Surviving Books*, 2nd edn. (London, 1964), and A. Watson, *Supplement to the Second Edition* (London, 1987); K. W. Humphreys, *The Friars' Libraries* (Corpus of British Medieval Library Catalogues; London, 1990); R. H. Rouse, M. A. Rouse, and R. A. B. Mynors, *Registrum Anglie de libris doctorum et auctorum veterum* (Corpus of Medieval Library Catalogues; London, 1991).

how few manuscripts have survived from medieval Franciscan and Dominican libraries in England.[87]

Losses from mendicant libraries

The case of the London Franciscan and Dominican convents conveys a warning to anyone who thinks that the modern pattern of survival is any kind of guide to the medieval situation. In a large Franciscan or Dominican convent one would expect a lot of manuscripts. The Dominican convent in London was large. In 1300, 92 friars lived there according to a recent study.[88] Of the few books surviving from their library, not one would be classed as a model sermon collection or preaching aid.[89]

It is the same with the Franciscans.[90] In 1300 there would seem to have been 76 of them in London.[91] Of the handful of surviving manuscripts from the library,[92] one, the 'Postillae' of Bertrand de la Tour, could count as a model sermon collection.[93] Another includes a few folios from a thirteenth-century sermon manuscript.[94] A third manuscript is a 'vocabulary of the Bible' and might count as a preaching aid if one stretched a point.[95]

Similarly with the Oxford Dominican house: according to the historian of the early Dominicans in England, the number of friars at Oxford 'fluctuates . . . between 60 and 96'.[96] Just three books have survived: Oxford, Merton College 132; Cambridge, Trinity College 347; and Oxford, Bodleian Lat. bib. d. 9.[97] None of these seems to be a sermon manuscript.[98]

[87] Rouse, Rouse, and Mynors, *Registrum Anglie*, cxlvii n. 66; Humphreys, *The Friars' Libraries*, xx.

[88] J. Röhrkasten, 'Mendikantische Armut in der Praxis: Das Beispiel London', in G. Melville and A. Kehnel (eds.), *In proposito paupertatis: Studien zum Armutsverständnis bei den mittelalterlichen Bettelorden* (Vita regularis: Ordnungen und Deutungen religiösen Lebens im Mittelalter, 13; Münster, 2001), 135–67 at 146.

[89] Ker, *Medieval Libraries*, 124.

[90] Ker, *Medieval Libraries*, 123; Watson, *Supplement*, 47.

[91] Röhrkasten, 'Mendikantische Armut in der Praxis', 146.

[92] Ker, *Medieval Libraries*, 123.

[93] MS London, BL Royal 4. D. iv.

[94] MS Oxford, Bodleian Library, Bodl. 429 = *Summary Catalogue* no. 2599.

[95] MS Oxford, Bodleian Library, Douce 239 = *Summary Catalogue* no. 21813.

[96] W. A. Hinnebusch, *The Early English Friars Preachers* (Institutum Historicum FF. Praedicatorum, Dissertationes Historicae, 14; Rome, 1951).

[97] Ker, *Medieval Libraries*, 142; Watson, *Supplement*, 52.

[98] The Bodleian manuscript, which formerly belonged to Neil Ker (see Ker and Watson, locc. citt.), is a Bible, almost certainly thirteenth century (personal exami-

So the known survival rate of sermon collections is nil for one big mendicant convent and a handful for another. Yet the number of sermon collections in each library in the Middle Ages must surely have been in three figures. In the Franciscan Library of Padua there were no fewer than 230 collections of sermons at the end of the medieval period, to judge by the 1499 catalogue.[99] Even if our three English friars' libraries were each half the size of Padua's, that still implies a loss rate on a notable scale, to put it mildly.

In the case of the Franciscans and Dominicans a further factor has to be taken into account, one which suggests that their loss rate taken as a whole must have been far greater than that of the older orders, however great that may have been. With the older orders, a book belonged to the library. Monks were assigned books, but normally they would read them within the monastery. The norm was for a fully professed monk to spend his whole life in the same monastery. Thus it would be easy for the librarian to keep track of library books. He might decide to destroy some books for their parchment, but he was not so likely simply to lose track of large numbers of books.

The same would be true of the books of Franciscans and Dominicans—but only when they were attached to libraries. As we have seen, the loss rate could be huge nevertheless: but this would be mainly because of the decision to recycle 'useless books' for their parchment, or because of the break-up of the convent and its library during the Reformation or a 'secularization'. Friars' books belonging to a convent library presumably faced much the same risks as Benedictine or Cistercian books. However, whole categories of friars' books were not attached to any library, and were consequently much more vulnerable.

nation); Trinity 347 is 'W. Woodford contra Wiclevum': M. R. James, *The Western Manuscripts in the Library of Trinity College, Cambridge* (4 vols.; Cambridge, 1900–4), i. 473–5. Merton 132 has a commentary on the Sentences and 'institutiones in sacram paginam' of Simon of Tournai: H. O. Coxe, *Catalogus codicum mss. qui in collegiis aulisque Oxoniensibus hodie adservantur* (2 pts.; Oxford, 1852), pt. 1. 57–8.

[99] K. W. Humphreys, *The Library of the Franciscans of the Convent of St. Antony, Padua, at the Beginning of the Fifteenth Century* (Studies in the History of Libraries and Librarianship, 3, Safaho-Monografien, 4; Amsterdam, 1966), 15. In this case many have survived: see Humphreys' concordance of catalogue entries and surviving manuscripts.

Books without libraries

As Neil Ker put it, 'The books individual friars had the use of might be the property of the order, or of the province, or of the custody, and were carried from house to house.' Ker was able to draw on Humphreys' careful study of the book provisions of the friars.[100] This makes it clear that books were not 'anchored' to any one library. A book unattached to a library is in danger in the long run, especially if it is small and unadorned. It is like a ship without a convoy in submarine-infested waters. Books could belong to provinces or in the Franciscan case also to custodies (subdivisions of Franciscan provinces) rather than to individual convents (Humphreys, 27–8, 52 n. 51). The Dominican provincial priors were supposed to 'keep a written list recording which books belong[ed] to the [provincial] community and to which brothers they [were] assigned' (ibid. 27 n. 59). This sort of regulation seldom works properly.

Clearly it was hard to keep track of both provincial books and conventual books out on loan. Humphreys quotes an order to the friars of the French Dominican province that

brothers who have books granted to them for their use, whether by the provincial priors or by any of the convents, are bound to inform in writing the same priors of convents or their deputies (vicariis), and the provincial prior so far as the books of the province are concerned, within a month from receipt of this memorandum, about the aforesaid books, or otherwise they are ipso facto deprived of the use of these books. (Humphreys, 28–9 n. 68)

In other words, there was no record of who had what. Even modern libraries with immaculate records have trouble with readers who forget what they have out. Despite the rather pathetic-sounding efforts to introduce some discipline into the borrowing system, it was a recipe for the loss of books, though from the point of view of the Dominicans' pastoral efficacy it was a perfectly sensible arrangement. Franciscans too take out books. It is worth quoting Humphreys' summary of regulations about what to do when a Franciscan friar died. They are a prudent librarian's nightmare:

The books of a friar dying when away from his native convent were to be collected by the custodian or by the warden and sent back to the of-

[100] K. W. Humphreys, *The Book Provisions of the Mediaeval Friars 1215–1400* (Amsterdam, 1964).

ficers in charge of the custodies where the books had been first issued. The convent, custody or province which assigned the books was to have such books returned; other volumes, i.e. gifts, or the personal books of a friar were to go to the convent at which the friar had first been received. If it was impossible to discover who had originally assigned the books, they were to be sent to the province from which the friar first came. Any friar who had lent a book to another should ensure that it was returned to the custodian or warden at the death of the borrower. (Humphreys, 52)

It is hard to imagine that this system worked like clockwork.

Though books belonged to Franciscan custodies, Humphreys points out (57) that there is no evidence that every custody had a library. If books lacked a physical home, it must have been difficult to keep track of them. Again, we know that books could be loaned to a Franciscan for life (ibid. 62). Friars could move around Europe a good deal in the course of their life, and books must have got lost in one way or another.

The implications should not be understated. No doubt some of these books were eventually incorporated into mendicant libraries, but often they would leave the order: books of deceased friars could be sold (Humphreys, 28, 53). Some were probably purchased by the older orders, which built up large collections of sermons in their libraries. This may explain why so many mendicant sermon collections survive in monastic libraries. There they would have a stable existence, unless recycled at the end of the Middle Ages for parchment. Books that went into private hands surely had much less chance of survival. It is a law that books outside libraries tend eventually to disappear. Of course, they were physically sturdy, so their nomadic existence could have continued for some time. Yet the very sturdiness of their parchment would in the end make them desirable to commercial bookbinders. One suspects that they were even more vulnerable to recycling than books in monastic libraries, because unwanted books are more of a nuisance to an individual and his heirs than to a large institution with continuity and a lot of space.

Quaterni

Even more vulnerable than books would have been the *quaterni* or unbound quires used by the friars. We know that friars used them. Roger Bacon says that the secular clergy with pastoral responsibilities[101] tended to have a weak formation in theology or preaching, so that when obliged to take on the task of preaching they 'borrow and beg the *quaterni* of the young friars'.[102] A 1267 regulation of the Roman province of the Dominican order banned friars from selling books or *quaterni* that they had written, unless they obtained the provincial prior's permission first.[103] Not only friars used *quaterni*: the Paris secular Jean d'Essômes left to the Sorbonne a manuscript of sermons and miscellanea which looks as if it was put together from originally independent *quaterni*.[104] (This is a reminder that highly educated members of the secular clergy count as 'honorary friars' for the purpose of this study.) A discussion by Gervase of Mont Saint-Éloi of originality in preaching says that great masters have been shamed by someone saying that 'I will show you in my *quaterno* the whole sermon you have given'.[105] 'Great masters' were supposed to compose their own sermons for some sorts of setting at least, whereas the imaginary critic would presumably have had the same sermon in his notebook to use as a model when preaching to a different sort of audience. In any case, it is further evidence that a *quaternus* was a normal way of carrying around sermons.

If a *quaternus* was not bound together with others into a book, its chances of survival would have been slight compared with, say, an illuminated Bible in a big Benedictine library. In fact, a *quaternus* written in 1300 probably had a lower chance of making it to 1500 than the illuminated Bible of making it from 1100 to 1500. Different genres of book paid different rates of interest to time, in the sense that the rate of attrition in one kind of book must have been much higher than with others. The attrition rate of friars' *quaterni*, as of friars' books unattached to a library, two categories which no doubt heavily overlapped, must have been particularly high: and sermon texts will have figured largely in both categories.

---

[101] The word he used is 'praelati', which seems to have included priests who had authority over a parish as well as 'prelates' in the modern sense: and I am assuming from the context that he is likely to have the former in mind.

[102] Roger Bacon, *Opus tertium*, in *Fr. Rogeri Bacon opera quaedam hactenus inedita*, ed. J. S. Brewer, i (Rolls Series; London, 1859), 309; d'Avray, *Medieval Marriage Sermons*, 19.

[103] Humphreys, *Book Provisions*, 26; d'Avray, *Medieval Marriage Sermons*, 26.

[104] MS Paris, BN lat. 16499: see d'Avray, *Medieval Marriage Sermons*, 235–7, for further references, especially to the findings of M. Mabille.

[105] Smalley, *English Friars*, 308.

The pecia *argument*

The last argument for a high loss rate is very technical: it involves a two-step inference from some surprising facts about transmission of sermon manuscripts by the *pecia* system (the system used to facilitate the copying of manuscripts in university milieux of the thirteenth and the first part of the fourteenth centuries). The details of the argument have been set out elsewhere and need not be repeated.[106] The following recapitulation only explains the general structure of the argument.

The first step is a demonstration that the loss rate of *pecia* manuscripts could be high by examining the transmission of a Franciscan sermon collection called *Legifer*. With the *pecia* system, a university 'stationer' had in his shop manuscripts of works believed to be in demand, in the form of loose quires. These shop manuscripts are called '*pecia* exemplars'. Their quires were hired out to people who wanted to copy the work. The copies are called '*pecia* copies'. Because the quires were loose, more than one scribe could be copying at the same time: one could be copying the first quire, another the second, another the third, and so on, although it was not likely to work out as simply as that since the scribes were operating independently, probably commissioned by different people. A more probable scenario would be that the scribe finished a quire and returned it to take out the next, only to find that someone else had it out. In that case he could take out the next one in the sequence, and leave an appropriate space to be filled later when the borrowed quire was back in the shop. Scribes often noted in the margins of their own manuscripts break points between quires in the *pecia* exemplar: they might write 'pe.' and a number. (Note that in a *pecia* copy the *pecia* marks will not normally coincide with the beginning of a quire.) Even when they did not, there are often tell-tale signs, such as a change of ink at the point where we know a new exemplar quire began, or compressed writing because they had left insufficient space for the contents of a quire copied out of sequence.

The system was first properly understood and explained by Jean Destrez, who devoted his life to it and travelled around European libraries looking for manuscripts with *pecia* indications, whether exemplars or copies. Few individuals have ever looked at so many medieval manuscripts in so many different libraries, and it is un-

---

[106] D'Avray, *Medieval Marriage Sermons*, 17–19; id., 'Printing, Mass Communication and Religious Reformation', 52–6.

likely that anyone since has developed such a sharp eye for a *pecia* indication. He published a big book[107] long before his manuscript work was complete, and so many of his later findings never got into print, but fortunately he left his voluminous notes in good order, and they may be consulted today in the Dominican study centre of Le Saulchoir in Paris.

Since Destrez, scholars have worked out some more details of how the system worked. They have been able to show how some *pecia* exemplars had to be duplicated, presumably because of demand, and how others had to be remade in part, presumably because some parts had become soiled or damaged by over-use. The Franciscan sermon collection called *Legifer* is one such collection. We have an exemplar and a copy, but the marginal numbers in the copy do not coincide with the quire numbers of the exemplar all the way through. The natural inference is that the original exemplar was so heavily used that parts had to be remade.

If so, many copies were made from it. However, Destrez found only one *pecia* copy. Now, he must have missed some manuscripts with *pecia* indications. As indicated above, manuscripts copied from *pecia* exemplars did not necessarily have the tell-tale numbers in the margin, and the other *pecia* indications are easier to miss. Still, Destrez had the best eye in the world for such indications and devoted his working life to looking for them. Thus it is thought-provoking that he did not find more *pecia* copies of this work. The natural explanation is that many others have disappeared: again, an indication of a high loss rate.[108]

There is a second step to the argument. *Pecia* transmission accounts for only a small proportion of surviving sermon manuscripts. So one may say this: if surviving *pecia* manuscripts represent only the tip of the small iceberg of those that once existed, surviving sermon manuscripts *tout court* represent only a tiny proportion of the number of sermon manuscripts *tout court* that once existed. This complex argument would not be overwhelming on its own. There are too many links in the chain of inference for

[107] J. Destrez, *La Pecia dans les manuscrits universitaires du XIIIe et du XIVe siècle* (Paris, 1935).
[108] I set out a converging argument about the *pecia* transmission of the sermons of Pierre de Reims in *Medieval Marriage Sermons*, 17–18. It is not the only hypothesis that fits the data, but it is the hypothesis with the most comfortable fit. As an argument for a large loss rate it would not stand on its own, but it reinforces and draws strength from the other arguments.

certainty. Still, it fits very well with the other evidence and adds significant support to an already strong case.

Here the subject is sermon manuscripts and model sermons, but it should be said again that the implications extend to other genres of manuscripts of this period, some of which survive in far more copies than the sermon collections studied here.[109] The implication is that their original diffusion was proportionally larger. So the concept of late medieval mass communication should not be confined to the friars or to model sermon collections and preaching aids—though it should be remembered that only these were further systematically multiplied by repeated oral events.

Convergence

Each of the foregoing arguments—the great book massacre, the vanished mendicant libraries, books without libraries, *quaterni* without books, *pecia* inferences—has considerable force, but they also support one another more or less independently. The onus of proof should be on those who deny a colossal loss rate of mendicant manuscripts like model sermons, and other manuscripts facing similar perils. Quantification would be quite artificial, but, despite the talk of tips of icebergs, one in ten would surely be too optimistic by far. It is perfectly possible that only one in fifty got through to our day: perhaps even fewer. Even with fifteenth-century printed books, the survival rate averages only about 1.2 per cent for small-format books,[110] and these books have had fewer centuries to survive and would have been less attractive to bookbinders seeking strong scrap materials. The low figure is eloquent. It is all the more remarkable that we still have so many thirteenth- and fourteenth-century sermon collections in books of this format: just the size that friars could have carried easily with them when they moved to a different

---

[109] This was stressed in Robert Lerner's review of *Medieval Marriage Sermons* in *Speculum*. He intended it as a *reductio ad absurdum*: the absurd conclusion being that medieval books which survive to this day in hundreds of manuscripts could have originally been transmitted by thousands of manuscripts. But in fact there is nothing absurd about this conclusion, though it runs against some assumptions which are as prevalent as they are ungrounded in evidence.

[110] '. . . bei Oktavbänden allerdings nur bis zu 3% (Durchschnittswert 1,2%) [erhalten]' (Neddermeyer, *Von der Handschrift zum gedruckten Buch*, 75); 'Schmale Bände sind fast ausnahmslos nur noch vereinzelt vohanden. . . . Oktavbände [sind] heute in jedem Fall sehr selten' (ibid. 76).

house or province.[111] Common though they still are, there may have been a hundred times more of them, or still more than that, at the start of the fourteenth century.

Production of manuscripts by friars
If so many manuscripts have been lost, they must have been first produced. How could they have been produced in such numbers without the help of printing? In essence, the answer is that a double labour force was at work. On the one hand, there were professional scribes. There has been an idea in the air in the oral culture of modern manuscript scholars that such commercial scribes took over the work of monastic scriptoria entirely. However it may be with monastic scriptoria, which lie outside the scope of the present study, it is a mistake to think that the new orders of friars relied only on the products of commercial scribes. They certainly got many of their books this way.[112] (Other books originally copied by paid scribes for someone else would have been passed on as gifts to mendicant convents.) There is no doubt that very many manuscripts used by friars were produced by this first labour force of paid scribes. However, the second labour force consisted of the friars themselves, who copied their own manuscripts. It also included any other literate priests who copied sermon collections for their own use and—this is important—the use of others.

There is a good deal of direct evidence for the copying activity of friars: chronicle evidence and their own regulations.[113] Then there is a quite different kind of evidence which converges towards the same conclusion: the nature of variants in many sermon manuscripts. In some manuscripts there are many free and independent variants: not mistakes but voluntary changes that make sense. They represent an independent attitude on the part of the scribe, and this has considerable implications.

Such variants may be found in the critical apparatus of *Medieval Marriage Sermons*, more or less *passim*. They are also more clearly

---

[111] D'Avray , 'Portable *Vademecum* Books Containing Franciscan and Dominican Texts'.
[112] M. Mulchahey, 'More Notes on the Education of the *Fratres communes* in the Dominican Order: Elias de Ferreriis of Salagnac's *Libellus de doctrina fratrum*', in J. Brown and W. P. Stoneman (eds.), *A Distinct Voice: Medieval Studies in Honor of Leonard E. Boyle, O.P.* (Notre Dame, Ind., 1997), 328–69 at 338.
[113] Collected in d'Avray, *Medieval Marriage Sermons*, 25–8.

illustrated in another study,[114] and some more evidence of the same kind is provided in Documents **1. 4–8.** The changes are not necessarily drastic. Small unnecessary modifications betray an attitude to the text different from that of hired scribes.

These independent variants are not a peculiarity of Franciscan and Dominican sermon manuscripts. In vernacular texts they are exceedingly common, and they may also be found in other genres of Latin text.[115] There is a whole spectrum from the scribe-author who rewrites the whole thing to a copyist who feels free to change the wording occasionally, but deliberately (so I am not counting simple inversions of words, which can occur even when a scribe is trying to copy exactly, word for word).

On the other hand, many texts do not have any semi-authorial or independent-minded interventions. A majority of the manuscripts collated for *Medieval Marriage Sermons* try to give a standard text. I would be amazed to find such improvisation in a copy made from *pecia* exemplars at university stationers;[116] it is not normal in canon-law manuscripts.[117]

The following principles are in tune with common sense and may confidently be proposed as hypotheses which no one is likely to succeed in falsifying.[118]

(1) Manuscripts of works by authors of known authority, when copied by commercial scribes working for hire, would seldom if ever have independent, deliberate, nonconformist variants. Like any copies, they will have errors, but we should not find improvisation. The reason: if you pay someone to copy a work, you do not expect him to alter the text as he goes along. So, for instance, a *pecia* copy of a sermon collection in the university stationer's shop will necessarily be conformist.

(2) Consequently, when the text of a manuscript varies freely from the standard one, not in error but deliberately, it was probably not copied by a commercial scribe. (Or if it was, it descends from a manuscript which was not the work of a commercial scribe.) The reason: if you are not working for money and feel

---

[114] D'Avray, 'Printing, Mass Communication and Religious Reformation', 69–70.

[115] See d'Avray, *Medieval Marriage Sermons*, 23 n. 62.

[116] My instinct was confirmed by conversation with Kent Emery (who knows the *pecia* transmission of Henry of Ghent).

[117] My own impression confirmed by conversation with Dr Martin Bertram.

[118] This should be interpreted as an invitation to try.

at home with the material, you are not obliged to follow the exemplar slavishly. So a sermon collection copied by a friar who was an experienced preacher could have nonconformist variants.

(3) A manuscript with a script of professional quality and where the text is conformist could *either* be the work of a commercial scribe *or* of someone working on his own account. The reason: a commercial scribe had to be conformist, but a person working on his own account and without pay could be conformist too: nonconformity was not an obligation. So a sermon collection with a conformist text might or might not have been copied by a friar.

These principles are an appeal to common sense. The way to falsify them would be to find a substantial number of manuscripts of Latin works where the scribe was demonstrably working for hire but where the text nevertheless contains nonconformist variants. Until or unless the principles are falsified, the hypothesis holding the field is that both commercial scribes and friars copied mendicant model sermon collections.

To clear up any misunderstanding: free scribal variations are *not* in themselves evidence of mass communication. Works with a minute diffusion could be copied this way. The free variants are evidence of a second labour force alongside professional scribes, pointing to an explanation of how such a high rate of production was possible. This fact also shows how the production of so many manuscripts could be economically viable despite the relatively high cost of medieval books.[119] If friars rather than paid scribes did the copying, the greater part of the cost of a book would be saved. Louis-Jacques Bataillon has provided evidence suggesting that in the later thirteenth century parchment represented about 20 per cent of the cost of a book.[120] This would have made the economics of large-scale book production viable for friars. It must be remembered that the cost of parchment varied a lot.[121] MS BN Lat.

[119] I am indebted to Robert Lerner for raising the question of the cost of book production.

[120] L.-J. Bataillon, 'Les conditions de travail des maîtres de l'université de Paris au XIIIᵉ siècle', *Revue des sciences philosophiques et théologiques*, 67 (1983), 417–32 at 423 n. 25.

[121] M. Gullick, 'From Parchmenter to Scribe: Some Observations on the Manufacture and Preparation of Medieval Parchment Based upon a Review of the Literary

16497 (written on cheap parchment) cost 12 sol. of Paris all told,[122] so the parchment would have cost between 2 and 3 sol., between a quarter and a third of a florin,[123] quite a modest sum. Alms given by Louis IX in 1256 give a relative idea of the cost of the parchment for this book. Thus pittances of bread and wine for fourteen days came to £38. 17s. 8d. in Paris currency, pittances from the kitchen for eighteen days came to £33. 2s. 6d., and alms for 200 poor on 14 August came to £20, a little short of the cost of the parchment for BN Lat. 16497 for each poor person.[124] On the assumption that the parchment was the main monetary cost because the labour cost only the future user's time, the book—of this sort and in these circumstances—becomes a relatively inexpensive article.

Another study notes a fifteenth-century English manuscript composed of parchment quires (sixteen pages per quire) which cost a penny-halfpenny each.[125] To put this in perspective by comparison with a peasant inventory from 1457: two buckets are valued at a shilling, which makes each worth four quires; a sheet cost 4d., more than two quires; two worn canvasses cost 4d., each more than a quire; a chair cost 3d., two quires.[126] Friars received substantial donations, and money on this scale would have been readily available. In the light of these figures, some of the ideas current among scholars about the minimum cost of a basic parchment book are exaggerated by orders of magnitude.

As just noted, manuscripts with maverick modifications of the text can be written as well as if they were produced by professional scribes. Whoever improvised upon the text did so in a physical form that others could use and copy. These maverick texts with nonconformist variants are not confined to personal preaching notebooks which could only be of use to the man who wrote them.

Here it is useful to invent a term: cul-de-sac books. A cul-de-sac

Evidence', in P. Rück, *Pergament: Geschichte, Struktur, Restaurierung, Herstellung* (Historische Hilfswissenschaften, 2; Sigmaringen, 1991), 145–57 at 147, 151.

[122] Bataillon, 'Les conditions de travail', 423 n. 24 (citing M. Mabille, 'Les manuscrits de Jean d'Essomes conservés à la Bibliothèque Nationale de Paris', *Bibliothèque de l'École des Chartes*, 130 (1972), 231–4).
[123] Cf. P. Spufford, with the assistance of W. Wilkinson and S. Tolley, *Handbook of Medieval Exchange* (Royal Historical Society Guides and Handbooks, 13; London, 1986), 168.
[124] E. M. Hallam, *Capetian France 987–1328* (London etc., 1980), 233, table 5.1.
[125] Cf. Gullick, 'From Parchmenter to Scribe', 151.
[126] C. Dyer, *Standards of Living in the Later Middle Ages: Social Change in England c. 1200–1520* (Cambridge, 1989), 170.

codex is a manuscript which is at the end of the line of tradition, because it is too untidy, informal, and personalized for anyone to use it as an exemplar. For the same reasons, it is unlikely to be passed on to new owners capable of using it in the same way as the man who wrote it. The manuscripts under discussion here were not cul-de-sac books. These model sermons could be the exemplars of further copies, and they could be used by other preachers, not only by the man who copied them. The point is really an answer to a potential objection: viz., that manuscripts with nonconformist variants were just private books, usable only by the man who made them and sterile in terms of the transmission of the text. The relevance to the mass communication thesis is thus real but indirect.[127]

To conclude. There may have been up to *c.*40,000 Franciscans and Dominicans in the early fourteenth century.[128] It was common for friars to copy sermon collections. Not all Franciscans and Dominicans did, we can be sure. On the other hand, there were also Carmelites, Augustinian Hermits, educated members of the secular clergy who could match the pastoral activity of the friars, and probably also some members of the older orders.[129] This formidable labour force worked alongside the commercial scribes who also copied sermon manuscripts. There has been a tendency to assume that the commercial scribes did all the work: hence the demonstration above that they did not carry the burden of copying alone. An enormous number of books to help preachers resulted. Even the number that has survived is huge, but it may be a tiny percentage, perhaps even as low as 1 per cent, of the number that once existed. The survival rate was probably quite uneven, biased against *quaterni* and friars' books not linked to libraries: though

---

[127] I am again putting right a misapprehension (for which I blame my lack of clarity) in the *Speculum* review by Lerner, who understood me to mean that maverick variants in a manuscript of professional appearance are evidence of a copying industry, which is not in fact my view.

[128] The estimate of R. Southern, *Western Society and the Church in the Middle Ages* (Harmondsworth, 1970), 285.

[129] '[A] certain number of monks, at least in the thirteenth century, went to Oxford to learn preaching, partly with the aim of dispensing with the services of friars in the cathedral priories, where friction had developed between the mendicants and the possessioners. Preaching in both Latin and English was contemplated' (D. Knowles, *The Religious Orders in Engand*, ii. *The End of the Middle Ages* (Cambridge, 1961), 24). I do not see why such monastic preachers should not have copied sermon manuscripts.

library books too were vulnerable to the great book massacre of
c.1500. Each of these innumerable model sermons on parchment
could have been used repeatedly for vernacular 'live' preaching
(the 'multiplier effect'). While we cannot even guess at the impact
of an individual sermon on an individual, the cumulative impact
of sermon topoi on the the sermon-going public cannot have been
slight. These considerations entitle us to regard mendicant preaching as a social force in the same kind of sense as a modern mass
medium. It remains to examine the content of the message where
marriage and marriage symbolism are concerned.

(d) The Message about Marriage

Marriage symbolism

Anyone who skims through the sermons edited and translated in
Medieval Marriage Sermons, or through the complementary corpus of sermons in the 'Documents' section corresponding to this
chapter, will realize that marriage symbolism is prominent and
perhaps usually predominant.[130] (The following analyses will be
based on these two dossiers, but one could carry out a similar exercise with late medieval sermons.) As a symbol, marriage is as
a rule overwhelmingly positive in preaching, but it can stand for
an intense commitment of any kind, including commitment to sin
or the Devil.[131] The sinful soul is 'the daughter and bride of the
Devil'.[132] The three stages that lead up to the finalization of a
marriage—initiation (engagement), ratification (present consent),
and consummation—stages which we shall meet again and again
and which are normally full of positive significance, can stand for
the three stages that finalize a sin. Thought or pleasure is initiation,
consent is ratification, deed is consummation.[133]

A detail of language should be noted. Pierre de Saint-Benoît

[130] The sermons did not have to take the approach they did, for they normally
start from the Gospel reading about the marriage feast of Cana, and instead of
exalting marriage on the literal and symbolic levels, the path they actually took,
they might have concentrated on an influential apocryphal story according to which
the bridegroom of Cana was St John the Evangelist, who opted for celibacy between wedding and consummation: see A. Volfing, *John the Evangelist and Medieval
German Writing: Imitating the Inimitable* (Oxford, 2001), 29–31.

[131] D'Avray, *Medieval Marriage Sermons*: Pierre de Saint-Benoît, para. 4/2/;
Gérard de Mailly paras. 3–7; Konrad Holtnicker: Document **1. 10. 8.**

[132] Konrad Holtnicker: Document **1. 10. 8.**

[133] D'Avray, *Medieval Marriage Sermons*: Pierre de Saint-Benoît, para. 4.

calls this evil marriage 'carnal marriage'. However, 'carnal' does not necessarily have negative associations. There are sermons where it is used in a positive sense.[134]

A common motif or topos is the marriage of Christ and human nature.[135] This is the incarnation, the union of divine and human 'in the womb of the Virgin', when the Lord 'took up our nature and completely united it to himself for ever'.[136] This is compared by one preacher[137] to the marriage between a woman of ill repute in the Old Testament and Osee (i.e. Hosea), who gave his name to the book of the Bible in which the story occurs. The woman is called Gomer. Pierre de Reims explains that the Hebrew name means 'taken up'. The idea is that human nature is 'taken up' and united to the saviour, Osee. The two natures become 'truly two in one flesh'.

The marriage feast of Cana took place 'on the third day', according to the words of the Gospel. Guibert de Tournai picks up on this detail and uses it in his symbolism. The first day is the age of nature: that is, before God gave the Law of the Old Testament to the Jews. The second day is the 'age of scripture', the age of the Old Testament. The third day is the age of grace, when divine and human nature were united in one person.[138] Guibert is interesting on the consummation of this marriage.[139] He understands it in two ways. First, there is the Passion of Jesus Christ. At the climax of the passion, Jesus said: 'It is consummated'. The other 'consummation' is the resurrection. Here one needs to be aware of thirteenth-century marriage law and theology to understand the implications of Guibert's comment. He says that after the resurrection, there will be no more division of Christ's body and soul or Divinity and Humanity.[140] Guibert shows his knowledge that it is only after consummation that Christian marriage becomes absolutely indissoluble. As we shall see in a later chapter, before that

---

[134] D'Avray, *Medieval Marriage Sermons*, 121, 134.

[135] See ibid.: Pierre de Reims, para. 2 (also p. 121, on the Angers version, and pp. 122, 122–3, on the Milan version); Guibert de Tournai, paras. 4, 6, 8 (and pp. 285 and 316, on the Assisi version); Jean Halgrin: Document **I. 9. 5**; Servasanto da Faenza: Document **I. II. 21–2**.

[136] Servasanto da Faenza: Document **I. II. 21**.

[137] D'Avray, *Medieval Marriage Sermons*: Pierre de Reims, para. 2.

[138] Ibid.: Guibert de Tournai, para. 4.   [139] Ibid., para. 6.

[140] As often with Guibert, he has not quite thought it through: of course the Divinity and Humanity, as opposed to body and soul, would have been inseparable right from the incarnation according to standard theology.

it could be dissolved at least by the entry of one partner into a
religious order.

Clearly connected with the 'marriage to human nature' topos is
the image of Christ's marriage to the Church: the two meanings are
imperfectly distinct. One version of Pierre de Reims puts it thus:
the marriage feast of Cana was 'a sign or sacrament of the joining
together of Christ and the Church: just as Christ did not lay down
human nature once he had taken it up, so too marriage is not divided
or sent away'.[141] However, the 'marriage to the Church' motif may
be analysed apart without doing violence to the data.[142]

The 'initiation–ratification–consummation' topos comes into
play again. The three stages of betrothal, consent in the present
tense, and sexual intercourse were, as already noted, a familiar
schema in theology and canon law, and through law affected practice. Familiarity with social practice will have enhanced the symbolism, as with Guibert de Tournai's reflection on 'consummation',
examined above. Pierre de Saint-Benoît comes close to echoing one
of Guibert's thoughts. He says that 'the matrimonial bond of this
marriage, that is, the marriage of Christ and the Church, was initiated in the promise of the Son of God which was made to the holy
fathers,[143] ratified in the incarnation, and consummated in Christ's
passion.'[144]

This takes him on to the Eucharist, the meal of Christ's body and
blood. It is the feast that goes with the marriage.[145] The Eucharist is
the wedding banquet again in another preacher's development of a
story from the Bible used frequently in marriage symbolism. This
is the story of Ahasuerus[146] and Esther, applied to the marriage of
Christ and the Church.[147] The proud consort of the king of the
Medes and Persians is replaced as queen by a beautiful Jewish girl.
In the biblical account revenge on the enemies of the Jews follows.

[141] D'Avray, *Medieval Marriage Sermons*, 121.

[142] In the corpus used for this analysis I note the following cases: d'Avray, *Medieval Marriage Sermons*: Hugues de Saint-Cher, para. 11, also p. 134; Pierre de
Saint-Benoît, paras. 7–9, and also, for the Trinity College Dublin manuscript,
p. 226; 'Documents': Konrad Holtnicker, 1. 10. 9; Servasanto da Faenza, 1. 11. 23.

[143] He means to the great men of Old Testament times.

[144] Pierre de Saint-Benoît, para. 8.

[145] D'Avray, *Medieval Marriage Sermons*: Pierre de Saint-Benoît, para. 9.

[146] Ahasuerus, Assuerus in the Latin Vulgate, corresponds to the historical Xerxes I.

[147] D'Avray, *Medieval Marriage Sermons*: Pierre de Saint-Benoît, para. 7; Konrad
Holtnicker: Document 1. 10. 9.

The preachers are not interested in that, but in the symbolism of the marriage. Vashti the first queen represents the synagogue, and Esther the Jewish girl stands for the Christian Church. Could this Vashti–Esther symbolism have undermined marital indissolubility? It seems unlikely. For one thing, the story is set in Old Testament times, when the rules were different, as preachers knew and could explain. Much more importantly, the whole emphasis is on the symbolism of salvation history and the point about the Old Testament dispensation and its replacement by the Christian Church, with the Old Testament narrative serving as an allegory. When the preacher moves into scriptural narrative as the basis for imagery, the change of discourse would probably have been evident to most attentive listeners, especially since supplementary clarification would have been possible in the 'live' sermon preached from the model if any necessity had been apparent. The message—replacement of Synagogue by Church—would have explained to the listener why the story was being used. When it came to types of discourse and changes of register in oral sermons, there is no reason to think late medieval listeners were obtuse, and there is an exotic tone to the story which marked it as belonging to the Old Testament 'other'. The line between this allegory and the analyses of Christian marriage, whether as a symbol or at the literal level, would not have been hard for most listeners to intuit.

The Esther story comes up again under our next heading: the marriage of the individual soul to Christ or God. In Guibert de Tournai this is linked with the 'initiation–ratification–consummation' topos:

The third marriage is the spiritual one of Christ and the faithful soul. This is the marriage of Assuerus with Esther. Esther 2: 17–18: 'the king made Esther reign in the place of Vashti, and he ordered that a banquet be prepared for the union and marriage with Esther'.

And this is what is said in today's Gospel: that the water was changed into wine, for the banquet of that marriage: the water, that is, of contrition, into the wine of consolation. For it is said in Mark 2: 19: 'Can the children of the marriage fast, as long as the bridegroom is with them?'

This marriage is initiated in good thought, ratified in consent, and consummated in good action.[148]

Guibert is quite eloquent in his section on the marriage of the

[148] D'Avray, *Medieval Marriage Sermons*: Guibert de Tournai, paras. 12–14.

soul. Some of the credit goes to the quotations he chooses,[149] but
no source is cited for the following passage: 'In good consent he
comes: not as a lord imposing labour, not as a judge striking fear,
not as a master correcting error, not as a doctor drastically curing
a disease, but as a bridegroom arousing love.'[150] This passage too
may be a quotation, of course—Guibert was derivative.[151] In this
'model sermon' genre it was unimportant: efficacy mattered more
than originality.

Even from the surviving Latin models one can guess that some
developments of the 'marriage to the soul' image could have sti-
mulated mental images in listeners. Pierre de Reims develops a
comparison between a soul who is betrothed to but then betrays
Christ and a poor girl betrothed to the son of a king but who
is unfaithful to him and loses everything. As he works through
the analogy, he evokes the social condition of a peasant girl. For
example: 'if she were free and responsible for herself, after all this
she might still be able to get a living for herself from somewhere or
other; but it is not so, because she has fallen into a great bondage.'[152]
This would be a much stronger image for listeners familiar with
the stigma of servile status in thirteenth-century France than it is
for a modern reader, unless the historian can reconstruct some of
the lost connotations.[153]

The imagery can be very simple. Jean Halgrin talks about the
soul who, forgetful of her engagement ring, does not keep the
faith of marriage, when women as a rule keep their engagement
ring throughout their life.[154] An image like this would not need
to be developed: the listeners would provide their own supplementary images. A much fuller image which could have triggered
associations precisely because it was analysed in greater depth
was that of the ideal husband, represented by Gérard de Mailly
in the corpus analysed here and in fact quite a widespread

[149] e.g. ibid., para. 17/7/ (the motif of the beautiful captive also used by Pierre de
Reims, paras. 19–20); and para. 18, a passage from St John Chrysostom which is
rather fine.
[150] Ibid., para. 14.
[151] Cf. D. L. d'Avray and M. Tausche, 'Marriage Sermons in *ad status* Collections
of the Central Middle Ages', in N. Bériou and D. L. d'Avray, with P. Cole, J.
Riley-Smith, and M. Tausche, *Modern Questions about Medieval Sermons: Essays
on Marriage, Death, History and Sanctity* (Spoleto etc., 1994), 77–134 at 94.
[152] D'Avray, *Medieval Marriage Sermons*: Pierre de Reims, para. 13/1/.
[153] As I tried to do in *Medieval Marriage Sermons*, 61–2.
[154] Jean Halgrin, Document **1. 9. 8.**

topos.[155] Gérard says that Christ has all the qualities of an ideal bridegroom: he is eloquent, wealthy, wise, attractive in appearance, powerful, noble—and immortal.[156] This last quality is clearly not for the human bridegroom, however idealized, but in general the list converges—perhaps more closely than coincidence can account for—with the image of the attractive knight found in the romances of Chrétien de Troyes.[157] That is not to say that Chrétien influenced the preacher. More probably, they both reflect generally current social assumptions. However, this means that Gérard's list would have struck cords in the imaginative and fantasy life of many listeners.

The image of the soul's marriage to God is turned by the Florentine Aldobrandino da Toscanella into a reflection on the nobility of man: it could be designated 'other-worldly humanism'. Explaining why the marriage of God and the soul really belongs to the next life, he gives a fascinating glimpse of his structured universe. Creatures are ranked in order of nobility, as are their settings in the elements. Thus plants go with earth; above them, fish with the nobler element of water; above them, the birds of the air, a still higher element. So 'those things which are fittingly grouped together in nature are fittingly grouped together in a place, as all plants are on earth' (and so on). But man has a likeness to God, so the marriage takes place in heaven. 'For . . . a noble pilgrim does not willingly contract a marriage in the land of his pilgrimage . . . but returns to the place of his birth.'[158]

This leads on to the general unsatisfactoriness of life in this world, where 'we are made sad, we grow heated, we get thirsty, we grieve, we get sick . . . For in this world there is no one who could have all good things without some evil. For some are good-looking, and yet poor; some are noble, but reduced to beggary; some are rich and noble, but suffer from ill health; some are rich and noble and healthy, but childless; but some, though they have children, nevertheless

[155] It is analysed in N. Bériou and D. L. d'Avray, 'The Image of the Ideal Husband in Thirteenth Century France' (1990), in Bériou and d'Avray, *Modern Questions about Medieval Sermons*, 31–61.
[156] For the explanation of the analogy see d'Avray, *Medieval Marriage Sermons*: Gérard de Mailly, paras. 21–9.
[157] See Bériou and d'Avray, 'The Image of the Ideal Husband in Thirteenth Century France', 42–6, for a fuller analysis of the parallels.
[158] See Aldobrandino da Toscanella, Document **1. 12. 5.**

have children who are foolish or evil; and if they are good, they are short-lived.'[159]

Aldobrandino de Toscanella has in effect located the marriage of the soul to God in heaven. Once again, the different kinds of symbolic marriage prove to be imperfectly distinct. With Pierre de Saint-Benoît the eternal marriage in heaven is a continuation of the marriage of Christ and the Church. In the present, the feast is the Eucharist, compared to a midday meal. In the future, that is in eternity in heaven, there is the evening feast.[160]

The marriage feast of the lamb in the Book of Revelations, or Apocalypse, is a favourite motif for this ultimate marriage.[161] The problem of representing heaven is overcome by using such scripturally inspired imagery. Another example: '[The Lord] satiates them with the flood of his pleasure, and he inebriates them with the wine of his plenty' (derived from Ps. 35: 9).[162]

One could give much more detail about marriage symbolism in preaching, but the argument does not require it. It should be sufficiently clear that it is important in model sermon collections of the thirteenth century (and the same could be demonstrated for model sermons circulating in the last two medieval centuries). That needs to be taken together with the previous demonstration that model sermons were a form of mass communication, so that they can be called a social force.

Symbolism's literal foundation

The next stage of the argument is that the symbolic use of marriage in these sermons rested securely on a literal-sense idea of marriage as good and holy: an idea propagated by the same sermons that transmitted marriage symbolism to the masses. The marriage symbolism was not dissociated from marriage in its mundane literal sense. A positive evaluation of 'real' marriage and the enthusiasm for marriage symbolism were complementary.

The fact that many marriage sermons bring instruction on marriage in the literal sense within the same frame as marriage symbolism has implications. One could have envisaged a genre of marriage

[159] Ibid. **1. 12. 7.** This passage sounds as though it could have been lifted from an earlier writer, but if so I have failed to find the source.
    [160] D'Avray, *Medieval Marriage Sermons*: Pierre de Saint-Benoît, para. 9.
    [161] Ibid., para. 24; Gérard de Mailly, para. 37; Konrad Holtnicker: Document **1. 10. 10**; Servasanto da Faenza: Document **1. 11. 25.**
    [162] Servasanto da Faenza: Document **1. 11. 24.**

symbolism which actually deprecated the ordinary human marriage of men and women. We actually find this view represented among the Cathars: 'spiritual' symbolic marriage between the soul and God, good; human marriage with sex, bad—not marriage at all but whoring.[163] Instead, many sermons for the second Sunday after Epiphany make vigorous propaganda for human marriage as well as developing the theme of symbolic marriage. This provided a solid literal base for the symbolic ideas.

Preaching and the sacralization of marriage

This line of thought needs to be extended beyond textual analysis. The propaganda for human marriage in this genre of preaching will have helped to sacralize the social institution. Preaching would have conferred a religious aura on marriage.

This would have been particularly important in parts of Europe where a religious marriage ceremony was not required by the Church. In parts of Italy couples could get married in a civil ceremony not only with full validity, but also with the full approval of the Church. There seems to have been no general rule about a religious ceremony in canon law—a fact often missed in the past by good scholars. After 1215 it is true that banns had to be read in order to stay within the rules, but the reading of banns would not have the same sort of psychological and religious impact as a religious ceremony.[164]

As a consequence, marriage could easily have seemed a very secular thing to the laity—had it not been for preaching. As it was, from the mid-thirteenth century at least it would have been hard for a layman or woman living in a town and attending mendicant sermons to avoid hearing every year or so sermons explaining the religious value of marriage, literally understood.

Attitudes to sex before and after the Cathars

In some sermons from our corpus symbolic marriage is the dominant theme and not much space is allotted to the goodness of marriage in the literal sense, but even when the point is made succinctly,

---

[163] M. G. Pegg, *The Corruption of Angels: The Great Inquisition of 1245–1246* (Princeton etc., 2001), 176 n. 27: report of the view of a Cathar believer.

[164] Here I am leaving out of account the whole question of clandestine marriages where the couple did not bother to have the banns read in advance. These will be discussed below, in Chapter 2.

the endorsement of the legal sexual union of men and women by these celibate preachers is unambiguous. To some degree this can be explained as a reaction to the Cathars, who had spread like wildfire in the twelfth century and who tended to think that sex was bad inside or outside marriage and that procreative sex was the worst kind.[165] In the Cathar *Book of Two Principles*, one of the few Cathar writings to survive systematic persecution, there is an interesting polemic (in its own terms dazzlingly skilful) by one Cathar sect against another in which the evilness of marriage is used as common ground from which a logical refutation can be mounted.[166] The logic of the system, so far as one can generalize about it, was that the whole material world was the product of an evil principle. Souls were seen as good, bodies as bad. Sex perpetuated the chain of bodies.

The goodness of marriage in the literal sense had been preached before the Cathars appeared on the scene. The following passage from Gregory the Great's *Regula pastoralis* deserves attention—it was not discussed before as it is not about marriage symbolism—for it undermines the assumption that the early medieval Church was generally negative about marriage. It comes from a section explaining, to quote its heading, that 'Those who are bound by marriage, and those who are free from the ties of marriage, are not to be given the same advice'.[167] It uses the Old Testament narrative of Lot's flight from Sodom as a sort of parable. He stopped off on the way to the mountains at a place called Segor:

Lot . . . finding Segor, by no means immediately ascended the mountains. Indeed, to flee from burning Sodom is to reject the illicit fires of the flesh. For the height of the mountains is the purity of those who are continent. Or truly, those people also are in effect [*quasi*] on the mountain who cleave to carnal union, but who are yet not weakened by any pleasure of the flesh over and above the intercourse that is due for begetting children. Indeed, to stand on the mountain is to seek only the fruit of procreation in the flesh. But since there are many who do indeed abandon the crimes of the flesh, and who, being in the state of matrimony, do not however keep to

[165] For further references on the Cathar attitude to marriage see d'Avray, *Medieval Marriage Sermons*, 11, citing Arno Borst on the Cathar condemnation and on what was apparently a more favourable attitude in a later phase, and Le Roy Ladurie for the idea of marriage as instrumentally useful but equivalent to fornication in value terms.

[166] For a convenient translation of the passage in question see W. L. Wakefield and A. P. Evans, *Heresies of the High Middle Ages* (New York etc., 1969), no. 59, p. 570.   [167] Migne, *PL* 77. 101.

the norms of that use of marriage which alone is proper, therefore did Lot indeed leave Sodom, but yet he did not reach the heights quickly, because now the way of life that earns damnation is left behind, but still the height of conjugal continence is not kept to in a rarefied way. For Segor is truly a city at a point midway, which can save the fugitive who is weak, namely because, when a married couple have intercourse through incontinence, they both flee the lapses of crimes [*scelerum*], and yet are saved through a pardon [*venia*]. They find as it were a little city in which they may be protected from the flames, because this conjugal life, while not marvellous in its virtues, is nevertheless safe from punishment. (Migne, *PL* 70. 102–3)

In short, marital sex motivated by the desire for children virtually puts married couples on the same level with monks and nuns; marital sex 'through incontinence' is only half-way to the heights, yet a means of salvation. It is quite possible that these ideas did get into some popular preaching in the early Middle Ages. So this passage may be more important for the history of marriage preaching than the defence of marriage at the beginning of Haymo of Auxerre's sermon on the Cana pericope.[168] (Haymo's homiliary was not primarily for popular preaching, as we have seen.[169]) So thirteenth-century preachers were drawing on tradition as well as reacting against Cathars. Nevertheless, the success of the Cathar movement probably helps to explain why some of them were so insistent about the goodness of marriage.

Thirteenth-century preachers allude to St Paul's prophecy that heretics would come and condemn marriage.[170] St Paul was probably attacking contemporary Gnostics. Early medieval homiliaries, notably that of Haymo of Auxerre,[171] picked up the passage but probably did not have any contemporary heretics in mind. Our thirteenth-century preachers, however, could hardly have failed to think that the Cathars, who briefly mounted such a serious challenge to Catholicism in southern France and Italy, were a fulfilment of the prophecy.

For our purposes the balance of tradition and reaction in the

[168] For the passage giving arguments for marriage see Haymo of Auxerre, homily 18, *Dominica II post Epiphaniam*, in Migne, *PL* 118. 126–37 at 126–7.

[169] See above, pp. 25–6.

[170] D'Avray, *Medieval Marriage Sermons*: Hugues de Saint-Cher, the sermon analysed but not edited, p. 132; Gérard de Mailly, para. 1; Guibert de Tournai, para. 1; Servasanto da Faenza: Document I. II. II.

[171] Haymo of Auxerre, homily 18, *Dominica II post Epiphaniam*, in Migne, *PL* 118. 126.

genesis of thirteenth-century preachers' attitudes to marriage matters less than the impact of their preaching. The great difference between the last three medieval centuries and the preceding period was that positive ideas about marriage were pumped out by a preaching system which was capable of bringing them to very large numbers of laypeople.

The following topoi become very familiar to anyone who reads a range of later medieval marriage sermons. Here they are illustrated only from the sermons transcribed in the Documents section below and those edited in *Medieval Marriage Sermons*, but the motifs are also common outside this double corpus.

God created marriage

'For it was instituted not by any contemptible person, not by a man, not by an angel, but by God.'[172] Sermons outside our corpus compare marriage favourably in this respect with the great religious orders.[173]

Marriage was made in Paradise

As Konrad Holtnicker put it, marriage was instituted 'not in a contemptible place, not in a corner, as clandestine marriages are made nowadays, but in Paradise'.[174] Holtnicker goes on to complain about people who 'contract marriage after many lapses and acts of fornication' (ibid.). Nevertheless, he sees marriage itself as noble: in sharp contrast to extramarital sex. Other sermons make the point about Paradise more simply.[175]

Marriage was instituted in a sinless world

This motif is obviously closely connected with the 'Paradise' topos. In sermons it tends to be just another compliment to marriage, but there was a reservoir of theological reflection in the background, on the nature of marriage in Paradise: whether it involved pleasure

---

[172] Konrad Holtnicker, Document **1. 10. 4**; cf. d'Avray, *Medieval Marriage Sermons*: Hugues de Saint-Cher, para. 1.

[173] N. Bériou and D. L. d'Avray, 'Henry of Provins, O.P.'s Comparison of the Dominican and Franciscan Orders with the "Order" of Matrimony', in Bériou and d'Avray, *Modern Questions about Medieval Sermons*, 71–5.

[174] Konrad Holtnicker: Document **1. 10. 4**.

[175] D'Avray, *Medieval Marriage Sermons*: Hugues de Saint-Cher, para. 1; Guibert de Tournai, para. 1; Jean Halgrin: Document **1. 9. 1**.

etc.[176] Probably preachers did not discuss in any depth the theology
of marriage in Paradise. Still, the topos implied that marriage went
with human nature in its pristine perfect state, and was not just a
remedy for concupiscence and lust.

The double cause

Preachers distinguish between the function of marriage before the
sin of Adam and Eve and after it. In the state of innocence, it was
for the sake of children (though they had not got as far as having
any before the first sin was committed), but after the original sin
marriage became a remedy for fornication also.[177] Behind this lies
the idea that the original sin disrupted the balance of human nature
and the control by mind and will over passion and desire. Marriage
acquired the supplementary function of regulating unruly passions.

Put like this, the preacher's view sounds unromantic. That would
be somewhat misleading. Their married love is not the love of
medieval romances, it is true: it is not an unstoppable emotional
force. Still, married love is a very central theme.[178] Guibert de
Tournai seems to have had a sense for it, writing that ' "Man will
leave [his father and mother]" by the privilege of love, for that love
by which husband and wife love one another is more vehement than
all carnal loves.'[179]

Christ was present at a marriage feast

The preachers argue that Christ's presence implies approval.[180]
Servasanto develops the argument thoroughly:

[176] M. Müller, *Die Lehre des hl. Augustinus von der Paradiesesehe und ihre Auswirkung in der Sexualethik des 12. und 13. Jahrhunderts bis Thomas von Aquin: Eine moralgeschichtliche Untersuchung* (Studien zur Geschichte der katholischen Moraltheologie, 1; Regensburg, 1954), 277–9. 'Yes' was the outcome of the debate.

[177] D'Avray, *Medieval Marriage Sermons*: Hugues de Saint-Cher, para. 1; cf. d'Avray and Tausche, 'Marriage Sermons in *ad status* Collections of the Central Middle Ages', 104–6.

[178] See d'Avray, *Medieval Marriage Sermons*, index, s.v. 'marriage, love and'; also id., 'The Gospel of the Marriage Feast of Cana and Marriage Preaching in France', in Bériou and d'Avray, *Modern Questions about Medieval Sermons*, 135–53 at 143–4.

[179] D'Avray, *Medieval Marriage Sermons*: Guibert de Tournai, para. 9; cf. d'Avray and Tausche, 'Marriage Sermons in *ad status* Collections of the Central Middle Ages', 128–31.

[180] D'Avray, *Medieval Marriage Sermons*: Hugues de Saint-Cher, para. 1; Pierre de Saint-Benoît, para. 1; Guibert de Tournai, para 1; Jean Halgrin: Document **1. 9. 1**; Konrad Holtnicker: Document **1. 10. 5**; Servasanto da Faenza: Document **1. 11. 13**.

Again, if marriage had been evil, the Lord would have taught that it is evil, nor would he have honoured it with his presence, nor eaten there, nor adorned it with so solemn a miracle, nor permitted his most holy mother to be present. Therefore in honouring a marriage with all these things, he showed that it was good.

Again, the canon says, and this is self-evident, that the error which is not resisted is approved, nor is a man who abandons the effort to resist a public wrong immune from suspicion of being secretly involved. Therefore, if marriage were evil, since the Lord was present at it, and did not resist that evil when it would have been possible for him to do so, and did confute it when he was the teacher of truth, in failing to obstruct evil, he approves it. But this is utterly impossible. Therefore so is the first point, namely, that marriage is evil. (Servasanto da Faenza: Document 1. 11. 12–13)

The miracle at Cana

Christ's endorsement of marriage is also demonstrated by the miracle worked at the wedding feast.[181]

Against the background of all these topoi, one or two preachers stand out for their more original or sophisticated apologias for marriage. Aldobrandino da Toscanella is unusual for his time in asserting that it confers grace. Until some point in the thirteenth century there was no consensus that marriage actually did confer grace: many thought that it was the one sacrament that did not.[182] By the second half of the thirteenth century the conviction that Christian marriage conferred grace had more or less won the day. However, it should not surprise us that preaching lagged behind theological development. Aldobrandino da Toscanella, though, had apparently been keeping up with academic theology. He puts it like this:

Again . . . in marriage grace is conferred. In so far as it is contracted in the faith of Christ, it has the power to confer the grace which helps with doing those works which are required in marriage. And we see an example of this in the field of natural philosophy, for whenever the power of doing something is given to anything, helps are also provided by means of which

[181] D'Avray, *Medieval Marriage Sermons*: Hugues de Saint-Cher, para. 1; Pierre de Saint-Benoît, para. 1; Guibert de Tournai, para. 1; Jean Halgrin: Document 1. 9. 1; Konrad Holtnicker: Document 1. 10. 6; Servasanto da Faenza: Document 1. 11. 12.

[182] D'Avray, 'The Gospel of the Marriage Feast of Cana and Marriage Preaching in France', 149, citing D. Burr, *The Persecution of Peter Olivi* (Transactions of the American Philosophical Society, NS 66, pt. 5; Philadelphia, 1976), 45–6.

those things may be attained. Therefore, since God has disposed it that man has the power in matrimony of using his wife for the procreation of children, he is also given the grace without which he cannot do it in a fitting way: just as God, or Nature, which gives the power of walking to an animal, gives it the instruments, namely legs, with which it may be able to walk. (Aldobrandino da Toscanella: Document 1. 13.

5)

Nature and Aristotle

Aldobrandino da Toscanella is keen on nature as well as grace, standing out from most preachers in the corpus for his special interest in it, except that Servasanto, the other Florentine preacher included, is very like him in this respect. In one of his sermons Aldobrandino celebrates nature in a passage where the precise train of thought, though not immediately evident in detail, is optimistic and evocative: for example, 'natural things are delightful, . . . Everything is a matter of delight in the time that belongs to it, like sweet wine in winter, dry wine in summer'.[183] The same paragraph eventually leads into the Aristotelian idea[184] that everything in nature strives towards the imperishable and the divine. Some things are imperishable in themselves so do not need to reproduce. Others have to achieve a sort of permanence by producing something like themselves.[185] Thus 'it may be preserved in something which is like itself because of the divine being, and thus it conserves nature'.

Servasanto da Faenza finds his way to the same idea, which he presents slightly differently, perhaps because refutation of the Cathars is at the forefront of his mind. His language and way of thinking are syllogistic and no less Aristotelian than Aldobrandino's, a warning not to attempt a sharp distinction between Franciscan and Dominican Florentine preaching.[186] He argues that if something has a good end (note the teleological thinking), then it too is good. But the end (i.e. the 'telos') of generation is to bring into the world children for the worship of God and to preserve in

---

[183] Aldobrandino da Toscanella: Document 1. 13. 3.

[184] Deriving probably from *De anima* bk. 2, 415^{a-b}.

[185] See *Aristotle's* De Anima *in the Version of William of Moerbeke and the Commentary of St. Thomas Aquinas*, ed. and trans. K. Foster, S. Humphries, and I. Thomas (London, 1951), 210 and 214–15, for the translation and/or commentary which Aldobrandino may have used.

[186] D. L. d'Avray, 'Philosophy in Preaching: The Case of a Franciscan Based in Thirteenth-Century Florence (Servasanto da Faenza)', in R. G. Newhauser and J. A. Alford (eds.), *Literature and Religion in the Later Middle Ages: Philological Studies in Honor of Siegfried Wenzel* (Binghampton, NY, 1995), 263–73.

them the being that comes from God. This is a good end. So procreation must be good. Then comes the Aristotle citation, as with Aldobrandino.[187]

Servasanto uses a series of other arguments from nature, notably: nothing made by nature is superfluous, so the sexual organs must be there to be used (properly, of course). Nature provided for reproduction, just as for nutrition; but if nutrition is good, so is reproduction. It is a greater thing to conserve the species than the individual; but nutrition preserves only the individual, reproduction the species; so the sexual act of generation is more necessary to the universe and not sinful.

All this has a relevance to the argument about the influence of marriage symbolism. The positive rationale for marriage in preaching converged with the symbolic message but will also have helped to foster social attitudes in the public which could give a secure base for the reception of the symbolism. The less that attitudes to marriage were coloured by religious approval, the weaker the base for religious marriage symbolism. Marriage would be a weaker symbol of union with God for people who thought that marriage in the normal human sense had nothing at all to do with their religion.

Conclusion

There is every reason to think that marriage symbolism became a powerful force in the lay world through preaching, from the thirteenth century on. The symbol of metaphor was intrinsically powerful, at least for many of those who had the basic religious beliefs and some positive experience of marriage.

Why did this not happen before the thirteenth century? The simple answer seems to be that an adequate delivery system for bringing marriage doctrine and marriage symbolism to the laity had not been in place. There was some popular preaching, but the Carolingian reforms had anticipated the preaching revolution of the thirteenth century on a relatively minute scale. The total volume of preaching material was very small in comparison with that of the last three medieval centuries. In any case a high proportion of ordinary priests were not well equipped educationally to make effective use of Latin homiliaries or sermons even if they had them. Furthermore, marriage symbolism seems to have played a relatively insignificant role in what preaching there was. Though the verdict

[187] Servasanto da Faenza: Document **1. 11. 5.**

has to be provisional until more research on early medieval preaching has been published, everything points to a watershed shortly after 1200, when university-trained clergy and above all the friars started preaching and producing model sermon collections. The sermons tended to include a marriage sermon in which propaganda for human marriage was combined with marriage symbolism.

Something similar might have come about much earlier if the Carolingian experiment had not fallen apart in the ninth century, owing to invasion, succession crises, and lack of a firm economic infrastructure for government. Weak economic infrastructure may also be the ultimate reason for the generally low level of clerical education, which would have limited the amount of preaching from model marriage sermons even if they had been available. The infrastructural frailties of the period before 1200 are the main reason why marriage symbolism had relatively little impact in the lay world before that date.

Even if it had done, the symbolism would have been undermined by marriage practices. Before the pontificate of Innocent III, the Church's official religious emphasis on the indissolubility of marriage had been undermined by the easy annulments. The male lay élite now accepted the principle and the authority of the Church's courts where the validity of marriage was concerned. Still they managed to change wives quite easily when they wanted to by discovering real or imaginary impediments which enabled them to get the marriage annulled. Before the Church courts gained a monopoly of such cases it had probably been even easier to end a marriage with a nominal annulment. All that changed in the thirteenth century, and as it happened marriage symbolism seems to have been a powerful force behind the change, which drastically affected the whole social institution of marriage.

I have argued that marriage symbolism became a social force when preaching became a medium of mass communication in the thirteenth century, but so far this has meant a force on people's minds, rather than on their behaviour. In the remainder of the book I shall look at the ways in which marriage symbolism worked through law to affect social practice. The chronology is roughly the same, the period around 1200 being decisive.

2
Indissolubility

(a) From the Roman Empire to the Carolingian Empire

Causes and effects

A potential cause may be neutralized for centuries by other social forces. If they are weakened, the cause is activated. One argument developed below is that Augustinian marriage symbolism's tendency to promote indissolubility was unlikely to take effect while so many of the clergy could identify with the sexually active lay male.

Then again, ideas may lie dormant for a long time, until influential persons infuse them with intensity and power. This began to happen when intellectuals at the proto-university of Paris revitalized Augustinian marriage symbolism. More decisive still was Innocent III's determination to turn symbolism into social fact. The degree to which he succeeded will be discussed, and I shall argue that Church tribunals did not make a mockery out of indissolubility after his time, as they had arguably done often in the twelfth century. So far as law can control life, Innocent and the symbolism behind his thinking left a deep mark on the social practice of marriage. Establishing that proposition will involve analysis of some comments by a great canonist (Hostiensis) that seem to show the opposite; analysis also of the meaning of the large class of 'pre-contract' cases in the church courts. The latter show that indissolubility overrode other considerations, including rules about marriage in church where they obtained. Indissolubility could furthermore be enforced by excommunication at the deserted spouse's request. Thus indissolubility had become a constraint on social behaviour. It limited or channelled sexual and emotional freedom to an extent unparalleled in most societies. The character of the constraint should not be misunderstood. In two important respects it did coexist with freedom. Legal separation was an option: sometimes there were even papal legal remedies to safeguard a wife's property in such circumstances. Again, indissolubility was the counterpart of a strong emphasis by the Church on real freedom at the point of commitment to marriage: another rather unusual feature of later medieval canon law in a broad comparative perspective.

Augustine of Hippo against the social world of late antiquity

A marriage system different from any other in the history of great civilizations was in large part produced by the reciprocal causal interplay of symbolism and social practice: but the process took 800 years, from Augustine of Hippo at the beginning of the fifth century to Innocent III at the start of the thirteenth.[1] The specific thing was marriage of one man to one woman for life. I have failed to find the combination of monogamy and indissolubility in any other major civilization. It is hard to overstate the importance of this. Hinduism has indissolubility with polygamy, pagan Rome monogamy with divorce, classical China the same but with status accorded to concubinage, Judaism and Islam allow both polygamy and divorce in principle.

Here we are talking about norms. Many people will always get around a social norm. On the other hand, to say that norms leave social behaviour unaffected would be an extreme view. Another qualification: in many or most societies monogamy for life may have been general practice without being a norm. Economics and sentiment both encourage it, countering the tendencies of men to use power to get sex and make alliances. The fact remains that there is something unusual about what happened in the West.

In explaining this development some familiar names will come up: especially Augustine of Hippo, Gregory VII, and Innocent III. However, it is first and foremost the history of an idea, a symbolic idea that came to give meaning to social practice. The idea itself is older than the medieval West and found in other civilizations, as we noted at the start of the book: the idea that the union of man and woman stands for the union of God and humans. We saw that it was an image for God's relation with his chosen people the Jews before it became a symbol of Christ's union with the Church. Augustine

[1] For a useful survey (from a Catholic point of view) of texts giving the mind of ecclesiastical writers from antiquity to the twelfth century see F. Delpini, *Indissolubilità matrimoniale e divorzio dal I al XII secolo* (Archivio ambrosiano, 37; Milan, 1979).

of Hippo was the man who turned the image into a social time
bomb.

In his treatise *On the Good of Marriage* (probably written in 401)
Augustine linked indissolubility with symbolism:

the bond of fellowship between spouses is so strong that though the purpose
of their attachment is for begetting children, the marriage is not dissolved
even in order to beget them. A man could put away a barren wife and marry
one by whom to have children, but that is not permitted . . . Admittedly if
an adulterous wife or husband were abandoned and one or other of them
married another, more persons would be born; yet if, as the divine law
seems to lay down, this is not permitted, who would not become alive to
the significance of so strong a marriage bond?

My belief is that the bond would certainly not have been so strong
had not some sacred symbol of something more profound than this feeble
mortality of ours become attached to it, and when people abandoned it
and were keen to dissolve it, it remained unshaken to punish them; for the
marriage alliance is not rescinded by the divorce [i.e. separation] which
comes between them, and so they remain wedded to each other even when
separated; and they commit adultery with those to whom they are attached
even after their divorce, whether the wife associates with a man, or the
husband with a woman. However, it is only 'in the city of our God, upon
his holy mountain' that this situation with a wife applies.[2]

The significance of Augustine's thinking was recognized in a
concise, acute, and little-known paper by R. Kuiters.[3] He noted
that Augustine did not explain indissolubility in terms of 'nature':

Augustine's logic led him to find in the relation of husband and wife to
the union of Christ and the Church the solid base on which he establishes
the indissolubility which is specific to Christian marriage. . . . To play its
role as a similitude, marriage must be adapted and brought nearer to the
original. . . . Divorce becomes . . . inconceivable and without effect, for
even though they are separated by their wills, the husband and wife remain
united in the City of God by a religious (sacramental) bond.[4] (Kuiters, 10,
my trans.)

---

[2] Augustine, *De bono coniugali*, 7, in *Augustine:* De bono coniugali*; De sancta virginitate*, ed. and trans. P. G. Walsh (Oxford, 2001), 17.

[3] R. Kuiters, 'Saint Augustin et l'indissolubilité du mariage', *Augustiniana*, 9 (1959), 5–11. Also good on Augustine is S. P. Heaney, *The Development of the Sacramentality of Marriage from Anselm of Laon to Thomas Aquinas*, (The Catholic University of America Studies in Sacred Theology, Second Series, 134; Washington, 1963), xiv.

[4] Augustine strengthened his idea in a work written a couple of decades later (419–20), 'On marriage and concupiscence': 'Les époux sont invités, voire moralement

A strikingly similar interpretation of Augustine was reached in a more recent study:[5]

Augustine believes . . . that God made marriage indissoluble so that it might symbolize the union between Christ and the Church. . . . the little sacrament (i.e., marriage bond) is a sacrament of the great sacrament (i.e., the mystery of the inseparable union between Christ and the Church). Indissolubility is the salient feature of the comparison and the point of assimilation.'[6]

The individual elements of Augustine's synthesis were not so new. Indissolubility of marriage was a well-established idea in the Christian writers of the first five centuries.[7] Similarly, the idea of symbolic marriage was important in the Christian ancient world before Augustine, as well as in biblical texts that would of course have been familiar. However, Augustine welded the two components into a combination that would eventually become socially powerful.

In his own day and for centuries after it, however, Augustine's ideas about indissolubility and symbolism had little to do with the law and social practice around him: neither reflecting nor much affecting them, so far as we can see. The Christian law of the expiring Western Empire and its resilient Byzantine counterpart allowed divorce.[8] Studying the history of texts, studying 'historical theology',

obligés d'être la réplique de l'union du Christ à son Église. . . . Le fondement (la *res*) de ce sacrement, c'est que l'homme et la femme sont inséparablement unis par le mariage pour toute leur vie. La continuité de ce sacrement est sauvegardée dans le Christ et l'Église' (Kuiters, p. 10).

[5] It was almost certainly independent, so the convergence confirms the truth of the interpretation.

[6] P. L. Reynolds, *Marriage in the Western Church: The Christianization of Marriage during the Patristic and Early Medieval Periods* (Leiden etc., 1994), 301.

[7] 'Parmi les auteurs des cinq premiers siècles considérés comme orthodoxes un seul donne donc clairement au mari trompé la permission de contracter à nouveau mariage, l'inconnu désigné sous le nom d'Ambrosiaster. Des signes d'une attitude moins rigide à l'égard des remariés peuvent être décelés dans le canon 10 du concile d'Arles et dans le canon 9 de Basile, mais rien ne permet de dire qu'ils acceptent ces secondes noces: seules le font les évêques blâmés par Origène' (H. Crouzel, 'Les Pères de l'Église ont-ils permis le remariage après séparation?', in id., *Mariage et divorce, célibat et caractère sacerdotaux dans l'église ancienne: études diverses* (Études d'histoire du culte et des institutions chrétiennes, 11; Turin, 1982), 3–43 at 43). Crouzel goes on to say that he is not personally an unquestioning advocate of absolute marital indissolubility, but the interpretation of patristic texts should not be affected by the modern scholar's personal views.

[8] Reynolds, *Marriage in the Western Church*, 49–65. Reynolds argues that the

can leave a false impression of continuity. Augustine's views run right through the subsequent history of thought, but only in the thirteenth century did social and legal practice move into line with the symbolic theology of marriage he worked out. Social practice converged slowly with the Augustinian ideal, the gap between them huge until the early thirteenth century.

Early medieval ménages

Beneath the stormy surface of political events in the age of Augustine and the successor states to Rome—the age held together in the mind by the writings of Peter Brown—a slow transformation of marriage structure occurred. A world of 'commensurable household units' evolved, a contrast with both classical and 'barbarian' society:[9]

> In classical society, mass slavery alone assured that some households might include scores or even hundreds of persons, while many slaves and poor freemen were denied any sort of independent domestic life. . . . The polygynous practices of the northern barbarians, the concentration of women in the households of the rich, also accentuated the differences in domestic organization up and down the social scale. (Herlihy, *Medieval Households*, 59)

The change from slavery to serfdom and the influence of Christianity evened up the differences between households, so that most men could live with a woman and only a few men had a lot of women (Herlihy, 59–62). 'The appearance of commensurable domestic units in the early Middle Ages, the formation of a symmetrical array of households encompassing the entire community, mark an epoch in the history of the European family' (ibid. 62).

This development should not be confused with a victory for indissolubility.[10] 'The Church' was not yet making any concerted or determined efforts against the practice of divorce. Even the legis-

---

aim of the Christian emperors 'was to make divorce more difficult, and to ensure that persons did not divorce without good cause' (62) and that 'they aimed to bring the law of divorce into line with Christian teaching, but that what they knew as the Christian doctrine of marriage was less dogmatic and less theological than the doctrine of men like Tertullian, Ambrose, Jerome and Augustine' (64).

[9] See D. Herlihy, *Medieval Households* (Cambridge, Mass., etc., 1985), ch. 3 ('commensurable units', p. 57; 'commensurate household units', p. 61).

[10] For the whole Frankish period see I. Fahrner, *Geschichte der Ehescheidung im kanonischen Recht*, i. *Geschichte des Unauflöslichkeitsprinzips und der vollkommenen Scheidung der Ehe* (Freiburg i.Br., 1903) 47–105; G. Fransen, 'La rupture du mariage', in Centro italiano di studi sull'alto medioevo, *Il matrimonio nella so-*

lation of church councils was not unanimous against divorce and remarriage: the Council of Angers in 453 permitted men to remarry and the Council of Vannes (465) accepted it apparently for either husband or wife if adultery was demonstrated.[11] In the following century the opposition of the Church to divorce was limp and in 506 the Council of Agde admitted the principle.[12] The early penitentials—a curious genre whose influence and setting in life are not easy to determine—are rigorous but 'in the seventh century Theodore of Tarsus, Archbishop of Canterbury, allowed divorce on grounds of adultery, desire to enter religion, desertion for five years, the reduction of either partner to slavery, or the wife's abduction into captivity'.[13]

If churchmen were not of one voice in condemning divorce, we should not expect greater rigour from lay authorities and do not find it. According to P. L. Reynolds, the law codes of the Germanic successor states 'contain remarkably little on the subject of the dissolution of marriage', but this 'may be due to the ease with which persons (especially men) could dissolve their marriages'.[14] For women, divorce after a properly formalized marriage may have become harder than in Roman times (ibid. 99–100). 'If an unfortunate Burgundian woman attempted to divorce her husband she was to be smothered in mire.'[15] Possibly it was easier in early

cietà altomedievale (2 vols.; Settimane di studio del centro italiano di studi sull'alto medieoevo, 24; Spoleto, 1977), ii. 603–30, esp. 623–6; J.-A. McNamara and S. F. Wemple, 'Marriage and Divorce in the Frankish Kingdom', in S. M. Stuard (ed.), *Women in Medieval Society* (Philadelphia, 1976), 96–124; J. Gaudemet, 'Deuxième partie: les incertitudes du haut Moyen Âge', in id., *Le Mariage en Occident: les mœurs et le droit* (Paris, 1987), 93–132; R. Le Jan, *Famille et pouvoir dans le monde franc (VIIe–Xe siècle): essai d'anthropologie sociale* (Paris, 1995), 277–85; and A. Esmyol, *Geliebte oder Ehefrau: Konkubinen im frühen Mittelalter* (Beihefte zum Archiv für Kulturgeschichte, 52; Cologne etc., 2002). The main thesis of the last-named work is to expose as a myth the idea of a type of marriage ('Friedelehe') between 'Muntehe' on the one hand (where a free woman passed from her family's control to her husband's with a corresponding property transaction) and concubinage on the other: which would normally be between a free man and an unfree woman, so that a free woman's status was drastically diminished if she entered into such a union.

[11] McNamara and Wemple, 'Marriage and Divorce in the Frankish Kingdom', 97–8.   [12] Ibid. 100.
[13] P. Stafford, *Queens, Concubines and Dowagers: The King's Wife in the Early Middle Ages* (London, 1983; repr. London etc., 1998), 80.
[14] Reynolds, *Marriage in the Western Church*, 99.
[15] McNamara and Wemple, 'Marriage and Divorce in the Frankish Kingdom', 100.

Anglo-Saxon England.[16] To return to the Continent: McNamara
and Wemple found that 'all the codes recognized that a man could
repudiate his wife for very slender reasons by requiring some monetary consolation for the unoffending wife thus left with her children'.[17]

It went beyond divorce. 'Traditions of polygamy died hard
among the Merovingians', noted Wallace-Hadrill, commenting on
the murder of King Chilperic's queen, at the instigation of a mistress it was said—'the mistresses of Chilperic saw no reason to
grant to the Visigothic princess the position of unique influence
she demanded'.[18]

Not only kings ignored the rules: Pippin of Herstal, the father of
Charles Martel, is a striking case.[19] In one of the few sources for
the period we read that 'Pippin took a second wife, the noble and
lovely Alpaida. She gave him a son, and they called him in his own
language Charles. And the child grew, and a proper child he undoubtedly was.'[20] The chronicler omits to mention at that point that
his wife Plectrudis was still alive. At Pippin's death 'his widow, the
before-mentioned lady Plectrudis, took everything under her control'.[21] One must not be too cut-and-dried in characterizing early
medieval relationships. Between the ideal-types of full monogamy

[16] ' . . . marriages were not regarded as indissoluble and it was not always the
wife who was discarded. In Æthelbert's code the woman who wanted to end her
marriage faced no legal obstacles. After clause 77, defining the man's right to return
the "fraudulent" woman, come clauses that spell out the property claims of the wife
who wishes to leave her husband; she may do so—and no grounds are specified—
taking with her half the goods and all the children; if the children stay with the
husband then the wife herself receives a child's share' (H. Leyser, *Medieval Women:
A Social History of Women in England 450–1500* (London, 1995), 45).

[17] McNamara and Wemple, 'Marriage and Divorce in the Frankish Kingdom',
100. Cf. Stafford, *Queens, Concubines and Dowagers*, 74: 'If doubt must hang over
polygamy, serial monogamy is crystal clear. . . . many kings repudiated one wife to
marry the next.'

[18] J. M. Wallace-Hadrill, *The Long-Haired Kings* (Toronto etc., 1982), 134. On
early medieval polygamy and concubinage see too M. Borgolte, 'Kulturelle Einheit und religiöse Differenz: Zur Verbreitung der Polygynie im mittelalterlichen
Europa', *Zeitschrift für historische Forschung*, 31 (2004), 1–36 at 10 and n. 41, with
further references.

[19] See *The Fourth Book of the Chronicle of Fredegar, with its Continuations*, ed.
J. M. Wallace-Hadrill (London etc., 1960), 86 (for the second wife) and 87–9 (for
the survival of the first). Paul Fouracre directed me to this case.

[20] Ibid. 86. Le Jan, *Famille et pouvoir dans le monde franc*, 271, comments in
connection with this case that 'Le système germanique répondait aux motivations
sociales de la polygamie'.

[21] *The Fourth Book of Fredegar*, ed. Wallace-Hadrill, 87.

and full bigamy or polygamy there are intermediate stages, not necessarily clearly distinguished from one another: concubinage where the woman was not just a mistress but had an official or semi-official position, or was a wife but not in the fullest sense, or where the line between wife and concubine was blurred.[22]

The evidence of formularies gives a glimpse of what were presumably regular social patterns and suggests that divorce was normal in the barbarian West, and not only at the top of the social scale. The following item in the formulary of Marculf is extremely significant:

Since not charity according to God but discord reigns between N. and his wife N., and because of this they are in no way able to live together, it was the will of each of them, that they should separate from the union of marriage, and this they have done. They have consequently had written and confirmed these two letters with the same content to be given to each other, so that each of them should be free to do what they wish: whether to enter the service of God in a monastery, or to enter into a marital union: and neither should have to answer to their neighbour [*proximi*] for it. But if either of the two parties should want to change this or make some claim against the other one of the couple, they must pay a pound of gold to the other, and, as they have agreed, they shall be kept away from their own marriage and shall remain with the party they have chosen.[23]

'Neighbour' here may be a clumsy way of referring to the other party in the dissolved marriage, or to third parties, but it makes no substantive difference. The meaning of the final clause is also clumsily formulated. It seems to say that if one party tries to reverse the agreement they must pay a penalty, and cannot interfere with their former partner's new relationship.

Thus it is hard to detect any influence of Augustine's ideas about marriage on the pre-Carolingian world. Conceivably this is because of the state of the sources, but more probably the influence was absent. No doubt Augustinian marriage symbolism found a place of some kind in the consciousness of some learned men.[24] Still, a chasm separated it from social practice.

---

[22] Cf. Le Jan, *Famille et pouvoir dans le monde franc*, 271–4, and J. Chélini, *L'Aube du Moyen Âge: naissance de la chrétienté occidentale. La vie religieuse des laïcs dans l'Europe carolingienne (750–900)* (Paris, 1991), 139, 140–1.

[23] *Marculfi formularum libri duo*, ed. A. Uddholm (Collectio Scriptorum Veterum Uppsaliensis; Uppsala, 1962), bk. 2, ch. 3, p. 273.

[24] J. Gaudemet, *Le Mariage en Occident: les mœurs et le droit* (Paris, 1987), 120 and nn. 46 and 47 for further references.

(b) *c.*800–*c.*1200

Carolingian contradictions

The place of the Carolingian era in the history of marriage is like
its place in medieval history generally: there are moments when
one could be in the thirteenth century, but the new social forms
and patterns do not quite come to anything. As with the revival of
trade, the power of the state, and the creative application of hard
questions to theological problems, so too with lifelong monogamy
or indissolubility: there are confident new beginnings, then it tails
off, and even when the forces of change look strong there are con-
tradictory tendencies.

With marriage the picture is confused. Councils legislate against
indissolubility, councils permit divorce, popes send mixed signals,
the practice of great men sometimes seems Merovingian and sometimes it could come straight out of the thirteenth century, when
people took church law very seriously.

Charlemagne's sexual history is not so different from the Merovingian pattern. His life was full of marriages and semi-official
liaisons with concubines, and at least one of the marriages involved
repudiation of an existing full wife: he had Himiltrud either as
a concubine or as a wife, then the daughter of Desiderius King
of the Lombards while Himiltrud was still living, then Hildegard
while the Lombard princess was still alive.[25] Things were very
different with his son and successor Louis the Pious. When his
wife was condemned for adultery in 830, Louis had to promise to
enter a monastery, which 'seems to demonstrate that by this time
the indissolubility even of adulterous marriages became generally
accepted'.[26] That might suggest a clear trend towards indissoluble
marriage at the highest level at least, but not so. A few decades
later Lothar II, king of the Middle Kingdom (of the successor
states of the Frankish empire), tried hard to change wives, though
as we shall see he was thwarted by a powerful pope.[27] That might

[25] Stafford, *Queens, Concubines and Dowagers*, 60; McNamara and Wemple, 'Marriage and Divorce in the Frankish Kingdom', 104–5; Gaudemet, *Le Mariage en
Occident*, 122.
[26] McNamara and Wemple, 'Marriage and Divorce in the Frankish Kingdom',
106.
[27] For the case see e.g. ibid. 108–11; Gaudemet, *Le Mariage en Occident*, 126–7;
and, for political context, see J. L. Nelson, *Charles the Bald* (London etc., 1992),
214–17.

of course fit the same trend, but there is no clear-cut direction: not long afterwards we find Charles the Bald making his son Louis the Stammerer divorce his wife Ansgard and marry a Burgundian noblewoman named Adelaide.[28] As we shall see, royal marriages continued to be very breakable after the Carolingian era. The secular and church legislation also sent mixed signals. It may or may not seem paradoxical that Charlemagne legislated in favour of indissolubility.[29] Under his successor, in 829, a council at Paris said that for a cuckolded husband to remarry was another adultery.[30] On the other hand, the council of Compiègne in 757 permitted divorce in the modern sense of allowing remarriage.[31]

It is the same story with the penitentials. The Jesuit scholar Joyce even thought that a penitential tradition deriving from Theodore, the Greek archbishop of Canterbury, was responsible for a growing tolerance for divorce.[32] Joyce was an impressive historian but almost certainly wrong on this point: he surely underestimated the prevalence of divorce with remarriage before Theodore. But still, a very soft line on indissolubility is characteristic of penitentials from around 700.[33] On the other hand, some late penitentials were more supportive of indissolubility.[34]

Mixed signals came even from Rome. On the one hand, two mid-eighth-century popes were strongly for indissolubility. A letter of Pope Zachary to Pippin took a hard line.[35] His successor

---

[28] Nelson, *Charles the Bald*, 232; Stafford, *Queens, Concubines and Dowagers*, 75.

[29] Bishops gathered by Charlemagne at Friuli ruled that adultery did not end a marriage, and 'This legislation was later incorporated into the Capitulary to the Missi in 802 extending it to the whole empire' (McNamara and Wemple, 'Marriage and Divorce in the Frankish Kingdom', 104). The Admonitio Generalis of 789 contained an indissolubility canon deriving from the Dionysio-Hadriana canon-law collection which had been sent by the pope in 774: Fahrner, *Geschichte des Unauflöslichkeitsprinzips und der vollkommenen Scheidung der Ehe*, 82.

[30] McNamara and Wemple, 'Marriage and Divorce in the Frankish Kingdom', 105.

[31] Ibid. 103; J. M. Wallace-Hadrill, *The Frankish Church* (Oxford, 1983), 171; Stafford, *Queens, Concubines and Dowagers*, 80. See also Fahrner, *Geschichte des Unauflöslichkeitsprinzips und der vollkommenen Scheidung der Ehe*, 75–7.

[32] G. H. Joyce, *Christian Marriage: An Historical and Doctrinal Study* (London etc., 1933), 337–41.

[33] Gaudemet, *Le Mariage en Occident*, 132; P. Daudet, *Études sur l'histoire de la juridiction matrimoniale: les origines carolingiennes de la compétence exclusive de l'Église — France et Germanie* (Paris, 1933), 62–4.

[34] Gaudemet, *Le mariage en Occident*, 132; Daudet, *Études sur l'histoire de la juridiction matrimoniale*, 64.

[35] Gaudemet, *Le Mariage en Occident*, 120 (note the error of ixe for viiie); McNa-

Stephen II allowed separation only if one spouse was possessed or suffering from leprosy: even so, the marriage was not dissolved.[36] On the other hand, it is possible that the Roman synod held by Pope Eugenius II in 826 permitted divorce on grounds of adultery (definitely forbidding it, however, on any other grounds).[37] This was a provincial synod, not a general council.[38] It has not given rise to the polemics aroused by Gregory II's letter to Boniface about a man whose wife was sick so that he could not (had never been able to?) have intercourse with her:[39] nor should it. Perhaps one could say that the doctrine of indissolubility was in about the same kind of state as the doctrine of the Trinity had been before Nicaea or the doctrine of Christ's divinity and humanity before Chalcedon: positions were possible that would later be excluded.

In parenthesis, another decree of this synod deserves mention. Decree 37 forbids any man to have two wives or concubines.[40] Nothing surprising about that—except that it was necessary to say

mara and Wemple, 'Marriage and Divorce in the Frankish Kingdom', 102; Chélini, *L'Aube du Moyen Âge*, 229; W. Kelly, *Pope Gregory II on Divorce and Remarriage* (Analecta Gregoriana, 203, Series Facultatis Iuris Canonici, Sectio B, 37; Rome, 1976), 71–2.

[36] Gaudemet, *Le Mariage en Occident*, 129.
[37] Concilium Romanum, 826, no. 36: 'De his, qui adhibitam sibi uxorem relinquerunt et aliam sociaverunt. Nulli liceat, excepta causa fornicationis, adhibitam uxorem relinquere et deinde aliam copulare; alioquin transgressorem priori convenit sociari coniugio' (*Concilia aevi Karolini*, ed. A. Werminghoff (2 vols.; Monumenta Germaniae Historica, Legum Sectio III, Concilia, 2. 1–2; Hanover, 1906–8), ii. 582). Fahrner commented on this that 'Dieser an sich zweideutige Kanon kann bei der Stellung der römischen Kirche nur dahin gedeutet werden, daß im Falle des Ehebruchs eine unvollkommene Scheidung gestattet ist' (Fahrner, *Geschichte des Unauflöslichkeitsprinzips und der vollkommenen Scheidung der Ehe*, 83 n. 3)—but permission to divorce (without qualification) on grounds of adultery is the most obvious sense of the Latin. On the synod in its context see T. F. X. Noble, 'The Place in Papal History of the Roman Synod of 826', *Church History*, 45 (1976), 434–54. The essence of Noble's argument is that the synod aimed to take the initiative in leading the reform of Christendom away from the Carolingians.
[38] It consisted of the pope and 'sixty-two bishops drawn from the Roman church province and from parts of what had been Lombard Italy' (Noble, 'The Place in Papal History of the Roman Synod of 826', 442); 'In the context of the synodal activity of the Carolingian period the Roman synod of 826 was, basically, a provincial synod' (ibid. 446).
[39] Kelly, *Pope Gregory II on Divorce and Remarriage*, esp. 315, where Kelly concludes that 'although the possibility that Gregory permitted divorce and remarriage cannot be completely ruled out, the likelihood that he did so must be considered to be remote'.
[40] Noble, 'The Place in Papal History of the Roman Synod of 826', 454, with further references.

so at all. One cannot invariably infer a practice from legislation against it, but as a rule of thumb the inference has much to be said for it. The decree does seem to imply that a tolerance of polygamy (or at least bigamy) was widespread enough in early eighth-century society to provoke ecclesiastical condemnation. An educated guess would be that at this time many men kept a semi-official concubine alongside their official wife.

A generation after the Roman synod indissolubility found a tenacious and powerful defender in Pope Nicholas I. He thwarted King Lothar II's attempted divorce from Theutberga with an intransigence hard to imagine in the Merovingian era. It was already a sign of changed times that Lothar got his clergy to make a canon-law case. Pope Nicholas I paid it no heed. He acted like a thirteenth century pope, except that an Innocent III would have laboriously considered the precise canon-law arguments at issue.[41] Otherwise, it could have been Innocent III frustrating Philip Augustus more than three centuries later.

Lothar II's queen, Theutberga, had found another defender in Hincmar of Reims,[42] the marriage guru of ninth-century Francia—

---

[41] Cf. R. Kottje, 'Kirchliches Recht und päpstlicher Autoritätsanspruch: Zu den Auseinandersetzungen über die Ehe Lothars II.', in H. Mordek (ed.), *Aus Kirche und Reich: Studien zu Theologie, Politik und Recht im Mittelalter. Festschrift für Friedrich Kempf zu seinem fünfundsiebzigsten Geburtstag und fünfzigjährigen Doktorjubiläum* (Sigmaringen, 1983), 97–103 at 103: 'Es mag sein, daß er Lothar und seine Anhänger besser durchschaut, ihre Motive klarer erkannt hat, als es uns die erhaltenen Zeugnisse der Auseinandersetzungen ermöglichen. Selbst dann ist als bemerkenswert festzuhalten, daß er nicht nur auf die — wenigstens formal — rechtlich begründeten Darlegungen der Partei Lothars nicht eingegangen, sondern auch seine Urteile nicht mit überliefertem kirchlichem Recht begründet hat'. Kottje inclines to the view that it was all about power for Nicholas, but the latter may have felt deep scepticism about the case without wanting or perhaps feeling equipped to wade into the quagmire of canon-law arguments. For a different perspective see Nelson, *Charles the Bald*, 199: 'Subsequently, Theutberga revealed her state of mind [in accepting a life of penance in a convent for alleged sins]: "I will say whatever they want—not because it's true but because I fear for my life"'. Letha Böhringer argued that 'Lothar seine Gemahlin 857 aufgrund von Ressentiments verstieß, deren Hintergrund wahrscheinlich ein tiefer Konflikt zwischen ihm und iherer Familie bildete. . . . Die mit dem Scheidungsgesuch Lothars befaßten Bischöfe . . .unterstützten ihren König . . . aus Loyalität' (Hincmar of Reims, *De divortio Lotharii regis et Theutbergae reginae*, ed. L. Böhringer (Monumenta Germaniae Historica, Concilia, 4, suppl. 1; Hanover, 1992), 17. Thus Kottje's reading—that assertion of papal power was the main reason why the divorce was prevented—should not be regarded as the last word on this case. For a recent discussion of the Lothar II–Nicholas I confrontation see Esmyol, *Geliebte oder Ehefrau*, 159–70.

[42] Not an unqualified defender: Böhringer points out that Hincmar 'gestattet . . . dem König grundsätzlich Scheidung und Wiederheirat (auch mit Waldrada!), wenn

'conseilleur matrimoniale', as Gaudemet called him.[43] The crisis led him to write a lengthy and important treatise on marriage.[44] Hincmar played an even more central role in another high-profile marriage case, that of Stephen of Auvergne.[45] That case anticipates the high Middle Ages in more than one respect. It suggests that the Church's rules had penetrated the consciousness of the higher nobility; it anticipates the emphasis on the mystical significance of consummation which became an essential element of marriage law and theology from the late twelfth century on; finally, it shows the power of symbolic reflection to shape the course of events.

Stephen of Auvergne had got himself into a position where he seemed doomed to choose between incest and the dissolution of a marriage to which he had consented. The woman's father brought him before a church council (Tusey). Hincmar extricated Stephen from the mess, arguing that it was morally impossible to consummate the marriage, which was thus necessarily null. The case and the way it was resolved show that the Church was on the way to becoming the rule-maker in marriage matters. We shall look again in a later chapter at the place of consummation in the argument. For the moment, however, we must note that 'Beyond the social aspect of marriage he sees a Christian mystery that reflects the Incarnation and Christ's marriage with his Church; and he sees it much as Augustine had seen it. Marriage, in a word, was a *signum* of the great and true mystery of Christ's incorporation in the church . . . a unique and irreversible gift'.[46] Hincmar was continuing the well-established tradition of taking marriage symbolism seriously,[47] but

Theutberga des Inzestes überführt wird' (Hincmar, *De divortio*, 19). But he 'äußert allerdings schwere Bedenken gegen das bisherige Verfahren und starke Zweifel an der Stichhaltigkeit der Vorwürfe. Solange der Sachverhalt nicht geklärt sei, betont er, dürfe die Ehe nicht gelöst werden' (ibid.).

[43] Gaudemet, *Le Mariage en Occident*, 125. On Hincmar and Lothar's divorce, see e.g. ibid. 126–7; McNamara and Wemple, 'Marriage and Divorce in the Frankish Kingdom', 108–11.

[44] Hincmar of Reims, *De divortio*.

[45] For a full analysis see Reynolds, *Marriage in the Western Church*, 348, 351, 354–61; for a different perspective, Nelson, *Charles the Bald*, 196–7.

[46] Wallace-Hadrill, *The Frankish Church*, 410.

[47] Cf. Gaudemet, *Le Mariage en Occident*, 120 (speaking about Hincmar but not about the particular case of Stephen of Auvergne): 'l'insistance mise sur le *sacramentum*, le symbole de l'union du Christ et de l'Église renforcent encore la doctrine de l'indissolubilité. Déjá Isidore de Séville avait qualifié le mariage d'"*inseparabile*

making it work to solve a real-life, high-profile case. It is typical of Carolingian history: ninth-century events foreshadowing structures of the thirteenth century and beyond, a moment anticipating a later *longue durée*.

The 'False Decretals' and the attitude of the Church establishment, c.850–1200

The indissolubility principle may have been strengthened in the long term by ideas about the episcopal office in the legal compilations called the 'False Decretals'. In these we find a stress on the marriage of the bishop to the church he ruled.[48] The False or Pseudo-Isidorian Decretals seem to have been put together in the mid-ninth century to strengthen the hand of ordinary bishops in dealing with metropolitan bishops who claimed authority over them.[49] It was a world in which bishops might be driven from their sees (perhaps because of their own shortcomings) and the symbolism of indissolubility delegitimized such expulsions: just as Christ is indissolubly married to the whole Church, so is the individual bishop indissolubly married to his see.[50] The symbolism of the bishop's marriage to his church was widely diffused by canon-law collections that drew on the False Decretals,[51] including the most influential collection of all, Gratian's *Decretum*.[52] Bishops were, needless to say, influential in the thought and life of Church and society. The False Decretals and the subsequent collections they influenced must have made bishops think more about marriage symbolism and indissolubility, in connection with their own office but also generally. It was not enough to transform society, but

sacramentum", en se référant à l'union indissociable du Christ et de son Église. On retrouve la même idée et la même justification chez beaucoup d'auteurs de l'époque carolingienne' (with further references).

[48] J. Gaudemet, 'Le symbolisme du mariage entre l'évêque et son église et ses consequences juridiques' (1985), repr. in id., *Droit de l'Église et vie sociale au Moyen Âge* (Northampton, 1989), no. IX, 110–23 at 113–14.

[49] The standard study is H. Fuhrmann, *Einfluß und Verbreitung der pseudoisidorischen Fälschungen: Von ihrem Auftauchen bis in die neuere Zeit* (3 vols.; Schriften der Monumenta Germaniae Historica, 24. 1–3; Stuttgart, 1972–4).

[50] Gaudemet, 'Le symbolisme du mariage', 114: 'Trop d'évêques, en ce milieu du IXᵉ siècle, sont indignes et leur peuple, scandalisé et outré, les chasse. C'est contre ce désordre et ces voies de fait que s'insurgent les Fausses-Décrétales. Le principe est celui de l'attache indéfectible au siège. Les textes sur l'union des époux viennent le fortifier' (the analogy breaks down in that the pope's power to remove a bishop is admitted).

[51] Ibid. 114–15.   [52] Note esp. Pars 2, C. 7, q. 1, c. 11.

it helped smooth the ground for the transformation that took place
in the central Middle Ages.

Celibacy and the attitude of the Church establishment, c.1050–1200

The effect of celibacy on the seriousness with which the Church establishment took indissolubility deserves greater prominence in the
history of marriage. Here we have to do with one of those forces that
neutralize, counteract, or remove another force that had until then
held a development in check. With this kind of causation definitive
proof is impossible. Equally, it is foolish to shut one's eyes to the
probability that it changed the situation. The development that was
held in check up to this point was the translation of Augustinian
marriage symbolism into the social practice of indissolubility. The
obstacle was the form of life of influential clergymen, or at any rate
many of them. Their way of life was too close to that of the average
sexually active upper-class layman for them to take a really hard
line with the latter.

This development came so late because the intense movement
in favour of clerical celibacy did not get under way until the papal reform of the mid-eleventh century; I would suggest that this
movement powerfully reinforced the psychological commitment of
bishops, senior churchmen, and the celibate masters of the urban
schools that can be described as pre-universities to the enforcement
of indissolubility on the laity.

The following general explanatory schema is not demonstrable
but it is adequate to explain the timing of the tightening of the
marriage law in the West. In societies where men hold most of the
power, it is to be expected that the law will tolerate relatively free
divorce, or polygamy, or official concubinage, or some combination
of the above. In patriarchal societies, a critical mass of men may
like the idea of having more than one woman. (The reverse pattern
would be predictable in a truly matriarchal society, but such societies are not common: matriarchal inheritance rules do not make
a matriarchal society.) Rulers especially are likely to want to exercise their power in the sexual domain too, and to be disinclined
towards either laborious clandestinity or loss of respectability. If
divorce is easy to obtain, the pressure for polygamy will be less.
Most modern societies fit that pattern. If polygamy or legal concubinage is allowed, the pressure for divorce will be less. Hindu India
definitely fits that pattern.

High-caste marriage in Hindu India is an interesting case for comparison. Hinduism has a marriage model in many ways reminiscent of the one that developed in the medieval period—so far as one can generalize about the variety of different tendencies and movements called 'Hinduism' for short. Marriage was sacramental and theoretically indissoluble; in most circumstances the first wife had a quite special status. Nevertheless, polygamy was normal for rulers and others who could afford it, and even divorce might be legitimated. A simple explanation is that the Brahman religious specialists who were the custodians of the religion were themselves sexually active males who could relate to and shared the sexual drives of the powerful men they advised.

As for religions such as Judaism and Islam, it is almost (actually not quite) a circular argument to say that rules laid down by charismatic religious leaders who were not themselves restricted to one woman are unlikely to impose monogamy and indissolubility.[53] For believers, this is because God revealed the rules to them. For unbelievers, their own form of life may have affected their thought on the subject.

In a society where power over marriage is held by celibates, however, a psychological barrier is removed. Men without any women at all may not have sympathy for other men who say they cannot manage with only one. The normal assumption that men will have a visceral sympathy with other men needs to be put into reverse. A genuinely celibate clerical hierarchy can helpfully be seen as a third gender where questions of divorce and polygyny are concerned—a thought that has received inadequate attention.[54]

---

[53] Cf. the following passage from the Koran: 'O prophet, we have allowed thee thy wives unto whom thou hast given their dower, and also the *slaves* which thy right hand possesseth, of the *booty* which GOD hath granted thee; and the daughters of thy uncle, and the daughters of thy aunts, both on thy father's side and on thy mother's side, who have fled with thee *from Mecca*, and any *other* believing woman, if she give herself unto the prophet; in case the prophet desireth to take her to wife. *This is* a peculiar privilege *granted* unto thee, above the rest of the true believers. We know what we have ordained them concerning their wives, and the *slaves* whom their right hands possess: lest it should be *deemed* a crime in thee *to make use of the privilege granted thee*; for GOD is gracious *and* merciful. Thou mayest postpone the turn of such of *thy wives* as thou shalt please, *in being called to thy bed*; and thou mayest take unto thee her whom thou shalt please, and her whom thou shalt desire of those whom thou shalt have *before* rejected: and *it shall be* no crime in thee' (*The Koran: Commonly Called the Alkoran of Mohammed*, ed. and trans. G. Sale (London etc., 1887), 318–19).

[54] However, it was suggested to me by S. Gaunt, *Gender and Genre in Medieval*

Until the mid-eleventh century many of the clergy in Western
Europe lived respectably if not perhaps quite legitimately under
a matrimonial or quasi-matrimonial regime not unlike that of the
laity. One symptomatic example: at the beginning of the eleventh
century we find an archbishop of Lyons and another bishop granting in return for rent a property to a certain Rozelin—a canon
and thus a clergyman with a substantial position—and to his partner Amandola.[55] The modern English usage of 'partner' precisely
renders the Latin word *fidelis*. There is no hint of disreputability.

By and large this was not untypical of the better-off clergy's
lifestyle in the early Middle Ages, so far as one can judge from
patchy evidence.[56] There is a change of atmosphere with the Gregorian reform in the mid to late eleventh century, a fierce attempt to
make clerical celibacy a reality.[57] Pope Gregory VII (Hildebrand)
was associated in people's minds with this campaign, though it
began well before he became pope. A little Ely chronicle says simply
that 'Hildebrand the archdeacon, elected as pope, himself banned
clerics, apart from the ones to whom the canons permitted it,[58]
from living with women'.[59] Even after Gregory VII put the full
force of his intense personality as well as the papal office behind
the campaign for clerical celibacy, it took quite a while to change
practice. Arguably, unrespectable concubinage at parish-priest level
remained common until the eighteenth or nineteenth century: but
it had no legitimation, and in some regions it was believed that

French Literature (Cambridge, 1995), which develops (pp. 94, 103) the analogous
argument that clerical writers of romances, like Chrétien de Troyes, cannot be
aligned with either the female or the male protagonists, because the latter are knights,
whose social status and values are quite different from their own; and I think the
idea of the clergy as a third gender is generally 'in the air' among scholars at present.

[55] *Die Urkunden der burgundischen Rudolfinger*, ed. T. Schieffer with H. E. Mayer
(Monumenta Germaniae Historica Regum Burgundiae e Stirpe Rudolfina, Diplomata et Acta; Munich, 1977), no. 152, p. 334.

[56] For a survey of the history of celibacy see G. Denzler, *Das Papsttum und der
Amtszölibat*, i. *Die Zeit bis zur Reformation* (Päpste und Papsttum, 5.1; Stuttgart,
1973).

[57] See e.g. C. N. L. Brooke, *The Medieval Idea of Marriage* (Oxford, 1989), 64.

[58] This presumably refers to clerics in minor orders. Cf. C. Mirbt, *Quellen zur
Geschichte des Papsttums und des römischen Katholizismus*, 5th edn. (Tübingen, 1934),
no. 291, pp. 151–2 (and no. 271, p. 143, item 3, for the celibacy decree of Pope Nico-
laus II at the Lateran synod of 1059); Denzler, *Das Papsttum und der Amtszölibat*,
i. 65.

[59] 'Hyldebrandus archidiaconus papa electus ipse [*ms. corrected and unclear*] in-
terdixit clericis cum mulieribus habitare nisi quas canones exceperunt' (MS BL
Cotton Domitian XV, fo. 6ᵛᵃ, new foliation).

anyone who received the kiss of peace from the 'priestess' had no part in the Mass.[60] Even at the relatively elevated level of canonries, however, marriage or *de facto* marriage was respectable deep into the twelfth century. Christopher Brooke has described the period 1090 to 1130 as 'the heyday of the married canons' at St Paul's Cathedral.[61] In Hereford it took longer for celibacy to take hold: until the end of the twelfth century.[62] Still, by the time Innocent III became pope the men who ran the Church mostly lived without women and sex. That was bound to make a difference to their attitude, to make them less indulgent towards the serial polygamy of patriarchal males. This is not the sort of explanation one can footnote. Without it, however, one is left with an unsolved problem. It may also appeal to those who think that social practice and 'forms of life' affect the intensity with which attitudes are held.

The establishment of celibacy coincided with the crystallization and professionalization of ecclesiastical courts, and it is the combination which was to be so deadly to polygyny. It was argued above that kings and nobles might have resisted church jurisdiction over marriage if they had not had the 'forbidden degrees' escape route to fall back on. When Innocent III put a stop to that, the church courts' control of suits about whether a marriage was firmly in place was taken for granted.

Divorce and law c.900–c.1200: the survival of patriarchal patterns

The change in attitude on the part of the Church establishment did not, however, succeed in changing the noble and royal habit of changing wives until the thirteenth century, and this time lag can be adequately explained. The following schema is another oversimplification, in that there were surely individuals who do not fit the crude generalizations: but it is close enough to the myriad facts on the ground, irrecoverable in all their details, to explain why the principle of monogamy and social practice stayed far apart until

[60] D. L. d'Avray and M. Tausche, 'Marriage Sermons in *ad status* Collections of the Central Middle Ages', in N. Bériou and D. L. d'Avray (with P. Cole, J. Riley-Smith, and M. Tausche), *Modern Questions about Medieval Sermons: Essays on Marriage, Death, History and Sanctity* (Spoleto etc., 1994), 77–134 at 126 n. 204.

[61] Brooke, *The Medieval Idea of Marriage*, 84.

[62] J. Barrow, 'Hereford Bishops and Married Clergy c.1130–1240', *Historical Research* [formerly *Bulletin of the Institute of Historical Research*], 60 (1987), 1–8. The cases she studies 'suggest that marriage of the higher clergy continued in parts of England to as late as 1200, a date about fifty years later than that suggested as the latest date for marriage among the higher clergy by Professor Brooke' (ibid. 4).

Innocent III. Here I leave aside areas on the borders of Latin Christian Europe and some long-Christianized areas within it in which polygamy of an old-fashioned sort seems to have been tenacious.[63] In the three centuries from *c*.900 to *c*.1200 great men continued to change wives without much difficulty, but the way in which they did so altered. In the late ninth and tenth centuries the Church had no monopoly of marriage cases. It looks as though marriages could be dissolved without consulting any church tribunal: the scanty data do not show us lay judges in action in marriage cases, but there is enough evidence to suggest that often powerful men just did what they wanted.[64] The marriage to Adelaïde of Louis V of France (not yet sole king—his father Lothar III was still in charge) is a good example.[65] Without jurisdiction, the Church had no control. Laypeople were not disrespectful of all church rules. On the contrary, they made astonishing efforts to comply with the rules against marrying kin.[66] This may be because churchmen had been attacking the marriage of kin quite vehemently for centuries,[67] and

[63] Borgolte, 'Kulturelle Einheit und religiöse Differenz', 10–23: a good corrective to the present chapter's concentration on the 'core' regions of Latin Europe.

[64] 'Les rares cas d'espèce que fournissent les très pauvres sources du xe siècle ne font plus apparaître le juge laïc. Mais, à côté de quelques efforts du juge ecclésiastique, on trouve encore la preuve d'un tel arbitraire de la part des maris que parler d'une compétence exclusive au profit des évêques semble finalement une gageure' (P. Daudet, *L'Établissement de la compétence de l'église en matière de divorce & de consanguinité (France — Xème–XIIème siècles)* (Études sur l'histoire de la juridiction matrimoniale; Paris, 1941), 18); 'A la fin du xe siècle l'on peut recueillir dans les chroniques plusieurs preuves que les laïques, tout au moins les grands, rompent à leur convenance les liens conjugaux, de façon plus ou moins arbitraire, au prix de plus ou moins de scandale, sans que l'autorité ecclésiastique soit consultée, sans qu'elle paraisse protester' (ibid. 21–2). Cf. Stafford, *Queens, Concubines and Dowagers*, 74–5: 'Edward the Elder probably dismissed Ælfflaed to marry Eadgifu; Henry the Fowler rid himself of Hatheburg to take Mathilda; Edgar disposed of Wulfthryth to marry Ælfthryth, if not Æthelflaed to marry Wulfthryth; and Robert the Pious summarily dismissed both Rozala and Bertha. Hugh of Arles, when he fled from Marozia in Rome, scarcely went through the formalities. A tiny minority . . . made a thorough job of it by murdering their wives. The majority found legitimate excuses for disposing of unwanted women.'

[65] Daudet, *L'Établissement de la compétence de l'église*, 22.

[66] 'After the "seven forbidden" degrees had been established as the norm in the early Middle Ages, in the later ninth and tenth centuries the greatest noble families, including Eleanor's and Louis's ancestors, had tried to avoid such marriages in the first place' (C. B. Bouchard, 'Eleanor's Divorce from Louis VII: The Uses of Consanguinity', in B. Wheeler and J. C. Parsons (eds.), *Eleanor of Aquitaine: Lord and Lady* (New York and Basingstoke, 2002), 223–35 at 225). Bouchard gives reference to her previous work on this issue and answers objections to it, to my mind convincingly—her findings are a remarkable achievement.

[67] ' . . . trat die frühmittelalterliche Kirche seit dem 6. Jahrhundert für die Durch-

the message may have begun to sink in after a long time lag (quite a good model for medieval lay religion in general). However, so far as one can judge from patchy evidence, magnates treated the principles of indissolubility and perhaps even monogamy with less respect, and prelates could not do much about it: nor do they seem to have tried very hard in the tenth century.[68]

If we move fast forward to the twelfth century,[69] we find a quite different state of affairs with a very similar outcome so far as ease of divorce was concerned. On the one hand, there was a new world of marriage jurisdiction. Throughout the century questions about the validity of marriage were deemed to belong to the Church. As the century progressed, church jurisdiction became rationalized in several ways. Decrees of popes and councils were synthesized in Gratian's *Decretum*, which took on the role of a legal code.[70] The result was analysed by keen legal minds. A functioning system of ecclesiastical courts began to crystallize, run by an emergent bureaucracy at the local level and at Rome. Towards the end of the twelfth century series of doubtful points about marriage law were tested by cases setting precedents.[71]

Yet this did not affect patterns of lay practice as much as one might expect. Kings and great nobles had stopped trying to obey

setzung des Verbotes geschlechtlicher Beziehungen zwischen blutsverwandten und verschwägerten Personen ein. Hatte man diese Delikte zwar auch schon vereinzelt in Konzilsbeschlüssen seit dem 4. Jahrhundert geahndet, so trat die Kirche seit dem 6. Jahrhundert doch mit zuvor unbekanntem Nachdruck für die kirchenrechtliche Durchsetzung der Inzest-Verbote ein' (H. Lutterbach, *Sexualität im Mittelalter: Eine Kulturstudie anhand von Bußbüchern des 6. bis 12. Jahrhunderts* (Cologne etc., 1999), 172 and sect. 2.3.3.2 *passim*, with further references, especially to the work of Paul Mikat and Mayke de Jong).

[68] Daudet, *L'Établissement*, pt. 1, ch. 1, sect. II. 11, *passim*.

[69] On marriage in the twelfth century in general, see Brooke, *The Medieval Idea of Marriage* (this splendidly readable and balanced synthesis is especially strong on the twelfth century); G. Duby, *Medieval Marriage: Two Models from Twelfth-Century France*, trans. E. Foster (Baltimore etc., 1978); id., *Le Chevalier, la femme et le prêtre: le mariage dans la France féodale* (Paris, 1981); and a brilliant essay, far more important than its brevity would suggest, by John Gillingham, 'Love, Marriage and Politics in the Twelfth Century' (1989), repr. in id., *Richard Cœur de Lion: Kingship, Chivalry and War in the Twelfth Century* (London etc., 1994), 243–55.

[70] See now A. Winroth, *The Making of Gratian's* Decretum (Cambridge, 2000).

[71] On these cases see the important study by V. Pfaff, 'Das kirchliche Eherecht am Ende des zwölften Jahrhunderts', *Zeitschrift der Savigny-Stiftung für Rechtsgeschichte*, 94 [*Zeitschrift für Rechtsgeschichte*, 107], kanonistische Abteilung, 63 (1977), 73–117.

the Church's rules on the forbidden degrees of kinship.[72] There may be various explanations, but one could be precisely that they had worked out a way of making the Church's own law work against itself. They played the 'forbidden degree' rules off against the indissolubility rules. If a king or nobleman married a woman related within the extensive forbidden degrees of consanguinity or affinity, and did not seek a dispensation, he had an annulment in his pocket.

John Baldwin found a remarkable passage in the writings of Peter the Chanter: a knight saying explicitly that he was going to marry a particular woman with a large dowry who was possibly related to him in the third degree of affinity, and that if she didn't please him he would be able to get the marriage dissolved.[73] It would be valid in church law: a church court would have to recognize it. This may explain why the laity so readily accepted church jurisdiction over marriage cases.

Between the tenth century and the twelfth we find what the foregoing would lead us to expect: the rise of ecclesiastical jurisdiction,[74] roughly coinciding with a decline in observance of 'forbidden de-

---

[72] Cf. Bouchard, 'Eleanor's Divorce from Louis VII', 225, speaking of the dissolution of Louis VII's marriage to Eleanor of Aquitaine: 'this divorce, a case of a prominent couple breaking up on the grounds of consanguinity with the divorce the husband's idea, not the bishops', was not typical of the entire Middle Ages, only of the twelfth century'.

[73] 'Sicut audivit magister militem quemdem [*recte* quemdam?] de uxore ducenda dicentem: Bene est michi quia magna est dos. In tercio genere affinitatis forsitan est illa mihi, et ideo non ita mihi proxima, quod ab ea separer. Sed si voluero et non placebit michi, per affinitatem illam discidium procurare potero. Ecce quanta derisio in ecclesia propter huiusmodi tradiciones' (quoted by J. W. Baldwin, *Masters, Princes, and Merchants: The Social Views of Peter the Chanter and his Circle* (2 vols.; Princeton, 1970), ii. 225 n. 179, and analysis at i. 335).

[74] 'Mesurons le chemin parcouru, en trente ans: en 1031, au concile de Bourges, le juge d'Église n'est pas mentionné lorsqu'est admis le divorce pour cause d'adultère; en 1060, au contraire, le concile de Tours investit l'évêque d'un pouvoir d'appréciation pratiquement sans limite, dans tous les cas de divorce et de séparation' (Daudet, *L'Établissement de la compétence de l'église*, 43); 'A l'époque d'Yves de Chartres, non seulement l'évêque est pleinement compétent, pour faire cesser une séparation non canoniquement motivée et, à l'inverse, pour séparer un mariage ou même pour le déclarer nul, mais encore la fermeté des lignes générales de la procédure suivie devant lui dénote déjà une pratique bien assise. Cette compétence pleine est aussi une compétence exclusive. Après plus d'un siècle de grave décadence doctrinale et judiciaire, l'épiscopat français a réclamé, en 1031, cette compétence; trente ans après il l'a posée comme une règle. Et si, durant la fin du xie siècle, certain fidèles ont pu tenter de se soustraire à la loi canonique, grâce à la force de leur situation personnelle, ils se sont finalement inclinés: les répudiations arbitraires sont impossible désormais, en droit sinon en fait' (ibid. 68).

gree' laws.[75] The more church justice blocked the path to divorce, the more the magnates tended to choose marriages which they knew could be annulled at need—whether or not by coincidence, perhaps with a half-awareness midway between innocence and calculation. The Church did not control the point of entry into a marriage. At the risk of a little disingenuity, the great laymen had it both ways: they could change wives and get religious legitimation.

It is worth pausing to reflect on these frequent annulments, which made the system look two-faced: unbreakable monogamy in principle, but a popular loophole to facilitate changing wives. How can this be squared with a very eminent specialist's statement that 'If you take the rough with the smooth—if you take a wider view of the nature of inheritance than just the production of a ceaseless flow of male heirs—the doctrine of legitimate monogamy [i.e. the medieval Church's model, including the ban on divorce] may produce very satisfactory results.'[76] Brooke is calling in question the assumption that easy divorce was in the interest, even the pragmatic interest, of medieval kings and nobles. Now it is true in a sense that indissoluble monogamy was arguably just as good for the class as a whole even in pragmatic terms: Brooke's insight is valid. However, the issue falls into a large class of cases where the willingness of some individuals to risk a sacrifice produces an aggregate and average advantage. His argument is structurally similar to 'everyone is better off if individuals don't cheat in paying taxes', 'waiting is more efficient in an orderly queue', 'interrogated prisoners will get lighter sentences if they manage not to inform on each other' (the famous 'Prisoner's Dilemma'). The problem that bedevils the 'rational choice theorists' who devote themselves to such issues is that this undoubted aggregate advantage will not necessarily be enough to make an individual accept a sacrifice. It can actually be in the individual interest of the toughest man in the queue to push his way to the front. You may know that another family's good fortune in acquiring your lands balances your unhappy awareness that

[75] 'In the eleventh century . . . [the greatest noble families] began to marry cousins, not first cousins or even generally second cousins, but often third cousins—the same degree of relationship as that between Louis and Eleanor' (Bouchard, 'Eleanor's Divorce from Louis VII', 225). Bouchard notes that 'several such unions . . . were dissolved against the wishes of the principals' (ibid.).

[76] C. N. L. Brooke, *Europe in the Central Middle Ages, 962–1154*, 3rd edn. (Harlow, 2000), 151. The first edition of this book was published in 1964, and already included a substantial discussion of the history of marriage. Brooke was in advance of the wave of scholarship from the 1970s on.

the territory will be lost to your family after your death, because you have no heir. That may not stop you thinking of marrying a new, younger, and more fertile wife, especially if your sexual drive encourages you. Other reasons may stop you: love for your wife, belief in 'till death do us part', but not pragmatic considerations. The Capetian policy of marrying early and often was not untypical.

It takes strong 'internalized norms' to produce the collectively rational system that Brooke describes, for pragmatism alone will not do it, and in the twelfth century not enough of the magnates had made the 'one-man-one-woman' model their own for the system to work that way.

In the sublimated regions of romantic fiction we find symptoms of the feeling that marriage was not necessarily for life. In the twelfth century there was still an idea that one was released from even a long-standing and consummated marriage if one's spouse entered a religious order. (This is the more comprehensible if we remember that not so very long before, in the early eighth century, this possibility had been timidly admitted even by the bishop and canon-law specialist Fulbert of Chartres.[77]) The feeling seems to have been quite powerful even in the second half of the twelfth century. We find it in the *Lai* by Marie de France called *Eliduc*. Here we have a version of the eternal triangle in which the wife becomes a nun to free her husband to marry the other woman.[78]

The similar plot line in the romance *Ille et Galeron* by Gautier d'Arras is worth a close look. Ille has left his wife Galeron after receiving a disfiguring wound, because he thought she would not be able to stand the sight of him. He underestimates her devotion. She travels far and wide looking for him, and finally finds him as he is about to marry another woman. She makes a sad speech and offers to enter a nunnery so that he can go ahead and marry the other woman:

[4124] Since then I have climbed down many a great hill, and up many a mountain, suffered many a hardship and offered up many a coin for your sake, and all of this strikes me as very little. When I saw that I could not find you and that all my men were dead, I came away to the pope here in

---

[77] Daudet, *L'Établissement de la compétence de l'église*, 26–30. Daudet notes that 'l'évêque n'exclut, en principe, ni l'entrée d'Aude, en religion, ni le mariage nouveau de Galeran' (ibid. 28).

[78] R. L. Krueger, 'Questions of Gender in Old French Romance', in ead. (ed.), *The Cambridge Companion to Medieval Romance* (Cambridge, 2000), ch. 8 at p. 139.

Rome; I bared my conscience to him, and he imposed a penance on me. I have been in this town ever since: it will be four years this summer. So help me God, whose servant I am, there was never anyone who gave me any news of you until today; but now I have news which I know is good and welcome to you and all your friends. . . . [4145] My lord, I can see very well that I am keeping you too long: you are due to marry the king's daughter. For God's sake, may I be in your thoughts and in your wife's, so that for the sake of God and his countenance the pope may do this much for me, and find a place for me in an abbey. May God sanctify and bless you! I intend to pray God night and day to grant you a place in Paradise when our souls leave our bodies, when evil doers will be left outside.[79]

She takes it for granted that her entry into a nunnery will leave him free to remarry. Entry into the religious life would end the marriage, which had definitely been consummated.[80] Gautier had earlier told his readers that 'Ille, who had longed for her so much, shared one bed with Galeron, and they experienced such joy and such delight that it defies description' (ibid. 53). As it happens, Ille does not take up her offer. He still loves Galeron and the marriage to the other woman is called off.

Furthermore, the whole atmosphere is religiously charged, and there is no hint of unorthodoxy. On the contrary, Galeron assumes the pope will be involved. This is not a courtly love counter-culture. The passage reflects genuine unclarity among pious laypeople about the indissolubility doctrine held by the higher clergy.

That becomes doubly evident later in the poem, when Galeron takes a vow in childbirth to enter a nunnery (ibid. 178–9) and Ille can consider marrying the other woman, whom he also loves. Ille was confused about his emotions. The poet compares his heart to a tower:

Who was inside? The first love, which held it by force of custom; except that his love for the maiden, which was outside, frequently accused her, saying that she had no right to be there inside, and intended to demonstrate logically and prove that love for a nun has no title to the heart of a castellan, a duke, a count or a king, and that it is on the contrary wholly unreasonable that it should be allowed, that it should be permitted to be there. It was Ille who suffered, Ille who felt the effects of this. The first love was difficult to overcome, and did not know what on earth to reply, but what she did say

---

[79] Gautier d'Arras, *Ille et Galeron*, ed. and trans. P. Eley (King's College London Medieval Studies, 13; London, 1996), 139.
[80] In a later chapter it will be explained that an unconsummated marriage could be dissolved by entry into a monastery.

was that she was the rightful occupant; this is what her title deed said; and the second replied that it was null and void from the moment she became a nun: what use does a nun have for a castle? [5653] But a king's daughter does, who has the power to give and to take away, and let the nun read her psalter in the abbey and in the church! (*Ille et Galeron*, trans. Eley, 191)

Ille eventually marries the second lady, after rescuing her from an unwanted suitor and his army. The religious legitimacy of the marriage is stressed:

All the Romans eagerly endeavoured to see to it that Ille the noble warrior should have the crown; they were all well aware that his wife was a nun. Duke Ille wanted it very much, and the prospect did not displease Ganor [the other woman] in the least; the pope used his best endeavours; so there was no alternative but for it to be done. The pope celebrated their marriage; Rome was glad and rejoiced at it. (*Ille et Galeron*, trans. Eley, 221)

Abelard and Héloïse

Abelard or the Abelard persona in Letter 4 of the famous correspondence with Héloïse had thought differently, and this was the view that would ultimately prevail. When they were both committed by vows to the religious life, he had still been able to write:

Come too, my inseparable companion, and join me in thanksgiving, you who were made my partner both in guilt and in grace. For the Lord is not unmindful also of your own salvation, indeed, he has you much in mind, for by a kind of holy presage of his name he marked you out to be especially his when he named you Héloïse, after his own name, Elohim. In his mercy, I say, he intended to provide for two people in one, the two whom the devil sought to destroy in one; since a short while before this happening he had bound us together by the indissoluble bond of the marriage sacrament.[81]

Most scholars at present think that the correspondence is genuine[82] or at least that it is an only semi-fictionalized literary composition by Abelard and Héloïse themselves.[83] Abelard died in 1142/3, so the

---

[81] *The Letters of Abelard and Heloise*, trans. B. Radice (Harmondsworth etc., 1974), 149 (in the revised edition by M. Clanchy (2003) the passage will be found under 'Letter 5', p. 83).

[82] M. T. Clanchy, *Abelard: A Medieval Life* (Oxford, 1997), 15, 154–5.

[83] D. Luscombe, 'From Paris to the Paraclete: The Correspondence of Abelard and Heloise', *Proceedings of the British Academy*, 74 (1988), 247–83, esp. 270, and also 278, where he raises the attractive and plausible possibility of a 'compact between Heloise and Abelard jointly to share, compose and exchange their thoughts, experiences and principles in fictive correspondence'.

view he expresses definitely antedates the attitudes in *Eliduc* and *Ille et Galeron*. It is not surprising that the author of a Latin text (let alone the immensely learned Abelard) should be more in touch with the long theoretical tradition that marriage was indissoluble than vernacular romances.

The attitude of Abelard and Héloïse to indissolubility may be symptomatic of a gradual but general shift of attitudes towards divorce in the twelfth century, preparing the way for the transformation of law and consequently society effected by Innocent III, to be discussed below. It is actually rather surprising how few marriages are dissolved in vernacular romances: Marie de France and Gautier d'Arras apart, instances of true divorce in the modern sense are extremely difficult to find. Exceptions tend to prove the rule. Thus in Chrétien de Troyes's romance *Cligès* the marriage of the heroine to the emperor in Constantinople is never consummated, a fact that she regards as crucial. Poems like Chrétien's *Erec and Eneide* or *Yvain*, or Wolfram von Eschenbach's *Parzifal*, suggest that the idea of durable married love had great appeal in literature even if great men found it constricting in practice.

In the twelfth century the lay élite show signs of accepting the theory that the clergy were trying to turn into law, but maintained traditional habits of serial polygamy by using a loophole in the Church's own rules. Paradoxically, this may have played a part in the eventual triumph of indissolubility. It enabled the nobility to get used to ecclesiastical domination of marriage without changing the pattern of their legitimized sex lives too much. By the time they were compelled to do so, they had been paying lip-service to indissolubility and working within canon-law rules for so long that they could not easily justify resistance after the convenient loophole had been closed. There were few ideological obstacles to be overcome in lay minds when a new wave of clerical intensity washed over Western marriage. It drew much of its impetus from the proto-university schools.

(c) The Age of Innocent III

Symbolism, the schools, and Innocent III

A wind of change was getting up among academics in the twelfth century. Peter Lombard brought out clearly the connection between marriage symbolism and indissolubility. He took up Augustine's

100   *Chapter 2*

ideas and recharged them with influence. After the Lombard's place in the tradition had become secure, and then for more than a century, every serious theologian would be steered towards reflection on the subject. Their conclusions have been closely analysed in a neglected book by Tomas Rincón.[84] The most important thing about Rincón's findings for our purposes is that they provide the background which makes sense of some epoch-making decisions by Pope Innocent III, who made this symbolic reasoning about marriage his own. Against the background of twelfth-century thought reconstructed by Rincón, this was explicable, almost predictable. Thus Peter of Poitiers uses language which we shall meet again in Innocent's decretal *Debitum* (X. 1. 21. 5). Peter says that 'The sacrament is here the consent of minds and carnal joining, and there are not two sacraments, but one sacrament: of the union of Christ to the Church which comes about through charity, and of the bodily union which comes about through conformity of nature—of which the sign is carnal joining, just as consent of minds is the sign of spiritual union.'[85] Peter was a prominent Paris theologian in the late twelfth century.[86] He would have been teaching when the young Lothario Segni, the future Innocent III, was a student there.[87] However, the whole tradition of thought about marriage symbolism in twelfth-century Paris is a relevant context to Innocent's decisions.[88]

[84] T. Rincón, *El matrimonio, misterio y signo: siglos IX–XIII* (Pamplona, 1971). Rincón deals with canonists as well as theologians.

[85] Peter of Poitiers, *Sententiarum libri quinque*, 5. 14 (Migne, *PL* 211. 1257), cited by Rincón, *El matrimonio*, 208 and n. 308. Note that the Migne edition has 'consensus animorum' then 'consensus animarum'; Rincón silently emends.

[86] On Peter of Poitiers, and for further references, see F. Robb, 'Intellectual Tradition and Misunderstanding: The Development of Academic Theology on the Trinity in the Twelfth and Thirteenth Centuries' (unpublished Ph.D. thesis, University College London, 1993), 108–9. The work from which this is taken was influential: see ibid. 108.

[87] On the future Innocent III's time as a student in Paris see W. Imkamp, *Das Kirchenbild Innocenz' III.* (*1198–1216*) (Päpste und Papsttum, 22; Stuttgart, 1983), 24: 'dürfte sein Pariser Studienaufenthalt in die ersten beiden Drittel der 80er Jahre des 12. Jahrhunderts fallen'; and Baldwin, *Masters, Princes, and Merchants*, i. 44: 'Peter of Poitiers . . . acceded to the theological chair left vacant by Peter Comestor in 1169, was made chancellor of Notre-Dame in 1193'.

[88] On this see Rincón, *El matrimonio*, pt. 2, ch. 2, and the conclusions on p. 212, which are worth quoting since the book is hard to obtain: '1.ª El matrimonio es un vínculo indisoluble por ser sacramento de la unión indisoluble de Cristo con la Iglesia. 2.ª El divorcio es pecado porque rompe esta significación. 3.ª La unión de Cristo con la Iglesia se realizó de doble forma: por el amor y por la carne. Lo primero se significa por el consentimiento, lo segundo por la cópula. El matrimonio-signo,

We see symbolic reasoning at work when Innocent refused to annul the marriage of Peter I of Aragon to Maria de Montpellier. Explaining his decision, he explicitly links the sacrament of human marriage with the sacrament of the union of Christ with the Church, of God with the faithful soul, and of the second person of the Trinity with human nature.[89] The decision is hard to explain in terms of *Realpolitik*, as a recent careful analysis by Martin Aurell has demonstrated.[90] Consequently, the reason Innocent gives looks like the real explanation. We know that Innocent liked marriage as a spiritual metaphor—it is the basis of one of his allegorical treatises and of an important sermon on the anniversary of his coronation[91]—but symbolism which shapes action is something different. The central theme of the present study is of course that marriage symbolism became a force in the real social and political world, with Innocent III's pontificate marking a turning point.

The symbolic reasoning that surfaces briefly in Innocent's expla-

en efecto, debe plegarse jurídica y vitalmente a las exigencias dimanantes de la *cosa significada*. 4.ª Es plena y estrictamente sacramento el matrimonio integrado por los dos elementos. Es sacramento en sentido amplio cuando media sólo un vínculo consensual.' Rincón's pt. 2, ch. 3, on 'La significación en las fuentes canónicas del siglo XII', is also important as backround to Innocent III. For Innocent III's thought on marriage generally see M. Maccarrone, 'Sacramentalità e indissolubilità del matrimonio nella dottrina di Innocenzo III', *Lateranum*, 44 (1978), 449–514.

[89] '. . . et maxime ubi agitur de matrimonii sacramento, quod ante peccatum in paradiso a Domino institutum, praeter propagationis humani generis fructum, illud ineffabile sacramentum, conjunctionis Christi videlicet ad sanctam Ecclesiam Dei ad fidelem animam, et ipsius verbi ad humanam naturam, noscitur figurare', cited by Inkamp, *Das Kirchenbild Innocenz' III.*, 224 n. 130.

[90] 'Innocent III n'avait pas un préjugé particulièrement favorable pour Maria . . . Tous semblaient contre la dame: ses ennemis étaient sûrs d'obtenir sa destitution. Elle décida alors de changer le cours des événements, en défendant personnellement ses droits à Rome' (M. Aurelle, *Les Noces du comté: mariage et pouvoir en Catalogne (753–1213)* (Paris, 1995), 456–7 (Aurell summarizes the grounds for the decision ibid. 457). He notes that Peter I was an ally of Innocent in his Languedoc policy (ibid. 458), and comments that 'Le verdict ne répondait pas à la pressante conjoncture politique, mais bien plutôt à l'application stricte de la législation canonique: le mariage de Pere Iᵉʳ avec Marie de Montferrat aurait parfaitement convenu à la croisade en Terre sainte, préconisée de longue date par le Saint Siège, tout comme l'union avec Marie de France serait la bienvenue à l'époque où Innocent III prônait une solution pacifique à la crise albigeoise. Le tribunal, indifférent aux subtilités de la diplomatie, ne s'arrêta pas à ce genre de considérations. Profondément enraciné dans la conscience des juges romains, le modèle matrimonial chrétien avait pris le dessus sur les contingentes stratégies temporelles' (ibid. 458).

[91] R. Kay, 'Innocent III as Canonist and Theologian: The Case of Spiritual Matrimony', in J. C. Moore (ed.), *Pope Innocent III and his World* (Aldershot etc., 1999), 35–49.

nation of this decision is set out in detail in his decretal *Debitum*, which will be discussed in more detail in the chapter on bigamy: it is a key text.[92] As will become clear there, this intellectually gifted ecclesiastical politician had a coherent and consistent symbolic rationale in mind. Granted his ability to turn ideas into action, we should not be surprised to find him behind the most thoroughgoing attempt—probably in human history up to that point—to impose a 'one man to one woman for life' model of marriage on a large literate society.

Innocent's intransigence towards royal matrimonial wishes showed the way things were going. Even more remarkable than his decision to confirm Marie de Montpellier's marriage was his refusal after much diplomatic delay to grant an annulment to Philip II Augustus of France.[93] Innocent needed Philip as an ally. In the early thirteenth century Philip made himself the most powerful ruler in Europe. The empire was divided by a succession crisis and had no serious centralized revenues by comparison with France. The Angevin empire under King John suffered a humiliating defeat and a massive loss of land to Philip. Behind his success was wealth.[94] Innocent was trying to get a pro-papal candidate made Holy Roman Emperor; in 1207 he imposed his candidate as archbishop of Canterbury after a disputed election, and found himself locked in a serious conflict with the king of England. By inflexibility towards Philip he was taking a risk. In hindsight, we know he could afford to, but he could not have been so sure in advance: the other crises were too serious. The rejected girl was a Danish princess. Staying on good terms with Denmark was desirable, but good relations with France were more important by far: in the early 1200s France had achieved a position comparable to that of the United States from the 1990s: not the only power that mattered, but far

[92] As Rincón recognized: 'En la exposición detallada que acabamos de hacer, ha quedado, a nuestro juicio, incuestablemente patente la relevancia jurídica de la significación sacramental del matrimonio, debido, en gran manera, al peso magisterial y jurídico de la decretal *Debitum* de Inocencio III' (*El matrimonio*, 403).

[93] In addition to works cited below, see J. Gaudemet. 'Le dossier canonique sur mariage de Philippe Auguste et d'Ingeburge de Danemark (1193–1213)', *Revue historique de droit français et étranger*, 62 (1984), 15–29, repr. in id., *Droit de l'Église et vie sociale au Moyen Âge*, no. XIV.

[94] For instance, to judge by the accounts of 1202/3, 'An overwhelming surplus was . . . available for the costs of the "hotel" and the military campaign against John' (J. W. Baldwin, *The Government of Philip Augustus: Foundations of French Royal Power in the Middle Ages* (Berkely etc., 1986), 174).

stronger than any other.[95] After conquering Normandy and other domains of King John of England, in 1204 Philip stood alone in terms of power. Innocent showed a conciliatory spirit by legitimating Philip's children by his mistress.[96] The tone and intensity of his pressure on Philip varied with the configurations of church power politics.[97] But nothing would make Innocent actually dissolve the

[95] There is more to be said about the Danish side of the crisis, and Frederik Pedersen has this in hand. Though he emphasizes Denmark's influence more, our positions are not far apart. In a personal communication he agrees 'that the case could never have ended in a victory for Philip. Innocent was far too committed to the consensual theory of marriage and too clever a politician to fall for the rather lame excuses Philip presented as reasons for his wish for the dissolution of his marriage to Ingeborg'.

[96] Of this, Georges Duby wrote that 'the most important consideration for Rome was the increase in power that might accrue to it from the ascension to the French throne of a bastard legitimized by the pope' (*Medieval Marriage*, 78). This is an instance of Duby's tendency to over-explain. The desire to please Philip at that critical time is a sufficient explanation. Anyway, it was not as if legitimation could be withdrawn, so it would not have given a future pope much of a hold over a future king who might not inherit anyway (and did not: in the event, Philip's son by a previous marriage to a wife who had died succeeded him as Louis VIII). Again, what of the power that would have accrued to Rome from the marriage of the king to a mistress turned into a queen by the pope's decision? Such arguments are shadow-boxing either way: with a scholar of Duby's fame and a widely read work like this the danger is that some people might assume that there is positive evidence.

[97] This led a nineteenth-century historian of the case to think that Innocent III's overriding priorities were political: 'zu einem sofortigen energischen Vorgehen, wie er es gegen einen minder mächtigen Fürsten in dieser Zeit übte, mochte sich Innocenz gegen den König von Frankreich bei der unklaren Lage der Dinge im Reich, die ihm gute Beziehungen zu Philipp wertvoll machen mußten, doch nicht entschließen können' (R. Davidsohn, *Philipp II. August von Frankreich und Ingeborg* (Stuttgart, 1888), 71); 'mußte sich eine Angelegenheit geistlichen Zwanges, in der es nur gegolten hätte, die moralische Hoheit des apostolischen Amtes zur Geltung zu bringen, mit den Interessen weltlicher Politik des Papsttums kreuzen, mußte sie durch diese bestimmt und vielfach gehemmt werden. Wo die Pflicht des Oberhirten schnelles Einschreiten gefordert hätte, erheischte das Interesse politischer Machtstellung kluges Abwarten' (ibid. 74–5). Davidsohn did not grasp that, for Innocent, indissolubility was a value not up for negotiation, whereas such matters of timing, tone, and sanctions were the objects of instrumental calculation. Innocent had a 'Verantwortlichkeitsethik' anchored in some fixed values rather than a 'Gesinnungsethik' which would have compelled him to treat each decision as an absolute moral imperative. For a better insight into Innocent's mind see R. H. Tenbrock, *Eherecht und Ehepolitik bei Innocenz III.* (doctoral dissertation for the University of Münster; Dortmund-Hörde, [1933?]), 99: 'es kennzeichnet die Größe dieses Papstes und Staatsmannes, daß er im Grunde niemals bewußt von dem Wege des Rechts abwich. Er verlangsamte wohl den Schritt auf diesem steilen und rauhen Wege, um Ausschau zu halten nach Nebenpfaden, die ihn zwar nicht vom Ziele wegführten, aber ihm gestatteten, manchen Vorteil für die Kirche zu erlangen. Das bedeutete freilich oft ein Zurückweichen vor den Schwierigkeiten und eine Angst, gewisse äußere Erfolge, Erfolge des Politikers, des Mannes, der der Welt "zugewandt" ist,

marriage. Innocent really is a confusing figure for historians who divide great men into idealists and power-brokers.

Thus Innocent III took the exalted idea of indissolubility out of the ivory tower and into the world of power politics. At the end of his pontificate he tried to make it a more general norm in practice. At the Fourth Lateran Council the loopholes which had permitted not only monarchs but also many lesser noblemen to get out of marriages were closed. The circle of forbidden degrees was drawn much smaller. The ban had extended up to the seventh degree of consanguinity: anyone with a great-great-great-great-great-grandparent in common, any sixth cousin, that is. The same rule applied to affinity: one could not marry the widow, widower, or former sexual partner of a sixth cousin. Both affinity and consanguinity were now reduced from seven degrees to four: one could not marry a third cousin or anyone who had slept with one or been married to a deceased third cousin, but beyond that there was no problem; obscure extra modes of affinity were abolished altogether.[98]

aufgeben zu müssen. Aber gerade dadurch war es ihm beschieden, "seine Papstidee in die reale Wirklichkeit zu übersetzen und die Macht des Papsttums aufs höchste zu steigern".' An excellent brief treatment in context is in Baldwin, *Masters, Princes, and Merchants*, i. 235 and ii. 225–6. M.-B. Bruguière, 'Le mariage de Philippe-Auguste et d'Isambour de Danemark: aspects canoniques et politiques', in Université des Sciences Sociales de Toulouse, *Mélanges offerts à Jean Dauvillier* (Toulouse, 1979), 135–56 (I am grateful to Alexandra Sanmark for drawing my attention to this), and ead., 'Canon Law and Royal Weddings, Theory and Practice: The French Example, 987–1215', in S. Chodorow (ed.), *Proceedings of the Eighth International Congress of Medieval Canon Law* (Monumenta Iuris Canonici, Series C, Subsidia, 9; Vatican City, 1992), 473–96, makes some surprising assertions and assumptions. She thinks that Innocent's legitimation of Philip's children by Agnes of Méran 'n'est guère susceptible que d'une explication: depuis son accession au trône de saint Pierre, il avait découvert le bien fondé de la requête de Philippe Auguste . . . et il ne pouvait plus mettre en péril sans raison valable la succession au trône de France' ('Le mariage de Philippe-Auguste et d'Isambour de Danemark', 145–6). This will not do. Legitimacy was not a matter of principle like indissolubility. The fundamental implausibility is that forbidden degrees that would have annulled the marriage without difficulty were ascertainable but not used by Philip Augustus, who, she suggests astonishingly, was not really trying after his initial effort. A secondary implausibility is that fear of offending Denmark was a major reason for frustrating Philip Augustus: a topsy-turvy sense of power realities in the early thirteenth century. (As noted above, however, Frederik Pedersen has in press a paper emphasizing the importance of Denmark.) I hope to return to these questions in detail.

[98] Gaudemet, *Le Mariage en Occident*, 205–6; Baldwin, *Masters, Princes, and Merchants*, i. 336–7. Baldwin gives fascinating evidence that Innocent was influenced by Peter the Chanter: see ibid. 332–7 (Gaudemet, *Le Mariage en Occident*, 205, comments, 'On peut en discuter'). Baldwin, i. 336, is probably mistaken in thinking that hearsay testimony was banned by Lateran IV: see below.

The change in the consanguinity laws dovetailed with another measure designed to prevent annulments by precluding invalid marriages. This was Canon 51, on clandestine marriages.[99] It laid down that banns must be read in advance of a marriage, to give time for any impediments to come to light. This gave neighbours who heard the banns time to bring up a problem if there was one, and gave the priests time to investigate whether there was any impediment. Note that this decree did not require marriage in church or by a priest, as some good historians have assumed.[100] It was not about sacralizing the ritual of entry into marriage, which varied from one part of Europe to another: in parts of Italy a purely secular marriage contract was quite acceptable in the eyes of the Church. Marriage was a sacrament whether or not a priest was present. The decree was part of a determined effort to block the twelfth-century nobles' favourite escape route from marriage. The smaller the circle of possible impediments, the easier it would be to discover them; furthermore, there would be time to discover them and a public request for anyone who knew of one to make it known before the marriage.

The Fourth Lateran Council did not go so far as to declare marriage invalid if the banns had not been read. Perhaps there was uncertainty about the limits of the Church's power to add a condition of validity to a sacrament; or more probably there was fear that marriage practices were too varied and ingrained and that such a rule would create many invalid marriages; or perhaps the problems were not thought through. At any rate plenty of people did get married clandestinely, without having the banns read, as we shall see. Nevertheless, it is clear that Innocent and the Council were in earnest in their effort to make annulment much harder.

Tighter rules about proof

In addition to redrawing the limits of consanguinity and generalizing the system of banns, Innocent III, or rather the Fourth Lateran Council, made it harder to prove in court, tightening up the evidence requirements.[101] Hearsay evidence had been allowed before

[99] *Conciliorum oecumenicorum decreta*, ed. J. Alberigo *et al.*, 3rd edn. (Bologna, 1973), 258.
[100] See D. L. d'Avray, 'Marriage Ceremonies and the Church in Italy after 1215', in T. Dean and K. J. P. Lowe (eds.), *Marriage in Italy 1300–1650* (Cambridge, 1998), 107–15 at 107–9, for historians' views.
[101] The best starting point on this topic is R. H. Helmholz, *Marriage Litigation in Medieval England* (Cambridge, 1974), 81–2.

because it had been so hard to reconstruct genealogies linking sixth cousins going back to great-great-great-great-great-grandparents: now it was still allowed, but rigorous requirements had to be observed.

For a certain tolerance of less than rigorous evidence had been acceptable when dealing with the distant past, rather as scholars nowadays allow a little more leeway to early than to late medieval historians when it comes to rigorous demonstration. Reduction of the forbidden degrees to four brought the family facts in question nearer to the present. A couple related in the fourth degree would have a great-great-grandparent in common, and they might even be still alive. In noble families couples could afford to marry shortly after puberty. An elementary calculation brings the implications home. Pregnancy and childbirth at 16 were possible and respectable. Suppose this happened in two lines coming down from a common ancestor. A woman could be a great-great-grandmother at 64. Seven years later her great-great-great-grandchildren might be the subject of marriage negotiations. (Betrothal was acceptable after the age of reason had been reached.[102]) At that point the families involved could consider whether there were any canonical impediments. The common ancestor linking the couple in the fourth degree of consanguinity could be alive.

It is unlikely that common ancestors of fourth-degree relatives often actually lived to see an annulment process between their great-great-grandchildren. Suppose that the young couple became engaged without anyone bothering about the impediment, and married without the banns being read (or without anyone being so tactless as to protest). The great-great-grandmother would be elderly by the time they got married. Possibly she would be dead by then. If the husband sought an annulment a few years later (perhaps because he wanted to make a new political marriage alliance), more time still would have elapsed and our great-great-grand-maternal common ancestor would very probably be dead. Even so, many people alive would have known her and they could have sworn to the genealogy at first hand, with no need for hearsay evidence.

Not all 'forbidden degree' cases would have presented so few

---

[102] 'Aquinas', Supplement to *Summa theologica*, 43. 2, in *Sancti Thomae Aquinatis . . . opera omnia, iussu . . . Leonis XIII P.M. edita*, xii (Rome, 1906), 83–4 ('Supplementum' section, which is separately paginated): an interesting essay in developmental child psychology.

problems of proof. If children were born in both lines coming down from the common ancestor at thirty-year intervals between the generations rather than sixteen-year intervals, the genealogy would stretch back into a more distant past. For this reason, no doubt, the decree did allow hearsay evidence, but only under the stringent conditions to which we must now turn.

These conditions are set out with forceful directness by Hostiensis, Henry of Susa (Latin Segusium) or Henricus de Bartholomaeis, doyen of thirteenth-century canonists (in a career full of success he also rose high in the service of King Henry III of England and ended up a cardinal), in an important passage which is edited below (Document **2. 2. 1**). Hostiensis comments directly on the decree of Lateran IV: it had been incorporated into the Decretals of Gregory IX, which put it before the eyes of every canon lawyer. It was natural for Hostiensis to discuss it at length in his great *Lectura* on the Decretals, and his own remarks would have reached a wide and respectful professional audience.[103] Witnesses giving indirect evidence must be of good repute, must have learnt of the forbidden degree relationship before the beginning of the legal case, and must have learnt it from 'elders' (*antiquioribus*). There must be more than one witness of good repute, reporting the testimony of more than one source of good repute. The witnesses in the annulment case must not be motivated by hatred, love, fear, or advantage. They must be able to identify properly the individuals in the genealogy to which they bear witness, and they must know how to count the degrees of consanguinity or affinity. They must swear that they heard the facts to which they bear witness from their elders, and believe them personally, and they must have seen some of the people in the kin group they reconstruct acting as relatives.

No paraphrase is as forceful as Hostiensis's own words, which give judges a numbered checklist and deserve to be quoted:

The first thing is that one should consider whether the witness carries weight or not. Second, whether he or she learnt the things to which testimony is given before the beginning of the lawsuit. Third, whether the witness heard this from his or her elders. Fourth, whether the witness heard it from at least two people. Fifth, whether the two were suspicious types or of bad reputation, or whether they were trustworthy and unexceptionable.

[103] K. Pennington, 'An Earlier Recension of Hostiensis's *Lectura* on the Decretals' (1987), repr. in id., *Popes, Canonists and Texts, 1150–1550* (Aldershot etc., 1993), no. XVII (retaining the original pagination: 77–90), at 79.

Sixth, whether only one person heard this from several people, even if they were of good reputation, or whether several witnesses of evil repute heard it from men even of good repute. Seventh, granted that there are several of good repute, who heard it from several of good repute, whether they are motivated by hatred, affection, fear, or advantage. Eighth, whether they have described the persons by their own names or at least by adequate periphrases. Ninth, whether they distinguish the individual degrees on both sides, counting them out clearly. Tenth, whether they conclude by swearing that their depositions are based on what they have heard from their elders. Eleventh, whether they believe that it is so. Twelfth, whether they have seen some of the persons of the degrees which they have counted out acting as relatives.

These are the twelve things, in the order specified above, which are to be absolutely kept before the mind; it is by questioning the witnesses about the greater part of these things that the enquiry should be conducted. If one of them should be lacking, the testimony is held to be insufficient, as is made clear at the beginning of this passage. And when there is an annulment case turning on consanguinity or affinity, the judge should memorize these twelve questions, and he should question every witness about them or the majority of them, in such a way as not to leave out even one of them, indeed he should conduct his examination with the utmost rigour even if the case is contested.[104] For the argument, see below: 'Concerning a man who has intercourse with a blood relative of his wife', *Super eo*; . . . (Document **2. 1. 2–3**)

(d) Indissolubility in Practice

How far were the rules about proof observed?

Hostiensis feels very strongly about the need for rigour in annulment cases. He suddenly breaks out of his normal dry and technical manner of writing to say with outrage that these rules for evidence in annulment cases had been widely disregarded by the judges of his own time:

So far, however, the judges of our time have kept this badly, caring little or nothing for such things. Therefore they despise the canonical form and pass many sentences of annulment contrary to God and justice, not without dangers to their souls and the souls of many others, dangers which

---

[104] My interpretation here is that the judge must obviously conduct a careful interrogation when the case is not contested, because of the danger of collusion, but that he must still do so even if the case is adversarial and one party is casting doubt on the claims of the other.

we solemnly entreat them not to neglect in the future, but to hold before their minds. (Document **2. 1. 4**)

The tone is reminiscent of protests against the ease of annulments in the United States in the late twentieth century[105]—and indeed, we shall have to consider the possibility that the experience which sparked off Hostiensis's protest was localized, since the situation he describes does not fit very easily with what we know from church court records, where we have them. He was a man experienced in the world's affairs, but there is no tolerant cynicism here: his warning about the danger to the souls of the judges and many others seems to come from the heart.

Hostiensis uses the word *actenus* (so far), as if he expected the situation to change, and perhaps it did. He was himself an enormously influential man and probably did not underestimate the effect of his vehement protest on readers and pupils—for in the nature of the case it is likely that he expressed himself with still greater freedom, which is saying a lot, in his academic teaching.

Discussions during academic teaching may lie behind the objections Hostiensis raises. An imaginary interlocutor challenges him by saying that the law normally tries to make as much proof as possible available: so why not in annulment cases? Hostiensis has two answers. The first is much the same as the point made earlier, namely that proof had become much easier since the number of forbidden degrees had been reduced to four, so that strict standards should now be expected. His second argument is an allusion to the 'examples' of how hearsay evidence could be abused. The decretal which gave rise to the whole discussion had referred to the many examples that showed the danger of hearsay evidence and the consequent need for rigour.[106] An earlier passage in Hostiensis's commentary takes this remark as a cue for the remarkable story of Raymund Barellus, of the diocese of Nice (printed below as Document **2. 1. 1**).

Barellus worked the following scam to get marriages dissolved. He was old, and claimed to be able to reconstruct practically any

---

[105] Cf. R. H. Vasoli, *What God Has Joined Together: The Annulment Crisis in American Catholicism* (New York and Oxford, 1998).

[106] 'quia tamen pluribus exemplis et certis experimentis didicimus, ex hoc multa pericula contra legitima provenisse coniugia, statuimus, ne super hoc recipiantur de cetero testes de auditu, quum iam quartum gradum prohibitio non excedat, nisi forte [*then the list of rigorous conditions begins*]' (X. 2. 20. 47).

genealogy (in the locality, obviously). However, as a single witness he would be unable to provide sufficient testimony: it was standard practice to require two. He would take a group of ten or a dozen people, tell them the genealogy, divide them into groups, and get people from different groups to relay the genealogy to other people who could then act as witnesses in the annulment suits, claiming that they heard the genealogy from their elders.

I have failed to identify this ingenious subverter of the law. It is possible that his interesting activities were carried on before 1215 and that Hostiensis only knows of him by reputation, but it seems much more likely that the canonist had direct knowledge of these machinations, and was genuinely shocked by their cynicism. He had been prior of the cathedral church of Antibes in the same general region. If applied with conscientious rigour, the detailed rules he gives for evidence would probably have stymied Barellus.

The next imaginary interlocutor suggests that this rigour might throw the baby out with the bathwater. If all the rules are observed to the letter, can a case ever be made for an annulment on grounds of consanguinity? Hostiensis responds strongly. The benefit of the doubt should always be given in favour of marriage. Better that a union within the forbidden degrees continue than that a valid one be dissolved. His position is quite similar *mutatis mutandis* to a traditional attitude to crime: better that a guilty man go free than that an innocent man be convicted.

Hostiensis explains his rationale. Indissolubility is a matter of divine law, the forbidden degrees are made by human ecclesiastical law. He makes it clear that he has in mind primarily the third or fourth degrees of consanguinity and affinity, which he is sure are not subject to an absolute divine prohibition; he indicates that the second degree might be in the same category, but he is being careful. He thinks that where the degrees are so close that divine law is an issue, the relationship will be so evident that witnesses would hardly be needed.

On the face of it, this passage gives clear evidence that 'soft' annulments were still the norm after 1215. That would be to go beyond the evidence. We too should exercise, as historians, the kind of rigour that Hostiensis liked in judges. It does not follow at all that the situation was the same as before 1215. To begin with, not all conscientious canonists would necessarily have gone all the way with him. He is not just saying that substantively valid marriages should not be undone with the help of formalities: he is saying that substantively invalid marriages should be allowed to stand if any part of the formal proof process is deficient. He views marriages in the way that a tenacious defence lawyer today views the innocence of clients: the prosecution should have to get every technicality right. He attacks a predecessor who put forward the following argument. If one witness proves that Martin is the son of John, and a different witness proves that Bertha is John's daughter, that is a sufficient demonstration that Martin and Bertha are siblings. Hostiensis will have none of it. The reasoning is against the wording of the decretal, and in any case there might be more than one John. We may well feel that the last point is weak, because it is only a thought experiment in which the identity of John might be presumed secure and unambiguous in the testimony of both witnesses. On the other hand, Hostiensis seems to be right about the literal meaning of the decretal. All the same, his opponent, on whom he pours scorn, was not trying to find an escape clause to allow unjustified annulments: he was just drawing a logical conclusion which makes sense in itself.[107]

More to the point, most of the surviving church court evidence is later than the time when Hostiensis was writing. As we shall see, it tells a different story, in which annulments on grounds of consanguinity are rare. Perhaps Hostiensis was generalizing from limited experience from one part of France at a time for which we have little court record evidence. It may be that there were great regional differences (just as *c*.2000 an extremely high proportion of Catholic annulments were from the United States). It is even possible that his own influence, or rather the great influence of his commentary, had an effect upon attitudes.

If so, we may note in passing that this is another instance of marriage symbolism affecting social practice. The next two chapters will show how deeply Hostiensis's thinking about 'bigamy' and consummation was bound up with marriage symbolism. In particular, a long passage about consummation shows that indissolubility was closely connected in his mind with the representation of Christ's union to the Church—a position familiar by now, but expressed with unusual power.

Whether or not Hostiensis was responsible for tougher treatment of consanguinity or affinity cases for annulment can only be

---

[107] For the foregoing, see below, Document **2. 2**.

guessed. The educated guess is surely that he must have had some
influence because of his great status, but could not have worked a
transformation on his own. However that may be, there is a good
deal of evidence that the 'forbidden degrees' loophole was no longer
a popular escape route from marriage in the fourteenth century, in
the areas where ecclesiastical court record evidence has survived
and has been studied.

Records of real cases from local church courts

Most of the evidence survives (or is known to survive) in England,
and the English evidence for marriage litigation has been the subject
of several fine studies. It is worth quoting some of the conclusions:

> *Helmholz*: 'It is all but irresistible to conclude that divorces were
> often procured under the system of kinship disqualification. The
> Church court records, however, do not support that conclusion.
> The hard fact is that there were few divorces on these grounds.'[108]

Helmholz provides various explanations: people tried to avoid marrying kin, they looked for wives outside their community, forbidden
degrees were hard to prove under the tough conditions of evidence
(ibid. 79–85).

> *Sheehan* (writing about a late fourteenth-century Ely consistory
> court register): 'the court's principal activity was the vindication
> and defence of the marriage bond; pleas of annulment occurred
> infrequently';[109] 'It becomes evident that marriages were not es-
> pecially threatened by impediments of consanguinity and affinity'
> (ibid. 75); 'the court was primarily a body for the proof and defence
> of marriage rather than an instrument of easy annulment' (ibid. 76).

> *Ingram*:

> Today the bulk of matrimonial litigation . . . relates to divorce. In late
> medieval and early modern England the situation was very different. It is
> true that, although legal divorce in the modern sense was unknown, it was
> possible on rigorously specified grounds to bring actions for the annulment
> of marriage or for separation from bed and board. However, all the avail-
> able evidence indicates that, throughout the period from the fourteenth to

---

[108] Helmholz, *Marriage Litigation in Medieval England*, 79.

[109] M. M. Sheehan, 'The Formation and Stability of Marriage in Fourteenth-
Century England: Evidence of an Ely Register' (1971), repr. in id., *Marriage, Family,
and Law in Medieval Europe: Collected Studies*, ed. J. K. Farge (Cardiff, 1996), 38–76
at 74.

the seventeenth centuries, such suits were comparatively infrequent: cases concerning the *formation* of marriage, not marital breakdown, normally constituted the bulk of matrimonial litigation in the English ecclesiastical courts.[110]

Pedersen (studying the fourteenth-century consistory court of York): 'Perhaps most surprising, however . . . is the fact that according to the cause papers no marriages were annulled because of consanguinity.'[111]

Three other scholars may be cited to show that the English situation was not exceptional—that annulments on grounds of consanguinity were rare on the Continent too:

Weigand:

'Consanguinity' and 'Affinity'. When one considers the extent of these impediments in the Middle Ages, even after the reduction in 1215 to the fourth degree according to the canonical and thus also the Germanic computation, one might presume that these impediments played a very great role. Indeed, occasionally one finds it written in the scholarly literature that these and other impediments would have been able to provide the interested parties with a rationale for dissolving the marriages which they could subsequently use pretty well whenever they wanted. In reality, however, they played only a subordinate role; furthermore, the annulment of a marriage occurred only on the basis of genuine proofs, and certainly not on the basis of mere assertion by the parties involved.[112]

[110] M. Ingram, 'Spousals Litigation in the English Ecclesiastical Courts *c.*1350–*c.*1640', in R. B. Outhwaite (ed.), *Marriage and Society: Studies in the Social History of Marriage* (London, 1981), 35–57 at 35–6.

[111] F. Pedersen, *Marriage Disputes in Medieval England* (London etc., 2000), 137.

[112] R. Weigand, 'Zur mittelalterlichen kirchlichen Ehegerichtsbarkeit: Rechtsvergleichende Untersuchung' (1981), repr. in id., *Liebe und Ehe im Mittelalter* (Bibliotheca Eruditorum, 7; Goldbach, 1993), new pagination at foot pp. 307*–341*, at 325*–326* (my translation). Weigand goes on to summarize the findings for individual church courts where records have survived. He notes among other things an interesting finding in a study of northern French dioceses. On the one hand, consanguinity cases were quite common. On the other, they seem not to have aimed at a dissolution of the marriage. Instead, the data show couples being instructed to obtain dispensations that would put their marriage right. There is reason to think that the papal Penitentiary dealt with such dispensations quite efficiently: for this aspect of its work see L. Schmugge, P. Hersperger, and B. Wiggenhauser, *Die Supplikenregister der päpstlichen Pönitentiarie aus der Zeit Pius' II. (1458–1464)* (Tübingen, 1996), 72–3, 80–8, and K. Salonen, *The Penitentiary as a Well of Grace in the Late Middle Ages: The Example of the Province of Uppsala 1448–1527* (Annales Academiae Scientiarum Fennicae, 313; Helsinki, 2001), 109–19.

Lombardi (writing about Florence at the end of the period and in the subsequent one):

If we consider the cases as a whole, it becomes evident that people did not for the most part have recourse to the tribunal for the purpose of breaking a matrimonial bond. More numerous were the cases which had to do with the formation of the bond.[113]

Donahue:

My own research has focussed on England and France. Anne Lefebvre has surveyed the surviving records from late medieval France. Professor Weigand and Klaus Lindner have worked on Germany. An international group on ecclesiastical court records has produced reports on the surviving records of Austria, Belgium, France, Hungary, The Netherlands, and Switzerland, and has made some preliminary soundings in Germany, Spain and Italy. While the patterns of these records and of their survival vary markedly from country to country, and considerably more work *in situ* needs to be done, the conclusions about incest cases[114] that Helmholz and Sheehan arrived at on the basis [of] a relatively small sample of English cases have held up remarkably well: Incest cases do not comprise a large portion of the marriage business of the medieval church courts. There are some such cases. . . . The number . . . however, pales in comparison with the number of instance cases in which one party is seeking to enforce a marriage legitimately—as he or she alleges—entered into or to obtain a separation on the ground of adultery or cruelty, or in comparison with the number of *ex officio* prosecutions of fornication or adultery. . . . First, the search has now been extended widely enough and has covered enough different types and levels of courts that we are probably safe in arguing that the records are not there. Second, with a bit more hesitancy, we can probably argue that the records never were there, i.e., that the sample is wide enough and the circumstances of its survival peculiar enough that we

[113] D. Lombardi, *Matrimoni di antico regime* (Annali dell'Istituto storico italo-germanico in Trento, Monografie, 34; Bologna, 2001), 171 (my translation). Cf. ibid. 175: 'il numero delle cause di nullità resta comunque limitato, finché, a partire dal ventennio 1670–1689, sparisce del tutto. Ne possiamo forse dedurre che il principio di indissolubilità si fosse profondamente radicato nelle coscienze dei fedeli, oltre che tra i guidici, sensibili alle esigenze di salvaguardia del vincolo.'

[114] Donahue means cases involving the forbidden degrees of kinship (consanguinity and affinity). I am not sure that the word incest in the sense that anthropologists use it, or indeed in the everyday sense, captures the way it was regarded in this period: except where very close kinship was concerned, the rules were seen increasingly as designed to produce on the aggregate a sociologically desirable harmony between extended families, rather than moral absolutes barring the way to pollution. See D. L. d'Avray, 'Lay Kinship Solidarity and Papal Law', in P. Stafford, J. L. Nelson, and J. Martindale (eds.), *Law, Laity and Solidarities: Essays in Honour of Susan Reynolds* (Manchester, 2001), 188–99.

are probably looking at a relatively unbiased sample of what once was. . . . Third, not only were relatively few cases of incest recorded, but there were relatively few such cases. . . . we can probably reject once and for all the suggestion that all medieval marriages were *de facto* dissoluble because of the incest rules.[115]

These converging investigations discredit the view once current that the forbidden degrees provided a let-out clause for most marriages in the Middle Ages. Of course it is possible that despite Donahue's confidence more records may come to light and that these might alter the picture. It is hard to know what may or may not survive in Italy because it was normal for ordinary notaries to keep ecclesiastical court records and to mingle them with perfectly secular documents.[116] So more Italian ecclesiastical court cases about marriage will probably be found from time to time and it is possible that they may lead future scholars to rethink Donahue's verdict— but it does not seem likely. One set of Italian church court records that seems to have escaped the scholars just quoted[117] reminds us that consanguinity cases need not be about the couple's desire to get out of a marriage, for in an Asti case of 1265 it is just the opposite.[118] A married couple, Pietro Rugio and Agnesina Rugna, were reported as being related in the forbidden degrees. There followed an investigation. Seven witnesses bore out the accusation, so the marriage was pronounced null. Then Pietro and Agnesina appeared and said under oath that they did not know themselves

---

[115] C. Donahue, Jr., 'The Monastic Judge: Social Practice, Formal Rule, and the Medieval Canon Law of Incest', in P. Landau, with M. Petzolt (eds.), *De iure canonico medii aevi: Festschrift für Rudolf Weigand* (Studia Gratiana, 27; Rome, 1996), 49–69 at 55–6.

[116] A case in point was drawn to my attention by Chris Wickham: marriage cases mixed with records of debt etc. in the records of Guglielmo Cassinese towards the end of the twelfth century: see *Guglielmo Cassinese (1190–1192)*, ed. M. W. Hall, H. C. Krueger, and R. L. Reynolds (2 vols.; Notai liguri del sec. XII, 2; Documenti e studi per la storia del commercio e del diritto commerziale italiano, 12–13; Turin, 1938). This has some interesting cases (e.g. vol. ii, no. 1293, pp. 70–1; no. 1467, pp. 138–40; no. 1641, pp. 212–13), though they do not affect the argument of this book either way.

[117] *Documenti capitolari del secolo XIII (1265–66, 1285–88, 1291, 1296–98)*, 'a cura di Pietro Dacquino', ed. A. M. Cotto Meluccio (Asti, 1987). (Trevor Dean directed me to this rich and fascinating set of documents.) The collection reinforces the conclusions of Donahue, Weigand, *et al.* A search through the entries listed in the index under 'Cause matrimoniali' did not reveal a single case of annulment on grounds of consanguinity or affinity. As with English material, to which these cases bear a striking resemblance, the disputes seem to turn on the formation of marriage: consent, pre-contract, etc. [118] Ibid., nos. 74 and 75, pp. 36–7.

to be blood relatives. They were released from excommunication. The investigation seems to have continued, and we do not know the outcome.

Consanguinity cases do not in themselves show that indissolubility was taken lightly. It they result from the initiative of local church authorities, rather than the husband, they attest only to zeal for the consanguinity rules. The large number of indissolubility cases from the Southern Burgundian Netherlands can be and have been explained in this way.[119] Though they do not conform to the general pattern described by Donahue, they do not resemble the twelfth-century pattern of easy annulments either: all the indications are that the couples wanted to stay married and that the local church's agenda was to enforce the 'forbidden degrees' legislation of 1215.

The 'easy annulments' theory works well for the long century before Lateran IV in 1215, but after that date it is a historians' myth which modern scholarship has dispelled. This needs to be said with some emphasis, for even so fine a historian as Robert Bartlett, in a recent standard work which goes up to 1225, suggests that 'aristocrats were adept at using the rules of consanguinity to get something like divorce on demand', without noting the transformation of the situation near the end of this period.[120]

The meaning of 'pre-contract' cases

Here an objection could be raised. In England at least, among the commonest sorts of case in later medieval church courts were 'pre-contract' cases, where a marriage was challenged by someone claiming a prior marriage to one of the partners. Behind such cases might lie an earlier clandestine marriage. If a man and a woman contracted a marriage by simple consent, without having banns read first, it was a sin but valid. If the court believed in the earlier marriage, the later one was dissolved. Did not pre-contract cases make a mockery of indissolubility? If so, that undermines the thesis that symbolism eventually brought about a transformation of marriage practice.

[119] M. Vleeschouwers-Van Melkebeek, 'Incestuous Marriages: Formal Rules and Social Practice in the Southern Burgundian Netherlands', in I. Davis, M. Müller, and S. Rees Jones (eds.), *Love, Marriage, and Family Ties in the Later Middle Ages* (International Medieval Research, 11; Turnhout, 2003), 77–95.
[120] R. Bartlett, *England under the Norman and Angevin Kings 1075–1225* (Oxford, 2000), 558. The examples he gives are all pre-1215.

On the contrary: pre-contract cases were premissed on the conviction that a marriage was indissoluble. The first marriage contract may have been informal, may have taken place in sinful circumstances, but even so, it overrode any subsequent marriage, however religious the ceremony. Marriage was so absolutely indissoluble that even a marriage contracted in an alehouse stood against a subsequent marriage solemnized by a papal legate in Canterbury Cathedral. According to the predominant view, widely publicized in pastoral manuals, the sacramentality of marriage did not require a religious ritual, merely the exchange of consent. Two influential English pastoral manuals from different halves of the fourteenth century deserve special attention. William of Pagula defines marriage thus:

Marriage is contracted by consent alone through words in the present tense, as when a man says: 'I take you to be my wife', or the woman says: 'I take you to be my man or husband'. Whether or not an oath is inserted, it is not permitted to contract another marriage.[121]

A little later he says:

Two things are necessary for a marriage to take place, namely, substance and form. For the substance, the consent is there. For the form, the words reckoned to express consent in the present tense, as when he says: 'I take you to be mine', and the woman says: 'I take you to be mine', or other words expressing consent in the present tense.[122]

Another extremely popular English priests' manual produced later in the fourteenth century, the *Pupilla oculi* of Johannes de Burgo, is even clearer:

With respect to the minister of this sacrament, it should be noted that no other minister is required apart from the couple contracting the marriage. . . . It is clear also that the ministry of a priest is not required for the conferral of this sacrament, and that the sacerdotal blessing which the priest is accustomed to pronounce over the husband and wife, or the other

---

[121] 'Contrahitur matrimonium solo consensu per verba de presenti, ut ubi dicit: "Accipio te in meam uxorem", vel mulier dicit: "Accipio te in meum virum vel maritum". Sive iuramentum sit interpositum vel non, non licet alteri ad alia vota transire' (MS BL Royal 8. B. XV, fo. 141ʳ).

[122] 'Duo sunt necessaria ad esse matrimonii, scilicet substantia et forma. Pro substantia, est ibi consensus. Pro forma, verba deputata ad exprimendum consensum de presenti, ut ubi dicit: "Accipio te in meam", et mulier dicit: "Accipio te in meum", vel alia verba consensum de presenti exprimentia' (ibid., fo. 142ᵛ).

prayers pronounced by him, are not the form of the sacrament, nor of its essence, but something sacramental pertaining to the adornment of the sacrament.[123]

A theologian here or there may have associated the Church's blessing with marriage's character as a sacrament, but it is mistaken to think that this was the general view, as has been suggested for England in a recent study.[124] Paradoxically, every pre-contract

[123] 'De ministro huius sacramenti est notandum quod non *requiritur alius minister distinctus ab ipsis contrahentibus. . . . Patet etiam quod ad collationem huius sacramenti non *requiritur ministerium sacerdotis, et quod illa benedictio sacerdotalis quam solet presbiter super coniuges proferre, sive alie orationes ab ipso prolate, non sunt forma sacramenti, nec de eius essentia, sed quid sacramentale ad ornatum pertinens sacramenti' (MS BL Royal 11. B. X, fo. 124ra).

[124] See the important and able article by Christine Peters, 'Gender, Sacrament and Ritual: The Making and Meaning of Marriage in Late Medieval and Early Modern England', *Past and Present*, 169 (2000), 63–96 at 67–9, where she argues that 'For Aquinas, the form of sacrament of marriage was exchange of consent in words of the present tense, the couple were the ministers of the sacrament, and other rituals merely contributed to its honour and dignity. For others, including Duns Scotus and Bonaventure, form comprised both exchange of consent using specified words and the blessing by the church. Practice in late medieval England suggests that it was this second view which was generally understood by clergy and laity alike' (67). The evidence of key English priests' manuals does not bear that out: see previous note. The argument Peters goes on to give is interesting but not decisive: it is conceivable that some writers located the sacrament in the blessing, but she does not produce enough evidence to outweigh the passages from priests' manuals cited above and to demonstrate a predominance in England of the view that the blessing rather than consent was the crucial sacramental element. That liturgical texts describe the nuptial blessing as 'benedictio sacramentalis' is inconclusive. As is shown in Chapter 3, sect. (b), this came to mean one short phrase, and one blessing among many, in the Sarum manual, the most important liturgy of later medieval England. About the canonist Bernard of Pavia Peters may be right (68 n. 12), but a learned analysis by J. A. Brundage seems to undermine her reading: see 'The Merry Widow's Serious Sister: Remarriage in Classical Canon Law', in R. R. Edwards and V. Ziegler (eds.), *Matrons and Marginal Women in Medieval Society* (Woodbridge, 1995), 33–48 at 40. Peters suggests (67 and n. 10) that important theologians thought that it was the priestly blessing that conferred the sacrament, but in fact this is far from clear: see the fundamental article by Gabriel Le Bras, 'Mariage. III. La doctrine du mariage chez les théologiens et canonistes depuis l'an mille', in *Dictionnaire de théologie catholique* (15 vols.; Paris, 1899–1950), ix (1926), 2123–223 at 2206–7. Peters cites a couple of striking pieces of evidence from England: views of Lollard heretics who (she argues) had to 'abjure the belief that mutual exchange of consent without the prescribed form of words and/or church solemnization was sufficient for the sacrament of marriage' (68–9 and n. 13). Now one of the cases she cites (N. Tanner, *Heresy Trials in the Diocese of Norwich 1428–31* (Camden Fourth Series, 20; London, 1977), 111) is not relevant to her general argument about sacramentality. John Reve had to withdraw the opinion that there could be the sacrament of matrimony 'withoute contract of wordes or solempnisacion yn churche'. This only proves that the Church insisted on solemnization or at least

case was an act of homage to the clergy's idea that marriage was unbreakable. These cases spoke a different language from the forbidden degrees cases of the twelfth century.

The big difference between such cases and annulments on grounds of forbidden degrees in the twelfth century is this: in the twelfth century laymen used the canon law against itself. The structure of the law sent conflicting signals, not in theory but in practice. The forbidden degrees loophole made it look as though the Church did not really mean what it said about indissolubility. To many it must have seemed like an ideal to which one had to pay lip-service, while working around it to achieve a realistic flexibility adapted to human weakness. Though the wide extension of the forbidden degrees had not actually come about to facilitate serial monogamy, that was the appearance. They had in fact arisen out of the reforming zeal of men like Peter Damian, who would have been shocked at the way they were used. Later reformers like Peter the Chanter, the academic, and Innocent III, the man in power, were evidently shocked too and did something about it.

Wherever there is a law that seriously aims to change behaviour, people will find ways to frustrate its intentions. The measures put in place under Innocent III to make marriages lifelong are no exception—the scam invented by Raymundus Barellus has already been noted. So: if you wanted to leave your spouse you could try to persuade a church court that you had been married to someone else first. (This would work especially well if you did actually want to marry that person.) We have remarked that this happened;[125] it may have been common. There is an exemplum about a man who married a woman and then did not want to take her as his wife. She took him to a church court with witnesses, proving her case. He countered by claiming that he had been married before to another woman. A date was set for him to prove it. On the day before the

verbal consent: which implies the assumption by the Church that verbal consent without a blessing was enough for the sacrament of marriage (special cases like mutes are not in the picture here.) The other case that Peters cites (71) does not seem to be an abjuration in the strict sense. John Pyrye is giving information about opinions he had learnt from the condemned heretic William White, one of which was 'quod solus mutuus consensus inter virum et mulierem sufficit ad sacramentum matrimonii sui'. Clearly this is regarded by the authorities as a bad idea. Could this simply be because the obligation to marry in church was heavily emphasized by the late medieval English Church, as a matter of positive law?

[125] See above, p. 116.

trial, he and the woman went through a form of marriage in front of the two witnesses he had persuaded to support him. At the hearing, the first witness swore that he had witnessed the contract, allegedly seven years earlier. The question was put to him: how did he have the circumstances so fresh in his mind? He answered (lying through his teeth) that it was no wonder, because on that same day one of his children had drowned. The other witness perjured himself just as plausibly. When asked how he had kept the circumstances so fresh in his mind for seven years, he said 'Lord, it is no wonder, because on the same day when I had to climb over a wall, I fell and broke one of my shins in the fall.'[126] Old-fashioned perjury frustrates any law. That is a different matter from the law frustrating the law. Perjurious and collusive pre-contract cases might have made contemporaries cynical about human nature. They would not induce cynicism about the Church's real intentions.

Evidence of papal registers

Again, sometimes pure corruption could frustrate the law. In 1234 Pope Gregory IX wrote to the archbishop of Vienne about the bishop of Orange. People were saying alarming things about him. He was a serial seducer, and assisted in this by a female helper whom he had installed and was supporting in church accommodation, committing simony in his disposal of benefices, denying justice, preventing appeals, and also taking money to annul good marriages and tolerate invalid ones.[127] The bishop at the centre of

---

[126] 'In eodem episcopatu [Norwich], in decanatu de Len, contigit quod quidam contraxit cum quadam muliere, et post illum contractum ipse eam in coniugem accipere noluit. Ipsa igitur coram ordinario loci [fo. 82va] et testibus productis [predictis *ms.*] ipsum petiit in maritum ac vendicavit. Igitur cum contra ipsum per testes esset probatum, excepit, dicens quod antea cum quadam alia contraxerat; et ad hoc probandum per testes diem certum assignavit. Die igitur illo probationis faciende statuto, cum muliere cum qua contraxisse se dixerat et duobus qui hoc testificare deberent die prefixo venit. Set priusquam ante ordinarium accederet, coram illis duobus mulierem per verba de presenti accepit in uxorem, eodem scilicet die quo debuit probationem suam facere. Iuratus igitur unus ex predictis, iuravit se vidisse dictum contractum, lapso iam septennio. Cui cum examinator eius diceret: "Qualiter ita recenter habes in memoria tales circumstantias?": et ille: "Domine, ne mireris, quia illo die quidam de filiis meis submersus est in aqua et periit." Post hec iuratus alius aperte testatur eadem. Cui cum examinator diceret: "Mirum michi videtur quod tales circumstantias per septennium tam recenter retinuisti", respondit: "Domine, non est mirum, quia eodem die cum debui transire murum cecidi, et ex casu illo confracta est una de tibiis meis."' (MS BL Add. 33956, fo. 82^{rb-va}; cf. MS BL Harley 2385, fo. 69vb).

[127] The printed calendar of the commission is as follows: 'Archiepiscopo Vien-

these alleged scandals was already excommunicated when the pope asked the archbishop to investigate. The annulments for bribes find their place among a series of accusations that mark this out as a dramatically untypical case.

For in general the papal registers tell much the same story as the local church court records studied by the scholars quoted above. In the thirteenth century at least, annulments are hard to find in them.[128] The overwhelming majority of cases are about dispensations to get married or stay married despite an impediment.[129]

Balance sheet

To sum up: Indissolubility was a reality of social life at least from the pontificate of Innocent III. No doubt there were other places and perhaps whole regions where easy annulments were possible for one reason or another. New evidence may be found which dilutes the strong conclusions of Donahue and others. Nevertheless, those conclusions look set to stand.

Enforcement

The indissolubility principle was extended: popes and lower ecclesiastical authorities provided the means for a deserted spouse to reel in the errant partner. Papal formularies include letters setting in motion proceedings to bring back a husband or wife who had

nensi, Apostolicae Sedis legato, mandat quatenus, ad Aurasicensem (=Arausicensem) civitatem accedens, de Aurasicensi episcopo inquirat, qui, . . . quamplures focarias habens, ut dicebatur; surripiens virginibus castitatis vinculum, pro quibus et aliis facilitate damnabili seducendis, quamdam miseram, in procurandis alienis lapsibus forte per proprios eruditam, [auxiliatricem] specialem sibi constituerat, eique unum de domiciliis Aurasicensis ecclesiae, cujus indigna pane vescebatur, deputaverat; ad ecclesias et ecclesiastica beneficia conferenda symoniacam advocans pravitatem; justitiam petentibus non impendens et emissis appellationibus super illatis ab ipso molestiis minime deferens; interventu pecuniae matrimonia legitima dirimens et prohibitis obstaculum non opponens; divina officia, licet excommunicationum sententiis innodatus, celebrare praesumens,—in multos excessus ceciderat; quae invenerit Summo Pontifici suis litteris fideliter rescribat' (*Les Registres de Grégoire IX*, ed. L. Auvray, i (Paris, 1896), no. 1709, col. 942.

[128] I read through the marriage cases in the École Française de Rome calendars of papal registers up to and including Boniface VIII, using the analytical indices for the registers where they exist. I have not attempted a systematic trawl of fourteenth-century registers.

[129] Royal annulments are a special case because of the pressure the parties could bring to bear. It is nevertheless my prima facie impression that even kings found it hard or impossible to get an annulment unless their case in law held water. The question requires further investigation and I hope to deal with it in a separate study.

moved out and tell the delinquent to treat deserted partners with 'marital affection'.[130] A letter from the bishop of Lincoln in 1298 shows the same attitude at work at episcopal level. Robert Huthe had married Mariot la Carter two decades before, lived with her nine years, and had six children with her. Then he left her for Agnes la Rus, defied excommunication by the archdeacon of Lincoln, and moved away to the area under the archdeacon of Ely. The latter is asked to pursue the matter.[131] One assumes that the deserted wife Mariot la Carter had set the process in motion.

An apparently real example of such an excommunication survives in a miscellaneous British Library manuscript:

Formula for an Excommunication. In the year of the Lord 1309, on Friday, 27 June, I, John, parish priest in Matray, since James/Jacob son of Hedbeigerius does not want to accept his wife Bridget, who had been adjudged to him by the sentence of the venerable father the Lord John bishop of Brixen (Brininen), and to treat her with marital affection, after being admonished by me three times on this matter in the presence of witnesses—and the witnesses should be named—exercising my authority I excommunicate him with this document.[132]

---

[130] 'Contra virum recedentem ab uxore et adultere adherentem. Iud. Sua nobis G. de .. mulier conquestione monstravit quod R. de .. laicus diocesis, ea dimissa, propria temeritate cuidam adultere inpudenter adheret. Mandamus quatenus, si est ita, dictum R. ut, adultera ipsa dimissa, nominatam uxorem suam recipiat et maritali, ut tenetur, affectione pertractet, monitione premissa per censuram ecclesiasticam iustitia exigente compellas' (MS BL Lansdowne 397, fo. 154ʳ (newer foliation)). The double dots in papal documents mean that a proper name has been omitted. 'Iud.' could be extended as 'Iudici' or 'Iudicibus'. If the latter, the last word would be extended as 'compellatis'. Cf. P. Herde, *Audientia litterarum contradictarum: Untersuchungen über die päpstlichen Justizbriefe und die päpstliche Delegationsgerichtsbarkeit vom 13. bis zum Beginn des 16. Jahrhunderts* (2 vols.; Bibliothek des Deutschen historischen Instituts in Rom, 31–2; Tübingen, 1970), ii. 302.

[131] *The Rolls and Register of Bishop Oliver Sutton, 1280–1299*, ed. R. M. T. Hill, vi. *Memoranda, May 19, 1297–September 12, 1299* (Lincoln, 1969), 84–5.

[132] 'Forma excommunicationis. Anno Domini M.° CCCIX.° proxima feria sexta post nativitatem sancti Baptiste, ego Iohannes, plebanus in Matray, quia Iacobus filius Hedbeigerii Brigidam uxorem suam sibi adiudicatam per sententiam venerabilis patris domini Iohannis Brixinensis episcopi non vult accipere et eam maritali affectione tractare, ter per per me monitus super hoc coram testibus—et nominentur testes—auctoritate qua fungor eum (*interlined*) excommmunico in hiis scriptis' (MS BL Add. 18347, fo. 40ʳ). The context is a small set of models for the correct form of an excommunication, but this one, at least, is so circumstantial that it is probably based on a real case.

Legal separation

The law of indissolubility did not force a couple to stay together in all circumstances, and this should be factored into any assessment of marriage in the age of papal monarchy. Church law was inflexible about remarriage but took a different attitude to legal separation, about which it could be quite flexible at least in the later medieval centuries, when indissolubility was being enforced (a chronology for the social history of legal separation in the preceding centuries has not been established).[133] To take a concrete example: legal separation was the outcome in a messy case that came before the vicar of the bishop of Asti.[134] The matter came to a head in 1265. A woman called Agnesina was ordered to return to her husband Guglielmo, who gave money as security that he would not injure her. There was a guarantor in case he did not pay. Some days later the guarantor withdrew, anxious about the husband's stupidity. Agnesina was released from excommunication for desertion. Her husband accused her of a long-term adulterous affair. She and a man named Bachino had been sleeping together in his shop and elsewhere for years, the husband alleged. Agnesina was very happy with the idea of a legal separation. A few days after this there seems to have been another change of mind. Guglielmo withdrew the charge of adultery and wanted his wife back. She was prepared to comply but wanted 'a good security with a substantial penalty':[135] presumably a way of ensuring that he paid punitive damages if he hurt her. However, that idea seems to have been dropped: within a few days the bishop's vicar in matters spiritual pronounced the legal separation, after Agnesina had admitted adultery. It is spelt out that neither party could remarry.

---

[133] For some good recent studies of legal separation, mainly covering the later Middle Ages and the early modern period, see S. S. Menchi and D. Quaglioni (eds.), *Coniugi nemici: i processi matrimoniali. La separazione in Italia dal XII al XVIII secolo* (I processi matrimoniali degli archivi ecclesiastici italiani, 1; Annali dell'Istituto storico italo-germanico in Trento, Quaderni, 53; Bologna, 2000), especially—for the Middle Ages—D. Quaglioni, '"Divortium a diversitate mentium": la separazione personale dei coniugi nelle dottrine di diritto comune (appunti per una discussione)', 95–118; C. Meek, '"Simone ha aderito alla fede di Maometto": la "fornicazione spirituale" come causa di separazione (Lucca 1424)', 121–39; and S. Chojnacki, 'Il divorzio di Cateruzza: rappresentazione femminile ed esito processuale (Venezia 1465)', 371–416.

[134] *Documenti capitolari del secolo XIII*, ed. Cotto Meluccio, nos. 48–51, pp. 24–6.

[135] 'bonam securitatem sub magna pena' (no. 50, p. 26).

If a woman (or a man, but it was more likely to be a woman) had difficulty in getting a legal separation, she could even go to the pope: there was a routine mechanism, probably necessary only in cases where local ecclesiastics were not trusted—for instance, if the husband was a friend of the bishop. A formulary of the *Audientia litterarum contradictarum*, the office through which routine litigation at the papal curia passed, gives an interesting example of a papal letter setting in motion the proceedings towards a legal separation.[136] It is clearly based on a real case, for the husband is named as a knight called Antonio de Luna of Zaragoza. The complaint had been made by his wife Alienor. Antonio had been a persistent adulterer and had apparently also treated her cruelly, so she was in physical danger living with him. She asks for a legal separation, *divortium quoad thorum et mutuam servitutem*. Furthermore, and this is important, she wants her dowry to be returned, together with anything else assigned to Antony as part of the marriage settlement. Thus property was involved. It was not just a matter of the couple splitting up and living apart: a legal settlement could hardly be avoided if Alienor wanted everything back, and the other side of the case would in fairness have to be heard. The pope—or rather the administrators acting with his authority—appoints the bishops of Barcelona and Vich as judges delegate, suspending the canon-law rules designed to make sure that judges and parties were not too far apart geographically.[137] One suspects that the husband was powerful locally and that judges from some distance away were appointed to ensure that the trial was fair to the wife.

Even with the possibility of legal separation, the medieval Church was asking more of married couples than most cultures and religions have done, since it did not permit remarriage so long as the first marriage was deemed to be genuine. This was clearly a demanding doctrine. The obverse was that the Church demanded a high level of freedom at the point of entry into marriage, so that any pressure that would frighten a reasonable person was enough to invalidate a marriage.

Indissolubility and free consent

Marriage was an unbreakable bond but it had to be accepted freely in the first place. In the Church's official thinking marriage was a

[136] Herde, *Audientia litterarum contradictarum*, 308–9.
[137] See ibid. 309 nn. 2 and 3.

strong, free, individual choice. There is a certain logic to this link between indissolubility and freedom. Because the commitment was for life, responsibility must be undiminished by family or other pressure. A choice that could not be revoked must not be imposed. This frame of mind, which was embodied in law, could not be further from the caricature of medieval marriage as nothing but a matter of families and property.

In the half century before Innocent III, the power to chose and freedom of consent seem to have come to the fore in Church thinking at the highest level.[138] Family or other external pressures continued throughout the Middle Ages and afterwards into recent times. The marriage of the Vanderbilt heiress to the duke of Marlborough in 1895 is a case of *de facto* coercion that should make modernists think about how much their period really differs from the Middle Ages.[139] A wealthy American woman was pressured by her parents into giving up the perfectly acceptable wealthy New York lawyer whom she loved, in order to marry an English peer whom she did not, for reasons which had nothing whatsoever to do with the legal power to choose. Social pressure is stronger than law. Such cases can still be found today, though the fashion for marrying American heiresses to British aristocrats is no longer an oppressive force. Nevertheless, it can hardly be denied that a law of free choice will make a real difference in many cases.

The canon-law compilation and textbook by Gratian gave a powerful impetus to the power to choose. As the classic article which brought out this feature of his thought put it:

Gratian recognized the place of individualistic, unsocial decision-making in the choice of spouses . . . Underlying this deference to the individual was the conviction that 'consent makes marriage'—not any consent, not merely lustful consent to intercourse, not merely intellectual consent to a shared life, but consent informed with that special quality that Gratian, drawing on the Roman law, denominated 'marital affection,' an emotion-coloured assent to the other as husband or wife. Neither Church nor feudal lord

---

[138] For the concept of consent in an earlier period see I. Weber, '"Consensus facit nuptias!" Überlegungen zum ehelichen Konsens in normativen Texten des Frühmittelalters', *Zeitschrift der Savigny-Stiftung für Rechtsgeschichte*, 118, kanonistische Abteilung, 87 (2001), 31–66.

[139] My source is the chapter on 'The *Financial Times* meets *Hello!*: Anglo-American Marital Relations 1870–1945', in a forthcoming history of Anglo-American relations by my colleague Professor Kathy Burk, to whom my thanks.

nor family could supply that element. Where it was wanting, there was no
marriage.[140]

Gratian's textbook was among the most influential books of the
Middle Ages: not just affecting thinking but also action, for it was
the handbook of the new professionalized church lawyers who ran
the well-organized hierarchy of ecclesiastical courts that came into
being around this time. Gratian's ideas about the power to choose
were therefore much more than ideals. They exercised power over
society.

The line of thought was taken further by a pope who left a mark
on church law almost as deep as Gratian's. This was Alexander III,
pope from 1159 to 1181. Gratian's synthesis of the law had left
many questions unanswered. The hardest cases about marriage
were often concluded by a papal decretal, which became case law
from then on. Alexander III issued many such decretals, notably
in marriage cases, and many were incorporated in the code of case
law issued in 1234, so that they remained legally binding and were
closely studied by practising church lawyers up to 1917 (when the
medieval church law was replaced).

The free consent doctrine of Alexander III is the subject of another classic article which converges towards the same general interpretation of later medieval marriage.[141] The two investigations
must have been pursued at around the same time, which would
make the similarity of the findings about adjacent topics all the
more striking.

Alexander III 'requires only the consent of the bride and groom
and rejects a requirement of the consent of anyone other than the
bride and groom'.[142] In previous legal tradition or traditions, 'the
family, the master, and in feudal times, the lord, play an important
role'.[143] Alexander's position may have vacillated a little during
his pontificate,[144] but the law he left to posterity put the couple,

---

[140] J. T. Noonan, 'Power to Choose', *Viator*, 4 (1973), 419–34 at 425.

[141] C. Donahue, Jr., 'The Policy of Alexander the Third's Consent Theory of
Marriage', in *Proceedings of the Fourth International Congress of Medieval Canon
Law, Toronto, 21–25 August 1972* (Monumenta Iuris Canonici, Series C, Subsidia,
5; Vatican City, 1976), 251–79.

[142] Ibid. 256; J. A. Brundage, *Law, Sex, and Christian Society in Medieval Europe*
(Chicago etc., 1987), 335–6.

[143] Donahue, 'The Policy of Alexander the Third's Consent Theory of Marriage', 256.

[144] For the problems of working out a coherent chronogical development of his

the man and the woman, at the centre of the stage without any supporting cast to upstage them. Donahue even made the intriguing and attractive suggestion that Alexander's marriage rules 'represent an unconscious attempt to incorporate the acceptable elements of courtly love into the law of the Church'.[145] Less tentatively, he argues that 'The coincidence . . . of an ethic of love which, in marked contrast to the general practice of society, puts a high premium on the consent of the woman, with a set of legal rules which make valid marriage by the consent of the parties alone is almost too extraordinary to arise by chance' (ibid.). The social forces pushing against free consent in practice must have been hard to withstand. Nevertheless, the influence of canon law on social practice should not be underestimated either. To quote Noonan again:

If a father beat his daughter severely to enforce his choice, the marriage was null, as a York case shows. . . . Attempts by parents to coerce might also be treated as sin and punished by refusal of the sacraments—a father, for example, might be denied absolution on his deathbed if his will disinherited a daughter refusing to marry as he directed.[146]

Local church court records are not common for the thirteenth century outside Italy, but they survive for thirteenth-century Pisa and a similar picture has emerged:

In a series of cases judged at the beginning of the thirteenth century by the episcopal court of Pisa, some women who had been betrothed refused to obey their own parents and guardians and rejected the marriages arranged by them, maintaining, as did Gherardesca, the daughter of Gherardo Magliolachi, that the choice of a husband for her 'was not and is not to her mind', and that 'she has not given her consent and does not intend to give it'.[147]

A couple of cases that went right up to the pope show aware-

thought as expressed in his decretals, see Brooke, *The Medieval Idea of Marriage*, 169–72, and also 133 n. 37.

[145] Donahue, 'The Policy of Alexander the Third's Consent Theory of Marriage', 279.

[146] Noonan, 'Power to Choose', 433–4.

[147] D. O. Hughes, 'Il matrimonio nell'Italia medievale', in M. De Giorgio and C. Klapisch-Zuber (eds.), *Storia del matrimonio* (Rome etc., 1996), 5–61 at 20–1 (my translation), citing *Das Imbreviaturbuch des Erzbischöflichen Gerichtsnotars Hubaldus aus Pisa (Mai bis August 1230)*, ed. G. Dolezalek (Forschungen zur neueren Privatrechtsgeschichte, 13; Cologne etc., 1969), 101–2.

ness of the rationale behind the rules. A woman named Gemma had a daughter whose name is simply given as 'T'. The daughter was betrothed to a boy when they were both less than seven, and a penalty clause was included in the arrangement. Still, when she grew up she married someone else. The father of her childhood fiancé attempted to enforce the penalty clause. In 1231 the pope gave delegates the power to stop him, because marriages should be free.[148] In a case of 1233 a French clergyman was able to bring in the pope to help a relative.[149] Her father had died and her guardian had arranged for her to marry the son of a certain Theobald, when the son came of age. If this son died first, she would marry another son. Theobald and the son specified under plan A both died; there was another son but he was not yet old enough to marry. So Theobald's widow seems to have imprisoned ('presumes to detain') the girl, who was now of marriageable age. The clergyman petitioned for her release and freedom to marry someone else. The pope commissioned the bishop of Le Mans to investigate and judge the case. If the facts turned out to be as stated, the girl was to be released, or else the woman holding her would face ecclesiastical censure. Again the pope states the rationale that 'marriages should be free', *matrimonia libera esse debeant.*[150]

The hard line on indissolubility needs to be set against the insistence on liberty. Marriage was for life, but it must be entered freely. We have seen—it is the theme of this chapter—that symbolism underlay the idea that marriage was for life. It seems also to connect with the thought that marriage must be free. To quote Noonan yet again:

Unwilling marriages usually brought bad results. But why was freedom a positive good? Reflection on the canons led to an answer put in the terms of the great mystery of the Epistle to the Ephesians, succinctly stated in 1457 by the last great commentator on Gratian, Juan de Torquemada: 'Marriage signifies the conjunction of Christ and the Church which is made through the liberty of love. Therefore, it cannot be made by coerced consent.'[151]

---

[148] 'cum vero libera matrimonia esse debeant': the phrase is from the calendar in *Les Registres de Grégoire IX*, ed. Auvray, vol. i, no. 719, col. 449, but it looks as though the editor has taken it from the words of the papal letter.

[149] 'proneptis': it can mean great-granddaughter, but in context 'great-niece' is more likely.

[150] *Les Registres de Grégoire IX*, ed. Auvray, vol. i, no. 1188, cols. 671–2.

[151] Noonan, 'Power to Choose', 434.

A similar formula is found in the 'Supplement' to the *Summa theologica* (further research may well show it to be a topos). In a question on 'Whether a coerced consent makes a marriage void' we meet the remark that 'marriage signifies the conjunction of Christ and the Church, which is brought about in the liberty of love. Therefore it cannot be brought about through a coerced consent'.[152]

Explanations

To conclude: the law of indissolubility became effective from the early thirteenth century on. Apparently contrary evidence—the strictures of Hostiensis, the plethora of pre-contract cases—fades away on closer examination. The law had teeth, but we need to remember that legal separation was possible and also that freedom at the point of entry into marriage was stressed, balancing the rule of strict indissolubility.

We have traced the path of this doctrine from theological into social history. Several compatible explanations have been given for the timing: the influence of the 'False Decretals', which emphasized the bishop's unbreakable 'marriage' to his church; the spread of celibacy in the power élite of the clergy; the flowering of canon law and church courts. All of these help to explain why indissolubility moved from theory into practice in the central Middle Ages. These forces account only for the timing, however, and a certain idea of marriage marked in advance the lines along which they ran. In history ideas can have a delayed-action impact. In recent centuries, for instance, ideas of human equality and rights have been applied to new categories of persons and situations gradually, long after the basic principle had become a social premiss. People pay lip-service to a principle for decades or centuries, but one day some group takes it seriously.

Without the principle of indissolubility, one man to one woman for life, the idea stretching back to Augustine and before, clerical energies and legal organization would have been pointed in a different direction. This takes us back to the beginning: the rationale

---

[152] 'matrimonium significat coniunctionem Christi ad Ecclesiam, quae fit secundum libertatem amoris. Ergo non potest fieri per consensum coactum' (Supplementum, q. 47, art. 3, in *Sancti Thomae Aquinatis . . . opera omnia, iussu . . . Leonis XIII P.M. edita*, xii (Roma 1906), 'Supplementum' section (separately paginated), 90. The remark comes in the 'Sed contra' section, which usually (as here) goes in the direction of the writer's own view, as expressed in the 'Respondeo dicendum' section.

of the principle as articulated lucidly by Augustine. The rationale is a symbol, the equation of Christ's union with the Church and the union of man and wife, symbolism which was released from the realm of texts and went on to transform law and society.

3
Bigamy

(a) Bigamy and Becoming a Priest

The meaning of 'bigamy'

Bigamy in this context does not mean having two wives at the same
time. It refers to a man's marriage to a widow or his remarriage
after his wife's death. For the laity it was legitimate in the Middle
Ages. It was not banned by the Church,[1] and in fact was extremely
common, as any social and political historian knows. On the other
hand there were rules about bigamy that may at first seem strange.
They have not been much studied though a few good publications
lay a solid foundation.[2] The key rules for our purposes are: (*a*) a
man who has been made a widower twice or whose deceased wife
was a widow is banned from the priesthood; (*b*) a central blessing

[1] P. Fedele, 'Vedovanza e seconde Nozze', in *Il matrimonio nella società altomedievale* (Settimane di Studio del Centro Italiano di Studi sull'alto Medioevo, 24; 2
vols.; Spoleto, 1977), ii. 820–43 at 825. B. Jussen, *Der Name der Witwe: Erkundungen
zur Semantik der mittelalterlichen Bußkultur* (Veröffentlichungen des Max-Planck-
Instituts für Geschichte, 158; Göttingen, 2000), is less relevant to the current investigation than might appear, perhaps surprisingly, since our general ideas about
history should be done are so similar. It tells an important monographic story about
the creation of the schema of differential afterlife rewards for virgins, widows, and
married people *c*.400 by writers like Jerome, the corresponding development in the
early Middle Ages of a distinct status group of women who had resolved not to remarry, and the metaphor of the penitential Church as a widow. It is not really about
widows who remarried, as was normal and respectable. For canon-law background
see J. A. Brundage, 'The Merry Widow's Serious Sister: Remarriage in Classical
Canon Law', in R. R. Edwards and V. Ziegler (eds.), *Matrons and Marginal Women
in Medieval Society* (Woodbridge, 1995), 33–48.

[2] See above all S. Kuttner, 'Pope Lucius III and the Bigamous Archbishop of
Palermo' (1961), repr. in id., *The History of Ideas and Doctrines of Canon Law
in the Middle Ages* (London, 1980), no. VII, pp. 409–53; H. Schadt, 'Die Arbores
bigamiae als heilsgeschichtliche Schemata: Zum Verhältnis von Kanonistik und
Kunstgeschichte', in W. Busch (ed.), *Kunst als Bedeutungsträger: Gedenkschrift für
Günter Bandmann* (Berlin, 1978), 129–47. Also useful are the article by J. Vergier-
Boimond, 'Bigamie (l'irrégularité de)', in R. Naz (ed.), *Dictionnaire de droit canonique*, ii (Paris, 1937), 853–88, and A. Esmein, *Le Mariage en droit canonique*, 2nd
edn., rev. R. Génestal and J. Dauvillier (2 vols.; Paris, 1929–35), ii. 119–25.

must be omitted from the marriage ceremony in the case of second marriages; and (*c*) a cleric in minor orders can be married but only once and only if his wife was a virgin. This section deals with the first of these three rules.

Marriage symbolism, bigamy, and eligibility for the priesthood

The rule against admitting double widowers and widowers of widows to the priesthood seems to derive ultimately from scriptural texts: from the New Testament, especially Titus 1: 5–7, which states that a presbyter should be the husband of one wife; and from the Old Testament, especially Leviticus 21: 13–14 and Ezechiel 44, which say that the high priest must not marry a widow (among other excluded categories). For our purposes it is not necessary to explain the origin of these prohibitions. Probably they can be accounted for along the lines pioneered by Mary Douglas.[3] The passage from Titus would in itself provide an explanation for the survival of the rules, though not a complete one because it could have been reinterpreted. Thus, it seems to imply a married priesthood, yet was not understood to mean that. So the 'one wife' could have been explained away too: she could have been the Church or God or Christ. Widows and widowers in the literal sense could have been taken out of the picture. We do not need to explain why they were left in it in the early Christian centuries, as our concern is the Middle Ages.

Why were the rules so important in the Middle Ages? Of Max Weber's famous four determinants of social action, tradition, emotion, value-rational motivation, and ends–means calculation,[4] the first, tradition, must surely have done much to keep the bigamy rules in operation. Their very antiquity must have discouraged the thought of simply abandoning them. That is taken for granted in this chapter. I attempt to show, however, that symbolic value rationality was another important reason and motive for respecting these traditions. A sign of the vitality of this symbolic value rationality is that it enabled development and modification of the rules. Their history is marked by vitality and change. Their symbolic rationale stimulates original reflections by famous writers. Tradition is thus

   [3] M. Douglas, *Purity and Danger: An Analysis of Concept[s] of Pollution and Taboo*, with a new preface by the author (London etc., 2002).
   [4] M. Weber, *Wirtschaft und Gesellschaft: Grundriß der verstehenden Soziologie*, ed. J. Winckelmann, 5th rev. edn. (3 vols.; Tübingen, 1976), i. 12.

necessary but not sufficient to explain the medieval history of the bigamy rules.

For historians of the Middle Ages, Augustine of Hippo's rationale in terms of Christ's marriage to the Church is a sufficient starting point for causal explanation in terms of symbolic values. In a passage that would run like a thread through the future law of bigamy, Augustine put it thus:

In the future, the one city will be composed of many souls who have 'one soul and one heart' in God, and after this earthly pilgrimage it will be the perfection of our unity, in which all men's thoughts will not be hidden from each other, and will in no way be opposed to each other. For this reason the sacrament of marriage has in our time been reduced to one husband and one wife, so that it is not possible for a man to be ordained minister of the Church if he has had more than one wife. This has been more clearly understood by those who have decreed that a man who as a catechumen or pagan had a second wife, should not be ordained. The concern here is with the sacrament, not with sinning. In baptism all sins are forgiven, but he who said 'If you have taken a wife, you have not sinned, and if a virgin marries, she does not sin', and 'Let her do what she wishes; she does not sin, let her marry' [1 Cor. 7: 28, 36], made it sufficiently clear that marriage is no sin. Now to ensure the sacred nature of the sacrament, a woman who has lost her virginity, even if she is a catechumen, cannot after baptism be consecrated among the virgins of God. So similarly it has not seemed out of place that a man who has had more than one wife, though not having committed any sin, has not observed the norm, so to say, of the sacrament, which was required not to gain the reward of a good life, but for the seal of ecclesiastical ordination.[5]

Augustine was writing at a time when priests could still have wives but were not supposed to have sex with them.[6] As the theory that priests should be unmarried gained acceptance, the rule would have come to refer to the categories just mentioned, twice widowed men and widowers of widows. It applied to bishops, priests, and deacons; in the Rome of late antiquity it seems to have extended to clerics in minor orders too, but this was not general in the West; the rule was extended to subdeacons in the course of the early Middle Ages.[7]

Where the early medieval centuries are concerned, it is hard to

---

[5] Augustine, *De bono coniugali*, 21 [XVIII], in *Augustine:* De bono coniugali; De sancta virginitate, ed. and trans. P. G. Walsh (Oxford, 2001), 39–41.

[6] H. C. Lea, *History of Sacerdotal Celibacy in the Christian Church*, 3rd rev. edn. (2 vols.; London, 1907), ch. 5, esp. 74–6.

[7] Kuttner, 'Pope Lucius III and the Bigamous Archbishop of Palermo', 411–12.

say how far the rules about 'bigamy' were enforced in practice.
Historians generally assume that the sexual abstinence of priests
was honoured in the breach rather than the observance, so one
might argue a fortiori that 'bigamy' rules were still less likely to be
obeyed—but that might be a false inference and a false assumption
about the relative gravity of the two deviations from the rules.
As with so many topics in the history of Europe before *c.*1000,
agnosticism is the only safe position.

Peter Damian

Rules about the clergy undoubtedly began to bite into social practice by the end of the eleventh century. Celibacy was taken in deadly
earnest by the leaders of the eleventh-century reform.[8] One of these
leaders also wrote some fascinating lines on bigamy, which tend to
suggest that the rules were taken seriously in his day. This was Peter
Damian, like Hildebrand himself a reformer of passionate intensity.
In a letter to a hermit about the mystical body of Christ,[9] in which
he explains how the words *Dominus vobiscum*, 'The Lord be with
you' in the plural, can meaningfully be used by someone who is on
his own, he points out that there are things in the Church which
seem otiose from the point of view of human reason, but which are
from God if one takes account of the *virtutis intimae . . . sacramentum*, a phrase hard to translate but which might from the passage
that follows be rendered: 'the mysterious symbol of intimate power'
(ibid. 264). The passage goes like this:

For who might not find it strange that it is laid down by provisions of canon
law that no 'bigamist'[10] may by any means be raised to the priesthood, but
that one who has lapsed and committed fornication, even if he is a priest,
may after he has completed his penance be restored to the office that
he held by right before? For indeed St Paul's opinion of fornication is
quite clear when we read that 'neither fornicators nor servers of idols nor
adulterers will possess the kingdom of God'. But on those who contract
second marriages, it continues as follows: 'A woman', he says, 'is bound
by the law as long as her husband lives, but if her husband dies, she is at

[8] They understood it as a ban on marriage, not just on sex with a wife with whom
one might have had children before becoming a priest.
[9] Peter Damian, Letter 28, to the Hermit Leo of Sitria, in *Die Briefe des Petrus
Damiani*, ed. K. Reindel, i (Monumenta Germaniae Historica: Die Briefe der
deutschen Kaiserzeit, 4; Munich, 1983), 248–78.
[10] 'digamum', which (just like 'bigamus') would include a man who had remarried
after his wife's death and a man who had married a widow who had then died.

liberty: let her marry whom she will, only in the Lord.' Without a doubt, with the words of the one passage and the other he shows clearly both that 'bigamists' do not break the rule of God's law and that fornicators are cut off at the peril of their soul from the kingdom of God on account of their lack of carnal restraint.

How to explain, then, that men who do not sin fall away from all hope of becoming priests, while men who are eliminated by ill-doing from the kingdom of God do not lose the prospect of ecclesiastical rank if they have completed their penance worthily? For this reason only: that with those who are joined in second marriages the focus is not on sin but on the symbol [*sacramentum*] of the Church. For just as Christ—who is the 'high priest of future goods' [Hebr. 9: 11], and the true 'priest according to the order of Melchisedech' [Ps. 109: 4], the one, that is, who offered the lamb of his own body on the altar of the cross to God the Father for the salvation of the world—is the husband of one bride, that is of the whole holy Church, which is without doubt a virgin, since it keeps the integrity of the faith inviolably: so too each and every priest is commanded to be the husband of one wife, so that he may seem to present the image of that supreme spouse. With 'bigamists', therefore, the issue is not the assessment of sin but rather the form of the sacrament, and when they are excluded, it is not that a crime is being punished, but that the mystical rule of the true priesthood[11] is kept: otherwise, how would something be counted among crimes that the doctrine of St Paul permits to take place licitly? But the sacred canons too designate those who condemn second marriages as belonging to the Novatian heresy. Therefore, in order that we may show we always hold the mystery of ecclesiastical unity, there can be no objection if we use a verbal expression even if it is not so very necessary. (Ibid. 464–5)

The train of reasoning would seem to be this. Second marriages rule out the priesthood not because there is anything wrong with second marriages *per se*, for on the contrary, they are entirely licit and it is heretical to deny that; even so, they are ruled out for priests in order to make a symbolic or mystical point about the union of Christ and the Church. God expresses himself in symbolic ways which do not quite make sense on the level of literal-minded human reasoning. Thus in the same way the plural expression *Dominus vobiscum* can be used in a context which would otherwise require the singular in order to make a point about the mystical unity of the Church.

---

[11] One manuscript cited in the apparatus criticus reads 'sacramenti'.

Innocent III's decretal Debitum

Peter Damian seems to take it for granted that the rule banning 'bigamists' from the priesthood is not a dead letter, and the conviction with which he expounds its symbolic meaning is unmistakable. The eleventh-century reformer thought along the same lines as St Augustine at the end of the Roman Empire. So did Innocent III in the early thirteenth century. In 1206 the symbolic rationale of the bigamy rules enabled him to solve a concrete case in a decision that would be incorporated into the canon-law compilation of 1234, a compilation that remained in force until 1917. Thus many commentators would reflect on the pope's reasoning. The decretal in question is known as *Debitum* (X. 1. 21. 5). It is important for the history of both bigamy and consummation, the subject of the next chapter. Innocent III's pivotal role in the history of marriage symbolism and its social impact will not have escaped notice.

A man marries a widow who had never had sex with her husband: she comes to him a virgin, and dies before him. Can he become a priest, or is he banned by the 'bigamy' rule? Innocent's answer is a meditation on the significance of the symbolism and at the same time a practical legal verdict. He reasons as follows:

Since there are two things in marriage, namely the consent of minds and the intercourse of bodies, one of which signifies the charity which obtains in spirit between God and the just soul . . . while the other signifies [*designat*] the conformity of flesh which obtains between Christ and the Church, to which second thing pertains that to which the Evangelist bears witness: 'The word was made flesh and dwelt among us': therefore a marriage which is not consummated by the intercourse of bodies is not suited to signify the marriage which was contracted between Christ and the Church by the mystery of the incarnation, in relation to which St Paul, expounding the words said by the first-made man, 'This now is bone of my bones and flesh of my flesh, and because of this a man will leave his father and his mother, and cleave to his wife, and they will be two in one flesh', immediately adds: 'But this I say is a great *sacramentum* [sacrament? symbol? mystery?] in Christ and the Church'. Since, therefore, it is forbidden because of the defect of the *sacramentum* for a twice married man [*bigamus*] or husband of a widow to presume to be elevated to holy orders, because she [the wife] is not the only woman of only one man, nor is he one belonging to one: therefore, where the mingling of bodies is lacking with spouses of this sort, this sign [*signaculum*] of the sacrament is not lacking. Therefore a man who marries a woman who has been married to another man without ever sleeping with him should not on this account be prevented from being elevated to the priesthood, since the woman did not divide her flesh into more than one part, and he did not do so either.

So symbolism solves a concrete case. Here the image works causally. Above all, a case like this is a symptom of how much in earnest intellectuals such as Innocent III were about marriage symbolism. This case will turn up again in the context of consummation.

Hostiensis and the 'Tree of Bigamy'

Apart from its immediate practical effects, this decretal of Innocent III is important for the history of 'bigamy' because it gave rise to an astonishingly elaborate visual and conceptual structure in the *Golden Summa* (*Summa aurea*) of Hostiensis, perhaps the greatest of the medieval canon lawyers. This is the 'Tree of Bigamy', which is accompanied by a lengthy textual commentary. Diagram and commentary have been thoroughly studied by Hermann Schadt,[12] who perceived their interest for art history, so that they need not delay us here, but they are a remarkable monument to legal marriage symbolism. On the right hand side of the diagram (heraldically speaking, or the left-hand side as one looks at it) are all the good marriages. Most are symbolic but one is the marriage of Adam and Eve. Hostiensis has human marriage in mind. He says it is one of the seven sacraments of the Church and the greatest in its signification (and he gives other reasons for the greatness and goodness of marriage).[13] So the literal base of the symbol is secured, but symbolic marriages dominate diagram and commentary, examples being the marriage of God and the Virgin Mary and that of Peter with the Church (ibid., fo. 42^{ra-b}). In the section or *cellula* on the marriage of the Son of God with the Church the rationale of the bigamy rule is spelt out: no one can marry the Church unless he is similar to his spouse.[14] We are treated to a

---

[12] Schadt, 'Die Arbores bigamiae als heilsgeschichtliche Schemata'.

[13] 'In secunda cellula ita scribitur matrimonium Ade et Eve in paradiso contractum. Hoc est unum de vii sacramentis ecclesie, quod est maius et dignius aliis quo ad significationem. Cum enim omnia alia sacramenta precedat, merito aliqua [*read* alia?] sequentia per ipsum habent significari non e contra. Hoc enim quod non est, significare non posset . . . Nota igitur quod hoc sacramentum in magna veneratione haberi debet, tum ratione autoris, qui ipsum instituit, scilicet dei' (and so on with other reasons) (Hostiensis/Henricus de Segusio, *Summa aurea* (Lyons, 1548 edn.), fo. 41vb; I have used BL C 66 K 7). Note that the *Summa* is a different work from the *Lectura*, used extensively in the previous chapter.

[14] 'nullus potest desponsare ecclesiam, nisi sit similis sponso suo' (ibid., fo. 42ra); cf. Schadt, 'Die Arbores bigamiae als heilsgeschichtliche Schemata', 134.

138 *Chapter 3*

dialogue between a bishop and a layman who wants to take holy orders:

BISHOP: Do you want to marry the Church, that is, do you want to take holy orders?
LAYMAN: I do.
BISHOP: Are you a 'bigamist', that is, have you married two wives in succession?
LAYMAN: I have.

The bishop's decision: 'You have to be rejected—even if you had married one wife who was not a virgin. For God the spouse of the Church had only one human partner, who was a virgin, nor did he divide the word made flesh into pieces'.[15]

On the opposite side of the diagram are evil unions, described as bonds, *vincula*, rather than *matrimonia*. They include the bond between hell and the Devil, man and sin, heresies and the Devil, etc. In these bonds there is no unity, but everything is division and schism. They are associated with bigamy, which denotes division, whereas the order of priesthood signifies unity: so the two cannot come together in the same person. Hostiensis uses strong words,[16] though he makes it clear that he is not talking about the ethics of 'bigamy' but rather of its signification.[17] Morals and symbolism are distinct registers. Successive 'bigamy' is morally unimpeachable and the problem is in the symbolic register.

In intellectual and cultural histories of the Middle Ages marriage symbolism goes with mysticism and monastic theology rather than with canon law (though the marriage symbolism of the episco-

[15] 'dicere potest episcopus: "Vis desponsare ecclesiam?", id est, "Vis ad ordines promoveri?". Responsio laici: "Volo". Interrogatio episcopi: "Es tu bigamus?", id est, "Duxisti duas uxores successive?". Responsio laici: "Duxi". Determinatio episcopi: "Repellendus es—etiam si unicam et corruptam uxorem carnalem duxisses. Nam deus sponsus ecclesie non habuit, nisi unicam humanam, et virginem, nec divisit verbum incarnatum in plures"' (Hostiensis/Henricus de Segusio, *Summa aurea*, fo. 42ra).

[16] 'In omnibus his vinculis vel ipsorum aliquo nulla unitas est, nulla firmitas, nulla integritas: sed totum divisio, totum schisma, totum falsitas, totum corruptio, et hoc per bigamiam representatur sive per bigamum qui divisus fuit sive corruptus in matrimonio, sicut precedentes in vinculis infernalibus, sive diabolicis; sicut ergo deus et diabolus in eundem subiectum simul, et semel, et eodem modo cadere non possunt, quia nemo potest servire deo et mammone, sic bigamia, que divisionem denotat, et ordo sacer, qui unitatem designat, in eundem subiectum simul et semel congrue cadere non possunt' (ibid., fo. 42vb).

[17] 'Ergo bigami in vinea [*read* linea?] ista cadunt et per ipsam presentantur: non quo ad vite meritum, sed quo ad ordinationis signaculum' (ibid.).

pal office has been thoroughly studied by legal historians).[18] This
is evidently a misleading segregation where marriage symbolism
is concerned. The symbolism is not an afterthought or a playful
decoration. It is an essential element in their thinking . This was
apparent in the history of indissolubility traced above, and it holds
good also for attitudes to 'bigamy' and consummation.

Bigamy and dispensation

Document 3. 1, from the mid-thirteenth-century canonist Johannes
de Deo's treatise on dispensations, is another example of a symbolic
analysis with practical social implications. Johannes sets out to explain why in his view a dispensation is possible in some 'bigamy'
cases and not in others. The passage is difficult because compressed,
but the sense of it seems to be as follows.With 'true' bigamy dispensation is impossible, because it would go against the words of
St Paul—he means the remarks about 'a husband of one wife'. (Incidentally, this view of Johannes would not prevail, but that is not
the issue here.) So when is a candidate for holy orders truly bigamous? The broad answer will be familiar by now. It is when the
sacramental symbolism is lacking from his previous married life,
because he has been married twice or married to a woman who had
been married at least once before. Johannes goes into a miniature
analysis of the type of sacramental symbolism which is not as it
should be with true bigamists. As for the undefective symbolism, it
is primarily the representation of Christ's union with the Church.
However, there is secondary symbolism too (*consignificatum est*).
He specifies the union of the divinity with Christ's flesh, a union
never broken. Then, as if by way of an afterthought, Johannes says
that there are three unions: the union of the Divinity to the flesh,
the union of the Divinity to the soul, and the union of soul to body.
Only this last one was ever divided—at the death of Christ. He adds
another union: that of the soul of the just person to God, a union
based on faith and charity, one that can sometimes be broken by
mortal sin.

This little analysis completed, Johannes returns to the practical
problem of when a dispensation by the pope is possible. His line
is that the sacramental symbolism is not defective in cases where
there are not two genuine marriages: that is, where one of the two is
invalid. He lists such cases. One seems to be bigamy in the modern

[18] By Kuttner, Benson, and Gaudemet: see Introduction, n. 69.

sense, when a man marries a second time during his first wife's
lifetime, so that the second marriage is invalid. Another situation
listed is that of a man in holy orders (probably he means a subdeacon
or someone of higher rank) who marries a woman who is not a
virgin. In this case the marriage is null. It would in fact have been
null even if the woman were a virgin. After 1139 it was clear law
that the marriage of a cleric in major orders (a subdeacon, deacon,
or priest) was not only illicit but also invalid. So why does John
raise the case in the context of 'bigamy' and what difference does it
make whether the woman was a virgin?

The fact that the woman is not a virgin may have been introduced by Johannes because a rigorist understanding of 'bigamy'
sometimes included marriages to women who had previously slept
with another man, whether or not they were widows. Reading between the lines, John's point may be this: if a priest invalidly marries
a virgin, he can after separating from the woman and undergoing
a long penance obtain a dispensation from a bishop to resume his
priestly office. On the other hand, if the woman had not been a
virgin, an episcopal dispensation would not be enough, because
the sexual union had been akin to bigamy, bigamy by extension so
to speak.

A casuistry of bigamy and its implications

If we take Innocent III's decretal *Debitum* and Johannes de Deo's
analysis together, an important conclusion about the social relevance of marriage symbolism begins to emerge. The rationality of
marriage symbolism was the basis of a casuistry of 'bigamy' cases,
providing the principles that could enable discrimination between
apparently similar cases and settle the law when its application
to ambiguous instances was unobvious. Incidentally, we have here
a criterion for distinguishing between unthinking 'tradition' and
'value rationality' as determinants of social action. Value rationality is not just about general principles, far from it, but they are an
important element, and can be invoked and applied by casuistry to
settle ambiguous concrete cases. Tradition alone could not provide
such a casuistry. Its social relevance was confined to men who had
been married and widowed.

The remainder of this chapter deals with people who did not seek
to become priests. Section (b) deals with second weddings, and the
final section with married clerics in minor orders. In neither case

is marriage symbolism the sole relevant factor but without taking account of marriage symbolism one cannot make sense of the social history of either.

(b) The Marriage Ceremony

Suspicion of second marriages and its ritual implications

Symbolism may not have been crucial to the history of second marriages until relatively late in our period. In the early period other rationales seem to have influenced attitudes more, and this background must be sketched in first. From an early period priestly intervention in second weddings was limited. Some such rule seems to be common to both Eastern and Western Christianity, in itself a symptom of antiquity.[19] So far as the West is concerned, a decisive moment was the reception of early fourth-century legislation of the Council of Neocaesarea[20] into the influential canon-law collection of Dionysius Exiguus, *c.*500, which would ensure its currency in the Latin Church. In the form in which we find it in Dionysius, it states:

It is inappropriate that a priest should join in the meal at the marriage of a person who has been married previously, for since the twice married person needs to do penance, what priest could give consent to such a marriage for the sake of a banquet?[21]

The need to do penance after a second marriage had already been spelt out in another decree of the same council, also adopted by Dionysius.[22]

---

[19] K. Ritzer, *Formen, Riten und religiöses Brauchtum der Eheschließung in den christlichen Kirchen des ersten Jahrtausends*, 2nd edn., ed. U. Hermann and W. Heckenbach (Liturgiewissenschaftliche Quellen und Forschungen; Münster Westfalen, 1981), index, s.v. 'Wiederverheiratung'.

[20] 'A Cappadocian Council of uncertain date (probably early 4th cent., before 325). It passed 15 canons concerned chiefly with disciplinary and marriage questions' (F. L. Cross and E. A. Livingstone (eds.), *The Oxford Dictionary of the Christian Church* (Oxford, 1997), 1136).

[21] 'Presbyterum in nuptiis bigami prandere non convenit, quia cum poenitentia bigamus egeat, quis erit presbyter qui propter convivium talibus nuptiis possit praebere consensum' (Dionysius Exiguus, *Codex Canonum Ecclesiasticorum*, 'Regulae prolatae in synodo Neocaesariensi XIV, no. LI, in Migne, *PL* 67. 156).

[22] 'De his qui in plurimas nuptias inciderunt, et tempus quidem praefinitum manifestum est, sed conversatio eorum, et fides, tempus abbreviat' (*Regulae . . .*, no. XLVII, in Migne, *PL* 67. 155). A more up-to-date and critical edition of Dionysius' canon-law collections is much to be desired.

If the twice-married person needed to do penance, it seems implied that there was something morally a little dubious about remarrying. Indeed that idea existed. Esmein's classic history of the canon law of marriage suggests two reasons. One was the rigorist view of sex that had some currency in the patristic period: if a person had to get married, once was enough; the other was an ideal of true monogamy, unspoilt by remarriage.[23] This second reason is close to the thinking of Brahman Hinduism about remarriage, but Esmein reminds us that pagan Roman religion had a counterpart for special cases and that Tacitus attributed a similar attitude to the Germans (ibid.).

The legitimacy of remarriage

An alternative view and the one that prevailed is that no moral stigma attached to second marriages.[24] Jerome put that view in no uncertain terms: not only a second but a fifth or a sixth marriage was licit.[25] Remarriage after a partner's death was absolutely normal throughout the Middle Ages. The papacy had no problem with that. In the central Middle Ages we find popes (Lucius III and Alexander IV) banning taxes imposed by abbots or a bishop on the remarriage of widows.[26] Peter Lombard said succinctly that 'not only first or second marriages are licit, but even third and fourth marriages should not be condemned'.[27] He quoted the passage from Jerome.

Twelfth-century authorities: Peter Lombard, Gratian, and two papal decrees

Even so, Lombard did quote a passage from pseudo-Ambrose ('Ambrosiaster'), which runs: 'first marriages only are instituted by God, whereas second marriages are permitted. And first mar-

[23] Esmein, *Le Mariage en droit canonique*, ii. 120.

[24] Ibid. 119–21. Cf. Jussen, *Der Name der Witwe*, 170–1 (granting the substantive point while stressing negativity about second marriages).

[25] *Epist.* 48 (ad Pammachium), para. 18 (Migne, *PL* 22. 508), cited by Ignatius Brady, the anonymous editor, in *Magistri Petri Lombardi Parisiensis Episcopi Sententiae in IV libris distinctae*, 3rd edn., ed. Patres Collegii S. Bonaventurae ad Claras Aquas (2 vols.; Spicilegium Bonaventurianum, 4–5; Grottaferrata, 1971–81), ii. *Liber III et IV*, 509 (listing the letter as number 43—presumably a slip).

[26] Esmein, *Le Mariage en droit canonique*, ii. 124–5 n. 5. In the same note Esmein points out that in 1391 the bishop of Chartres affirmed in Parlement that charivaris against the remarriage of widows were forbidden by synodal statutes.

[27] *Sententiae*, 4. 42. 7, ii. 508 Brady.

riages are celebrated above²⁸ with the blessing of God, whereas second marriages lack glory even in the present.'²⁹ The reference to 'blessing' may have influenced the later path of the limitation on priestly participation.

The ruling from the Roman Empire survived into Gratian's *Decretum*, verbally modified if the editions are to be trusted but substantially much the same.³⁰ Gratian prefaces this with the comment that 'There is a general ban on men and women contracting marriages frequently. Therefore priests ought not to take part in the marriage³¹ when it is a second wedding, as is read in the Council of Neocaesarea.'³²

Not everything in Gratian was treated as binding, but two later twelfth-century papal decretals reinforced the idea that second marriages should be treated differently, especially since both became incorporated in the 1234 canon-law collection that became the authoritative lawbook of Western Christendom. Pope Alexander III laid it down that a 'chaplain' who 'celebrated the blessing with a second [wife]'³³ was 'suspended from his office and benefice until absolved by the apostolic see'.³⁴ The reference to 'the blessing' marks this out from Gratian and the Council of Neocaesarea decree.

²⁸ 'sublimiter': probably meaning 'in heaven', though it may mean something vaguer: 'in the heights, sublimely'.

²⁹ 'primae nuptiae tantum a Domino sunt institutae, secundae vero sunt permissae. Et primae nuptiae sub benedictione Dei celebrantur sublimiter, secundae vero etiam in praesenti carent gloria' (Ambrosiaster on 1 Cor. 7: 10, in Migne, *PL* 17. 225; cited by Peter Lombard, *Sententiae*, 4. 42. 7, ii. 509 Brady).

³⁰ '*Fides et conuersatio penitenciam adbreuiet eorum, qui frequenter ducunt uxores.* De his, qui frequenter uxores ducunt, et de his, qui sepius nubunt, tempus quidem his manifestum constitutum est, sed conuersatio et fides eorum tempus adbreuiat. Presbiterum uero secundarum nuptiarum conubio interesse non debere; maxime cum precipiatur secundis nuptiis penitenciam tribuere: quis erit presbiter, qui propter conuiuium illis consentiat nuptiis?' (Decretum, Pars II, C. 31, q. 1, c. 8, in E. Friedberg, *Corpus iuris canonici* (2 vols.; Leipzig, 1879–81; repr. Graz, 1955), i. 1110).

³¹ 'conubio', but 'conuivio' in another edition: see 'Editio Romana' apparatus in Friedberg.

³² Decretum, Pars II, C. 31, q. 1, c. 7, in Friedberg, *Corpus iuris canonici*, i. 1110.

³³ 'secunda'.

³⁴ 'Capellanum . . . quem benedictionem cum secunda . . . constiterit celebrasse, ab officio beneficioque suspensum, cum literarum tuarum testimonio . . . ad sedem apostolicam nullatenus destinare postponas' (Decretals of Gregory IX, X. 4. 21. 1, in Friedberg, *Corpus iuris canonici*, ii. 730). The passages marked as omitted are those left out in the 1234 canon-law collection and supplied by Friedberg from other sources.

Perhaps it was influenced by the pseudo-Ambrose passage noted above. Urban III's decree also concentrates on 'the blessing'. 'A man or a woman, passing to a second marriage, ought not to be blessed by a priest, for, since they have been blessed on another occasion, their blessing should not be repeated.'[35] We shall shortly need to look more closely at what in terms of external ritual might be implied by 'the blessing'.

The meaning of the rules about the marriage blessing

More immediately, what was the thinking behind these decrees? No definitive answer can be given at present. It would be a good research topic. Canon-law commentaries on Gratian, *Decretum*, Pars II, C. 31, q. 1, cc. 7–8, could be collected with the aid of Kuttner's *Repertorium*,[36] the main Decretalist commentaries on Decretals of Gregory IX, X. 4. 21. 1 and 3, could be reviewed; commentaries on Peter Lombard, *Sentences*, 4. 42. 7, could be found with the aid of Stegmüller's *Repertorium*.[37] It would be a bonus for the argument of this book if symbolic reasoning turned out to be central, but I would not predict that. The most likely guess, no substitute for an investigation, is that the rationale behind the papal decrees was a mixture of tradition, respect for the attitude embodied in pseudo-Ambrose, and a sense that the blessing was a kind of ritual that should not be repeated. The last thought might be explicable in terms of the uncrystallized state of thought about marriage as a sacrament. Bernard of Parma in his standard gloss on the Decretals of Gregory IX suggested as a reason that a sacrament should not be repeated.[38] Other canonists rejected the idea that the nuptial blessing (as opposed to marriage itself) was a sacrament.[39] Thus Goffredus of Trani (writing in the years 1241–3) pointed out that

[35] 'Vir autem vel mulier, ad bigamiam transiens, non debet a presbytero benedici, quia, quum alia vice benedicti sint, eorum benedictio iterari non debet' (Decretals of Gregory IX, X. 4. 21. 3, in Friedberg, *Corpus iuris canonici*, ii. 731).

[36] S. Kuttner, *Repertorium der Kanonistik (1140–1234): Prodromos Corporis glossarum*, i (Studi e testi, 71; Vatican City, 1937).

[37] F. Stegmüller, *Repertorium commentariorum in Sententias Petri Lombardi* (2 vols.; Würzburg, 1947). The canny researcher would save time by following in the footsteps of P. Biller, *The Measure of Multitude: Population in Medieval Thought* (Oxford, 2000), ch. 7.2, pp. 166–77.

[38] Esmein, *Le Mariage en droit canonique*, ii. 123. For Bernard of Parma see P. Erdö, *Storia della scienza del diritto canonico: una introduzione* (Rome, 1999), 90.

[39] Esmein, *Le Mariage en droit canonique*, ii. 123 at n. 4.

the nuptial blessing was not a sacrament, though marriage itself was, and that some sacraments could be repeated.[40] One should also mention Hostiensis's suggestion that if one of the partners in a marriage had been blessed at a previous marriage the unity of flesh in the consummation of the second marriage would be enough to communicate the blessing to the unblessed partner, so that the second marriage did not require a reprise.[41] Was this idea also around in the twelfth century? The most likely overall hypothesis is that Alexander III and Urban III were not themselves absolutely clear in their minds and that it seemed safest to them to stick to a rule deemed traditional.

A feeling that the blessing should not be repeated because it was 'sacramental' or 'quasi-sacramental', and a certain stigma attached to second marriages, are the reasons for the rule given in the curious questions about marriage in MS BL Royal 11. A. XIV (see below, Document **3. 8. 20–1**). It may be significant, though, that there is a long passage nearby (**3. 8. 19**) which is full of marriage symbolism, drawing out the significance of the placing of the principal blessing shortly before communion in the mass:

. . . in the communion of the body and blood of Christ the lowest things are joined to the highest, that is, the human mind is joined to the body of Christ, in fact to God himself. Since, therefore, marital union [*copulatio*] signifies this joining, and indeed also the very union by which the same deity is united to the humanity as one person in Christ, who is most truly contained in the aforesaid sacrament [of the Eucharist], it was most fittingly laid down that the blessing which has the principal place in marriage be solemnly conferred before communion or the the reception of the same blessed body, as the sign before the signified.

Whether or not symbolism had been important in the thinking behind the rule originally, it was certainly important from the thirteenth century on. The analysis in Thomas Aquinas's widely diffused commentary on the *Sentences* deserves close attention.[42]

---

[40] Esmein, *Le Mariage en droit canonique*, ii. 123 and especially n. 5; for Goffredus see Erdö, *Storia della scienza del diritto canonico*, 98.

[41] Esmein, *Le Mariage en droit canonique*, ii. 124 and n. 3.

[42] In the extracts below I translate and paraphrase from the Latin text given in Thomas Aquinas, *Commentary on the* Sentences *of Peter Lombard*, qu. 3, art. 2, in *S. Tommaso d'Aquino: Commento alle Sentenze di Pietro Lombardo e testo integrale di Pietro Lombardo. Libro quarto. Distinzioni 24–42. L'Ordine, il Matrimonio*, trans. and ed. by the 'Redazione delle Edizioni Studio Domenicano' (Bologna, 2001), 888–90. For the commented text see Peter Lombard, *Sentences*, 4. 42. 7, ii. 508–9 Brady).

He is discussing the question of whether a second marriage is a
sacrament, concluding that it is and that consequently—this is the
interesting part—it is an obstacle to a priestly career. (He means
even after the second wife's death—otherwise the point would be
obvious in his context.) First come the arguments against regarding
a second marriage as a sacrament, the usual scholastic method of
beginning with what can be said against one's own point of view:

1. It seems that a second marriage is not a sacrament. For if someone
repeats a sacrament, he does an injury to it. But one should not do injury
to any sacrament. Therefore, if a second marriage were a sacrament, it
would certainly not be something to be repeated. 2. Besides, in every
sacrament some blessing plays a part. But not in a second marriage, as the
text [of Peter Lombard's *Sentences*] says. Therefore no sacrament happens
there. 3. Besides, signification is of the essence of a sacrament. But in a
second marriage the signification of marriage is not preserved: because it
is not a marriage of one to one, like Christ and the Church. Therefore
it is not a sacrament. 4. Besides, one sacrament is not an impediment to
the reception of another. But a second marriage is an impediment to the
reception of priestly orders[43] Therefore it is not a sacrament.

Then Aquinas begins to set out the reasons on the other side,
reasons why a second marriage is after all a sacrament:

On the other hand, sexual intercourse in a second marriage is excused from
sin, just as in a first marriage. But marital sexual intercourse is excused
by the three goods of marriage, which are faith, children, and sacrament.
Therefore a second marriage is a sacrament.

Besides, from a non-sacramental second union of man and woman, no
irregularity is contracted, as is evident with respect to fornication. But an
irregularity is contracted in a second marriage. Therefore it is sacramental.

Here Aquinas means that fornication by a widower does not make
him a 'bigamist' and bar him from holy orders: in effect his point is
that this happens with a second marriage only because it is a proper
sacramental union. This casts an interesting light on the issue of
clerical 'bigamy', discussed in the sections that precede and follow
this one. It is because of the high sacramental status of marriage
that two successive marriages rule out a priestly career even after
the second wife's death, and are incompatible with clerical status,
according to this reasoning. The 'irregularity' does not reflect badly
on marriage as a state: rather the contrary.

[43] Note: the subject of the first section of this chapter.

Now the main arguments for the sacramentality of second marriages begin:

I reply that one should say that wherever one finds the things which are of the essence of marriage, that is a true sacrament; so, since everything that is of the essence of the sacrament is found in a second marriage, because there is the matter required, which the legitimate status of the persons supplies, and the form required, that is the expression of internal consent through words: it is also clear that a second marriage is a sacrament just like a first one.

Next Aquinas disposes of the objections. The argument about repeatability is disposed of very easily. The objection applies only to sacraments whose effect is perpetual, where repetition might imply that the first administration of the sacrament did not work. Where the effect of a sacrament is not perpetual, this does not apply. Clearly it does not apply in the case of the sacrament of penance. In disposing of the remaining objections Aquinas allows symbolism to dominate his reasoning:

. . . although a second marriage taken in itself is a perfect sacrament, yet taken in relation to a first marriage it has something of a defect in the sacrament, since it does not have the full signification, since it is not of one woman to one man, as with the marriage of Christ and the Church; and by reason of this defect the blessing is withdrawn from second marriages. But this should be understood of the case where the second marriage is the second for both the man and the woman, or for the woman only. For if a virgin contracts marriage with a man who has had another wife, the marriage is blessed none the less: for the signification is in some way preserved even in relation to the first marriage, since Christ, even if he had a single Church as a bride, nevertheless has many persons within one Church as brides; but the soul cannot be the bride of any other but Christ, since with the demon it commits fornication, and there is no spiritual marriage there; and because of this, when a woman marries for the second time, the marriage is not blessed because of a defect of the sacrament.[44]

Aquinas's argument has taken him on to the issue of the blessing of second marriages. He has a symbolic rationale to explain why

[44] Aquinas's remaining arguments, or responses to arguments, do not add much for our purposes, though they continue the same line of symbolic thought: 'Ad tertium dicendum, quod significatio perfecta invenitur in secundo matrimonio secundum se considerato, non autem si consideretur in ordine ad praecedens matrimonium; et sic habet defectum sacramenti. Ad quartum dicendum, quod secundum matrimonium impedit sacramentum ordinis quantum ad id quod habet de defectu sacramenti, et non inquantum est sacramentum' (ibid. 890).

a marriage could be blessed if it was the first time for the bride even if not for the bridegroom. This practice does indeed seem to have been found 'in some churches'. Bernard of Pavia notes it, as does Hostiensis.[45] The same evidence proves that it was not the general rule.[46] The practice might be explained also in terms of the patriarchal assumption that properly speaking 'man is polygamous, woman is monogamous'. Aquinas finds a quite different meaning in it.

Meaning and reception: the 'inner side' of ritual

This raises the crucial question: do meanings imposed *a posteriori*—as this turn at least in Aquinas's argument may well have been—have any relevance to social history? I would suggest that the answer is: 'sometimes but not always' . For example, most of Aquinas's analysis is really relevant to the social history of bigamy, while the idea just mentioned—the explanation of why a marriage could be blessed when it was the wife's first marriage—may be interesting for the intellectual historian but not for the social historian, as being too much of an afterthought, too remote from practice.

To decide what is relevant to social history one needs to ask further questions. One was used in the preceding section, which suggested the following criterion: was the internal rationale used casuistically, as a way of classifying difficult or marginal practical cases? If it was doing that, then it was affecting practice, not just redescribing it. Here are two more questions. Was the new understanding of the social practice so widespread as to change it so to speak from the inside? Is this inner change revealed by external symptoms, minor in themselves but indicative of the new thinking that was altering the social meaning?

The notion that social practice has an 'inner side' which is the real object of the social scientist's (or historian's) research has been around for a long time. In the second half of the twentieth cen-

[45] See Esmein, *Le Mariage en droit canonique*, ii. 124–5, with references.
[46] Nor did it receive general approval. Hostiensis disapproved (see ibid.), and the interesting, probably fake bull attributed variously to Pope John XXII and Pope Benedict XII generously allowed the maximalist interpretation that if either of the couple in a second marriage had not been blessed in a previous marriage, the new marriage might be blessed: see the discussion by Johannes de Burgo, below, Document **3. 9. 5.**

tury there were classic expositions by Peter Winch[47] and Clifford Geertz.[48] Behind them lies Max Weber. Some key quotations: 'let human behaviour . . . be called "action" if and insofar as the person or persons who act connect it with a subjective meaning' (Weber);[49] 'Believing, with Max Weber, that man is an animal suspended in webs of significance he himself has spun, I take culture to be those webs, and the analysis of it to be therefore not an experimental science in search of law but an interpretive one in seach of meaning' (Geertz);[50] 'social interaction can more profitably be compared to the exchange of ideas in a conversation than to the interaction of forces in a physical system' (Winch).[51]

A brief consideration of the history of Christmas suggests that Weber, Winch, and Geertz were on the right lines. Christmas was celebrated at the winter solstice from Julius Caesar's time. The pagan religious significance grew. The sun came to be regarded by many as the divinity behind other gods. In 274 the emperor made 25 December the 'Birthday of the Unconquerable Sun'. The idea of Christ as 'the sun of righteousness' (Mal. 4: 2) enabled the transition to a Christian feast.[52] Then for centuries and for many still Christmas celebrated the birth of Christ. Now for many others it is instead a secular festival of good fellowship and the family. To take celebration of Christmas today as proof of religious feeling would be a mistake, just as it is a mistake to assume that its incorporation into Christian liturgy indicated the survival of pagan religion. What counts is the meaning behind the actions and rituals. Nevertheless, a text here and there is not enough to establish that a ritual has modified its meaning. The texts suggesting that need to be influential and popular. Furthermore, one would expect small but symptomatic changes in the mode of celebration. Thus a family

---

[47] P. Winch, *The Idea of a Social Science and its Relation to Philosophy* (London etc., 1958).

[48] e.g. C. Geertz, *The Interpretation of Cultures: Selected Essays* (London etc., 1973; repr. 1993).

[49] The sentence in full: ' "Handeln" soll dabei ein menschliches Verhalten (einerlei ob äußeres oder innerliches Tun, Unterlassen oder Dulden) heißen, wenn und insofern als der oder die Handelnden mit ihm einen subjektiven Sinn verbinden' (Weber, *Wirtschaft und Gesellschaft*, 1).

[50] C. Geertz, 'Thick Description: Toward an Interpretive Theory of Culture', in id., *The Interpretation of Cultures*, 3–30 at 5.

[51] Winch, *The Idea of a Social Science*, 128.

[52] The foregoing is taken from B. Blackburn and L. Holford-Strevens, *The Oxford Companion to the Year* (Oxford, 1999), 514–15.

today that is vaguely Christian but not churchgoing might go to a
carol service and join in heartily, whereas a wholly secular family
might not unless some other social obligation were involved. So the
fine print of practice can usually indicate a shift in the meanings
behind it.

Ritual changes and symbolic meaning

In the remainder of this section, therefore, I shall try to show that a
strong emphasis on a symbolic rationale correlated with change in
ritual, and that the symbolic rationale could have penetrated well
below the theological élite.

We shall be looking closely at the ritual of second weddings and
at how this ritual was interpeted at a level less exalted than that of
Thomas Aquinas. The social history of this ritual seems to have
received scholarly attention only on the margins of more general
histories of marriage liturgy,[53] and there is a need for a concentrated
study of it by a historical liturgiologist. The following reconstruction is only sketchy and tentative. It should also be said immediately
that there was clearly a great range of practice where the rituals of
second weddings are concerned.[54] We also need to remember that
there were parts of Europe where no church wedding ceremony
was required by the Church for a first marriage, apparently.[55] That
would make the ritual of the second marriage less important. The

---

[53] J.-B. Molin and P. Mutembe, *Le Rituel du mariage en France du XIIe au XVIe
siècle* (Théologie historique, 26; Paris, 1974), 236, 243–4, is useful but very brief.
There is a useful chapter in L. Duchesne, *Christian Worship, its Origin and Evolution:
A Study of the Latin Liturgy up to the Time of Charlemagne*, trans. M. L. McClure,
5th edn. (London, 1919), ch. 14, but it does not cover the period that mainly concerns us. Ritzer, *Formen, Riten und religiöses Brauchtum der Eheschließung*, has some
important pages: see index, s.v. 'Wiederverheiratung', but mainly pp. 160, 166, 168–
9 (Ritzer also discusses the history of second weddings in Eastern Christianity, but
these are not within the scope of this study). B. Binder, *Geschichte des feierlichen
Ehesegens von der Entstehung der Ritualien bis zur Gegenwart, mit Berücksichtigung
damit zusammenhängender Riten, Sitten und Bräuche: Eine liturgiegeschichtliche Untersuchung* (Metten, 1938), 84–8, provides a good miniature history of 'Segnung
bei zweiten Ehen'. He gives special attention to English rituals, commenting (88)
that 'Aus diesen kurzen Berichten ist bereits ersichtlich, wie schwierig und unklar
bezüglich dieser Frage die Verhältnisse lagen'. See too K. Stevenson, *Nuptial Blessing: A Study of Christian Marriage Rites* (Alcuin Club Collections, 64; London,
1982), 80–1, 82, and also (important background) 40–1, for the nuptial blessing in
the Gregorian Sacramentary.

[54] Esmein, *Le Mariage en droit canonique*, ii. 124–5. See also Johannnes de Burgo's
comment: 'nisi consuetudo alicuius ecclesie aliter obtineret. Tunc enim possent sine
periculo benedici' (Document **3. 9. 4**).

[55] D. L. d'Avray, 'Marriage Ceremonies and the Church in Italy after 1215', in

ceremony could be omitted altogether without anything seeming odd. Where this was the case the analysis that follows is less applicable. So the remarks that follow are certainly not meant to apply to Western Christendom generally; and indeed they bear particularly on England so far as the later Middle Ages are concerned.

So what significant patterns can one observe in the history of second weddings? For one thing, it looks as though the limitation on priestly participation became increasingly specific, in the sense that less and less was forbidden, with the consequence that the proverbial Martian observer would have found it harder and harder to tell a first wedding from a second wedding.

Back in the fourth century the contrast between first and second weddings may have been sharp. The decrees of the Council of Neocaesarea as transmitted by Dionysius Exiguus seem to ban priests altogether from participating in second weddings.[56] As for interpretation of the version in Gratian, Pars II, C. 31, q. 1, cc. 7–8, there is a problem of textual criticism to complicate things: there are variant readings, one implying a ban on participation in the wedding (*conubio*), another on participation in the banquet (*convivio*).[57] Perhaps the difference is not so important. Would it make sense to let a priest conduct a wedding but ban him from the banquet? More probably, the legislation would be taken to mean that the priest should just not be involved in a second wedding, though this is no more than a guess.

The papal decretals from the twelfth century are different and already more specific. They both forbid the priest to give 'the blessing', whatever that may mean. The natural assumption might be that 'the blessing' is shorthand for the whole celebration of a second marriage with a religious ritual. It was not, however, so understood, to judge by the texts printed as Documents **3. 8** and **3. 9,** and by the fascinating discussion in versions of the Sarum Manual.

An interesting and apparently unstudied text can tell us more about the rituals that went with marriage. The questions on Marriage in MS BL Royal 11. A. XIV (printed as Document **3. 8**) indicate that there are several blessings at and around a wedding. (Though this text may survive in only one manuscript and its

T. Dean and K. J. P. Lowe (eds.), *Marriage in Italy, 1300–1650* (Cambridge, 1998), 107–15.

[56] See above, p. 141.
[57] See the apparatus critici in Friedberg, *Corpus iuris canonici*, i. 1110.

author's theological views have no particular importance, the extract printed is valuable for the practices it describes.) Four blessings are listed as normal for first marriages: at the entrance of the church, at the beginning of the mass, before the kiss of peace, and at the marriage bed (Document **3. 8. 8**). The author says that he does not know of any authority which specifies what blessing Urban III intended in the decretal X. 4. 21. 3, and concludes that one must go by custom (Document **3. 8. 7**; cf. **3. 8. 27**). According to the common custom of the Church, the blessing forbidden by the decretal is the one after the *Agnus Dei* and before the kiss of peace (Document **3. 8. 8**).

This gives us a more precise idea of the effect of the decretals about second marriages. They were not understood to mean that such marriages should be without a religious ceremony. Indeed, the nuptial mass would seem to have been quite acceptable at a second marriage. One particular blessing is omitted, but the priest is crucially involved in the wedding throughout. This is a quite different picture from what one finds in the Council of Neocaesarea legislation as preserved by Dionysius Exiguus and in Gratian. It is clear from this document that couples who had been married before were not relegated to a dry or secular ceremony. They had plenty of religious ritual. However it may have been in late antiquity or even in subsequent centuries, any idea that the priest must distance himself from second weddings seems to have disappeared.

The evidence of the Sarum Manual

The Sarum manual of the dominant liturgical rite in England casts even more light on what actually went on in first and second wedding ceremonies. It is helpfully explicit and has been edited in a critical and thorough manner, so it is useful to follow the relevant section in detail.[58] During the canon of the mass, the central section that includes the consecration, the bride and groom prostrate themselves before the altar.[59] If they are both getting married for the first time, four clerics in surplices hold a cloak (*pallium*) over them, each cleric holding a corner. This eye-catching ritual was apparently to be left out of second marriages. That may have been a disappointment to some couples on those occasions.

[58] See *Manuale ad usum percelebris Ecclesie Sarisburiensis*, ed. A. J. Collins (Henry Bradshaw Society, 91; London, 1960), 53–8.
[59] 'ad gradum altaris' (ibid. 53).

Textually, however, the difference between first and second marriage seems to come down to one section of one blessing. The section is the part in which marriage is compared to the marriage of Christ and the Church. The canon of the mass is completed and the Lord's Prayer is said. In a normal mass the *Agnus Dei* ('Lamb of God who takest away the sins of the world . . .') and the kiss of peace would follow, but the marriage liturgy inserts special blessings at this point, after a prayer to God to help the new union. The words are as follows, with the blessing that especially concerns us in bold:

Let us pray. O God, who by the power of your might made everything from nothing, who, after ordering the first elements [*exordiis*] of the universe, established for man, made in the image of God, the inseparable assistance of woman in order that you might give to the female body a beginning from male flesh, teaching that what[60] it was pleasing to establish from one it would never be right to put asunder: **O God, who consecrated conjugal union [*copulam*] with such an excellent mystery so that you might prefigure [*presignares*] the sacrament of Christ and the Church in the covenant [*federe*] of a marriage [*nuptiarum*]**; O God, through whom woman is joined to man and a social bond ordained from the beginning has bestowed on it that blessing which alone was not removed either by the punishment of original sin or by the sentence of the Flood: look favourably on this your maidservant who is to be joined in the partnership of marriage and[61] asks to be strengthened by your protection. May the bond of love and peace be in her: may she marry as one faithful and chaste in Christ: and may she continue to follow the example of holy women. May she be lovable as Rachel was to her husband: wise as Rebecca: long-lived and faithful as Sara. [*The prayer for the bride continues for some lines.*]

The Sarum manual seems to differ from the anonymous author of the questions in MS BL Royal 11. A. XIV (Document **3. 8**) by omitting still less of the ritual for a first marriage.[62] Instead of leaving out the whole blessing, the Sarum rite seems to cut only the few words that I have printed in bold. Before these words in the manual we find the note: 'Here begins the sacramental blessing',[63] and after it the words 'Here the sacramental blessing ends'.[64] At

---

[60] The Latin really requires 'quod quod' here, but the second 'quod' may have been omitted because it is inelegant.

[61] I am emending the edition from 'tua que' to 'tuaque' as the sense requires.

[62] For what follows see too Stevenson, *Nuptial Blessing*, 80–1. By his account the Hereford and York rites are in line with the Sarum rite, the only one I have examined myself.   [63] 'Hic incipit benedictio sacramentalis' (53 Collins).

[64] 'Hic finitur benedictio sacramentalis' (54 Collins).

the end of the whole prayer we find the following: 'Note that the clause "O God, who . . . with such an excellent mystery" to "O God, through whom woman is joined to man" is not said in second marriages.'

The Sarum manual cites Urban III's decree (X. 4. 21. 3) about the blessing of second marriages by the priest in such a way as to imply that the decree was directed only at this one short clause. The explanation given is that 'the flesh that has been blessed draws to itself the flesh that has not been blessed' (56 Collins).

The manual has not finished. It seems it cannot leave the topic of second marriages alone, for there is plenty more. The author quotes pseudo-Ambrose's negative comments about second marriages, remarks that there are a number of blessings associated with marriage, from that at the entrance to that of the marriage bed in the evening,[65] and returns to the question of which blessing should be omitted.

Now his attention is on the prayer beginning 'O God who by the power of your might . . .', which includes two more 'O God who . . .' clauses, including the one printed above in bold type. According to this long rubric, each of these 'O God who . . .' clauses is a separate blessing. One imagines, then, that the priest would make the sign of the cross three times over the couple during this prayer.

It is the middle 'O God who . . .' blessing that must be omitted in second marriages, we are told, and presumably on those occasions the sign of the cross would be made only twice. The prohibition on blessing such marriages has been reduced to the omission of this short clause: 'O God, who consecrated conjugal union [*copulam*] with such an excellent mystery, so that you might prefigure the sacrament of Christ and the Church in the covenant of a marriage.' The reason for narrowing it down to this point is that only this clause was about the symbolism of Christ's union with the Church.

To put it another way: the interpretation of the prohibition's rationale as symbolic had the practical ritual consequence of retaining almost all of the words of the marriage service apart from this brief clause. It is a symptom that the symbolism is not just epiphenomenal, not merely a surface coating: it has affected the social meaning of marriage.

No accident, then, that the manual cites at this point the decretal

---

[65] 'plures benedictiones sunt in nuptiis celebrandis .scilicet. in introitu ecclesie et super pallium et post missam et super thorum in sero' (56 Collins).

Debitum of Innocent III, discussed in the previous section, perhaps the single most important document for medieval marriage symbolism as a practical social force. It will be remembered that this was the decretal that prompted Hostiensis's amazing Tree of Bigamy, that visual monument to marriage symbolism. The attention shifts briefly from symbolism, as the manual's rubric now moves on to the question of which marriages precisely are affected by the prohibition, and to a full quotation of the strange, probably fake, papal bull[66] that purported to settle such questions. The bull also removed the obligation of priests to seek absolution from the pope if they had broken the rule. This forgery is a fascinating little problem in its own right, but not necessarily relevant to the theme of marriage symbolism. The Sarum manual has only temporarily let go of that theme, however, and returns with another substantial piece of symbolic reasoning before moving on. The passage in question is none other than one from Aquinas which was quoted above,[67] in which Aquinas explains that a second marriage is a perfect sacrament taken in itself, but defective in relation to a first marriage because it is not of one woman to one man and thus imperfectly represents the marriage of Christ and the Church.

The rubrics in the Sarum manual illuminate the thinking behind the ritual practice and explain how the prohibition against blessing second marriages could be interpreted as omission of one small clause. This may have been peculiar to England.[68]

---

[66] See the excellent discussion of the bull in *Manuale*, ed. Collins, 54–6 at n. 65. The 'papal bull' in question was called *Concertationi antique*, from its opening words. If forged, the perpetrator knew that discourse. John XXII and Benedict XII both used similar language in documents aiming to put an end to controversy. A decretal of John XXII settling the question of whether entry into holy orders (as opposed to entry into a religious order) dissolved an unconsummated marriage begins: 'Antiquae concertationi finem cupientes imponere' (Extrav. Jo. XXII 6. i, ii. 1212 Friedberg). The same pope's 'Cum inter nonnullos' has 'Nos huic concertationi finem imponere cupientes' (C. Mirbt, *Quellen zur Geschichte des Papsttums und des römischen Katholizismus*, 5th edn. (Tübingen, 1934), no. 379, p. 219); see also Benedict XII, 'Benedictus Deus': 'praedecessor noster . . . ad decisionem concertationum huiusmodi se pararet' (Mirbt, *Quellen*, no. 382, p. 222). Even so, the consensus is that this strange document, brought to England by 'Master John Haysted' according to the Sarum Missal, is a forgery.

[67] See above, pp. 145–8, esp. 147. As the editor of the Sarum manual points out, the words 'Ad hoc dico' are substituted for Aquinas's 'Ad secundum dicendum' (omitted from my translation above) (*Manuale*, ed. Collins, 58 n. 82).

[68] Molin and Mutembe, *Le Rituel du mariage en France*, 243–4, suggest that in France the changes were more substantial, though they find that at Narbonne and Saint-Pons 'on ne supprime que la formule de bénédiction *Deus qui potestate*'

The evidence of the Pupilla oculi

Where England is concerned, the evidence of the Sarum Missal is complemented by that of Johannes de Burgo, author of the *Pupilla oculi*, 'The Pupil of the Eye' (the title is an allusion to the earlier 'Eye of the Priest' by William of Pagula), a late fourteenth-century priests' manual that was influential, to judge by its wide diffusion.[69] The Sarum rubrics etc. had probably got into the Sarum books before the appearance of the *Pupilla*,[70] but the popular pastoral handbook would have reinforced the message of the liturgical books.

It was in fact a practically identical message. The following passage from Johannes de Burgo is extremely close to the wording of a passage from the Sarum rubric translated above:

But since several blessings are given at a wedding, that is, over the couple getting married at the entrance of the church, over a cloak after mass, and over the marriage bed in the evening, it should therefore be noted that all the blessings or prayers of blessing that are said at a first marriage, are said also at a second one—even where both spouses or one of them had previously been blessed—apart from the one that begins: *O God, who consecrated conjugal union* [copulam] *with such an excellent mystery* up to *O God, through whom woman*, in which the theme is the unity of Christ and the Church which is represented in a first marriage, but not in a second: see Decretals of Gregory IX, *De bigamis*, the chapter *Debitum*.[71]

These explanations show that the symbolic rationale could have penetrated well below the level of the ivory-tower élite, one of the criteria suggested above as a ground for treating it as part of the social meaning of the ritual practice. This conclusion is strengthened if one bears in mind a finding of the first chapter: that the loss rate of manuscripts was huge, for some genres of book especially. Pastoral handbooks which would lie around a parish priest's house and liturgical books that were functional rather than for show, used

(243)—that is, all three 'O God who . . .' clauses were suppressed, but no other words—which would bring them into line with the questions in MS BL Royal 11. A. XIV.

[69] On this work see W. A. Pantin, *The English Church in the Fourteenth Century*, 2nd edn. (1962; repr. Toronto etc., 1980), 213–14; see also introduction to Document **3. 9** for further references. The author was quite an important man: chancellor of Cambridge University.

[70] 'Almost certainly . . . these rubrics, etc., were already in the Sarum books when the *Pupilla* appeared, having probably been introduced before 1370' (*Manuale*, ed. Collins, 56 (n. 65 from p. 54)).

[71] Document **3. 9. 8**: compare with *Manuale*, ed. Collins, 56, lines 6–end.

at parish level rather than in cathedral or monastic churches, are among the genres of book that would have been vulnerable. Since the *Pupilla oculi*, at least, nevertheless survives in a large number of manuscripts, we can be fairly sure that its impact in late medieval England was massive.

The other criterion for detecting a change in social meaning from within—an external change symptomatic of the symbolic meaning of the ritual practice—was satisfied above: the narrowing down of the prohibition, in England at least, to a few words about the marriage of Christ and the Church. So whatever the origins of the liturgical rules about second marriages, symbolism was part of their social meaning in late medieval England. Other parts of Europe deserve fuller investigation, but we must now turn to a different strand of marriage symbolism's social meaning and to married clerics in minor orders.

(c) Clerics in Minor Orders

Clerics in minor orders as a status group

The first part of this chapter looked at men who wanted to become priests or at least to be elevated to the higher orders of subdeacon or deacon. The second part dealt with the ceremonies for second marriages of laypeople. We may now turn to a third category, a status group somewhat neglected by historians: the legimately married clerics in minor orders. Of the rungs on the ladder up to holy orders the top three were for subdeacons, deacons, and priests, in ascending order. Perched on the lower rungs were large numbers of legitimately married clerics. We have little idea how many. It may have been a substantial class.

Marriage barred them from ecclesiastical benefices[72] but not from the considerable privileges of a separate status group. One important privilege was immunitiy from prosecution in secular courts. Ecclesiastical courts did not use the death penalty, so this privilege could literally be a life-saver. Another advantage was heavy spiritual protection against physical assault: anyone who laid violent hands on a cleric was under an anathema until he sought absolution from the pope; a bishop could not absolve him; only at the point of death

---

[72] 'Decretals of Gregory IX', X. 3. 3. 2 seems to say that a married cleric who vowed perpetual chastity might perhaps be eligible for benefices. Such a vow would require the wife's consent, though this decretal does not discuss the matter.

could the rule be relaxed.[73] Some of the documents to be discussed later on point to further advantages.

Papal bulls to kings of France

The first document relating to this section (Document **3. 4**) is relevant to our investigation for a different reason. It is a bull of pope Alexander IV,[74] a response to a request by King Louis IX. To judge from the response, the request was uncontroversial: if married clergy committed some dreadful crime and if they had already been stripped of their clerical status for some other reason, the prelates of France should not prevent the king's men from bringing these malefactors to justice. Even Thomas Becket would not have minded this because the criminals were not being judged twice for the same offence.

The bull is relevant because it uses the following formula: 'clerics who are bigamous and husbands of widows and also other married clerics'. Assuming that the papal document echoes the original request, as was normal, why did Louis IX not simply say 'married clergy'? That would have included the 'bigamous and husbands of widows'. Why mention them separately?

The following explanation, which does not claim to be more than a hypothesis, is that he did so to give his request the most favourable spin. Bigamous clergy and husbands of widows were marginal categories whose right to ecclesiastical justice even for a first crime was, as we shall see, questioned by influential canon lawyers. By listing them first, the king would have softened any possible impression of a Church–State conflict. The phrase (which may well have been formulaic) put a 'consensus spin' on the request.

The other papal bulls edited in the documents section of this chapter (Documents **3. 5–7**) seem to do the same thing. (I continue to assume that they too echo the wording of royal requests to which they are responding.) They all say 'married clerics whether bigamous or monogamous', where 'married clerics' would have sufficed. Explicit mention of bigamous clerics subtly emphasized the unreasonableness of objecting, even from a high ecclesiastical standpoint: rather as if it were said today that 'asylum-seekers who first entered the country illegally or who declared themselves at an immigration point should be obliged to carry an electronic tag'.

[73] Gratian, Pars II, C. 27, q. 4, c. 29.
[74] The original is now Paris, Archives Nationales J 709 no. 296.

This first point about minor orders is a modest one: a hypothesis that marriage symbolism had an indirect effect on French royal diplomatic practice. It presupposes the findings about 'bigamy' and symbolism set out in the first two sections, especially the first. The sequence of thought is: marriage symbolism put 'bigamous' clerics in a bad light so far as the Church was concerned, French kings knew this, so they put an effective rhetorical spin on requests to the pope by making an unnecessary allusion to bigamous clerics.

The ruling of the Second Council of Lyons and its origins

The next point relates to a larger issue: in 1274 'bigamous' clerics in minor orders were stripped of the privileges of their clerical status by the Second Council of Lyons,[75] a decision that had major social consequences. As should by now be predictable, the decree groups together men who had remarried after their first wife's death and men who had married widows. As we shall see, its force could also be extended to clerics who married a woman who was not a virgin. However, a cleric in minor orders who had been married only once, and to a virgin, could continue to enjoy clerical privileges. Here we have a legal situation that makes absolutely no sense from the outside.

Up to a point it can be explained by the desire of kings, especially the king of France, to extend royal jurisdiction as far as possible. (Just before the council Philip III had obtained from the pope an instruction to the French bishops to treat the 'bigamous' as laymen, but there had been a loophole in this preliminary document.[76]) The death of Becket had turned the tide in favour of clerical immunity, but this does not mean that monarchs were happy with the development. Married clerics especially were less likely than beneficed priests and the like to be deterred by purely ecclesiastical justice: an excommunication by a church court could cut a man off from the income from his benefice and block his career, but none of that applied to clerics in minor orders.[77] In effect they fell between two stools if they were not subject to secular justice either. They were a potentially disruptive element.

---

[75] B. Roberg, *Das zweite Konzil von Lyon [1274]* (Paderborn etc., 1990), 319–21.
[76] Ibid. 320.
[77] For the consequences of excommunication, the great sanction of ecclesiastical justice, for benefice holders and career prospects, see E. Vodola, *Excommunication in the Middle Ages* (Berkeley, 1986), 58.

Again, it is not so surprising that the papacy was compliant with the wishes of kings in relation to married clerics. Popes did not hold any particular brief for this awkward marginal category. It is likely that the celibate higher clergy generally looked down on them for having things both ways. So if the papacy had simply agreed to reclassify married clerics as subject to secular justice, adequate explanations in terms of power interests and ingrained prejudices would be at hand and one would not have to bring marriage symbolism into the account.

It is clear, however, that popes did not feel they could simply turn a large category of clerics over to secular justice without implicitly abandoning the idea that only the church courts judged the clergy. That idea was clearly stronger than any prejudice there may have been against clerics who could not cope with celibacy. The popes could not abandon married clerics purely because they were married: so long as the marriage was not against canon law, they would be abandoning them as clerics.

The 'bigamy' theory helped the popes to meet monarchs half way. It gave them a principled rationale for giving kings some of what they wanted without running the risk of conceding the thin end of the wedge. Their cooperation with kings could be quite genuinely presented as a stiffening of canon-law principle rather than a dilution of it.

In fact, a strong current of academic canon-law opinion seems to have been in favour of some such change, though it was not the only view.[78] The commentary on the Decretals of Gregory IX by Innocent IV (Sinibaldo dei Fieschi) was apparently written when he was already pope (incredibly enough, and an encouragement to all administrators with academic urges). He argues thus in the passage printed below as Document **3. 2.** If a cleric in minor orders does something altogether contrary to his status, he loses it. The examples are: marrying for a second time or marrying a woman not a virgin; or becoming a knight and employing violence (*seva exercuerit*)—by which he presumably means becoming a real fighting knight as opposed to acquiring this status for the sake of social esteem, administrative office, etc. On the other hand, if someone became the kind of knight who did not use violence or if he married a virgin, he could keep his clerical status. The fact that Innocent IV apparently assumes that one could be a knight and a

---

[78] Vergier-Boimond, 'Bigamie (l'irrégularité de)', 872.

cleric at the same time is an indication of how large this class of clerics in minor orders may have been: it could have extended far beyond the boundaries of what modern historians normally think of as 'the clergy'. However, the immediately relevant point is the canonist pope's conviction that it was fine to be a married cleric, but to marry twice or to marry a non-virgin was totally contrary to clerical status.

The suspicion that symbolism informs this sharp distinction is confirmed if one turns to Innocent IV's commentary on the Decretals of Gregory IX, X. 1. 21. 5, the decree *Debitum* of his predecessor but one, Innocent III, a key text in this history. Innocent IV was hard-headed as a canonist[79] just as he was as a political decision-maker, but there is nothing pragmatic about his analysis of bigamy in the commentary on this decretal (see Document **3. 3** below), which is full of symbolism. Interestingly, he uses the word *sacramentum* to mean something close to 'representation' (or perhaps the union that is represented, for as with the text on which he is commenting there is a little ambiguity). Thus carnal union between a husband and a wife is a 'sacrament' of Christ's incarnation. Only in a marriage between two spouses, and not more than two, is there a representation of one Church subject to one Christ.

Innocent IV asks how one gets this 'sacrament' out of the authority, by which he seems to mean the Genesis passage (2: 23–4)[80] to which the Pauline Ephesians 5: 30 refers. Innocent points to the use of the grammmatical singular for 'bone', 'flesh', and 'wife', and to the sentence 'they shall be two in one flesh'.

Moving down the decretal he is explaining, Innocent IV comments that 'between two only'—indicating that this is the only marriage for each partner—symbolizes the one Church subject to one husband. In a second marriage this *sacramentum*, representation, is lacking. Such a marriage could actually signify that a plurality of Churches were attached to one husband. He is in effect saying that a second marriage symbolically misrepresents the unity of the Church, an idea familiar by now.

If we take together the two extracts from Innocent IV's commentary, we can say the following. Here we have a work which enjoyed

[79] Cf. J. F. von Schulte, *Die Geschichte der Quellen und Literatur des canonischen Rechts*, ii (Stuttgart, 1877; repr. Graz, 1956), 92, on his extremely practical outlook.
[80] 'And Adam said: This is bone of my bones, and flesh of my flesh; . . . Wherefore a man shall leave his father and mother, and shall cleave to his wife; they shall be two in one flesh.'

a 'full and general authority' until long after the Second Council of Lyons.[81] He is for eliminating from the married minor clergy this one category: the bigamists, men whose wife was not the first, or who had been married before, or even who had not been a virgin before the marriage. The Second Council of Lyons duly eliminates the bigamists, definitively dislodging from their status a major section of the minor clergy. This was surely not due to the pope-canonist's individual influence alone, but he was a particularly powerful representative of a strong current of canonistic opinion. In giving his views on bigamy and the married minor clergy Innocent does not discuss its symbolic rationale, but the symbolic underpinnings of his ideas about bigamy are unmistakable in his comments on his namesake's decree *Debitum*, which deals with candidates for the priesthood, rather than with the married clergy who did not aspire to rise above minor orders, but where the issue of defining what is defective about a bigamist is identical.

At the risk of repetition, it should be stressed that marriage symbolism did not necessarily provide the impetus for removing large numbers of men from the privileged ranks of the minor clergy, and that the trigger for the change was probably the French king's desire to extend his jurisdiction: but symbolism provided the rationale for the new clear line that was drawn and determined its contours. Without the symbolism there is no reason to think that the border would have been redrawn in that way at that time, however much monarchs may have wanted to get as many individuals as possible onto their side of the legal border, and however little popes may have cared about the minor clergy as such.

Consequences in England

The explanation of the new borderline may lie in the realms of symbolism, but its consequences can be called brutally practical, notably in England. In no time at all King Edward I passed the 'Statute on Bigamists', turning the council's new ruling into English common law.[82] A concrete case from the reign of Edward's

---

[81] 'Man kann ihm [his *Apparatus in quinque libros decretalium*] in der That kaum einen zweiten Kommentar der Dekretalen als ganz ebenbürtig zur Seite stellen. Seine innere Bedeutung und das Ansehen seines Verfassers verschafften ihm eine volle und allgemeine Autorität bis zu den Zeiten, wo eine gänzlich unwissenschaftliche und geistlose Richtung im kirchlichen Forum den Sieg erlangt hatte' (von Schulte, *Die Geschichte der Quellen und Literatur des canonischen Rechts*, ii. 92).

[82] F. Pollock and F. W. Maitland, *The History of English Law before the Time of*

son Edward II, printed below as Document **3. 10,** shows what a difference could be made in practice—literally between life and death.[83]

At the centre of the case is a fairly big-time criminal named John of Worcester (variously 'Wyrettstre' and 'Wyrecestre'). He was apparently responsible for some major coups of robbery and burglary: for instance, he took goods and chattels to the value of £100 from a house (in London) of the bishop of Bath and Wells. He also robbed the chancellor of the exchequer, no less, of £40. These were large sums in the currency of the time, though he could have been hanged for much less, or indeed even for the attempt to rob or burgle.[84] When John was captured, he argued that he was a cleric and exempt from royal jurisdiction. That would have saved his skin, since church courts did not have the death penalty.

He would have got away with it. The authorities had an answer, however: John was a bigamist, the husband of a widow. A jury found that his wife Alice had indeed been married previously, to a man called William of Thurston who had died in the Tower of London. Despite some further legal moves, John's last good hope was gone. He was hanged almost certainly in 1320.[85] In a way, he was killed by symbolic reasoning.

The results of the 1274 'bigamy' ruling have been especially well studied for France, by Génestal.[86] He relates cases which would be grist to the hermeneutic anthropologist's mill, and which will be

---

Edward I, ed. S. F. C. Milsom (2 vols.; Cambridge, 1968), bk. 2, ch. 2, §5, i. 445; L. C. Gabel, *Benefit of Clergy in England in the Later Middle Ages* (Smith College Studies in History, 14. 1–4; New York, 1969), 88.

[83] I must have been led to this case via Gabel, *Benefit*, 89 n. 108, listing references to examples of cases involving bigamy from the gaol delivery rolls. She uses an outdated numbering system, so the match is not evident.

[84] 'In neither burglary nor robbery was the value of the goods stolen of any relevance to the charge. To have taken nothing at all was immaterial; the mere attempting to rob, or simply breaking into a house with that or another felonious intent was sufficient, if proven, to warrant a sentence of death' (J. G. Bellamy, *The Criminal Trial in Later Medieval England: Felony before the Courts from Edward I to the Sixteenth Century* (Stroud, 1998), 77.

[85] He abandoned his last legal move on the Saturday after the feast of the Translation of the Martyr (Becket) in the fourteenth regnal year. Edward II's fourteenth regnal year started on 8 July 1320. The feast in question falls on 7 July, so in 1320 the Saturday following it was 12 July. See C. R. Cheney and M. Jones, *A Handbook of Dates for Students of British History* (Royal Historical Society Guides and Handbooks, 4; Cambridge, 2000), 34, 85, 173. I am assuming the execution was not much further delayed.

[86] R. Génestal, *Le Privilegium fori en France du décret de Gratien à la fin du XIV*[e]

discussed in the next chapter because they involve consummation. It will be apparent already that the topics of bigamy and consummation are closely related.

There is reason to think that the implications of the 1274 decision extended beyond exemption from secular justice. We have already noted that clerical status afforded a spiritual defence against physical attack, in that anyone who laid violent hands on a cleric could only be absolved by the pope (except at point of death). In losing that privilege, bigamous clerics, or ex-clerics as they would now be, lost a lot in their violent society. Were there other privileges as well? The matter has not been sufficiently studied, but some pieces of evidence suggest that there may have been. Specimens of the evidence will be discussed below, but there is an earlier decretal of Honorius III that seems to anticipate their main message. It was subsequently included in the Decretals of Gregory IX (X. 3. 3. 9), in a truncated form, but it is the fuller form that concerns us here. Interestingly, it is addressed to Berengaria, the widow of Richard I of England, who appears to be living at or around Le Mans, on lands received at her marriage.[87]

Honorius is responding to a complaint that many *literati*, having abandoned their clerical tonsure, entered into marriage, and involved themselves in secular business, have then resumed their tonsure and clerical status in order to avoid the customary *justitiae* and the due *obsequia*. (Others never abandon their tonsure, for the same reason.) The *justitiae* could simply be their subjection to the secular courts, but what does the word *obsequia* refer to?

An *obsequium* can mean a service and also a payment. That strongly suggests that the advantages of being a cleric extended beyond legal exemption in the narrower sense of *privilegium fori* (the right to be tried in an ecclesiastical rather than a secular tribunal).

siècle (2 vols.; Bibliothèque de l'École des hautes études, Sciences religieuses, 35, 39; Paris, 1921–4), i. 62–80.

[87] Friedberg, *Corpus iuris canonici*, i. 459; *Regesta pontificum Romanorum inde ab a. post Christum natum 1198 ad a. 1304*, ed. A. Potthast, i (Berlin, 1874), no. 5755, p. 506; E. Hallam, 'Berengaria', in H. C. G. Matthew and B. Harrison (eds.), *The Oxford Dictionary of National Biography* (60 vols.; Oxford, 2004), v. 321–2; *Regesta Honorii Papae III*, ed. P. Pressuti, i (Rome, 1888; repr. Hildesheim etc., 1978), no. 1224, p. 202.

*Advantages beyond 'benefit of clergy': bulls to French kings and
Penitentiary evidence*

In slightly different language, Documents 3. 5–7 below suggest
much the same. In these cases a pope writes to a French king who
has clearly asked for the bull in question; and the bulls (1273, 1317,
and 1322) follow the same pattern. The king has drawn the pope's
attention to an abuse. Clerics 'both bigamous and monogamous' in
his land have given up their tonsure and have taken on secular jobs,
acting as *échevins* and the like in towns and other places and as *bail-
lis* etc. of princes. The popes reel off a list of names of secular offices
which could involve the shedding of blood (which was forbidden
to clerics). Now, we may note in passing that the king has apparently used the device discussed above of mentioning that some of
the clerics are bigamous, presumably to get the pope's sympathy.
Nevertheless, it is what follows that mainly concerns us: they use
their clerical status as a pretext to deprive the king of *consuetae
iustitiae* and *debita servitia*, customary 'justices' and due 'services'.
What are these 'services'? It sounds as though they are financial
but in any case it looks like a perk for being a cleric in addition to
exemption from trial in a secular court.

Some much later documents about bigamy confirm the impression that the advantages of being a cleric transcended 'benefit of
clergy' as normally understood. They are early sixteenth-century
requests by bigamous clerics to the papal Penitentiary to grant dispensations so that they could retain their clerical status.[88] Though
a negative is hard to prove, it looks as though such dispensations
were not part of the Penitentiary's business much before the date
of these entries in the Penitentiary registers.[89] It is not known why
the papacy started granting such dispensations around this time.
There is reason to think that bishops could grant 'bigamy' dispensations to clerics in minor orders when there was grave cause.[90]

[88] On the registers of the *Penitenzieria apostolica* see e.g. L. Schmugge, P. Hersperger, and B. Wiggenhauser, *Die Supplikenregister der päpstlichen Pönitentiarie aus
der Zeit Pius' II.* (*1458–1464*) (Tübingen, 1996), and K. Salonen, *The Penitentiary
as a Well of Grace in the Late Middle Ages: The Example of the Province of Uppsala
1448–1527* (Annales Academiae Scientiarum Fennicae, 313; Helsinki, 2001).

[89] I have asked excellent specialists in the pre-1500 Penitentiary (Prof. Ludwig
Schmugge, Dr Kirsi Salonen, Dr Peter Clarke) if they have noticed such cases in
the registers on which they have worked, and they do not remember doing so.

[90] See the following papal Penitentiary regulations relating to clerical 'irregularity': '§ Qui duas uxores simul vel successive habuerit. . . . § Qui contrahit cum vidua
vel corrupta . . . § Et nota quod qui duxit viduam a primo viro intactam vel qui

Probably it was that or nothing until around this time. Bishops may have granted dispensations readily in straightforward cases; in cases where several 'bigamies' were involved, there may have been nothing to be done. For whatever reason, in the early sixteenth century characters like Five-Wife Francis (Document **3. 11**) started going to the top and asked the Penitentiary. In his case his multiple 'bigamies' would probably have made a dispensation from the bishop impossible. Even in milder cases like our second one (Document **3. 12**) the petitioner probably came to the Penitentiary because he had failed with the bishop or knew he had no chance. The question of why these cases start to appear is in any case unimportant for the immediate purpose.

'Five-Wife Francis', Franciscus Sola from Gerona, had successively married no fewer than five women after becoming a cleric: three virgins and two widows. Nevertheless, he asked for a dispensation. Pedro Martorel of Barcelona was only a double bigamist, so to speak. He had married a virgin after becoming a widower, then after her death he had married a widow.

These two cases also imply that a bigamous cleric in minor orders lost more than just immunity from secular prosecution. To scrutinize the formulae: Five-Wife Francis asked that he might use all the 'privileges, graces, concessions, and indults [*omnibus et singulis privilegiis, gratiis, concessionibus et indultis*]' enjoyed by clerics who are married for the first time, to a woman who had been a virgin before marriage. Pedro Martorel's list is a little longer: he wants to use 'all privileges, immunities, exemptions, graces, favours, concessions, pre-eminences, liberties, and indults [*omnibus et singulis privilegiis, immunitatibus, exemptionibus, gratiis, favoribus concessionibus, pre-eminentiis, libertatibus et indultis*]' of such clerics. These formulae suggest that the advantages of clerical status even for married men in minor orders were multiple, and extended well beyond immunity from secular criminal prosecution.

---

duas habuit uxores, sed mortua prima in|cognita [*fo. 36ᵛ*] non est bigamus . . . § Qui cum virgine contraxit si eam post adulterium cognovit . . . § Qui infra sacros ordines de facto contraxit . . . [§] Qui post votum castitatis emisssum professione regulari contenta de facto matrimonium contraxit. . . . § In istis quinque casibus bigamie episcopus potest dispensare: in minoribus ordinibus tantum, propter necessitatem: xxiiii. Di. *Lator* [*sic ms. in error*] (probably Gratian, Pars I, D. 34, c. 18) et c. *Si subditus* [*sic ms. in error*] (probably Gratian, Pars I, D. 34, c. 17). Et Di. prima *Placuit* [*not found*]' (MS Vatican City, Biblioteca Apostolica Vaticana Vat. Lat. 3994, fo. 36ʳ⁻ᵛ).

Both these cases are from Spain. Perhaps clerical status made even more difference there than elsewhere. The tangible and intangible advantages of legitimately married clerics is a subject crying out for more research. One would like to know, for instance, how much difference if any clerical status made to secular financial obligations to local and central government in the various regions of Europe. The intangible advantages should not be forgotten either. Married clerics had a special status in the Weberian sense: they were set apart from other laypeople in their own and other people's estimation. A first step, however, would be to investigate systematically the practical pay-offs.

The more we learn about the advantages married clerics enjoyed over other married men, the more we should appreciate the social relevance of marriage symbolism. These advantages were forfeited by remarriage, marriage to a widow, even marriage to a woman no longer a virgin, and the rationale for that was the symbolic defectiveness of the clerics' marriage. For by the thirteenth century, when the rule about clerics in minor orders was laid down, the symbolic grounds for the rules seem solidly established.

Bigamy and the Wife of Bath

Chaucer scholars could learn something from reflection on these developments. Much has been written about the Wife of Bath's last husband, Jankyn, and the 'Book of Wicked Wives' with which he nourished a sturdy anti-feminism. Scholars seem not to have made the following connections, of which it seems likely that Chaucer was aware. The husband in question had been a 'clerk' (cleric) of Oxford. The Wife of Bath had got through several husbands before him, and when the Oxford man married her he was automatically declassified from clerical status. Some of Chaucer's contemporary readers would surely have been more attuned to these implications than modern literary scholars.

'Bigamy' is an elegant illustration of the thesis that life affected marriage symbolism and marriage symbolism life. Consummation is another such case.

4

Consummation

(a) Consummation and the Medieval Church's Idea of Sex

Bigamy and consummation

A consummated marriage symbolizes the union of Christ and the Church, an unconsummated one only the union of God with the just soul. So if a woman marries a man but never has sexual intercourse with him, and then after his death marries another man and does sleep with him, her flesh has not been divided: she is uniquely his in flesh and he uniquely hers. Thus the symbolism of the sacrament of marriage is not defective, so if she dies, the man is no 'bigamist' and may become a priest. That is Innocent III's argument in the decretal *Debitum*.[1]

Similar reasoning could affect the fate of married clerics in minor orders. 'Bigamy' would normally lose them clerical status and immunity, but if the wife's previous marriage had not been consummated (or, according to a strict interpretation, if she had never lost her virginity), there was no problem. The man remained a cleric, out of reach of secular criminal justice.

The historian of clerical privilege in France has studied practical consequences in concrete cases.[2] There was a cleric named Imbert who had been put in a secular prison. The archbishop of Lyons demanded that he be surrendered. The royal procurator objected that he was a 'bigamist'. The archbishop replied that Imbert's wife had not been married before, or that if she had, the marriage had never been consummated. The procurator still thought that the presumption of law was against Imbert, and it may have been to avoid such an argument that another cleric called Perrin took an extreme precaution. Since the friends of the girl he planned to

---

[1] X. 1. 21. 5.
[2] I follow R. Génestal, *Le Privilegium fori en France du décret de Gratien à la fin du XIVe siècle* (2 vols.; Bibliothèque de l'École des hautes études, Sciences religieuses, 35, 39; Paris, 1921–4), i. 73–4.

marry told him that she was still a virgin, he set in motion a formal legal enquiry to establish her virginity. It was not her virginity as such that he was worried about. He wanted to establish 'the privilege of his tonsure'.[3] These are quirky cases, exotic curiosities. Bizarre-seeming behaviour by people in other cultures is always a cue for historical analysis, a challenge to make sense of it by 'thick description'. In the cases just examined, the inner logic is the rationality of marriage symbolism, and consummation is at the centre of the symbolism.

The Church's endorsement of marital sex

It is worth pausing to reflect on the implications of this. The ideas and practices discussed in this chapter amount to a massive objection to the widespread assumption that the medieval Church tolerated sex only grudgingly, as a lesser evil.[4] This modern view is so deeply embedded in unscholarly and even scholarly writings that it will probably always survive the overwhelming evidence against it, but there is no real excuse for retaining it as a generalization.

There is an excuse for the misconception. Medieval religious writers were indeed ambiguous about pleasure as a *motive* for sex, but in the thirteenth century and after, pleasure was deemed legitimate as an *effect* of marital sex. (An analogy would be the instinct quite current today that it is natural to feel good after performing a kind act but wrong to perform a kind act in order to feel good about oneself. Their attitude was Kantian, *avant le mot.*) From Peter Abelard on, medieval scholasticism moved away from Augustine's view that sexual pleasure did not exist before original sin.

[3] *Grand coutumier*, quoted by Génestal, *Le Privilegium fori*, i. 74 n. 2.
[4] Here it is worth quoting P. Toxé, 'La *copula carnalis* chez les canonistes médiévaux', in M. Rouche (ed.), *Mariage et sexualité au Moyen Âge: accord ou crise?* (Cultures et civilisations médiévales, 21; Paris, 2000), 123–33 at 129: 'Si les canonistes ont répugné à une conception trop spiritualiste du mariage qui ne serait fondéé que sur le seul échange des consentements, ce n'est pas seulement pour faire droit à la mentalité ou aux mœurs du temps pour lesquelles la *copulatio* joue un rôle majeur, mais aussi et surtout à cause d'une conception symbolique, spirituelle de l'acte charnel, dans le mariage. Quoiqu'on en dise, il y a une valorisation positive de cet acte qui n'est pas nécessaire à l'union des cœurs (les théologiens et canonistes sont d'accord sur ce point et citent l'exemple du mariage de la Vierge Marie) mais qui peut l'exprimer et aider à y parvenir. La *copulatio* a pour ces auteurs une dimension symbolique, spirituelle, sacramentelle, et c'est pourquoi elle n'est pas un élément parmi d'autres des obligations du mariage. . . . L'union charnelle seule, signifie l'union du Christ et de son Église, indissoluble. Et c'est pourquoi l'union dont le mariage consommé est désormais le signe ne peut être dissoute.'

Sexual pleasure was natural for humans and sex in Paradise, before original sin, would have been pleasurable.[5] More gradually, in the period of 'High Scholasticism', the thought gained ground that sexual pleasure need not be wrong at all.[6] John Gillingham's brilliant short synthesis on twelfth-century marriage illustrates this point from sources that escape the historians of scholasticism. He quotes Matthew Paris's formula for a proper marriage: 'Law connects them, love and sexual compatibility',[7] and notes Innocent III's advice to Philip Augustus—that 'It was not enough to give Ingeborg the public status of a queen. He must also sleep with her, for "nothing could be more honourable or more holy than this"' (ibid.). The data about consummation's powerful symbolic status converge with these findings.

Hinduism and Catholicism

In fact medieval Christianity resembled some Hindu sects in the central importance accorded to sexual intercourse as a symbol of human union with the divine. In both cases the meaning attaches to real sexual intercourse: more is involved than a literary topos.[8] There are important affinities between the Hindu and the Catholic conception of marriage: in addition to the religious meaning attached to sex, there is a common emphasis on indissolubility. A big difference, of course, is the medieval Church's emphasis on the union of one to one, absolutely excluding polygamy, as the symbol of Christ's union with the Church.[9]

[5] M. Müller, *Die Lehre des hl. Augustinus von der Paradiesesehe und ihre Auswirkung in der Sexualethik des 12. und 13. Jahrhunderts bis Thomas von Aquin: Eine moralgeschichtliche Untersuchung* (Studien zur Geschichte der katholischen Moraltheologie, 1; Regensburg, 1954), 276–9.

[6] Ibid. 285–6; P. J. Payer, *The Bridling of Desire: Views of Sex in the Later Middle Ages* (Toronto etc., 1993), 82–3. Cf. e.g. the supplement to the *Summa theologica* of Thomas Aquinas, q. 41, art. 3–4 (*Sancti Thomae Aquinatis . . . opera omnia, iussu . . . Leonis XIII P.M. edita*, xii (Rome, 1906), 79–80) and q. 49, art. 1 and 4 (ibid. 92–3, 94–5). On Albert the Great, see L. Brandl, *Die Sexualethik des heiligen Albertus Magnus: Eine moralgeschichtliche Untersuchung* (Studien zur Geschichte der katholischen Moraltheologie, 2; Regensburg, 1955).

[7] J. Gillingham, 'Love, Marriage and Politics in the Twelfth Century' (1989), repr. in id., *Richard Cœur de Lion: Kingship, Chivalry and War in the Twelfth Century* (London etc., 1994), 243–55 at 251; 'sexual compatibility' translates 'concordia lecti' in Gillingham's paraphrase.

[8] M. Weber, *Die Wirtschaftsethik der Weltreligionen: Hinduismus und Buddhismus* (1916–20), repr. in *Gesammelte Aufsätze zur Religionssoziologie*, ii. *Hinduismus und Buddhismus* (Tübingen, 1988), esp. 326–50.

[9] Or a symbol of his union with human nature: but this is not a separate meaning— it is the basis of his union with the Church.

Consummation in marriage symbolism

These are points that need to be emphasized, but they lie somewhat to the side of our central theme. As in the last two chapters, the effects on law and through law on social practice will be singled out for special attention. It is appropriate to end with consummation because it is a central junction in the network of ideas explored in this book. We have just noted its connection with 'bigamy' symbolism. It is a common motif in the marriage symbolism transmitted to the masses by preaching, as was noted in Chapter 1. (The formula of 'initiation, ratification, and consummation' comes up again and again. Confining ourselves to the six texts edited in *Medieval Marriage Sermons*, we find it used as a basis for marriage symbolism in Jean de la Rochelle (*passim*), Pierre de Saint-Benoît (paragraphs 4– 10), Gérard de Mailly (5–7),[10] and Guibert de Tournai (6 and 14).) The present chapter will explore more closely its intimate links with indissolubility, the theme of Chapter 2. There the efforts of Philip Augustus to extricate himself from his marriage to Ingeborg of Denmark were briefly described. One of the lines he tried was the following: the marriage was never consummated, and she will go into a religious order, so that the marriage can be ended and a new marriage becomes possible. Pope Innocent III was unimpressed, but not because he rejected the principle. He was simply sceptical about the alleged facts in this particular case: non-consummation and the queen's willingness to become a nun. Much of the current chapter will turn on the case law made by Pope Alexander III that the French king was trying to use for his purpose.

Consummation is also central in a genre that this study has deliberately neglected as lying at some distance from social history: scholastic theology. By way of compensation two 'questions' from the later thirteenth-century theologian Ricardus de Mediavilla[11] are printed below as Documents **4. 2** and **4. 3**. They show the theological importance that he invests in consummation.

In the 'question' printed as Document **4. 3** Ricardus asks whether the marriage of Mary and Joseph was perfect. From a medieval theologian one would hardly expect anything but an un-

---

[10] Here in a negative sense, symbolizing the stages of marriage to sin.
[11] For a good bibliography on Richard, whose biography is obscure but whose intellectual influence was great, see article on 'Richard of Middleton', in F. L. Cross and E. A. Livingstone (eds.), *The Oxford Dictionary of the Christian Church*, 3rd edn. (Oxford, 1997), 1396.

qualified 'yes!' to this question.[12] This a priori expectation is misleading: instead we get a very qualified 'yes' together with a distinction between two different sorts of perfection. There is perfection in matters pertaining to the essence of a thing and there are perfections that do not pertain to the essence. The marriage of Mary and Joseph had the first kind but not the second, because it did not represent the unity of Christ and Church as perfectly as does a consummated marriage. This was not just a hypothesis of élite ivory-tower theology. Document **4. 6,** from the *Pupilla oculi*, the popular fourteenth-century priests' manual by Johannes de Burgo, shows how the idea could be diffused to a wider circle.

Ricardus manages to cite the authority of Peter Lombard, who was of course the doyen of twelfth-century theologians. In fact, however, Peter's emphasis had been subtly different.[13] The reader could come away thinking that a marriage without sex was holier than a consummated one, and that the perfect signification of a consummated marriage was secondary to that.[14] It is a nuance, but not a trivial one. Earlier on the Lombard had said outright of the marriage of Mary and Joseph that it was holier and more perfect because it was without sex.[15]

Another of the 'questions' by Ricardus de Mediavilla (below, Document **4. 2**) may explain why he took a different view of unconsummated marriages from Peter Lombard. Here he asks whether

---

[12] On this issue see P. S. Gold, 'The Marriage of Mary and Joseph in the Twelfth-Century Ideology of Marriage', in V. L. Bullough and J. A. Brundage (eds.), *Sexual Practices and the Medieval Church* (1982; repr. Amherst, NY, 1994), 102–17 and 249–51. This is an honest and intelligent piece of work but leaves out some important pieces of the jigsaw, in particular Alexander III's decision about unconsummated marriages and Gaudemet's work on its origins (both discussed in sect. (b) of the current chapter).

[13] Peter Lombard, *Sentences*, 4. 30. 2, in *Magistri Petri Lombardi Parisiensis Episcopi Sententiae in IV libris distinctae*, 3rd edn., ed. Patres Collegii S. Bonaventurae [I. Brady] (2 vols.; Spicilegium Bonaventurianum, 4–5; Grottaferrata, 1971–81), ii. 439–41.

[14] 'Inter quos, ut ait Augustinus, perfectum fuit coniugium: perfectum quidem non in significatione, sed in sanctitate. Sanctiora enim sunt coniugia pari voto continentium' (Peter Lombard, *Sentences*, 4. 30. 2, ii. 440 Brady); 'Sed intelligendum est coniugium perfici commixtione corporali non quantum ad veritatem vel sanctitatem coniugii, sed quantum ad significationem, quia perfectius unionem Christi et Ecclesiae tunc figurat' (ibid., ii. 440–1 Brady).

[15] 'Hanc si secundum superficiem verborum quis acceperit, inducitur in errorem tantum ut dicat sine carnali copula non posse contrahi matrimonium, et inter Mariam et Ioseph non fuisse coniugium, vel non fuisse perfectum. Quod nefas est sentire: tanto enim sanctius fuit atque perfectius, quanto a carnali opere immunius' (Peter Lombard, *Sentences*, 4. 26. 6, ii. 421 Brady).

a non-consummated marriage can be dissolved by one partner's entry into a religious order. The answer is yes. His explanation involves symbolism and is akin to his comments about the marriage of Mary and Joseph. An unconsummated marriage is still a spiritual union only. It can be dissolved when one party dies to the world by entering the religious life. This is in accordance with the meaning or symbolism of such a marriage: it stands only for the breakable union between God and the soul, not for the indissoluble union of human nature to the person of the Son of God. He cites canon law: cases decided by the pope and setting precedents.[16]

Ricardus cites two decisions by Pope Alexander III that are central to the argument of this chapter. It was the decision of Alexander III (1159–81) that an unconsummated marriage could be dissolved, really dissolved after really existing, dissolved as by a divorce in the modern sense, so that remarriage was allowed, if one partner entered a religious order. The letters are worth quoting. Neither seems to be precisely datable, so we shall follow the order in which they were inserted into the Decretals of Gregory IX. The first is addressed to the bishop of Salerno. These are the the critical words:

It is true that after legitimate consent in the present tense, it is permitted to one partner, even against the will of the other, to choose a monastery (just as certain saints were called away from weddings), so long as they have not had carnal intercourse; and it is permitted to the other who remains to marry again, if he or she does not want to keep continence after being admonished to do so. For since they have not been made one flesh, one may well cross over to God, and the other remain in the world.[17]

The second is addressed to the bishop of Brescia. The wife had been excommunicated for refusing to return to her husband and

[16] X. 3. 32. 2 and 7. Though neither these cases nor Ricardus de Mediavilla's ideas actually contradict Inga Persson's comment that 'Nur das kanonische Ehemodell spricht einer Ehe auch ohne *copula* umfassende Gültigkeit, Perfektion und volle Sakramentalität zu' (I. Persson, *Ehe und Zeichen: Studien zu Eheschließung und Ehepraxis anhand der frühmittelhochdeutschen religiösen Lehrdichtungen 'Vom Rechte', 'Hochzeit' und 'Schopf von dem lône'* (Göppinger Arbeiten zur Germanistik, 617; Göppingen, 1995), 127), for although an unconsummated marriage was indeed valid and sacramental and in a sense perfect, her formula underplays the crucial significance of consummation in canon law and theology.

[17] X. 3. 32. 2, in E. Friedberg, *Corpus iuris canonici* (2 vols.; Leipzig, 1879–81; repr. Graz, 1955), ii. 579; cf. *Regesta pontificum Romanorum ab condita Ecclesia ad annum post Christum natum MCXCVIII*, ed P. Jaffé, W. Wattenbach, *et al.*, 2nd edn. (2 vols., Leipzig, 1885–8), ii, no. 14091 (9141), p. 394.

show him 'marital affection'. Alexander says that she need not do
so provided that the marriage had not yet been consummated and
that she enters a religious order. After she has done so, the husband
can remarry. The passage that matters most is as follows (note that
the words in italics were in the original letter but were not included
in the Decretals of Gregory IX):[18]

. . . since *the aforesaid woman*, though married[19] to the aforesaid man,
nevertheless has not yet had intercourse with him, as she asserts, we order,
commanding you, brother, through apostolic writings, that, if the aforesaid
man has not known this *woman* carnally, and the same *woman, as we are
informed by you*, wishes to enter a religous order, you should—after receiving from her sufficient guarantee that she should either enter the religious
life or return to her husband before two months have elapsed—absolve her
from the sentence which binds her, *no objection or appeal being permitted*,
in such a way that if she enters the religious life, each should restore to
the other person what they are known to have received from that person,
*and the husband himself, while she takes the habit, should have the freedom
to remarry*. Indeed, when the Lord says in the Gospel that a man is not
allowed to send away his wife except on account of fornication, it is to be
understood, if one draws out the meaning of the Scripture, to refer to those
whose marriage has been consummated by carnal union.[20]

The possibility of remarriage is explicit in both letters, though the
second would have lost clarity as transmitted in the Decretals of
Gregory IX because of the omission of the words 'should have
the freedom to remarry'. There is no such unclarity in the letter
to the bishop of Salerno as transmitted in the Decretals, whose
gender symmetry is also important. On the other hand, the second
decretal, to the bishop of Brescia, left all subsequent canonists to
reflect on the idea that the difference between a consummated and
unconsummated marriage was rooted in the Gospel itself.

---

[18] I follow the scholarly edition of the Decretals: see Friedberg, *Corpus iuris
canonici*, ii, Prolegomena, p. xlv: 'Ut vero quae inserui [from other sources for
the document] a Gregoriano textu discerni possent, illa italicis quos vocant typis
exprimenda curavi.' It was unhelpful of Friedberg to hide this line, absolutely
crucial for the use of his edition, in the middle of a paragraph of a lengthy introduction.

[19] The word is *desponsata*, which can also mean betrothed, but that meaning does
not seem possible in the context.

[20] X. 3. 32. 7: Friedberg, *Corpus iuris canonici*, ii. 581; *Regesta pontificum Romanorum*, ed. Jaffé et al., ii, no. 13787 (8854), p. 371.

Consummation 175

The implications of Alexander III's decision

Alexander III's emphasis on consummation has long been recognized as decisive for the long-term history of marriage in the Catholic Church.[21] Even so, there is room for clarification, since the point has not been spelt out in two of the best books on the history of marriage, one linking it too closely for complete clarity with the distinct issue of annulment on grounds of impotence (distinct because in the cases just discussed there is no indication of impotence),[22] another just missing it out, though mentioning annulment for impotence and impediment of affinity.[23] So it is worth re-emphasizing that although all cases of impotence must have been non-consummation cases, the converse does not hold. With many non-consummation cases the ability of the spouses to consummate the marriage was not in doubt and not the issue.

The idea that the marriage of Mary and Joseph was in a certain sense imperfect because unconsummated percolated down from speculative to pastoral theology. We find it in the late fourteenth-century priests' manual discussed above and also in connection with 'Bigamy': the *Pupilla oculi*, by Johannes de Burgo, chancellor of the University of Cambridge.[24] The passage is printed and translated below, as Document **4. 6.** These remarks would have reached a relatively wide public, far beyond that of academic theologians and theology students, for it was well adapted to its task, and transmitted in many manuscripts and then later in print.

It seems likely that papal case law prompted by actual situations

[21] Cf. e.g. G. H. Joyce, *Christian Marriage: An Historical and Doctrinal Study* (London etc., 1933), 428–9, 449–63.
[22] C. N. L. Brooke, *The Medieval Idea of Marriage* (Oxford, 1989), 132–3 and n. 37.
[23] D. Lombardi, *Matrimoni di antico regime* (Annali dell'Istituto storico italo-germanico in Trento, Monografie, 34; Bologna, 2001), 30: 'La questione di più difficile soluzione era quando una persona, dopo aver contratto matrimonio *per verba de praesenti*, ne contraeva un altro, con un secondo partner, e lo consumava. Quale dei due vincoli era valido? Le risposte date da Alessandro III mostravano ancora qualche segno di incertezza. In diverse decretali expresse la validità del primo, puramente consensuale, . . . In altre decretali, invece, Alessandro insistette sul valore della consumazione. Stabilì che il rapporto sessuale intervenuto tra i partner e un parente dell'altro, prima del matrimonio, impedisse la conclusione del matrimonio. O, ancora, che la non consumazione, a causa dell'impotenza di uno dei coniugi, rendesse nullo il matrimonio.' Nothing here about the dissolution of the *matrimonium ratum sed non consummatum*.
[24] W. A. Pantin, *The English Church in the Fourteenth Century*, 2nd edn. (1962; repr. Toronto etc., 1980), 213–14 (and on Johannes also above, pp. 156–7 and 172).

helped deflect theological tradition into a new channel. The following fascinating comment by Stephen Langton caught Sir Maurice
Powicke's acute eye long ago:

> We say that it is not our business nor is it possible to define how far
> [*quantum*] the pope can go. For who would have dared to say before the time
> of pope Alexander that a woman who had not consummated her marriage
> could transfer herself to the monastic life? Who would not have denied that
> the lord pope, in the light of the saying in the gospel, 'whomsoever God
> hath joined let no man put asunder,' could give dispensation in a matter of
> this kind? But afterwards when the decretal was issued, any man who had
> previously denied it would say that the lord pope could dispense.[25]

Alexander's decision was unexpected but it did not come out of
nowhere. A long tradition of thought about symbolism, consummation, and indissolubility lies behind it and makes sense of it.
Alexander must have been aware of this tradition if only because
it showed itself in the most influential canon-law text of his time,
Gratian's *Decretum*. The relevant passage is in the section on the
conversion of married people to the religious life, the part of the
work directly relevant to the case Alexander decided.[26]

(b) The Dissolution of the Unconsummated Marriage: From Hincmar to Alexander III

'*One flesh*' and the '*great mystery*'

Perhaps the ultimate origins of the developments described here
lie in the 'one flesh' passages in the Gospels[27] combined with St
Paul's 'great mystery' passage at Ephesians 5: 32. Did a marriage
where the couple had not become one in flesh mirror the marriage
of Christ to the Church as perfectly as after consummation? The
eventual answer given in our period should not astonish us, in view
of these New Testament passages, with which clerical writers about
marriage were naturally familiar. Nevertheless, it was a long time
before theological thought turned in this direction. The process has
been traced in a fundamental and little-known paper by the legal
historian Jean Gaudemet, and the next few paragraphs are largely
a précis of his findings.[28]

---

[25] Langton, quoted in F. M. Powicke, *Stephen Langton* (Oxford, 1928), 140.
[26] Pars II, C. 27, q. 2, c. 7.   [27] e.g. Matt. 19: 5.
[28] 'Recherche sur les origines historiques de la faculté de rompre le mariage

Pope Leo I

A key text in the story is a passage from Pope Leo I's decretal letter
to Rusticus of Narbonne:

Not every woman joined to a man is the man's wife, for not every son
is his father's heir. The bonds of marriage between free men and women
follow the rule of law and are between equals, as the Lord established,
long before the beginning of Roman law. Therefore a wife is one thing, a
concubine is another, just as a slave girl is one thing, and a free woman
another. . . . Therefore since the society of marriage was established from
the beginning in such a way that it should have in it, beyond the union
of the sexes, the symbol [*sacramentum*] of Christ and the Church, there is
no doubt that a woman of whom we learn that the nuptial mystery [*mysterium*] has been lacking has nothing to do with marriage. Therefore, if
a cleric anywhere has given his daughter in marriage to a man who has
a concubine, it should not be treated as if he has given her to a married
man, unless perchance that woman has been freed, and given a dowry
in accordance with the law, and accorded the honour of a public wedding.[29]

One of the issues was: when is a marriage not a marriage but
a sexual partnership? The question arose because in one or more
cases the daughter of a priest or deacon under Bishop Rusticus's
authority had been heading for marriage with a man who already
had a partner. Should the partner be counted as a wife? Pope
Leo gives criteria for deciding whether this existing partner is
a wife. If she is a slave who has not been freed, she is judged
not to be a wife. (Why does the bishop not extend his question to daughters of laypeople too? Probably because his practical authority over marriage did not extend beyond the clergy.)
Behind the assumption that a slave girl was not a wife lay the
whole tradition of classical antiquity. It was taken for granted
that slaves could not marry. The only way to marry a female
slave was to set her free. Christianity's doctrine of equality before God had not yet eroded this assumption. If we look forward
to the Council of Châlons-sur-Saone in 813, we see that in the

non consommé', in S. Kuttner and K. Pennington (eds.), *Proceedings of the Fifth
International Congress of Medieval Canon Law* (Monumenta Iuris Canonici, Series
C, Subsidia, 6; Vatican City, 1980), 309–31.

[29] *Ep.* 167. 4, Migne, *PL* 54. 1204–5, cited by Gaudemet, 'Recherche sur les
origines historiques', 309.

long run the Church rejected the exclusion of unfreed slaves from marriage.[30]

To return to the text. It shows that priests and deacons had daughters and were presumably still married. The discipline of the Western Church at this date was that a a man in holy orders should live chastely with his wife. One may guess at the following pattern. A man becomes a 'cleric' and embarks on the road to becoming a priest, relatively young. He marries and has children. On one of the ritual stages on the way to becoming a priest, the diaconate or the subdiaconate,[31] he supposedly stops having sex with his wife.

What does the sentence about the *sacramentum* of Christ and the Church mean? Leo implies that a bodily union is not itself enough to make a marriage. A true marriage is a mirror of the union of Christ and the Church. The signs that such a marriage has taken place are that the couple are free (freed if necessary), that the woman has a dowry (which she could not have if she were a slave and ineligible for matrimony), and a public ceremony. Sexual partnership is not enough to symbolize the mystery of Christ and the Church.

Hincmar of Reims to Gratian

In the ninth century Hincmar, the powerful archbishop of Reims, modified the Latin and the sense of Leo's text to produce a completely different meaning: namely, that until the couple have sexual intercourse, marriage does not properly symbolize the union of Christ and the Church. He developed this new reading in the context of a real problem, a case touched on briefly in Chapter 2. A nobleman called Stephen of Auvergne had been through a marriage ceremony with a woman when he had slept with a close relative of hers. By the rules of the time, this made it a sin to sleep with his wife. Hincmar was called in to decide what should be done. He said that the marriage could be ended. It could not be consummated morally. Until it was consummated it did not mirror the union of Christ and the Church, so it could be dissolved.[32]

---

[30] *Concilia aevi Karolini*, ed. A. Werminghoff (2 vols.; Monumenta Germaniae Historica, Legum Sectio III, Concilia, 2. 1–2; Hanover etc., 1906–8), no. 30, i/1. 279.

[31] We may leave aside here the question of whether or when the rule about chastity was applied to subdeacons (the subdiaconate being the antepenultimate rung on the ladder of priestly orders). The requirement seems to have included deacons as well as priests more or less from its introduction.

[32] Gaudemet, 'Recherche sur les origines historiques', 315–18.

Gaudemet shows that this rereading of the text of Leo did not have any impact until the twelfth century. Then some books of church law start altering Leo's text in the same kind of way as Hincmar had done. One of them was Gratian's *Decretum*. Gaudemet is cautious about the connection between the Hincmar–Stephen of Auvergne case in the ninth century and Gratian in the twelfth.[33] He thinks that the influence of Hincmar's text on Gratian is not direct and that the chain of texts linking them cannot be reconstructed: too many links are missing. Nevertheless, he agrees that Hincmar was the intellectual ancestor of the text in Gratian, Pars II, C. 27, q. 2, c. 17, a transformed version of Leo the Great's remark, that reads as follows:

Since the social bond of marriage was instituted from the beginning in such a way that without sexual intercourse marriages would not contain the symbol of the union of Christ and the Church, there is no doubt that a woman whom we learn to have been without the nuptial mystery does not pertain to marriage.

Gaudemet concludes his paper with the comment that the interpolated passage would 'leave its impress thenceforward on the canonical doctrine of marriage'.[34] He sees this as decisive in the history of the origins of the power to break a non-consummated marriage (the title of his paper is 'Investigation into the historical origins of the power to break a non-consummated marriage'). If he is right, as I believe he is, symbolism was crucial to the reasoning behind the development.

---

[33] So careful and dense is Gaudemet's wording, in fact, that one can read his text several times without being absolutely sure how much or how little he is claiming.

[34] His overall conclusion is worth quoting: 'Doctrine commune des Pères, le consensualisme matrimonial est scrupuleusement conservé par les collections canoniques jusqu'aux années 1123–1130. Hincmar, pour résoudre une grave difficulté, y fait échec afin de permettre la rupture d'une union non consommée. Mais le traitement qu'il infligea au *responsum* de Léon n'atteignit pas la transmission du texte dans les collections canoniques. La doctrine avancée par l'archevêque de Reims reparaît entre 1123 et 1130 dans une collection qui du coup interpole le texte de Léon. Interpolation que l'on retrouve dans le Décret de Gratien et qui marquera désormais la doctrine canonique du mariage' ('Recherche sur les origines historiques', 331).

(c) The Social Effects of Alexander III's Decision

John XXII and the count of Anguillaria

A genuine but unconsummated marriage, then, could be broken if one spouse entered a religious order.[35] Does it matter much to the social historian? Is it more than a minor curiosity in the history of canon-law doctrines? Did it affect more than a tiny number of couples, where one spouse had suddenly died before the marriage could be consummated?

Here it helps to move forward for a moment to the early fourteenth century, to a concrete case that can be reconstructed in detail and casts light on the dynamics of marriages between ratification and consummation. The transcriptions from a register of Pope John XXII printed as Document **4. 4** are enough to suggest that Alexander's decision could have serious social implications. The letters relate to a marriage between the count of Anguillaria and the daughter of Stefano da Colonna—a member of the great family which turns up repeatedly in papal history. In this case the pope badly needed Colonna's help against his arch-opponent Ludwig of Bavaria, and may have earned it partly by intervention in the marriage. The details are summarized in the introduction to the set of documents, but the essence of the situation was as follows.

The count of Anguillaria had placed Colonna's daughter Agnes in an impossible position by postponing consummation. We have no reason to think that the count was contemplating entry into a religious order, which would have released Agnes. The only way out would be for her to become a nun herself, which was probably the last thing she wanted to do. It would also have enabled the count to marry another woman, adding insult to injury. In this case the pope helped out by putting pressure on the count to consummate the marriage and thus make it indissoluble.

The case points to an unintended effect of Alexander III's decision. If the consummation was postponed for any reason, the husband was left with a great deal of leverage over the bride and her family. Presumably fathers who knew their way around tried to take precautions to prevent this situation when arranging a marriage. Conversely, delay in consummating could have been a way

---

[35] I leave aside the question of whether any solemn vow of chastity even apart from entry into a religious order dissolved a marriage: but see P. Glorieux, 'Le Quodlibet de Pierre de Tarentaise', *Recherches de théologie anciennne et médievale*, 9 (1937), 237–80 at 243–4. I owe this reference to Patrick Nold.

to put pressure on the father of the bride to pay the dowry. Thus Alexander III's decision will have been a causal factor not only in cases where the marriage was never consummated, but also in cases where it was ultimately consummated but only after a significant time lag.

Last-minute conversion to a life without sex

Moving to a more idealistic level, there may have been more last-minute conversions to perpetual chastity than one would imagine, for the ideal was widely diffused in vernacular literature. It was constantly reinforced by one of the most successful stories current in the medieval West, the legend of St Alexis. It survives in many vernacular versions, in addition to the Latin ones.[36] The core of the story is that Alexis is pressured into marriage by his father, leaves to pursue a life of poverty before consummating the marriage, returns to his father's house as a beggar without being recognized, where he is given a sort of shelter until his death, after which he is recognized and a written explanation of his life is found in his clenched hand. According to one version, only his wife is able to remove the document.[37]

The Alexis story is famous among students of medieval heresy. According to an account of the origins of the Waldensian movement, one of the great heretical movements of the Middle Ages, surviving to this day, the founder underwent his conversion when he heard the legend of St Alexis being told by a *jongleur*. It is a symptom of the story's wide diffusion. Little though it appeals to most modern sensibilities, it could have influenced people, just as Goethe's *Die Leiden des jungen Werther* apparently caused a vogue for Romantic suicides.

One real-life counterpart to the story of St Alexis is the case of Christina of Markyate.[38] Her parents put heavy pressure on her

---

[36] A. Gieysztor, '*Pauper sum et peregrinus*: la légende de saint Alexis en Occident. Un idéal de pauvreté', in M. Mollat (ed.), *Études sur l'histoire de la pauvreté* (Publications de la Sorbonne, série 'Etudes', 8; Paris, 1974), 125–39 at 126. For a sensitive exploration of the ideas about marriage in one of the versions, see N. Cartlidge, *Medieval Marriage: Literary Approaches, 1100–1300* (Woodbridge etc., 1997), 77–106.

[37] Gieysztor, '*Pauper sum et peregrinus*', 127. In the canonical version, equally interestingly, only the pope is able to take the document from his hand (ibid. 136).

[38] For two vivid retellings of the story see Brooke, *The Medieval Idea of Marriage*, 144–8, and R. Bartlett, *England under the Norman and Angevin Kings 1075–1225* (Oxford, 2000), 550–1.

to marry, though she wanted a celibate life devoted only to God. They eventually got her to go through with the ceremony, but she absolutely refused to consummate the marriage. Her husband Burthred made various attempts. On one occasion she managed to dissuade him. He lost face with his friends, and on another occasion burst into her room with a group of them, but she hid. In the end the marriage was never consummated and she was able to have the life she wanted. It was just the kind of case for which Alexander III's law was designed, though it came too late to help her.

The question remains: was a time lag between present consent and consummation at all common? If it was not, the dissolution of a non-consummated marriage would seldom be an issue because most newly-weds would hardly have time to reconsider. Christina of Markyate was clear in her mind from the start that she did not want to consummate her marriage, but unless there was a time lag, second thoughts would rarely have a chance to take root.

Consummation delayed because of youth

In fact, however, there is quite a lot of evidence that a significant delay between marriage and consummation was normal. There were a number of reasons why this was so. One might be the youth of the couple or at least of the bride. It was common for women to marry young, not long after puberty.[39] The bride's parents might well prefer to keep her at home for a time, while delaying the exchange of present consent would carry with it the risk of the bridegroom changing his mind and marrying someone else.

Proxy marriages

Another reason might be that the words of present consent were given by proxy. It had been so with the marriage of the count of Anguillaria to Stefano da Colonna's daughter.[40] An earlier example is King Henry III of England's invalid marriage to Joan of Ponthieu.[41] When the abortive marriage was annulled long after, the reason given was that Henry and Joan were related within the forbidden degrees. This must have been known when the words of con-

---

[39] D. Herlihy, *Medieval Households* (Cambridge, Mass., etc., 1985), 103–7.

[40] See Document 4. 2 below, first full paragraph after the table of contents.

[41] The whole story is laid out in a massive papal bull, preserved in MS BL Cotton Cleopatra E. 1, fos. 194^v–195^r: see D. L. d'Avray, 'Authentication of Marital Status: A Thirteenth Century English Royal Annulment Process and Later Medieval Cases from the Papal Penitentiary', *English Historical Review*, forthcoming.

sent were exchanged. Henry was seeking a dispensation from the impediment, and dropped the attempt when the marriage ceased to seem desirable. It is significant that he nevertheless stressed during the annulment proceedings that the marriage had not been consummated.[42]

Dowry and delay

Other reasons will be illustrated as the data are presented below: the bridegroom might delay consummation until the bride's father had paid the dowry; consent might be exchanged during one of the liturgical periods when marriages could not be celebrated, or consummation postponed until after a church wedding. Whatever the reasons, there is plenty of evidence that sexual intercourse by no means always followed quickly on the exchange of consent, even though a couple were married from that point on.

At least so far as Italy is concerned, the convention of a gap between consent and consummation has already been noted by some historians. Following earlier studies, Brundage notes that couples commonly had to wait until the dowry had been paid before sleeping with each other.[43] According to another study, there might be a gap of at least a year between the exchange of present consent in front of a notary and the church ceremony. In the interval the bride continued to live with her parents, presumably without sleeping with her husband.[44] To this one might add the throwaway line by Hostiensis,[45] to the effect that it had been normal in Modena for a second, consummated marriage to out-trump a first, unconsummated one (see Document **4. 1**). This comment makes no sense if a time lag had not been fairly common in the city.

Three English cases

These fairly firm findings can be complemented with evidence from England, at the other end of Europe. The twelfth-century Anstey

[42] Line 33 of the papal bull.

[43] J. A. Brundage, *Law, Sex, and Christian Society in Medieval Europe* (Chicago and London, 1987), 504: 'Consummation was also frequently linked to property considerations. In Italian towns couples often initiated conjugal relations only when the dowry had been paid' (he gives further references to works by C. Klapisch-Zuber and J. Heers).

[44] E. Hall, *The Arnolfini Betrothal: Medieval Marriage and the Enigma of Van Eyck's Double Portrait* (Berkeley etc., 1994), 53.

[45] Alluding to X. 4. 4. 5, as Patrick Nold kindly pointed out to me.

case, rather famous among historians of marriage because it established the principle that consent makes a marriage, might never have happened had there not been a long delay between present consent and consummation. The following passage is central to the history of medieval marriage as well as being directly relevant to our specific problem:

> As to your question concerning the sacrament of marriage, I give you this brief answer. With regard to the lady who you said was given in marriage by her father, and was returned into her father's keeping by the man to whom she had been given until on a day appointed he should take her into his own house, I say that, if it was done by lawful consent, she was a wife from the moment when by her promise freely given she consented to be his wife. For it was not a promise for the future, but a present arrangement with immediate effect.[46]

Here we see a decision that present consent alone makes a valid marriage. It is also mentioned as if quite normal that the wife went back to live in her father's house for a time. What looks like a similar arrangement is agreed in a later thirteenth-century original charter in the British Library. It is a marriage agreement, but some complex financial arrangements between the fathers of bride and groom are included in it. For our purposes what matters is a provision that the bride, Maud, would remain with her father for a year after her marriage before joining her husband.[47]

The dowry theme discussed above in connection with Italy is made explicit in a Berkshire case from the mid-thirteenth century. We read that

> Alexander . . . says that he did not keep any of the chattels of the aforesaid

---

[46] The words are purportedly those of Pope Innocent II, as quoted in a letter of the bishop of Winchester, quoted in a letter by Archbishop Theobald of Canterbury, actually composed by his aide John of Salisbury! See *The Letters of John of Salisbury*, ed. W. J. Millor, SJ, H. E. Butler, and C. N. L. Brooke, i. *The Early Letters (1153–1161)* (Oxford, 1986), 228–9. For background see Brooke, *The Medieval Idea of Marriage*, 148–52.

[47] 'Et por cestes choses le dit Monser Barthe' dorra au dit Monser Robert mil' et deux centz mars a paier, cest a saver deux centz mars lendemein de la seint Johan prochein avenir, a quen iour le dit monser Robert fera la dite reconisaunce de vint mil' mars et deux centz mars ala seint Jake prochein suant a quen iour est acorde qe le mariage se fera entre les avantditz Robert et Maud, et deux centz mars au Noel prochein suant, deux centz mars ala Pasque prochein suant, deux centz mars ala seint Johan prochein suant, et deux centz mars ala seint Michel prochein suant. Et la dite Maud demorra en la garde le dit monser Barthe' a ses custages un an apres le iour du mariage' (MS BL Harley Charter 45. F. 11, lines 18–23 (unprinted so far as I know)).

Stephen from him, indeed he says that in truth the aforesaid Stephen
was espoused to the daughter of the aforesaid Walter, and since the same
Stephen did not want to take his aforesaid wife home after he had espoused
her, until the aforesaid Walter paid him back twenty shillings that he owed
him . . .[48]

Here a debt is the reason for the delay in consummating the marriage.

A legal way to end delay: the Audientia litterarum contradictarum

In such cases an enterprising spouse might have recourse to a rou-
tinized procedure at the papal court. We know about it through
a formulary of the *Audientia litterarum contradictarum*, the papal
court that dealt with routine cases which would be passed on to
judges delegate.[49] Different form letters deal with several variants
of the problem.[50] Thus, the girl might refuse to join her husband,[51]
or her father might prevent her,[52] or again the wife might use the

[48] 'Et Alexander venit et deffendit vim et injuriam quando etc., et dicit quod nulla
catalla predicti Stephani ei detinet immo dicit quod revera predictus Stephanus
disponsavit filiam predicti Walteri, et quia idem Stephanus noluit predictam uxorem
suam postquam ipsam desponsaverat ad hospicium suum ducere donec predictus
Walterus redderet ei xx solidos quod ei debuit' (*The Roll and Writ File of the
Berkshire Eyre of 1248*, ed. M. T. Clanchy (London, 1973), 195). I have used the
word 'espoused' to translate 'desponsare', to capture the ambiguity of a word which
can mean either 'marry' or 'betroth', but the use of the word 'wife', *uxor*, makes it
overwhelmingly probable that the espousal had been in words of the present tense,
so constituting the 'ratification' of a true marriage according to the Church.

[49] On the system see P. Herde, *Audientia litterarum contradictarum: Untersuchungen über die päpstlichen Justizbriefe und die päpstliche Delegationsgerichtsbarkeit vom
13. bis zum Beginn des 16. Jahrhunderts* (2 vols.; Bibliothek des deutschen historischen Instituts in Rom, 31–2; Tübingen, 1970). The system, which cannot be
described here, was a brilliant administrative creation, enabling a combination of
local knowledge and central authority hard to parallel in world history before the
twentieth century: though the English system of royal writs and local juries did
the same over a smaller geographical area. The formulary could be compared to a
register of writs in England.

[50] Herde, *Audientia litterarum contradictarum*, ii. 298–302. One variant (ibid.,
K 155a, ii. 300–1) specifies that the marriage had been consummated. In the other
variants it would appear that it had not.

[51] '*Episcopo*. Sua nobis . . laicus petitione monstravit, quod, cum ipse cum M.
filia . . matrimonium per verba legitime contraxerit de presenti, eadem tamen M.
ab ipso non patitur se traduci.—mandamus, quatinus, si est ita, predictam M.,
quod ab eodem viro se traduci libere patiatur, monitione premissa per censuram
ecclesiasticam, sicut iustum fuerit, appellatione remota compellas' (ibid., K 152,
ii. 298).

[52] '*Episcopo*. Conquestus est nobis . . laicus, quod, licet ipse cum M. muliere . .
diocesis matrimonium legitime per verba contraxerit de presenti, tamen eadem ab

procedure when her husband would not let her come to live with him after the marriage had been contracted.[53] All these situations imply a time lag. The *Audientia* evidence shows that something could be done about a time lag unwelcome to one partner, but the remedy would hardly have been rapid.

The evidence that consummation did not always follow swiftly on marriage by present consent may be concluded with two cases from Spain, from the very end of the medieval period. They come from the registers of the Apostolic Penitentiary, and both read like one-paragraph novels.

Cases from the papal Penitentiary registers

The first (Document **4. 7**) also raises complex legal issues. It was handled in 1499. The petitioner and central figure was a woman called Constance of Padilla, who was in the service of a nobleman named Bonadilla. This man seems to have taken violent exception to a marriage that she had contracted by words of the present tense, and acted before the couple could consummate it. A likely scenario is that her new husband was someone of higher social status, for whom her noble master had other plans. This would explain why the couple did not live together after getting married. If Bonadilla had been informed in advance, presumably he would have tried to prevent the exchange of consent. However, the rule that consent alone was enough for a valid marriage made it hard to stop a determined couple. Bonadilla's solution was to force Constance to enter a Conceptionist nunnery (the Conceptionists were a branch of the Franciscan order). As we shall see, it would be crucial to Constance's case that she had been compelled to join the Conceptionists: it was not a free choice. Nevertheless, she made the normal profession as a nun. She could not tolerate the religious life, however, and she left. By this time the man she had married by 'present

ipso contra iustitiam non patitur se traduci patre mulieris eiusdem id presumente temere impedire.—mandamus, quatinus, si est ita, prefatam mulierem, ut se ab eodem viro suo, ut tenetur, libere traduci permittat, et prefatum patrem eius, quod ab huiusmodi impedimento desistat, monitione premissa per censuram ecclesiasticam appellatione remota previa ratione compellas' (ibid., K 154, ii. 299–300).

[53] '*Episcopo*. Sua nobis B. de . . mulier petitione monstravit, quod, cum I. de . . laicus tue diocesis cum ipsa legitime matrimonium per verba contraxerit de presenti, idem tamen I. eam non curat, ut tenetur, traducere in uxorem (*vel aliter*: eam non curat traducere, ut tenetur).—mandamus, quatinus, si est ita, dictum I., ut eam traducere studeat, monitione premissa per censuram ecclesiasticam, sicut iustum fuerit, appellatione remota compellas' (ibid., K 156, ii. 301–2).

consent' had remarried, and this time he had consummated the union. Yet when Constance ran away from her life as a nun, he clearly wanted her still: the whole point of the case is to allow them to live as man and wife.

How could this possibly be allowed in church law? One would have thought that Alexander III's rulings stood against it: entry into a religious order would have dissolved the first unconsummated marriage, the second marriage was consummated and so indissoluble. The key to her case, however, is that she entered the order under compulsion. Becoming a nun was like getting married in that true freedom of choice was required and the lack of it made the decision void. Constance's case was that she did not truly consent to the religious life, so that her first marriage had after all never been dissolved, with the consequence that her husband's second marriage was invalid. The whole story makes vivid another way in which the consummation of a marriage might be delayed, as well as the interaction of Alexander's decision in the twelfth century with social life centuries later (and with another canon-law principle: free consent before lifelong commitment to a religious order). The case was committed to judges delegate. If they found the facts to be as stated, and if her husband got his second marriage annulled, the judges were to give her the means of authenticating her marriage to any ignorant persons who called it into question.

The second case (Document 4. 8) concerns a Juan Sams (?) of Burgos diocese. He had married Catherine, daughter of Juan Gomez. They did not consummate the marriage immediately, and in the interval she slept with another man. Evidently this changed everything, and 'induced by penitence or for some other reason' she entered the Order of the Holy Trinity. At least, she made profession of the rule of the order without entering one of its monasteries, but it must have been enough to bring her within the scope of Alexander III's decrees. Juan Sams had got as far as getting engaged to a woman who is named in the petition. However, he wanted something to show the ignorant that he could go ahead and marry her validly. This is yet another scenario of how Alexander III's judgment might be applied in practice.

It should be clear from the above that non-consummation cases were different socially, as well as legally, from impotence cases. The legal difference was in itself profound. Where permanent impotence could be established, the marriage would be annulled. That would be a declaration that it had never existed. Non-consummated marriages were real marriages from the moment the words of present consent were spoken. Thus their dissolution was more like a divorce in the modern sense. (The medieval word *divortium* normally means either an annulment or a legal separation.) So much for the legal difference. The social difference is that the couple had probably never lived together in non-consummation cases. We have seen that a variety of situations explain why that might be so.

Thus there is every reason to think that delay was a common occurrence, and consequently that the late twelfth-century decision of Alexander III opened up an option for a larger proportion of newly married couples than one might initially suppose. From the fifteenth century on the opening was widened. Reflection in the intervening period on the symbolic rationale for Alexander's decision would open the way to a wide papal discretion to dissolve (rather than annul) unconsummated marriages.

(d) Long-Term Developments

Holy orders

The symbolic rationale continued to work like a yeast within medieval marriage doctrine, producing practical consequences for which the thirteenth-century papacy clearly did not feel ready. Symbolism was a powerful and active intellectual ingredient, stimulating speculation by the Church's intellectuals. In the early fourteenth century the Dominican theologian John of Naples considered the question of whether holy orders dissolved an unconsummated marriage just as entering a religious order did, concluding that a future papal decision was needed to settle the problem. A decision by Pope John XXII did in fact follow: holy orders did not dissolve an unconsummated marriage unless the man also entered a religious order. The pope's decision marked the difference between the priesthood and the religious life, but perhaps left open the further question of whether a pope could change the law so that in future entry into the priesthood had the same effect as becoming a religious: we are on a borderland between doctrine and law here.[54] So this flurry of

---

[54] In the foregoing I have plagiarized my own discussion in D. L. d'Avray, 'Christendom: Medieval Christianity', in P. Byrne and L. Houlden (eds.), *Companion En-*

debate led to no practical difference. That would come later and in a somewhat different form, as will become apparent.

Contrasting cases from the thirteenth and seventeenth centuries

Between Alexander III's decision in the late twelfth century and the fifteenth century there is no new substantial change in practice as a consequence of symbolic reflection. Then, after this long time lag the speculation was translated into more social change. The process seems to have begun in the fifteenth century but gathered strength in the early modern period. The fifteenth-century changes will be discussed shortly, but a good sense of the trajectory and its direction can be obtained by confronting an early thirteenth-century case with one from the early seventeenth century. The contrast brings out more clearly than a detailed narrative the difference between the period from the late twelfth century to the early fifteenth, on the one hand, and the subsequent period (continuing to this day in Catholic marriage law) on the other.

The thirteenth-century case had come to Pope Innocent III because of its complexity and the unsolved legal problem it raised. Because it set a precedent, it was preserved in the Decretals of Gregory IX (X. 4. 15. 6), published in 1234. Innocent's letter itself was sent on 3 July 1206.[55] It was addressed to the bishop of Auxerre, as the ordinary responsible. The case turned on a woman who had been unable to consummate her marriage.

The rules for annulments on grounds of impotence were followed. Married women inspected her to determine whether she really was unable to consummate a marriage, and concluded that she was. The bishop annulled the marriage, and persuaded her to make a promise to enter a religious order. Whether she simply made a promise, or took a solemn vow and entered a religious order, seems to have been empirically unclear to Innocent, who would go on to give solutions for either case.

cyclopedia of Theology (London etc., 1995), 206–29 at 220. Dr Patrick Nold has in hand a study of the whole problem, on the basis of unpublished opinions by theologians consulted by the pope before his decision. He pointed out to me that the question related to deacons and subdeacons as well as priests. Examining the ideas of theologians consulted by John XXII, he has found interesting discussion of the putative unconsummated marriage—at Cana in Galilee—of John the Evangelist. That theme does not seem to play much part in the causal sequences studied in the present book.

[55] Friedberg, *Corpus iuris canonici*, ii. 706–7.

The husband apparently remarried, as he was entitled to do after the first marriage had been declared null and void. So far, so simple. Complications began when the woman encountered a man with whom she found she could have sexual intercourse. They got married (whether or not after they had slept together, the letter does not say). Her second man appears to have been the bearer of the letter to the pope, asking for the marriage to be regularized. It was not to happen. Innocent evidently felt that his hands were tied by the principle of indissolubility. He could not decide the case on sympathy, and drive a wedge through the whole principle of the unbreakability of marriage. He therefore gave a decision that would bear hard on the woman, who had apparently found happiness.[56]

Characteristically, Innocent's analysis was like a precision tool. The annulment had been based on an empirical conclusion subsequently falsified. The court had thought the woman was frigid, unable to have intercourse with a man, and that had been proved wrong. Consequently, the court's verdict had to be reversed. Ecclesiastical courts, even the papal court, were not deemed infallible in annulment cases, any more than we think our secular courts are infallible. The judges had to decide as best they could on the evidence. They did not have the power to *make* a marriage invalid, any more than a judge now has the power to make a man guilty of murder. They could only declare the proven truth as they saw it. If they were proved wrong afterwards, the judgment had to be reversed. That would reinstate the first marriage, with one proviso.

The proviso is the rule that entry into a religious order dissolves an unconsummated marriage. If the woman had really done that, Innocent reasons, then the first marriage was dissolved. This would not be an annulment, for it would have been a real valid marriage, and a null marriage is a marriage existing only in appearance, but still the marriage would cease to be one. On that assumption the first man was free to stay with his new wife. On the other hand, the woman would not be free to remarry because she would have taken a vow of perpetual chastity. So her second marriage would be invalid.

On the other hand, Innocent is far from sure whether the woman did more than promise to enter a religious order. He clearly thinks

---

[56] A small caveat here. One never knows exactly what lies behind such legal cases. It is conceivable that the woman and her second husband actually wanted that marriage declared null and the first reinstated. But it does not seem likely.

she may have stopped short of actually committing herself solemnly to that life. If she did not make such a commitment, the picture changes, and the first marriage is not after all dissolved. If the first marriage is reinstated, the original couple find that they are married after all. Both have to leave their current partner.

It was a hard decision for the parties, one must imagine. On the face of it, no one ended up with the desired partner. But we need to look at the situation from Innocent's point of view: he could not change his ethical principles because of a hard case, or let the hard case make a bad law. The rationality of the pope's decision can hardly be questioned, within the terms of his own ethical and religious system. The judgement of impotence had been mistaken, and even an unconsummated marriage could not be dissolved except by undertaking a solemn vow of chastity.

If we move fast forward four centuries we find a similar case treated differently: the principles of Innocent have not been jettisoned, in fact a style of reasoning dear to him has been at work, but the outcome has been to create more room for manœuvre. The case was decided by the 'Congregation of the Council', a body which was responsible for implementing the decrees of the Council of Trent and whose activity curiously parallels the stream of papal case law in the twelfth and thirteenth centuries. (The ideal-type which elucidates both phenomena is that reform legislation requires concrete clarification.) It is reported by the interesting seventeenth-century theologian and canon lawyer Jacob Pignatelli.[57]

The case concerned a Spanish couple, García de Vargas and Elizabeth de Lezano. They got married when he was 16 and she was 14, but she found herself unable to consummate the union. As with the thirteenth-century case from Auxerre, she was examined by matrons who confirmed that she was too 'narrow' for intercourse. The bishop seems not to have waited for the usual three years of cohabitation (to test whether the impotence was permanent) before judging the case. The marriage annulled, the man married another woman. Evidently she died, so he married again. Then that wife died, and so he married yet again; García seems to have

---

[57] J. Pignatelli, *Consultationes canonicae*, i (Venice, 1736), consultation 148, pp. 184–6 at 186. I was led to this important source by Joyce, *Christian Marriage*, 446 n. 2. On Pignatelli see H. Hurter, *Nomenclator literarius theologiae Catholicae theologos exhibens aetate, natione, disciplinis distinctos*, 3rd edn. (5 vols.; Innsbruck, 1903–13; repr. New York, n.d.), iv. *Aetas recens: Seculum secundum post celebratum Concilium Tridentinum. Ab anno 1664–1763* (1910), 264–5.

been unlucky with his marriages. By the time the case came to the Congregation of the Council, Elizabeth was 30. It seems that time had cured the problem of narrowness, and now she wanted to marry and have children.[58] The case is virtually the same as the previous one from the thirteenth century, except that no mention is made by Pignatelli of entry into a religious order. For Innocent III there would presumably have been only one answer: the annulment had been granted in error, the first marriage thus remained valid, and so García must give up his current wife and return to Elizabeth. Instead we get a different outcome. The local bishop is told to make sure that the whole story is correct. On that assumption, the congregation grants a dispensation to dissolve the marriage, provided that this is what both Elizabeth and García want.[59] A new kind of reasoning about non-consummation cases lies behind this outcome.[60] For Innocent III there were two straightforward questions: was the woman really unable to have sex, and had she taken a vow of perpetual chastity as a nun? In the early modern period the calculations become much more complicated. They come under Max Weber's much-misunderstood rubric *Zweckra-*

[58] 'Concinit alia declaratio in una Seguntina, in qua narrabatur, *quod alias fuerat contractum, matrimonium inter Garziam de Vargas in aetate sexdecim annorum, et Elisabetham de Lezano annorum quatuordecim, et quod mulier reperta est arcta, ita ut a matronis post inspectionem relatum fuerit eam ad hujusmodi matrimonium esse inhabilem. Unde Ordinarius non expectata triennali cohabitatione, matrimonium nullum declaravit, et viro licentiam dedit, ut aliam uxorem duceret, prout successive cum duabus aliis fecit, et prolem suscepit, et de praesenti cum secunda uxore vivit. Quoniam vero dictam Elizabeth annorum triginta, et grandior effecta nunc a viro cognosci potest, ut matronae, quae illam inspexere, referunt, cupiens esse mater supplicat pro dispensatione, ut matrimonium cum alio contrahere posset'* (Pignatelli, *Consultationes canonicae*, loc. cit.).
[59] 'Die 12. Septembris 1609. Sacra, etc. *censuit, hujusmodi dispensationem esse concedendam. Id est committendum Episcopo, ut si sibi constiterit Elisabetham hodie esse cognoscibilem, veraque esse caetera in supplicatione narrata, atque etiam tam ipsam quam Garziam, a quo post matrimonium per verba de praesenti contractum, tanquam arcta per sententiam diffinitivam separata fuit, concorditer supplicare, petitam dispensationem concedat'* (ibid.).
[60] E. Saurwein, *Der Ursprung des Rechtsinstituts der päpstlichen Dispens von der nicht vollzogenen Ehe: Eine interpretation der Dekretalen Alexanders III. und Urbans III.* (Analecta Gregoriana, 125, Series Facultatis Iuris Canonici, Sectio B, 43; Rome, 1980), argues that the principle that non-consummated marriages might be dissolved for reasons other than entry into a religious order was already embodied in the legislation of Alexander III. That view has much to be said for it, but it can take a long time before an implicit consequence is fully realized and translated into practice, and Innocent III certainly does not seem to have felt ready to do so.

tionalität: the weighing up of causes and effects, pros and cons, in a space left free, but yet usually (as here) defined and constrained by values.[61] Pignatelli gives us an imaginary illustration at the beginning of the same 'consultation'. A young couple who have barely reached sexual maturity get married. The husband's parents were not informed and are enraged on finding out. Great hostility between them and the wife's parents ensues, and the couple themselves become hostile towards each other. There is more. The man is unable to consummate the marriage, though they live together for five months and he tries hard to do it. Moreover, it turns out that he is subject to insane rages. This mental instability and the hatred that he has now conceived for his wife lead her to fear that he might kill her, and so she leaves him. There seems no hope of resolving the situation. The anger on all sides only increases. Can the marriage be dissolved?[62]

Note that the obvious solution, annulment on grounds of impotence, seems ruled out by the fear for the woman's physical safety. The medieval Church was quite happy with the idea of a legal separation, but it would condemn her to lifelong celibacy, for the couple had not cohabited long enough for his impotence to be proved in canon law.

Pignatelli concludes that dissolution of the marriage by papal

[61] 'Zweckrational handelt, wer sein Handeln nach Zweck, Mitteln und Nebenfolgen orientiert und dabei sowohl die Mittel gegen die Zwecke, wie die Zwecke gegen die Nebenfolgen, wie endlich auch die verschiedenen möglichen Zwecke gegeneinander rational abwägt . . . Absolute Zweckrationalität des Handelns ist aber . . . nur ein im wesentlichen konstruktiver Grenzfall' (M. Weber, *Wirtschaft und Gesellchaft: Grundriß der verstehenden Soziologie*, ed. J. Winckelmann, 5th rev. edn. (3 vols.; Tübingen, 1976), i. 13).

[62] 'Quidam juvenes optimates, vix pubertatem excedentes matrimonium per verba de praesenti contraxerunt, insciis viri parentibus, quorum indignatio tanta fuit, ut inter illos, et parentes uxoris, ac deinde inter ipsos conjuges odium immane, et crudele exortum fuerit, ac propterea magnus timor accesserit scandalorum, et infelicis exitus matrimonii absque spe remedii. Item vir spatio quinque mensium quibus cum conjuge post celebratum matrimonium cohabitavit, detectus fuit nedum impotens, eo quia matrimonium, quamvis studiose operam copulae dederit, consummare non potuit, verum etiam furiosus, et talia furoris habere intervalla, ut probabiliter dubitaretur, quod hujusmodi furore aliquando correptus, juncto odio penitus insito, eandem uxorem esset occisurus, quam ob causam se separarunt. Furor autem viri, et odium diuturnum tam inter ipsos conjuges, quam inter eorum parentes, et consanguineos nequit vel precibus mitigari, vel tempore, communique utilitate deponi, vel vetustate sedari: quinimmo in dies magis magisque discordia ira acerbior, intimo odio, et corde obstinato concepta exardescit. Quapropter consensu omnium exposcitur ejusdem matrimonii dissolutio' (Pignatelli, *Consultationes canonicae*, consultation 148, p. 184).

dispensation is justified in view of the serious circumstances he has outlined.[63] His reasoning is of the sort that modern secular divorce court judges might use. On the one hand, to dissolve a marriage is a grave thing, not to be done without powerful reasons; but on the other hand, the reasons are weighty, for the marriage has irretrievably broken down, and is the source of great animosity. For a consummated marriage such reasoning would be inconceivable in this tradition.

The reasons are set out why consequences can be weighed with unconsummated marriages while pure principle rules the law on consummated marriages. God gave a dispensing power to his vicar in matters which are inferred remotely rather than proximately from the principles of natural law and which contain an element of human rather than divine regulation; at least where ratified (non-consummated) marriages are concerned, the power is a way of putting an end to scandals and strengthening peace in the state; after all, the signification of marriage is incomplete before consummation; before that it merely stands for the union of God and the soul through charity, but afterwards, Christ's union with the Church; the Lord's saying (Matt. 19: 6) that 'What God has joined together, let no one put asunder' comes *after* the words 'and they will be two in one flesh'; again, St Paul's reference in Ephesians 5 to 'the great sacrament' comes *after* the words 'they will be two in one flesh'; then Pignatelli quotes the passage of Leo the Great which was analysed in the first half of this chapter, naturally in the form which made the commingling of the sexes a sort of *sine qua non* of marriage's proper representation of Christ and the Church.[64] It is

---

[63] Ibid., *passim*, esp. pp. 185–6.

[64] I am paraphrasing the following passage: 'Quod attinet ad potestatem Pontificis dispensandi non est dubitandum ex communi Canonistarum sententia, qui omnes, uno vel altero discrepante, docent, posse Summum Pontificem potestate quidem ordinaria matrimonium ratum ex causa dirimere. Quia Pontifex potest divina authoritate dispensare in aliquibus, quae non deducuntur proxime ex principiis juris naturae, sed remote, et quae habent admixtum aliquid obligationis humanae. Credibileque omnino est, Deum suo Vicario hanc potestatem contulisse, quae regimini Ecclesiae necessaria erat. Nam hac ratione, saltem in matrimoniiis ratis, multa scandala cessant, pax in Republica stabilitur, sine qua matrimonium est pactio servitutis. Quandoquidem matrimonii Sacramentum, quoad significationem non est completum usque ad carnalem copulam inclusive; ita quod matrimonium contractum sive ratum significet conjunctionem Dei ad animam per charitatem, consummatum vero conjunctionem Christi ad Ecclesiam. Prima autem conjunctio est solubilis, non secunda; ideoque matrimonium ratum solvi potest, non vero consummatum. Unde Dominus, Matth. 19. non dixit: *Quos Deus* [p. 185] *conjunxit homo non separet*, nisi

consummation with its attendant symbolism that takes indissolubility from the realm of calculated consequences into the realm of
unshakeable principle.

The fifteenth century: from theory to practice

We have noted several milestones in the history of consummation:
prelates judging cases where theological theory intersected with
concrete social practice and developed in consequence. Hincmar of
Reims was one such milestone and Alexander III another. Somewhere in the four hundred years between the two cases narrated
at the start of this section there must have been another milestone.
Quite probably it was Martin V (1417–31), the first pope after the
Great Schism. George Joyce noted long ago a claim by St Antoninus of Florence to have seen bulls by Martin V and Eugenius IV
which actually exercised the power to dissolve unconsummated
marriages.[65] Much more recently direct evidence of real cases from
Martin V's pontificate was brought to light by K. A. Fink.[66] The
second of the two cases he printed may not have been successful
(ibid. 436), and the third could have been reformulated as a case
for annulment on grounds of defective consent,[67] but the first and
earliest case is a perfect example, and everything suggests that it
would have gone through if the facts stated were borne out by the
investigation that the pope entrusted to the bishop of Augsburg.[68]
   The events to be investigated took place in Munich, or at least
that was the home town of the protagonists, Stefan Puetrich and
Ursula, daughter of Heinrich Part. According to the documents,
the story is as follows. The couple were from important families,

post illa verba: *et erunt duo in carne una.* Et Apostolus *ad Ephes.* 5 non dixit hoc
Sacramentum magnum in Christo, et Ecclesia, nisi post illa verba *Et erunt duo in
carne una.* Et ideo Leo Pontifex, inquit, ut referunt Magister *in 2 d.* 1 et Gratian. 27
q. 1 *Societas nuptialis ita est a principio instituta, ut praeter commixtionem sexuum non
habeat Christi, et Ecclesiae Sacramentum.* Textus est *in cap. Ex publico,* ubi Gloss. *v.
Consummatum de convers. conjug.*' (ibid., pp. 184–5).

[65] Joyce, *Christian Marriage,* 434. Joyce's treatment of the whole matter, in his
ch. 10, is as usual remarkably well informed.
[66] K. A. Fink, 'Frühe urkundliche Belege für die Auflösung des matrimonium
ratum consumatum durch päpstliche Dispensation', *Zeitschrift der Savigny-Stiftung
für Rechtsgeschichte,* 77 [*Zeitschrift für Rechtsgeschichte,* 90], kanonistische Abteilung, 46 (1960), 434–42.
[67] 'licet ad iussum matris sue purum emisit consensum, ipsa tamen corde et animo
semper dissensit' (ibid. 441).
[68] Fink prints all the documents he found bearing on the case, ibid. 437–9.

since the three dukes of Bavaria would intervene with the pope to try to obtain a resolution after the marriage had gone sour, emphasizing the power of the two families involved and the danger to peace resulting from the break-up. The couple had got married by present consent but had not immediately started living and sleeping together. (As we have seen, there was nothing abnormal about this.) Before that could happen, Stefan had a nasty shock: it turned out that Ursula was very pregnant. He knew he could not be the father. In fact she gave birth to a child only about five weeks after the marriage. How he had failed to notice her condition is not explained. Perhaps she dressed carefully and perhaps he assumed she had a full figure. When the truth came out he was apparently enraged, and refused to proceed to solemnize the marriage. (This presumably means that the church service had been held over after the exchange of present consent, fitting a pattern of marriage–delay–church service–consummation.) He would not accept her as his bedfellow (*conthoralem*). Relations between the two powerful families became so bad that deaths and injuries were feared. It is the kind of story that historians are tempted to tell with a smile on their lips, but the humiliation and anger cannot have been amusing for anyone involved.

Could the pope provide a solution? There was no case for an annulment here: undisclosed pregnancy was not among the grounds deemed sufficient to vitiate consent. The pope's preferred solution was for Stefan or Ursula or both to enter a religious order, thus dissolving the marriage in the by now time-honoured way. He realized, however, that this might not be acceptable to either of them. He was therefore prepared to dissolve the marriage on his own authority, once he was assured that both parties wanted that.

The symbolic rationale: William of Pagula

The symbolic rationale for this remarkable power may by this time have become a commonplace in theory. In the extract printed here as Document **4. 5,** from the fourteenth-century priests' manual by William of Pagula, a work in a pastoral genre drawing on both theology and canon law,[69] we find a cautious intermediate position, before stating the by now familiar symbolic reasons: 'A marriage

---

[69] See the classic unpublished thesis by L. E. Boyle, 'A Study of the Works Attributed to William of Pagula: With Special Reference to the *Oculus sacerdotis* and *Summa summarum*' (D.Phil. thesis, Oxford University, 1956).

can be dissolved before the consummation of the marriage, *say* by entering a religious order' (emphasis added). The single word 'say' (*puta*) has large implications. It indicates that entry into a religious order may not be the only reason for dissolving an unconsummated marriage. It is probably significant that William of Pagula was a trained canon lawyer. The influence of canon lawyers was surely central in the development we have analysed, for by and large canonists admitted the theory behind Martin V's decision long before his pontificate, whereas the weight of theological opinion seems to have been rather against it.[70] This might seem like a stereotyped clash between pragmatic lawyers and idealistic theologians, but in fact the canon-law reasoning is highly theological, and furthermore symbolically theological. The analysis of the views about 'bigamy' of Hostiensis should have prepared us for this. He is perhaps the best person to analyse in this connection too, for his influence and reputation were enormous—he even gets a mention in Dante's *Paradiso* (12. 82–97).[71] His opinion would have carried great weight with subsequent canon lawyers and popes.

The symbolic rationale in detail: Hostiensis

A remarkable passage is printed below as Document **4. 1**.[72] It follows a long and complex discussion in which symbolism also figures largely, but to follow its twists and turns would be a distraction from the central points stated in the passage selected. This passage has its twists and turns too: sometimes the canonist narrows the focus to dissolution by entry into an order, at other moments he is thinking about the general power to dissolve, but really he seems to have both in mind. Hostiensis concludes, towards the end of the analysis, that the pope has the power to dissolve unconsummated marriages provided that the partners consent. The implication is that he can do this with his 'unbounded' (*absoluta*) power even without a special reason. However, the rule that a marriage can be dissolved before consummation by one partner's entry into a religious order is a much more normal thing, coming within the pope's bounded (*ordinata*) power. Hostiensis assimilates this to the papacy's power to

---

[70] Joyce, *Christian Marriage*, 431–6 (noting important exceptions in each camp).
[71] Pointed out by J. A. Brundage, *Medieval Canon Law* (London etc., 1995), 214.
[72] For Hostiensis's discussion of the issue in his other synthesis, the *Summa aurea*, see Joyce, *Christian Marriage*, 432–3.

tighten or relax impediments to marriage, saying that a particular cardinal whom he names had convinced him of this. Keeping the focus for the moment on the rule about entry into a religious order, he argues that the unconsummated marriage symbolizes only the marriage of God and soul through charity. (At this point he makes explicit his debt to Innocent III's decretal *Debitum* (X. 1. 21. 5), which keeps turning up in the history of marriage symbolism as a social force.) The union of God and soul is not diminished but enhanced by entry into a religious order, he argues. This he links with another thought: the Virgin Mary was able to be Joseph's spouse and at the same time truly married to God. The implication is that this was possible because the marriage of Mary and Joseph was unconsummated. The parallel lines between symbol and symbolized seem to come together in these points about virginity and marriage to God. Probably he is breaking some basic rule of symbolic discourse, but in any case his train of thought moves off again to the power of the Church to dissolve unconsummated marriages not only because of entry into a religious order, but for any just cause. Is this against Scripture—'What God has joined together let no man put asunder'? No, because that commandment refers to consummated marriages. Where a marriage is not consummated, we (here he is speaking as if with the pope's voice) can decree what we like about it. In practice the pope should use his bounded rather than his unbounded power and only dissolve such marriages for a good reason: laxity is not what Hostiensis wants. He is envisaging the weighing of consequences or arguments: to outweigh the great undesirability of ending a marriage, there should be proportionately strong reasons. If, however, the marriage has been consummated, the situation is transformed because it symbolizes something that cannot be broken. To suggest that a consummated marriage could be dissolved by entry into a religious order is like suggesting that another faith or Church might replace the one Christ married, and this suggestion would be heretical.

It is a strong statement: divorce and remarriage after consummation would be like Christ discarding the Church and replacing it with a new one. Throughout the passage symbolism is decisive. Is this just a rhetorical ornament? Far from it: Hostiensis seems to take it with extreme seriousness. Without the symbolic rationale, the law could have been left with a fossilized rule: entering a religious order ends an unconsummated marriage. With the symbolic argument, the intellectual situation was still fluid, leaving open the possibility of a further crystallization of practical law in the fifteenth century. Marriage symbolism in Hostiensis and the tradition he represents is not a discourse of mysticism or a literary trope, and it goes far beyond the allegorical interpretation of Scripture that we find everywhere in medieval and patristic writings. As has been argued throughout, it is a force capable ultimately of shaping social practice, as we have seen it was in the case of indissolubility and 'bigamy'.

Conclusion

Synopsis

Behind all the detail, this book has developed some simple and straightforward ideas which can be summarized in a small space as a series of propositions. Marriage symbolism is common in many religions. There are some close parallels between medieval marriage symbolism and the marriage/love symbolism of Hinduism in particular, but the parallels are still closer with the ancient Hebrew idea of the people of Israel as spouse of God, an idea which was of course a lineal ancestor of Christian marriage symbolism.

Marriage symbolism was not preached to a mass public in the early Middle Ages. Preaching became a system of mass communication in the age of the friars and marriage symbolism was highly developed in a genre of preaching from the thirteenth century onwards. Only then did preaching about marriage symbolism reach a huge public and become a social force in the same kind of way that radio is today (that is, not so powerful as television, but still a mass medium to be reckoned with). In marriage preaching the symbolism rested securely on a literal-sense idea of marriage as good and holy.

Augustine of Hippo developed remarks from the New Testament into a strongly stated theology of marriage symbolism, deriving indissolubility from the analogy between human marriage and the union of Christ and the Church. A wide gulf separated this theory from social practice for centuries, but by the end of the Middle Ages it had turned into a social force underpinning the unbreakability of the marriage bond.

Marriage symbolism conditioned the rules about who could become a priest. It changed the meaning of wedding ritual from within. In the thirteenth century it helped reclassify a class of minor clerics as laymen.

Consummation was central to the idea of marriage in the later medieval centuries. Symbolic reasoning going back to Hincmar of Reims lay behind Pope Alexander III's judgement that a non-consummated marriage could be dissolved by the entry of one partner into a religious order. This decision had a social impact. Symbolic reflection continued in its wake, eventually enabling popes to dissolve unconsummated marriages in the light of instrumental calculation.

Disclaimers

There have been so many studies of medieval marriage in recent years that in this book it has been possible to develop an argument and present fresh data without writing a general history of the subject to provide context and balance. The general books that are available complement each other well, so the danger of imbalance is diminished. Ideally, this book would be read after or together with Brooke's *Medieval Idea of Marriage*, which looks at the subject from many angles, without concentrating on one single thesis. The present study is, however, monographic, not monocausal. I am not saying that symbolism is all that mattered in the social history of medieval marriage, far from it. Symbolism deserves a central place in medieval marriage's social history, not the central place (if such exists). I have merely tried to show how powerful symbolism was even outside the areas studied by historians of religious thought.

The main vehicles of symbolism's power in the world, the world outside texts, were preaching and law, both of which affected all social classes and both genders (even the law being gender-symmetrical to a greater degree than with the other great systems of sacred law). Nevertheless, it seems likely that different classes and genders were affected in different ways. Again, one would expect urbanization to affect the overall picture. The evidence I have found is, however, too patchy to pursue these lines of investigation systematically. I hope someone in the future may do better.

So far as gender is concerned, this study has not contributed much to the recent but already distinguished tradition of analysing symbolism in gender terms. There are reasons. The Church as bride of Christ is composed of men as well as women. The soul as bride of Christ is the soul of a man as much as the soul of a woman. The bride can stand for Christ and the bridegroom for the Church.[1] This in itself diminishes the impact of the symbolism on real gender relations. Furthermore, the point of the symbolism ana-

---

[1] The analogy between Christ and the Church could be taken both ways: Christ

lysed throughout this book is not about gender specificity so much as unity and indissolubility. Some of the texts used in this study could certainly bear a little more gender analysis in the context of a different investigation, but it might be somewhat peripheral to their principal significance.

Narrative

It is an interesting exercise to rerun in précis form the preceding (primarily) analytical and social history as a narrative, including the 'great men'. An obvious starting point would be Augustine of Hippo, *c*.400. With clarity and force he linked marriage symbolism and indissolubility. He also set out lucidly the principles behind the rules about 'bigamy' in its technical sense.

Next would come Hincmar, in the mid-ninth century. He put consummation in the foreground as crucial to the meaning of marriage. He anticipated later developments and had an influence on them. Like so much about the Carolingians and their 'renaissance', future transformations are adumbrated without being actualized, except transitorily.

Then come Peter Lombard and Gratian in the mid-twelfth century. They helped put the ideas of Augustine and Hincmar before the élite who ran the western Church. After the Lombard's *Sentences* had become a standard textbook, every serious theology student would be likely to come across Augustine's ideas about symbolism and the nature of Christian marriage. The symbolic reasons for thinking consummation changed the meaning of marriage were inescapably available in Gratian's *Decretum*. He made Hincmar's line of thought widely accessible, and almost certainly

---

as the man or Christ as the woman: '*vidue*, id est, corrupte, quia licet fuisset vidua, dummodo non corrupta, non prohibetur . . . Sed quare exigitur maior castitas in uxore quam in viro, quia maritus corrupte, si cum ea una caro efficiatur promoveri non potest . . . Sed ille qui habuit concubinam post [potest *ms.*] uxorem vel ante promoveri potest, ut xxxiiii. [xxiiii *ms.*] Di. *Fraternitatis*. H. [=Huguccio?] dixit quod vir sig*nifi*cat ecclesiam, que in parte recessit a Christo adulterando recedendo a fide, etsi in parte virgo fuerit, et ideo non deest significatio sacramenti in viro quamvis non sit virgo. Uxor *vero sig*nifi*cat Christum, qui numquam ecclesiam dimisit, . . . Alii dicunt, et videtur melius, quod vir sig*nifi*cat Christum qui primo copulavit sibi sinagogam et postea ecclesiam, scilicet de gentibus, *militantem, in qua sunt boni et mali, et ideo non nocet si vir non fuerit virgo; uxor vero sig*nifi*cat ecclesiam triumphantem in qua non est macula' (Bernard of Parma, *glossa ordinaria* to Decretals, at X. 1. 21. 5, *Debitum*, in MS BL Royal 9. C. I, fo. 35rb, right-hand lower margin).

influenced Alexander III's decision about consummation and entry into a religious order.

Thus Alexander III (d. 1181) has a place in the 'great men' narrative. His authoritative decisions fixed the principle that consent makes a marriage, but that on the other hand only a consummated marriage between a baptized couple is indissoluble. This synthesis would be explained in coherent and rational symbolic terms by scholastic theologians.

Innocent III in the early thirteenth century has a pre-eminent position in the narrative. His thinking on marriage was demonstrably entwined with symbolic reasoning, which he translated into practice by enforcing indissolubility in the face of very powerful men who were his allies, and by changing canon law to close the largest loophole for annulments.

Innocent also approved the Franciscan and Dominican orders, whose preachers would popularize marriage symbolism, especially the 'initiation–ratification–consummation' schema. They will also have helped to imprint marriage symbolism on public opinion, helped by its convergence with social practices formed by a law influenced by the same symbolism.

Innocent III's new rules about evidence in annulment cases were not properly observed at first, and were quite probably never universally enforced. The canonist Hostiensis (d. 1271) not only remarked on this but made an impassioned plea to judges to take the rules with the utmost seriousness. Since he was widely studied and famous—he even has his place in Dante's *Divine Comedy*—he is not only a witness but in all probability an influence on thought and practice, so he too earns a place in the narrative. He adopted such a hard line about the rules of proof in annulment cases that we must take his strictures with a pinch of salt. The remarkable thing is how seriously indissolubility was enforced. Symbolism lay behind the seriousness.

Hostiensis's canonist contemporary Innocent IV reflected on the symbolic rationale of rules about marrying virgins (once only) and the path to the priesthood. He also reflected on which married clerics in minor orders should keep their status, and decided that the 'bigamous' should not. He represented a strong current of thirteenth-century church law opinion, and in 1274 a large number of legitimately married clerics in minor orders were deprived of their status because they were, in the technical sense, bigamous.

In the fourteenth century, if not earlier, the meaning of the marriage ceremony was changed, at least in England, to foreground symbolic reasons for changing the ritual of second marriages (details and definitions varying). Paradoxically, this tended to assimilate the ritual to that of first marriages, by pinpointing a specific symbolic clause that could be excised while the rest was retained.

In the fifteenth century, under Pope Martin V, we see the beginnings of a trend to enlarge the range of reasons for dissolving an unconsummated marriage (it should be stressed that the issue here is not impotence). This trend continued into the early modern period and afterwards. Symbolism provided the rationale.

In the sixteenth century popes began to grant dispensations for 'bigamous' clerics in minor orders to retain their clerical status in circumstances where a bishop was likely to refuse. The papal Penitentiary register entries that reveal this also hint at the wide range of privileges clerical status might entail, and which many would have lost because of bigamy symbolism.

All these curious details are symptoms of something bigger: a strong conviction that the analogy between marriage and Christ's union with the Church was far more than a figure of speech.

Explanations in a nutshell

How to explain the influence of marriage symbolism and its timing? The symbolic rationale had roots deep in the Christian past, so the delayed reaction is interesting.

In the case of preaching, the explanation is simply that there probably was relatively little marriage preaching, symbolic or otherwise, until the central Middle Ages.

In the case of indissolubility, popes were seldom in a position to enforce their strong line on a powerful laity. Acceptance of exclusive Church jurisdiction in marriage cases was practically a *sine qua non*. So was a religious leadership strong enough to stand up to kings and great nobles.

Why were they so ready to do so? A plausible if undemonstrable explanation has to do with the discipline of clerical celibacy. It had been in place in theory for centuries. However, from the late twelfth century the leadership of the Church systematically tried to impose celibacy on the clergy from the level of subdeacon upwards. By the end of the twelfth century a *de facto* wife or public mistress would have been an obstacle to high church office. A celibate clergy is likely to take a less tolerant attitude to sexual weakness by married males than a clergy in the same position as laymen. Brahmins, rabbis, muftis were married men and at some level must have sympathized with the predicament of other men who wanted to change wives for one reason or another. Celibate popes and bishops were more likely to feel that if they were doing without any women at all, laymen could make do with one. This explanation is an ideal-type. In so far as clerics lapsed from their ideal, the reasoning sketched out does not apply. Still, to say that clerical celibacy meant no more in the early thirteenth century than the early eleventh would be an extreme position. So the rise of celibacy would have given impetus to the force of marriage symbolism. One cannot footnote it but to many it will seem common sense.

In the case of 'bigamy', the sheer appeal of marriage symbolism to legal minds like Innocent III and Hostiensis seems to have been a considerable factor, paradoxical though it may seem. Alongside this, one may set harmonious relations obtaining between popes and English and French kings for much of the thirteenth century. The monarchs wanted 'bigamous' clerics out of the ecclesiastical courts, and churchmen could oblige because they were operating in a co-operative mode. That was not the whole story, however. Kings had learnt to use the language of 'bigamy' to put popes in the right frame of mind to make concessions, and churchmen could see the new rule about bigamous clerics in minor orders as a logical consequence of the rationale of marriage symbolism.

With consummation, the role of canon law as troubleshooter for theology is crucial. The position of consummation in marriage had been uncertain for centuries. Sooner or later concrete cases would turn on the theological questions. With the papacy operating at an increasing tempo as supreme court for problematic cases, it is not surprising that the question should be settled. If it was to be settled, the logic of marriage symbolism would provide the rationale. After it had been settled, the symbolic rationale was not forgotten.

Causal reciprocity of substructure and superstructure

Mary Douglas has written that 'without the relevant supporting classifications and values the material aspects of an organization would not be viable, and, vice versa, without the appropriate organization, the cultural values would make no sense. Culture and society are one as mind and brain.'[2]

Mary Douglas's model probably works for many societies. Even so, the interplay of marriage symbolism and practice in the late medieval West is not just another case of a common human pattern. The symbolism has priority in initiating the system of reciprocal forces: it sets the whole thing going. That is not so easy to find in other civilizations (scholarly readers are urged to try: I shall be glad if they succeed). Symbolic reasoning about marriage had to overcome tendencies which are strong in most societies: the desire of many men and women (especially men) to change spouses or have more than one. The defeat of these tendencies at the institutional level was a deep cut against the social grain. Only then, after symbolism had cut society into a new shape, did social structure serve the symbolism, strengthening the force that had made it what it was. Perhaps the more usual human pattern is for the structure of the symbolism to mould itself to the structure of society, though with most societies studied by twentieth-century social anthropologists there was a dearth of historical data about the development of the system studied. At any rate, in the medieval West the causal influence flowed in the opposite direction, symbolism moulding social structure.

For once the historian has the advantage over anthropologists. It is possible to reconstruct the genesis of this system of mutual causality. It turns out that intellectuals played a crucial part in the process. The reciprocal cycle is started by ideas which had remained in a rarefied world until turned into practice by serious energetic men who took them seriously. Once they had done so, the flow of causation began to go both ways. Symbolism starts the process but eventually the process becomes reciprocal.

In the Middle Ages, then, it was on the whole the marriage symbolism that came first, and gradually moulded law and thus society in its image. However, that made a difference to the symbolism.

[2] M. Douglas, *A Feeling for Hierarchy* (Dayton, Oh., 2002), 27. Mary Douglas is very good on this this kind of interplay: to quote her slightly out of context, the work of anthropologists, 'especially the French', shows 'how the categories of the world are established by being embedded in daily practice. This is a marvellously dynamic and interactive view of the relation of knowledge to behaviour: the analogies from practice justify the knowledge and the knowledge justifies the action' (M. Douglas, 'Raisonnements circulaires: retour nostalgique à Lévy-Bruhl', *Gradhiva*, 30–1 (2001–2), 1–14 at 8 (this 'translation' is in fact Douglas's original English version, which she kindly showed me).

Always a strong image, the union of man and woman, it came to be rooted also in social practice, which made it concrete in a different way. When ideas are embodied in social practice, they take on a new force, even if they helped to create the social practice in the first place.

Documents

The first digit of each document's number identifies the chapter whose arguments it illustrates.

Documents Relating to Chapter 1: Mass Communication

1. 1. Marriage symbolism in the Bavarian Homiliary

This is one of the few examples found of a homily addressed apparently to an ultimate lay audience containing marriage symbolism. It comes from a collection of Bavarian origin, composed in the ninth century probably for the churches of Salzburg and Augsburg, and relatively widely diffused as homily collections of this period go.[1]

MS Munich, Bayerische Staatsbibliothek, Clm. 3833[2]

Parchment manuscript, 192 folios, 'in fol.', two columns (unlike the other sermon from the same manuscript, printed below as Document **1. 2**), date *c.*1000 (the Staatsbibliothek catalogue dates it to the tenth century, Barré to the first half of the eleventh). The use of '&' to mean 'et' within a word, the 'ae' as well as the 'e caudata', and the 'cc' type 'a', as in 'la&tificccr&', p. 43, line 7, together with the absence of spacing between some words, favour the earlier date, though these indications are not decisive. According to the catalogue, the homiliary is preceded by 'capitula sermonum'.

Note. The 'e caudata' is here represented thus: '**ae**'.

Pp. 57 col. a–59 col. a:

Omelia. Lectionis eiusdem

1. In lectione quae nobis recitata est, fratres karissimi, audivimus Dominum dicentem (Mt. 25: 1): '*Simile est regnum caelorum decem virginibus quae accipientes lampades suas, exierunt obviam sponso et

---

[1] All this from H. Barré, *Les Homéliaires carolingiens de l'école d'Auxerre: authenticité — inventaire — tableaux comparatifs — initia* (Studi e testi, 225; Vatican City, 1962), 26.

[2] Description based on C. F. Halm *et al.. Catalogus codicum Latinorum Bibliothecae Regiae Monacensis (secundum Andreae Schmelleri indices)*, 2nd rev. edn. (2 vols.; Munich, 1892–4), i/2, *Codices num. 2501–5250 complectens* (1894), 143; on Barré, *Les Homéliaires carolingiens*, 26; and on microfilm printout of the homily.

sponsae'. Haec ³si secundum litteram tantum intellegimus nimirum durum videtur et asperum. Absit hoc a sensibus christianis ut tam parvus numerus veniat ad vitam aeternam. Et ideo quia nulla ratione secundum litteram intellegi debet, quia et revera ipse Dominus similitudinem esse dixit, requiramus quare quinque dictae sunt fatuae aut quinque prudentes. Illae enim quinque prudentes significant omnes sanctos qui cum Christo sunt regnaturi.

2. E contrario, illae quinque fatuae figuram habere videntur christianorum malorum qui sine operibus bonis de solo tantum christiano nomine gloriantur. Ideo autem et ille fatuae quinque et ille prudentes quinque dicuntur, quia quinque sensus in omnibus hominibus esse probantur, visus videlicet, [*p. 57 col. b*] auditus, gustus, odoratus, et tactus, et quia per istos sensus, velut per quasdam ianuas vel fenestras, aut vita aut mors ingreditur ad animas nostras. De quibus et propheta dicit (Jerem. 9: 21): Intravit 'mors per fenestras nostras'. Ideo et ibi quinque virgines dicuntur prudentes quae istis sensibus bene utuntur, et ibi quinque fatuae quae per istos quinque sensus magis mortem quam vitam excipiunt.

3. Quomodo autem isti quinque sensus, velut quinque virgines, aut virginitatem custodiant, aut corruptioni subiaceant, diligentius requira-

…t filiam alienam, servum
…er aspexerit, corrupta est
…rporis in secretum cordis
…e ⁴religiosus clericus sive
…tiosos et cantica luxuriosa
…n delectatione placido au-
. *58 col. a*] . . . Et revera,
…ie si in corpore virginitas
…cordis integritas violatur?
…em, et in omnibus sensi-
…s quae 'agnum ⁶secuntur'
…ium, quia solam virgini-

tatem corporis servaverunt: denique, cum dixisset (Apoc. 14: 4): 'Hi [*p. 58 col. b*] sunt qui cum mulieribus non coinquinaverunt ⁷se', adiunxit (Apoc. 14: 5): 'Et non ⁸est inventum in ore eorum mendacium: sine macula sunt.' Qui ergo de sola castitate corporis gloriatur, diligenter *attendat quia si mendacium diligit, cum illis sanctis virginibus

---

³ si] *interlined*
⁴ religiosus clericus] *possibly corrected by subsequent punctuation to* religiosus, clericus, *which would change the meaning from* 'whether a religious cleric or a layman' *to* 'whether a religious, a cleric, or a layman'
⁵ vel] velut *ms., but probably corrected*
⁶ secuntur] *physical lacuna follows in ms.*
⁷ se] *physical lacuna follows in ms.*
⁸ est] *added as correction?*

Christum sequi non poterit. Nulla ergo virgo de sola corporis virginitate presumat, quia si inoboediens fuerit, aut linguosa, ab illo thalamo sponsi caelestis se noverit excludendam.

4. Cum ergo virgo centesimum gradum teneat, et mulier coniugata tricesimum,[9] melior tamen est mulier casta quam virgo superba. Illa enim casta mulier, marito serviens, tricesimum possidet gradum: virgini superbae nec unus gradus remanebit. Adimpletur in illa quod ait psalmista (Ps. 17: 28): 'Tu populum humilem salvum facies, et oculos superborum humiliabis'. Et quia totam ecclesiam catholicam beatus Apostolus virginem vocat, non solas in ea considerans corpore virgines, sed [10]incorruptas omnium desiderans mentes, ita dicens (2 Cor. 11: 2): '[11]Aptavi vos uni viro virginem castam exhibere Christo', non solum [12]sanctarum monialium, sed etiam omnium virorum vel mulierum [13]animae, si [14]cum castitate corporis in illis supradictis quinque sensibus virginitatem servare voluerint, sponsas Christi se esse non dubitent. Non enim corporum [*p. 59 col. a*] sed animarum sponsus intellegendus est Christus. Et ideo, fratres karissimi, tam viri quam feminae, tam pueri quam puelle, si virginitatem usque ad nuptias servant, et per istos quinque sensus, id est, visus, auditus, gustus, odoratus, vel tactus, dum eis bene utuntur, suas animas non corrumpunt, in die iudicii, apertis [15]ianuis, ad eternum sponsi thalamum feliciter merebuntur intrare. Illi vero qui et corpora sua ante nuptias adulterina coniunctione corrumpunt, et postea per totam vitam suam male vivendo, male audiendo, male loquendo, animas suas vulnerare non desinunt, si eis fructuosa et digna paenitentia non subvenerit, clausis ianuis sine causa clamabunt: 'Domine, Domine, aperi nobis' (Mt. 25: 11; cf. Luke 13: 25).—'Amen, dico vobis, nescio vos, unde sitis' (Mt. 25: 12; Luke 13: 25).

5. Haec ergo, fratres karissimi, [16]si fideliter et diligenter adtendimus et cum [17]castitate corporis etiam integritatem cordis auxiliante Domino custodiamus, non cum fatuis proiciemur 'in tenebras exteriores. Ibi erit fletus et stridor dentium' (Mt. 8 12; 22: 13; 25: 30):—sed cum sapientibus ad spiritales nuptias intromissi audire merebimur: 'Euge, serve bone et fidelis, intra in gaudium domini tui' (Mt. 25: 21 and 23).

---

[9] Cf. Mark 4: 20.
[10] incorruptas] incorruptas esse *understood?*
[11] Aptavi] Despondi *in Vulgate*
[12] sanctarum] *after correction*
[13] animae] *guessed from sense—in ms. corrected and hard to read*
[14] cum castitate] castitatem *ms.*
[15] ianuis] ianuus *ms.*
[16] si] *added in margin*
[17] castitate] *corr. from* castate

1. 2. Homily on the text 'Nuptiae factae sunt' (John 2: 1) in the Bavarian Homiliary

See Document 1. 1. This text from the same manuscript illustrates the same points.

MS Munich, Bayerische Staatsbibliothek, Clm. 3833
For description see Document 1.1. Note that this sermon, unlike the previous text, is in one column.

Pp. 43–46:

In illo tempore nuptiae factae sunt in Chana Galileae, et erat mater Iesu ibi et reliq.[1]

OMELIA LECTIONIS EIUSDEM

1. Quod Dominus atque salvator noster ad nuptias vocatus non solum venire[2] sed et miraculum ibidem quo convivas laetificaret facere dignatus est, audivit in presenti lectione dilectio vestra. 'Nuptiae', inquit, 'factae sunt in Chana Galileae et erat mater Iesu ibi. Vocatus est autem Iesus et discipuli eius ad nuptias.' Magna quidem humilitas est Domini nostri quod ad humanas nuptias venire dignatus est. Sed tamen magnum ibidem gessit mysterium.

2. Venit igitur ad nuptias carnali more caelebratas in terra Dominus et salvator noster qui, ad copulandam sibi spiritali amore ecclesiam, de caelo descendit ad terras. Cuius quidem thalamus incorruptae virginis uterus fuit, in quo deus humanae naturae coniunctus, et ex quo ad sociandam sibi fidelium ecclesiam natus processit. Vocatus est autem ad has nuptias semper ab initio mundi per sanctos viros et iustos, qui eum tota intentione deprecati sunt ut humani generis redemptionem, quam promisit, impleret.

3. 'Et deficiente vino, dixit mater Iesu ad eum: "Vinum non habent"' (John 2: 4). Veniente autem Domino ad has nuptias in hunc mundum, multas pro fidelibus suis iniurias et tribulationes sustinens, [3][e]os ab aeterna morte redemit, et ad regnum caeleste perduxit, cum deficiebat vinum veteris observantiae legis ut vinum nobis gratiae spiritalis largiretur, per quam omnia secreta legis a nobis spiritaliter intellegerentur, et per miracula sua, quae operatus est latenter in homine, divinitatis suae potentiam demonstraret, et credentium in eum fides aucta proficeret.

4. Sed audiamus quod sequitur. 'Dicit ei Iesus: "Quid mihi et tibi est, mulier? Nondum venit hora mea"'. Neque enim matrem suam inhono-

---

[1] *Above the line, in small script:* 'Vocatus est autem Iesus et discipuli eius cum eo ad' (*the remainder has probably been cut off by the binder*)
[2] venire] xv *added in margin* (*later script?*)
[3] [e]os] *lacuna in ms., filled from the sense*

ravit, qui nos iubet honorare patrem et matrem, nec eam sibi matrem
negavit esse, ex cuius virginitate carnem suscipere non dispexit. Sed
'Quid mihi et tibi est, mulier? Nondum venit hora mea' ita intellegen-
dum est, ac si diceret: 'Quid divinitati quam ex patre semper habui,
cum tua carne commune est ex qua carnem suscepi? [*p. 44*] quia divini-
tatem meam quae *facit miraculum non tu genuisti, sed infirmitatem
meam peperisti. Nondum venit hora passionis meae, in qua pro salute
mundi mori disposui. Sed ante sunt fideles elegendi, ante sanitatum
mirabilia facienda, ante evangelium est predicandum, et sic humanitatis meae ostendenda infirmitas [4]in passione, ut mox divinitatis meae
potentia clarescat in resurrectione'.

5. 'Dicit mater Iesu ministris: "Quodcumque dixerit vobis facite". Erant
autem ibi lapideae hydriae sex positae, secundum purificationem [5]Iu-
daeorum. Et dicit Iesus: "Implete hydrias aqua" (John 2: 5–7). Et
impleverunt eas usque ad summum.' Hydriae vocantur vasa aquae re-
ceptui preparata. Sex ergo hydrie sex aetates huius seculi designant, in
quibus omnibus electos suos Dominus suo semper erudivit precepto,
quae [6]precepta omnia insipida velut aqua fuerunt antequam Christus
veniens ea in vinum, id est, in spiritalem intellectum, convertit.

6. Prima ergo aetas ab Adam usque ad Noe atque diluvium. Secunda a
Noe usque ad Abraham. Tertia ab Abraham usque ad David. Quarta
a David usque ad captivitatem populi dei. Quinta ab ipsa captivitate
usque ad Christum. Sexta a nativitate Christi modo agitur usque in
finem saeculi. Per has ergo sex aetates, precepta Domini semper data
[7]fuerunt ad electos quosque quae omnia Christus, cum veniret, in
vinum convertit, id est, spiritaliter intellegenda [8]monstravit.

7. Audiamus ergo eamdem aquam, id est, divinam scripturam, in vinum
[9]nobis suavissimum, spiritu sancto monstrante, Christoque operante,
[10]conversam.

8. In prima aetate seculi, Abel iustum frater invidens occidit, et ab hoc
ipse perpetua *martyrum gloria beatus, fratricida impius aeterna male-
dictione damnatus est. Quicumque hoc audiens formidat cum impiis
damnari, cupiens cum electis beatificari, omnem fomitem odii et in-
vidie [11]festinet abicere, deoque placere per sacrificium iustitiae, per
modestiam [12]innocentiae, per virtutem innocentiae, procurat, aquam

[4] in] *interlined, perhaps in a later hand*
[5] Iudaeorum] *corr. from* idaeorum
[6] precepta] cepta *ms.*
[7] Fuerunt] *corr. from* funt
[8] monstravit] *corr. from* mostravit
[9] nobis] *corr. from* nos
[10] conversam] conversum *ms.*
[11] festinet] *read* festinat (*in line with* formidat *and* procurat)?
[12] innocentiae . . . innocentiae] *sic*

hydriae primae in vinum spiritale [13]conversam habet, quia innocentia
Abel iusti imitando Christum sequitur, qui innocens et sine causa
damnatus, nobis innocentiae bonum demonstravit exemplum. Qui
vero [14]cum fratricida invidia stimulatur, etiam quicquid boni operatur
per invidiam consumitur, quia per invidiam omne malum nascitur, et
per innocentiam magnum malum extinguitur, et magnum perficitur
[*p. 45*] bonum.

9. Secunda aetate seculi inchoante deletus est diluvio mundus ob magni-
tudinem criminum. Sed solus Noe propter iustitiam cum domo sua
liberatur in arca. Audita ergo hac vastatione horribili, paucorumque
liberatione mirabili, quisquis bonis moribus vivere coeperit, timens
perire cum reprobis, desiderans liberari cum electis, secundam hy-
driam aquae qua mundaretur accipit in vinum spiritalis intellegentiae
[15]conversam. Nos vero post baptismum, quod diluvium significat, nonnisi per iustitiae opera a peccatorum nexibus eripi meremur. Ideo
iustitiam in omnibus et super omnia diligamus, per quam ad vitam
perveniamus sempiternam.

10. In tertia aetate, deus Abrahae temptavit oboedientiam, eique filium
unicum iussit immolare, sed pro filio aries immolatur. Hoc quasi aqua
nihil profectus fieri videtur antequam hoc Christus in vinum spiritalis [16]intelligentiae convertit. Nam Abraham significat deum patrem,
qui pro nobis unicum [17]tradidit filium, qui factus est oboediens patri
usque ad mortem, et mortuus est propter delicta nostra, sicut Abraham non filium immolavit sed arietem, quia non divinitas Christi mori
potuit, sed humanitas, quam pro nobis suscipere dignatus est. Audiens
quisque quanta virtus est oboedientiae, quam meliorem sacrificio esse
Dominus testatur, ipsam oboedientiam pro Domino subire et adimplere satagerit, [18]perpetuae benedictionis hereditatem cum Abraham
consequi delectatur, habet aquam tertiae hydriae in spiritale vinum
[19]conversam.

11. Quarta aetate David gigantem proprio occidit [20]gladio. Quid nobis
auditum profuit? Sed Christus, per quem David significatur, antiquum
hostem humani generis propria sua morte prostravit, nosque ab aeterna morte liberavit. Ecce, hic aquam quartae hydriae in vinum spiritalis intellegentiae conversam habemus! Quisquis igitur haec audiens,
Christum imitari desiderans qui pro nobis mori dignatus est, non pro

[13] conversam] conversum *ms.*
[14] cum] cam *ms.*
[15] conversam] conversum *ms.*
[16] intelligentiae] *corr. from* intellentiae
[17] tradidit] *letters obscured in ms.*
[18] perpetuae] *read* et perpetuae?
[19] conversam] conversum *ms.*
[20] gladio] *unclear in ms.*

Christo corporis mortem subire necesse est, sed mori concupiscentiis carnis et desideriis huius mundi studeat, regnum a Christo percipiet sempiternum.

12. Quinta aetate populus dei in Babylonia tenebatur captivus, et per Hiesum sacerdotem magnum eiusque socios ad terram repromissionis adductus. Hoc cum nobis dicitur quasi aquae saporem sentimus. Si ergo intellegimus quod totus mundus captivus tenebatur sub potestate diaboli, antequam per Iesum Christum liberaretur et [*p. 46*] vitae aeterne nobis ianuae panderentur, habemus aquam quintae hydriae in spiritalem conversam saporem.

13. Sexta aetate Christus resurrexit a mortuis et ascendit in caelos. Significat quod deus pater, qui illum suscitavit a mortuis, omnes quoque credentes et in fide eius perseverantes a morte resuscitavit aeterna et consedere secum facit in caelesti regno cum Christo.

14. Nobis ergo fratres karissimi, ut audistis, Christus fecit vinum de aqua, quando per sanctos doctores demonstravit quid spiritalis sensus in veteri lege latuit. Praeparemus ergo corda nostra ut digna sint accipere gratiam spiritalem. Mundemus corda et corpora nostra ab omni carnali concupiscentia. Abstineamus nos ab omni immunditia, teneamus fidem rectam, et totam spem nostram in dei promissionem et eius misericordiam dirigamus. Caritatem dei et proximi super omnia et in omnibus observemus. Deprecamur indesinenter misericordiam dei ut omnes actus nostros et desideria in suam dirigat voluntatem, et tota intentione cordis eius inhereamur preceptis, ut post hanc presentem vitam aeterna gaudia cum Christo et omnibus sanctis habere mereamur, per eum qui vivit et regnat deus per omnia saecula seculorum, Amen.

1. 3. Marriage symbolism in the Beaune Homiliary

This is another of the small number of known cases of marriage symbolism in early medieval popular preaching.

MS Paris, BN Lat. 3794[1]

A parchment manuscript, 290 × 185/190 mm., 169 folios, twelfth century, in 'Plusieurs mains de style allemand' according to the catalogue. The provenance is the Hôtel Dieu of Beaune. The manuscript contains homilies and sermons.

Though for the sake of overall consistency I have maintained the policy of normalizing 'n' to 'm' in words where there is no standard medieval

[1] Description based on Bibliothèque Nationale, *Catalogue général des manuscrits latins*, vii. (*N°s 3776 à 3835*): *Homéliaires* (Paris, 1988), 155–66 (a very full description), and on microfilm of the sermon.

orthography and the letter is often swallowed up in an abbreviation, it would not have been justified for this scribe alone as he has a distinct preference for 'n': e.g. for 'inmutatio' rather than 'immutatio'. The Bibliothèque Nationale catalogue classifies the manuscript under the general heading of 'Homéliaires' and describes it as a 'Sermonarium'. As noted in the text, the Beaune Homiliary seems to have been for popular preaching. 'O holy brothers' in the final paragraph may suggest that this was at least originally addressed to monks.

Fos. 5ᵛ–7ʳ:

Sermo post Epiphaniam

1. Audivimus fratres carissimi cum sacrum legeretur evangelium quod die tertia nuptie facte sunt in Chana Galileae. Quae sunt ille nuptiae nisi nostra adquisitio? Quae sunt illa convivia, nisi nostrae salutis gaudia, quae die tertia facta sunt, quia tertio mundi tempore huius convivii facta est letitia? Nam unum fuit tempus nature, aliud celestium gratiae, quo Christus, ad nuptias invitatus, ²se ut latentem in homine deum, operum virtute detexeret, et ex volubilitate gentium stabilem sibi coniungeret sponsam. Sed inter nuptiales prophetarum simphonias, vinum gratiae deficiebat. Quod mater querimoniis [*fo. 6ʳ*] agit cum filio, ut et filii gloria innotesceret, et convivis vinum sufficeret. Cui filius non indignando negavit, sed veritatem proferendo respondit: 'Quid michi et tibi est mulier? Nondum venit hora mea.' Ad quamdam horam in veritate rursum agnovit, quasi dixisset: 'Quod de me facit miraculum, non tu genuisti, sed quia genuisti infirmitatem meam, tunc illam agnosces cum illa pendebit in cruce. Tunc et te cognoscam etiam ex illa natura quae mori non potest. Sed ante sunt discipuli eligendi; ante sunt sanitates perficiende; ante evangelium predicandum: et sic est humanitatis ostendenda infirmitas in passione, ut mox divinitatis potentia clarescat in resurrectione.'

2. Post haec tamen veritatis oracula, produnt deum pietatis miracula. Nam statuuntur hydriae sex, et insipide legis aqua implentur, quae mox in ferventis gratiae vina mutantur. Nec aquis aliquid minuitur, dum virtus saporis augetur. Ita legalis iota non solvitur, dum evangelicus apex apponitur, sed moriens legis littera, spiritu vivificatur gratiae. Et ideo ubi vinum defecit, Christus vinum fecit, quia umbra removetur, et veritas presentatur. Credit lex, et gratia succedit, carnalia spiritalibus commutantur, in novum testamentum observatio vetusta transfunditur, vetera transierunt, [*fo. 6ᵛ*] facta sunt omnia nova. Vino deficiente, vinum aliud ministratur, quia lex novum odorem vite reddidit in gratia, et quae in sola littera evanescit, spiritali intellectu reviviscit.

___
² se] *om. ms.—conjecture*

3. Sex autem hidriae ille, sex significant aetates, quae aetates quasi vasa
inania permanent, nisi a Christo implerentur. In quibus singulis prophetiae non defuerunt de sponso et ³sponsa, quae in Christo manife-
state, ad omnium gentium intendebant salutem.
4. Quis in prima hydria per Adam et Eva figuratur, nisi Christus et aec-
clesia? Et quis in secunda monstratur, in qua Noe misticam regebat
archam, nisi idem Christus in ligno crucis sponsam sibi aecclesiam
ex omnibus coniungens gentibus? Et quis in tertia ostenditur hydria,
ubi Abraham unicum ducebat ad immolandum, nisi unicus filius dei
⁴traditus a deo patre, pro salute omnium immolandus? Qui crucem
passionis suae, ut Isaac ligna, propriis portavit humeris? Et quis per
David in quarta designatur hydria, nisi Christus noster bellator, qui
superbissimum diabolicae potentiae caput suo potentissimo mucrone
truncavit? Cui dictum est per eumdem David ex quo carnem habuit:
'Exurge deus, iudica terram: tu hereditabis in omnibus gentibus' (Ps.
81: 8). In quinta hydria Danihel vidit lapidem precisum de monte sine
manibus, et fregisse omnia regna terrarum (Daniel 2 esp. 34 & 44–5).
Lapis iste est quem reprobaverunt aedificantes: [*fo. 7ʳ*] in caput anguli
factus est (Ps. 117: 22), qui facit utraque unum, et non est in alio aliquo
salus (Act. 4: 12). Sexta hydria Iohannes Baptista clamat: 'Ecce agnus
dei! Ecce qui tollit peccata mundi' (John 1: 29).
5. Ad Christum vero et advocationem gentium sex hydriarum prophetiae
pertinebant, quae singule metretas binas vel ternas tenebant, et vel in
preputio et circumcisione, vel in tribus mundi divisionibus ⁵designantur,
quia Christus sponsus ex omni gente et ex omni genere hominum sibi
unam sponsam eligere venit, cui gratie vinum miscuit, quod ab architri-
clino, id est, sanctorum choro doctorum, probatur, et omnibus prioris
seculi deliciis prefertur: quia in prophetia umbra tegebat, in evangelio veritas aperuit; in illa figuratio, in ⁶hoc manifestatio; illa predixit,
hoc retexit; illa promisit, hoc reddidit. Ideo obtimum servatum vinum,
usque dum venit auxilium divinum, et factus est liber, qui fuit servus.
Et non solum de penali ereptus est miseria, sed etiam caelesti insertus
est felicitati. Ecce vera, carissimi, ecce predicanda miracula, quae in nos
cotidie clementia gerit divina, quando de filiis tenebrarum filios lucis
efficit. Haec est vero 'immutatio dextere excelsi' (Psalm 76: 11), quod
ipse in nobis, O fratres sancti, efficere dignetur, qui cum patre et spiritu
sancto vivit et regnat deus per omnia secula seculorum, Amen.

³ sponsa] sponsae *ms.*
⁴ traditus] traditur *ms.*
⁵ designantur] designatur *ms.*
⁶ hoc] illa *ms.*

1. 4. Nonconformist variants in Hugues de Saint-Cher

This extract, together with Documents **1. 5–8**, illustrates the argument in Chapter 1 that many sermon manuscripts were written by intelligent users (like friars) rather than scribes working for pay, who would have not felt entitled to modify the text as if it belonged to them. This implies an army of friars and other such people copying sermon manuscripts, alongside paid scribes, so that there was a double labour force that can explain the large number of sermon manuscripts which must have been in circulation.

TEXT

13/1/ Primum est ut sit iusta et in se discreta per refrenationem illicitorum et punitionem uitiorum. /2/ Osee ii (19): 'Sponsabo te michi in iustitia et iudicio'—ecce primum quo ad se; et bene addidit 'in iudicio', quia sine discretione et iudicio iustitiam exercere de carne non prodest. /3/ Eccli. xxxiii (31): 'Si est tibi servus fidelis, sit tibi quasi anima tua', etc. 14/1/ Secundum est ut sit misericors et leta quoad familiam et amicos sponsi. /2/ Unde sequitur in auctoritate premissa: 'in misericordia et miserationibus'—ecce secundum quoad proximum, ut dicatur misericordia in compassione cordis et miseratio in exibitione operis.

(For a translation, see *Medieval Marriage Sermons*, 159.)

FREE VARIANTS

13/1/ iusta . . . uitiorum] munda et iusta in se per resecationem illicitorum et discreta ad aliqua licitorum *M*   in se] tamen *Be*   refrenationem] districtionem *Vo* 13/2/–14/2/ (*all*)] Unde sponsabo te michi in iustitia et iudicio—ecce prima duo.—Ut sit misericors et leta quo ad familiam et amicos sponsi. Unde sequitur: In misericordia et miserationibus. Ecce tertium. Misericordia notatur in cordis compassione, miseratio in exibitione operis *M*

1. 5. Nonconformist variants in Jean de la Rochelle

See introductory comments on **1. 4.**

TEXT

4/1/ Secunde nuptie significate sunt in desponsatione Ysaac cum Rebecca, Gen. xxiiii, et ibidem (Gen. 24: 63) dicitur quod Ysaac exivit in agro ad meditandum, et ideo per ipsum significatur spiritus, qui ad meditandum exivit in agro contemplationis, in quo est proprie meditatio.

(For a translation, see *Medieval Marriage Sermons*, 187.)

FREE VARIANT

significatur . . . meditatio] significantur nuptie spectantes ad meditandum in agro contemplationis, ad quem agrum exire oportet *Mu*

1. 6. Nonconformist variants in Pierre de Saint-Benoît

See introductory comments on 1. 4.

TEXT

9/1/ Cuius matrimonii convivium celebratur cotidie in convivio eucharistie. /2/ Sed iste nuptie non solum habent convivium in presenti, sed etiam in futuro. /3/ Ita enim sollempnes sunt quod nec in presenti nec in futuro deficiunt, sed in presenti habent quasi prandium matutinum, in futuro quasi cenam vespertinam, et ille sunt nuptie eternales.

(For a translation, see *Medieval Marriage Sermons*, 217.)

FREE VARIANTS

9/1/ convivio] sacramento *M* eucharistie] Quarte nuptie sunt nuptie glorie *added in Pv*: Quarte sunt nuptie eternales *added in V, which omits* 9/2–3/   9/2–3/ (*all*)] Sed iste nuptie non solum habent convivium in presenti, sive prandium matutinum, sed in futuro habent quasi cenam, et iste sunt nuptie eternales *M*   9/3/ deficiunt] desinunt *Pv*   et ille . . . eternales] Item quarte sunt nuptie eternales *Wi*

1. 7. Nonconformist variants in Gérard de Mailly

See introductory comments on 1. 4.

TEXT

31/1/ Propter quod preceptum est in Levit. 21 (13–14) quod sacerdos, id est Christus, 'virginem ducat uxorem; viduam autem et repudiatam et sordidam et meretricem non accipiat'. /2/ Per 'meretricem' intelligitur anima que omnibus immunditiis et peccatis mortalibus se exponit. /3/ Per 'sordidam', illa que, licet a peccatis mortalibus se abstineat, adhuc habet sordidas affectiones, quia adhuc nimium afficitur circa temporalia. /4/ De qua dicitur Tren. primo (9): 'sordes eius in pedibus eius'. /5/ Per 'repudiatam' intelligitur anima que licet non afficiatur circa temporalia uel carnalia, hoc tamen non est quia ea repudiaverit, immo potius quia ab ipsis repudiata est; et libenter se ingereret adhuc si posset recipi—sicut lecatores nutriti in curiis, quando eiciuntur per unum hostium, redeunt per aliud. /6/ Per 'viduam' intelligitur anima cui mundus mortuus est, sed non ipsa mundo, que adhuc libenter de mundanis et carnalibus loquitur et cogitat, sicut vidua de marito mortuo, licet fuerit ei pessimus.

(For a translation, see *Medieval Marriage Sermons*, 265 and 267.)

FREE VARIANTS

31/1/ Propter . . . 21] Leui. xxi precipitur *P7*   Propter quod] Propter hoc *Pr* 31/2–6/ (*all*) Vidua appellatur anima peccatrix que separata est a Christo. Repudiata, quia derelicta a deo. Sordida, quia maculata peccato. Meretrix, quia exposita dyabolo *P7*   31/2/ mortalibus] etiam mortalibus *Pr*   31/3/ adhuc] tamen adhuc *Pr*   31/5/ afficiatur] multum afficiatur *Pr*   immo] sed *Pr*

1. 8. Nonconformist variants in Guibert de Tournai

See introductory comments on **1. 4**.

TEXT

15/1/ Debet autem sponsa que vocatur ad has nuptias esse casta quo ad carnis aut saltem mentis integritatem, quia, Levit. xxi (10–13), summus pontifex ducit tantum virginem.

(For a translation, see *Medieval Marriage Sermons*, 307.)

FREE VARIANT

15/1/ (*all*)] Sed advertendum quod anima sive sponsa que ad has nuptias invitatur debet esse multipliciter ornata, scilicet anima [natura *ms.?*] debet esse casta quo ad carnis et mentis integritatem; debet esse discreta per veram humilitatem; debet esse maxime libera per ipsam caritatem. Primo dico quod anima debet esse, etc. *A2*

1. 9. A sermon on marriage by Jean Halgrin d'Abbeville[1]

This sermon emphasizes marriage symbolism and at the same time the goodness of marriage on the human and literal level. The sermon and collection belong to the 'model sermon' genre. To judge from the date of manuscripts of it that I have seen over the years, the collection seems to have been popular in the generation immediately before the friars' collections became widely diffused: indeed, it was possibly the most popular of its generation. Jean Halgrin d'Abbeville was a learned member of the secular clergy and a trusted agent of papal policy. A generation later he might well have been a friar.

MS BL Arundel 132[2]

A parchment manuscript, 315 × 194 mm., last folio number 145, 2 columns, probably second quarter of the thirteenth century. Palmer, *Zisterzienser*, puts it in the third quarter, but the writing is above the top line, and where the 'a' has two compartments, the top one is not closed, so a slightly earlier date is more probable. Note the reversed-'c' 'con-' sign, another early indication except with German manuscripts (there seems no reason to think that this book was made in Germany, though it ended up in the library of the Cistercian monastery of Eberbach). From spot checks at the beginning and end, it seems that the manuscript is filled

---

[1] Second sermon on the text *Nuptie facte sunt* (J. B. Schneyer, *Repertorium der lateinischen Sermones des Mittelalters für die Zeit von 1150–1350* (11 vols.; Münster, 1969–90), iii. 512, Johannes Halgrinus de Abbatisvilla, no. 32).

[2] Description based on personal examination, and on N. F. Palmer, *Zisterzienser und ihre Bücher: Die mittelalterliche Bibliotheksgeschichte von Kloster Eberbach im Rheingau unter besonderer Berücksichtigung der in Oxford und London aufbewahrten Handschriften* (Regensburg, 1998), 282.

with the Sermones de tempore of Jean Halgrin/'Johannes Halgrinus de Abbatisvilla'.

Fos. 23va–24rb:

1. 'Nuptie facte sunt in Chana Galilee, et erat mater Iesu ibi', etc. Prima est inter religiones matrimonium, quod Dominus noster instituit in paradyso, et ante peccatum, et nuptias sua presentia honoravit, et signorum suorum initio, quod fecit coram discipulis suis. Declaratur autem et religio matrimonii designatione loci, in quo facte sunt nuptie, et miraculi qualitate. Facte sunt quidem nuptie in Chana, vico Galylee. Chana zelus interpretatur,[3] et proprie zelus est amor coniugis ad coniugem. Zelatur enim alter alterum tamquam sibi soli proprium, et in hoc fides coniugii designatur. Galylea transmigratio interpretatur,[4] et in coniugio unus coniugum transmigrat in alterius potestatem, dicente Apostolo,[5] prima ad Chor. vii (4): 'vir non habet potestatem sui corporis, sed mulier', et e converso.

2. Aque in vinum muta|tio [*fo. 23vb*] signi*fica*t quod tantum debet distare vita coniugatorum a vita ante coniugium, quantum distat aqua a vino, quoniam carnalis societas ante coniugium comparatur aque, que fluit sine ordine. Inordinatus est enim cursus fluvii et distortus. Vinum vero non sine ordine fluit, sed cum ordine et mensura, et signi*fica*t coniunctionem viri et mulieris in matrimonio. Nam in carnali commixtione matrimonii, tempus, locus, voluntas, et actus: omnia debent esse ordinata.

3. 'Mater Iesu erat ibi': in quo ostenditur castitas et fecunditas. Non enim propter fecunditatem in matrimonio perit castitas. De qua dicit angelus ad Thobiam, reddens rationem quare diabolus interfecisset vii viros qui Saram filiam Raguel duxerant, dicens (Tob. 6: 14): 'Hii namque qui ita suscipiunt coniugium ut deum a sua mente excludant, et libidini vacent, in hiis potestatem habet demonium'. Et iterum Tobias [6]viii (9) orans ad Dominum ait: 'Et vero Domine, tu scis quod non libidinis causa accipio sororem meam, sed sola dilectione posteritatis, in qua nomen tuum sit benedictum in secula.' Hoc etenim fine desideranda est posteritas, ut educatur proles ad cultum dei, et parentes filios, quos genuerunt ad huius seculi miseriam, per malam doctrinam non generent ad gehennam.

4. 'Vocatus est Iesus et discipuli eius ad nuptias', ostendens qui debeant vocari ad convivium nuptiale, scilicet pauperes et boni, non scurre et

---

[3] 'Chana "zelus" vel "emulatio" vel "possedis eos" aut "possessio eorum"' (MS BL Add. 31,830, fo. 447ra).
[4] 'Galilea "rota" vel "volubilis" sive "transmeans" aut "transmigratio mea"' (ibid., fo. 452ra).
[5] *With* apl' *in margin*
[6] viii] vii *ms.*

hystriones. Sed hodie, sicut habetur in Exodo viii, Egypti rane intrant in cibos pharaonis, scilicet hystriones garruli et clamosi qui intrant in reliquias ciborum et vestimentorum nobilium que debent pauperibus erogare.

5. Nuptie iste signi*fic*ant nuptias divinitatis et humanitatis in utero virginis celebratas. In hiis nuptiis erat vinum quamdiu apostoli gaudebant de presentia sponsi, dicente Domino in Matheo ix (15): 'Non possunt filii ⁷nuptiarum lugere quamdiu cum eis presens est sponsus.

6. Defecit vinum cum Dominus, transiturus ad patrem, dixit eis, Ioh. xvi (20): 'Amen, dico vobis, plorabitis et flebitis, mundus autem gaudebit; vos contristabimini'; conversa est aqua in vinum cum dixit: 'Tristitia vestra vertetur in gaudium'.

7. Item hee nuptie signi*fic*ant nuptias Christi et fidelis anime, quod matrimonium describit, Osee ii (20 & 19), dicens: 'Sponsabo te in fide; sponsabo te in iustitia et iudicio et in misericordia et miserationibus; sponsabo te in sempiternum'. Ter dicit 'sponsabo' ut ostendat illud matrimonium initiatum, ratum et ⁸consummatum.

8. Initiatur enim in fide, per quam anima dei sponsa efficitur, anulo fidei subarrata, de quo Ihere. ii (32): 'Numquid obliviscetur virgo ornamenti sui, id est, anuli desponsationis sue, aut sponsa fascie pectoralis sue', tu autem 'oblita es mei in diebus innumeris'. Arguit animam que, oblita anuli de|sponsationis, [*fo. 24ʳᵃ*] fidem non servat coniugii, cum mulieres consueverint servare anulum desponsationis sue toto tempore vite sue'.

9. Ratum et consumatum efficitur hoc matrimonium 'in iustitia et iudicio et misericordia et miserationibus'. Iudicium est in discussione boni et mali et duorum malorum inter se; iustitia in punitione culpe. Sunt multi qui bene iudicant, sed non sunt boni iustitiarii: peccata sua condempnant sed districte non vindicant. Unde Ysaias ⁹xxviii (17) 'Ponam iudicium in pondere et iustitiam in mensura'. Iudicium quasi in statera diiudicat pondera, et penam culpe commensurat iustitia. Misericordia est in eorumdem compassione. Miseratio, in beneficii datione. Et precedit misericordia miserationem. Unde 'iustus miseretur et tribuet' (Ps. 36: 21), et 'plus est compati ex corde quam dare', sicut dicit Gregorius.¹⁰ Consumatur autem matrimonium in eternitate, sed in quo sit consumatio non dicit propheta Osee, sed hoc tantum: 'Sponsabo te in sempiternum', ostendens quod ineffabilis est consumati matrimonii beata delectatio.

10. In hiis nuptiis vinum deficit, scilicet amor huius seculi inebrians, de quo Ysa. xvi (10) 'Auferetur letitia et exultatio de Carmelo'. Carmelus,

⁷ nuptiarum] sponsi *in Vulgate*
⁸ consummatum] confirmatum *ms.*
⁹ xxviii] xxii *ms.*
¹⁰ Gregory the Great, *Moralia in Job*, 36 (Migne, *PL* 76. 180).

'mons fertilis', sign*ifica*t sterilitatem bonorum temporalium, et interpretatur 'mollis' vel 'tener', et 'ab omni rigore per delicias dissolutus':[11]
a quibus auferetur letitia et exultatio, data ipsis gratia penitentie. Sequitur (ibid.): 'vinum non culcabit in torculari'. Qui calcare consue-
verat, calcans in torculari multo labore vinum exprimit, et seipsum
totum polluit in exprimendo: et amator huius seculi vix a suis la-
boribus modicum delectationis exprimet, et hoc non habebit sine peccati macula.

11. 'Deficiente vino dicit mater Iesu: "Vinum non habent". Et ait Iesus:
"Quid michi et tibi est, mulier?"', quasi dicat: 'Quid a te accepi, per
quod vinum eis miraculose dare possim? A te quidem accepi carnem
que velut uva premetur in cruce, et fluet vinum sanguinis mei: sed
numdum venit hora, quia nondum Iudas extendit [12]calcaneum super
uvam. [13]Siquidem beata virgo vitis. Unde in Ecc(li) xxiiii (23) habetur:
'Ego quasi vitis fructificavi suavitatem odoris, et flores mei fructus
honoris et honestatis', scilicet Christum, qui duo attulit unguenta,
unum contra infirmitatem anime, aliud contra infirmitatem corporis.
Sanavit enim infirmitatem anime unguento gratie remittentis peccata,
et sanabit infirmitatem corporis immortalitatis et incorruptibilitatis
unguento. Unde in Cant(ico canticorum) (1: 2–3): 'in odore unguento-
rum tuorum [14]curremus; adolescentule dilexerunt te nimis'. Bene dicit
'in odore'. Semper enim canis venaticus nasum habet in odore illius
fere quam querit. In hunc modum, qui querit Dominum ab odore
suavitatis eius non recedit, donec invenerit et plene perceperit quod
intendit.

12. Sequitur: 'Dicit Iesus: "Implete ydrias aqua"'. Ydrie sunt corda nostra, ab 'ydor', quod est aqua. Non enim debent esse corda nostra
vasa vinaria, sed aquatica, lacrimis scilicet compunctionis plena, non
[*fo. 24*[rb]] vino terrene delectationis, et debent impleri ydrie iste usque
ad summum, quia in pleno non amplius apponi potest, in semipleno
autem potest, quia si plenum fuerit cor hominis lacrimis contritionis,
non poterit diabolus infundere venenum prave suggestionis.

13. Sex autem ydrie dicte sunt propter sex facies sive peccatorum latera,
que designantur in sex lateribus lapidis quadrati, de quibus in Trenis
(3: 9): 'conclusit vias meas lapidibus quadris'. Sunt enim peccatis
propriis concluse vie peccatoris, ut clausus peccati carcere prodire
non possit cum voluerit. Sex autem peccati latera sunt consensus in

---

[11] I have checked a thirteenth-century version of the *Interpretationes nominum
Hebraicorum*, but found only the following, an imperfect match: 'Carmelus "mollis"
vel "tenellus" sive "cognoscens circumcisionem" aut "scientia circumcisionis"' (MS
BL Add. 31,830, fo. 446[ra]).

[12] calcaneum] calneum *ms*.

[13] Siquidem] *ms. unclear*

[14] curremus] *Vulgate*: currimus *ms*.

peccatum, consuetudo vel iteratio mali operis, gloriatio de peccato, excusatio peccati, postremo desperatio venie vel nimia presumptio venie, que peccandi securitatem inducit.

14. Capiunt autem singule ydrie metretas binas vel ternas. Due metrete sunt contritio et confessio, que sufficiunt exeuntibus de seculo. Tres metrete sunt confessio, contritio, satisfactio, que manentibus in hac vita sunt necessaria.

15. Igitur ydrie cordium, que sex varietatibus peccatorum deformantur, predictis aquis per compunctionem impleri iubentur. Si autem hiis aquis implete fuerint ydrie iste, Dominus aquas convertet in vinum et tristitiam penitentie commutabit in gaudium et letitiam felicitatis, et glorie sempiterne. Quod nobis prestare dignetur, etc.

1. 10. A sermon on marriage by Konrad Holtnicker[1]

This sermon also illustrates the combination of marriage symbolism and emphasis on the holiness of marriage on a literal and human level. The sermon and collection belong to the 'model sermon' genre. The author was a thirteenth-century German Franciscan.

MS Munich, Bayerische Staatsbibliothek Clm 2946 (=*M*), with occasional corrections from MS Paris, BN lat. 3742 (=*P*)

M[2] is a parchment manuscript, 'in 4°', of 308 folios. The catalogue dates it to the fourteenth century; I would put it in the first or even second half of the thirteenth. In addition to the 'de tempore' sermon collection from which this comes, and what looks from the description like an index applying the sermons to liturgical slots, it contains the 'Liber scintillarum', presumably the work by Defensor of Liège. It came to the Staatsbibliothek from the Bridgettine nunnery of Altmünster.

There is an exemplary scholarly description of *P* in Bibliothèque Nationale, *Catalogue général des manuscrits latins*, vi. (*N*^{os} *3536 à 3775*^{*B*}) (Paris, 1975), 701–5.

M, fo. 28^{ra–va}, corrected from *P*, fos. x^r–xi^r:

1. 'Nuptie facte sunt' et cetera, Io. 2 (1). Nota quod sunt nuptie officiose, perniciose, gratiose, gloriose. Prime sunt viri et mulieris cohabitantis, secunde sunt anime peccantis et dyaboli, tertie sunt Christi et ecclesie militantis, quarte sunt Christi et ecclesie triumphantis.

2. Prime igitur sunt nuptie officiose viri et mulieris contrahentis. [3]Tob. 9 (12): Cum timore Domini nuptiarum convivium exercebant. Expone

---

[1] Schneyer, *Repertorium*, i. 751, 'Conradus Holtnicker de Saxonia OM', no. 54.
[2] Description based on Hahn *et al.*, *Catalogus codicum Latinorum Bibliothecae Regiae Monacensis*, i/2. 52, and on a microfilm printout of the sermon.
[3] Tob. 9] Iob. 49 *M*.

hystoriam quomodo 7 viros Sare demonium occidit, et quomodo tribus noctibus orationi vacabant.

3. Has nuptias honoravit Dominus quadrupliciter: scilicet:

4. Institutione. Institute [4]enim sunt non a vili persona, non ab homine, non ab angelo, sed a deo. Institute sunt non in vili loco, non in stabulo, non in angulo, sicut iam fiunt [5]clandestina matrimonia, sed in paradyso. Institute sunt non in statu culpe, sed innocentie, non post lapsum hominis, sed ante. Sed heu, modo post multos lapsus et fornicationes multi contrahunt.

5. Associatione, quia Iesus et mater et discipuli eius in nuptiis erant, non histriones, non corizantes, ut modo.

6. Operatione, quia in nuptiis aquam in vinum convertit. Sed heu, modo magice artes non divine exercentur in nuptiis.

7. Significatione. Eph. 5 (32): Sacramentum hoc magnum est. Augustinus: Bone sunt nuptie in quibus tanto sunt meliores coniugati, quam castiores ac fideliores deum timent, maxime si filios carnaliter desiderant, spiritualiter [6]nutriunt.

8. Secunde sunt nuptie perniciose, scilicet dyaboli et anime peccantis. 1 [7]Macc. 9 (41): 'Converse sunt nuptie in luctum et vox musicorum in lamentum'. Nota hystoriam, quomodo filii Zambri cum tympanis et musicis adduxerunt sponsam filiam unam de magnis principibus Chanaan, super quos irruit Ionathas et interfecit eos. Zambri Luciferum [8]significat. Interpretatur enim 'dies amaricans'.[9] Lucifer autem ante lapsum dies fuit, post lapsum vero [10]amaricans totum mundum. Sap. [11]2 (24) 'Invidia dyaboli mors intravit in orbem', etc. Huius filii sunt demones, non natura sed imitatione. Ps. (143: 11): 'Erue me de manu filiorum alienorum'. Chanaan mundum significat. Interpretatur enim 'commutatus'.[12] Mutatio [13]est autem mundi primo per aquam diluvii, in fine per ignem iudicii, medio autem tempore per aquam baptismi et ig|nem [*fo. 28rb*] spiritus sancti. 'Hec mutatio dextere excelse' (Ps. 76: 11). Principes Chanaan sunt demones. Eph. 6 (12): 'Non est nobis colluctatio (adversus carnem et sanguinem: sed adversus principes, et potestates, adversus mundi rectores tenebrarum harum, contra spiritualia nequitie, in celestibus)' etc. Anima ergo pec-

---

[4] enim sunt] sunt enim sunt *M*
[5] clandestina] clamdestina *M*
[6] nutriunt] nutriantur *M*: nutriant *P*
[7] Macc.] Mach. *corrected from* Mich. *in M*
[8] significat] signat *is also a possible extension of the abbreviation*
[9] 'Zambri, "iste lacescans" vel "iste amaricans"' (MS BL Add. 31,830, fo. 470ra).
[10] amaricans] amorificans *M*
[11] 2] 1 *M*
[12] 'Canaam "commutatus" vel "commutatio"' (BL Add. 31,830, fo. 446ra).
[13] est autem] *corrected from* autem est *in M*

catrix filia est et sponsa dyaboli, que nunc dyabolo [14]cum mundanis gaudiis adducitur. Sed Ionatha, id est Christo, in morte vel in iudicio superveniente mala societas dampnatione percutitur. Iob [15]21 (12–13): 'Tenent tympanum et cytharam', etc., usque 'et in puncto ad inferna descendunt'. In hiis nuptiis non aqua in vinum, sed vinum temporalis lascivie in aquam eterni fletus convertitur. Unde supra bene dicitur quod converse sunt nuptie in luctum. Bernardus:[16] 'Eia letare, iuvenis, in adolescentia tua, ut decedente pariter cum etate temporali letitia, succedat que te absorbeat eterna tristitia.'

9. [17]Tertie sunt nuptie gratiose, Christi scilicet et ecclesie militantis. Mt 22 (2): 'Simile factum est regnum celorum homini regi qui fecit nuptias filio suo', id est, Christo, cuius sponsa est ecclesia sive anima fidelis. Io. 3 (29): 'Qui habet sponsam, sponsus est'. Sicut autem in nuptiis convivium [18]constituitur, vestes et dona largiuntur, sic et Christus fecit, sicut [19]signatum est Hester 2 (18), ubi dicitur quod iussit Assuerus 'convivium preparari [20]permagnificum pro coniunctione et nuptiis Hester': 'dona largitus est', etc. Assuerus Christum, Hester ecclesiam [21]significat, quam pro Vasti, id est synagoga reprobata assumpsit. Convivium [22]permagnificum est in quo corpus suum ad comedendum et sanguinem ad bibendum dat. Largitus est etiam dona in cruce ubi sponsam duxit. Dedit enim corpus tortori, spiritum patri, matrem Iohanni, paradysum latroni. Sed postmodum etiam dedit dona. [23]Spiritus sancti, Ps. (67: 19), dedit 'dona hominibus'; vestes etiam dedit et nudus in cruce remansit. In hiis nuptiis aqua in vinum convertitur cum lacrimas doloris gratia spiritus sancti sequitur. Ps. (103: 15): 'Vinum letificet cor hominis'. Crisostomus: 'Dominus ipse est qui consolatur flentes, dolentes curat, penitentes [24]informat'.[25]

10. [26]Quarte sunt nuptie gloriose, Christi scilicet et ecclesie triumphantis. Mt. 25 (10): 'Que parate erant, intraverunt cum eo ad nuptias'. Omnem iocunditatem et delectationem quam visus, auditus, gustus aut omnium hominum sensus omnes habent vel habebunt in omnibus

---

[14] cum] *P*: etiam *M?*
[15] 21] 31 *M*
[16] Bernard of Clairvaux, *Ep.* 2. 10, in *Sancti Bernardi opera*, ed. J. Leclercq and H. Rochais, vii. *Epistolae, I: corpus epistolarum 1–180* (Rome, 1974), 20–1.
[17] Tertie] Tertio *M?*
[18] constituitur] *P*: construitur *M*
[19] signatum] significatum *also a possible extension of the abbreviation*
[20] permagnificum] per manus per magnificum *M*
[21] significat] *or* signat
[22] Permagnificum] permagnum *M?*
[23] Spiritus sancti, Ps. dedit] *P*: Spiritum s. dedit *M*
[24] informat] *corrected from* format *in M*
[25] Not found.
[26] Quarte] iiii *ms.*

nuptiis mundi que fuerunt et sunt et erunt, incomparabiliter excedit
gaudium nuptiale in celis. Apo. 19 (7): 'Gaudeamus et exultemus et
demus gloriam deo, quia venerunt nuptie agni'. In hiis nuptiis aqua in
vinum ²⁷con|vertitur [*fo. 28ᵛᵃ*] dum presens miseria in eternam iocun-
ditatem et in eternas delicias commutatur. Ieronimus: 'Miserie deliciis
et delicie miseriis commutantur. In nostro arbitrio est vel divitem sequi
vel Lazarum'.²⁸

1. 11. A sermon on marriage by Servasanto da Faenza¹

This text provides further illustration of the combination of marriage symbolism and emphasis on the holiness of marriage on a literal and human
level. Regarding the goodness of human marriage, note the attack on contemporary dualist heretics, the 'Patareni', clearly the Cathars. The Aristotelian colouring and the formal logic are also a striking feature, untypical
of thirteenth-century sermons generally, though the misnomer 'scholastic
preaching' has tended to obscure the general pattern. Servasanto was a
preacher active in Florence in the later thirteenth century.² The unusually
sophisticated lay audience there may have had a taste for rather intellectual sermons (more intellectual, paradoxically, than sermons for university
audiences of the same period at Paris, where there was a genre distinction
between preaching on the one hand and scholastic teaching with 'quaesti-
ones', logic, and philosophy on the other). This Florentine milieu could
have affected Servasanto's perception of a lay congregation's horizon of
expectation, even though his sermon collection is not just intended for a
Florentine public—it belongs to the genre of model sermon collections,
containing texts meant to be preached by friars and other preachers to
congregations anywhere.

MS Troyes, Bibliothèque Municipale 1440³

Parchment manuscript, 'In-quarto', 372 folios, two columns, coloured
initials. The manuscript is probably Italian, because it has the distinctive Italian superscript 'r' abbreviation, which looks like an 'a'with the

²⁷ convertitur] *concealed by crease but supplied from sense*
²⁸ Jerome, *Epistola* 48, para. 21 (Migne, *PL* 22. 511).
¹ Schneyer, *Repertorium*, v. 378, 'Servasanctus de Faenza OM', no. 32. There is
an incunable edition of this (1484), to which Carlo Delcorno and Nicole Bériou drew
my attention. I have examined it in the Reuttlingen, shelfmark IB. 10693, 'sermo
xxxii', but there is no reason to prefer it to the manuscript used here, which is a
couple of centuries earlier.
² See D. L. d'Avray, *The Preaching of the Friars: Sermons Diffused from Paris
before 1300* (Oxford, 1985), 76–7, 155 n. 2, 158.
³ Description based on Ministère de l'éducation nationale, *Catalogue général des
manuscrits des bibliothèques publiques des départements* (7 vols.; Paris, 1849–85), ii.
Troyes (1855), 603, and on microfilm printout of the sermon.

top sliced off, or like a 'u' (e.g. fo. 98ʳᵃ, 10 up, *honorare*) . The two-compartment 'a' is sometimes closed and sometimes not, which suggests a date in the mid- to late thirteenth century. The many paragraph marks also place it in the second half of the century rather than earlier. The fairly ample space between the lines and relative regularity of the script are more characteristic of thirteenth- than fourteenth-century hands. The manuscript contains a collection of sermons on the epistles and Gospels of the liturgical year.

Fos. 95ᵛᵇ–98ᵛᵃ:

1. 'Nuptie facte sunt in Chana Galilee, et erat mater Jesu ibi', Io. 2 (1). Tales sunt qui dampnant matrimonium quales sunt illi qui in die media impingunt in murum propter defectum luminis oculorum. Nam omni ceco ille magis cecus esse probatur qui oculos habens videre non sinitur. Adeo enim constat esse clarissimum, et veris testimoniis ⁴comprobatum, a deo esse matrimonium institutum, ut omni ceco fit cecior quicumque dicit contrarium. Nam matrimonium esse bonum probat natura; probat scriptura; et probant sanctorum exempla.

2. Dico quod primum argumentum sumitur ex natura. Natura enim refugit omne superfluum, nec admittit aliquid diminutum. Unde ⁵nec habundat superfluis, nec deficit in necessariis, nec aliquid frustra facit, sicut omnis *phylosophya dicit. Ergo, si natura ad generationem facit membra apta et congrua, et fecit ea non superflua neque frustra, ergo generare est de intentione nature. Sed quod naturale est, peccatum non est, si fiat [*fo. 96ʳᵃ*] eo modo quo institutum est. Actus ergo generative de se peccatum non est. Non ergo matrimonium malum est.

3. Item sicut natura dedit homini potentiam nutritivam, sic dedit et generativam. Sed non peccat homo si debito modo et tempore congruo satisfaciat *nutritive. Ergo non peccat si debito modo a deo ordinato tempore congruo et loco debito satisfaciat generative.

4. Item longe maius est et nobilius est et magis necessarium est speciem quam individuum conservare. Sed per generativam fit conservatio speciei, per nutritivam vero fit conservatio individui. Ergo universo magis est necessarius actus generative quam nutritive. Ergo si non peccatur in nutritiva, multo minus nec in generativa.

5. Item, cuius finis bonus est, ipsum quoque bonum est. Sed finis generative est ad cultum dei filios generare et divinum esse in successionibus conservare. Et constat hoc bonum esse. Ergo et bonum est generare.

---

⁴ comprobatum] comprobatur *ms.*
⁵ nec] *om. ms.*

Phylosophus:[6] Ad hoc data est homini vis generativa ut conservetur esse divinum.

6. Item, matrimonium esse ex instinctu nature [*fo. 96rb*] docent omnes sensibiles creature. Quis docuit omnia animalia aquatica, aerea, et [7]terrea ut coniungantur bina, masculus et femina? [8]Quis docuit ipsa animalia masculina esse zelotipa et unumquodque bellare pro sua femina? Quis docuit ipsa animalia masculina vindicare adulteria? Nonne leo pardum mortaliter odit, et eum persequitur et occidit, quia cum leena concumbit? Et ipsam suam feminam dum adulterium sentit, quod flatu cognoscit, verberibus afficit, et quandoque interimit? Quis docuit ciconiam masculam femine fidem thori servare, et in ea adulterum concubitum vindicare, quod ex solo cognoscit odore? Quis docuit turturem tantam fidem coniugi marito [9]servare, ut eo mortuo nulli umquam alteri se coniungat, sed omnem societatem refugiat, sola semper incedat, et amissum comparem semper gemat? Quis marinos pisces instruxit ut inter eos nulla adulteria committantur, sed sic unusquisque suo compari iungitur, ut numquam alteri uniatur?

7. Hec est igitur lex illa, quam natura docuit omnia animantia. Ex instinctu ergo nature sunt matrimonia, [*fo. 96va*] et ideo iusta et sancta, si debito fuerint modo servata.

8. Secundo patet hoc ipsum ex divina scriptura. Nam dicitur Mt. 19 (4) quod deus ab initio masculum et feminam fecit eos. [10]Sed non frustra fecit eos in sexu distincto, non incassum. Precepit eis ut crescerent, cum crescere nisi per mutuam coniunctionem non possent. Ergo ad hoc eos sic fecit, ut mutuo se coniungerent.

9. Item si matrimonium malum esset, eius separatio bona [11]est, quia cuius coniunctio mala est, eius divisio bona est. Sed Dominus dicit matrimonium preter adulterium nulla esse causa alia separandum. Ergo matrimonium non est malum. Et est malum vel bonum. Ergo est bonum. Minor probatur Mt. 19 (3–9), ubi pharisei querentes dixerunt: 'Si licet homini dimittere uxorem suam quacumque ex causa?' Quibus Dominus ait: 'Non legistis quia qui fecit homines, ab initio, masculum et feminam fecit eos? Propter quod', inquit, 'dimittet homo patrem et

---

[6] Perhaps Arist. *De anima*, 415^{a–b}, in William of Moerbeke's translation, 2. 7 (*Sancti Thoma Aquinatis . . . opera omnia, iussu Leonis XIII P.M. edita*, xlv/1. *Sentencia libri de anima*, ed. [R.-A. Gauthier] (Rome, 1984), 95 (the editor, who modestly left his name off the title-page, gives a critical edition of William of Moerbeke's translation of Aristotle as well as of Aquinas's commentary); *Aristotle's De anima in the Versions of William of Moerbeke and the Commentary of Thomas Aquinas*, ed. and trans. K. Foster, S. Humphries, and I. Thomas (London, 1951), 210.

[7] terrea] *read* terrena?

[8] Quis . . . femina] *supplied in margin*

[9] servare] *supplied in margin*

[10] Set non frustra fecit eos] *supplied in margin*

[11] est] *read* esset?

matrem et adherebit uxori sue, et erunt duo in carne una.' [*fo. 96vb*]
Et subdit: 'Quos ergo deus coniunxit, homo non separet.' Et illi e
contra dixerunt: 'Quid ergo Moyses mandavit dari libellum repudii
et ¹²dimitti?' Et Dominus: 'Ad duritiam cordis vestri permisit vobis
*dimittere uxores vestras. Ab initio autem non sic fuit. Dico ergo vobis
quia quicumque dimiserit uxorem suam nisi ob causam fornicationis,
et aliam duxerit, mechatur.' Quid istis expressius? Quid apertius? Est
igitur cecus qui doctrine tam aperte et solutioni tam solide a doctore
veritatis date nititur contraire.

10. Item Apostolus 1 Cor. 7 (2): 'Bonum est', inquit 'homini mulierem non
tangere. Sed propter fornicationem unusquisque suam uxorem habeat,
et unaqueque suum virum.' Nunc quero: aut propter fornicationem
vitandam, aut faciendam? ¹³Non utique faciendam, quia ipse alibi prohibet, 1 Cor. 6 (18): 'Fugite fornicationem'. Ergo uxorem haberi con-
cedit propter fornicationem vitandam. Ergo dum uxor cognoscitur,
peccatum vitatur. Matrimonium igitur bonum esse probatur. [*fo. 97ra*]
Nec te moveat quod dicit: 'bonum est mulierem non tangere' (1 Cor. 7:
1). Vult enim dicere quod melius est caste vivere quam non continere.
Unde subdit (1 Cor. 7: 9) 'Volo omnes homines esse sicut ego sum',
unde 'bonum est si sic permaneant sicut ego', sed 'si non continent,
nubant: melius est' inquit, 'nubere, quam uri'. Et multa apertissima
sunt ibi de materia ista.

11. Item 1 Ti. v (11): 'adolescentiores viduas devita', et subdit (1 ad Tim. 5:
14): 'Volo ergo iuniores viduas nubere, filios procreare, matresfamilias
esse'. Nichil istis apertius. Igitur errant qui matrimonium dampnant.
Unde dicitur 1 Ti. 4¹⁴ (1–3) 'Spiritus manifeste dicit quia in novissimis
temporibus discedent quidam a fide, attendentes spiritibus erroris ¹⁵et
doctrinis demoniorum in ypocrisi loquentium mendacium, et cauteri-
atam habentium suam conscientiam, prohibentium nubere et abstinere
a cibis quos deus creavit'. Manifestum est igitur quod omnes illi errant
qui nuptias dampnant et cibos aliis comedere vetant. Sed ista faciunt
Patareni. Isti igitur sunt illi heretici de quibus prophetavit spiritus
Apostoli.

12. Item, si nuptie male essent, Dominus ma|las [*fo. 97rb*] esse docuis-
set, nec eas sua presentia decorasset, nec ibi comedisset, nec eas tam
sollempni miraculo adornasset, nec matrem suam sanctissimam adesse
permisisset. Ergo dum istis omnibus nuptias decoravit, bonas eas esse
ostendit.

13. Item canon dixit, et hoc per se notum existit, quod error cui non

¹² dimitti] dimittere *in Vulgate*
¹³ Non utique faciendam] *supplied in margin*
¹⁴ Note that the scribe uses both roman and arabic numerals for biblical chapters:
the latter here, the former a couple of lines above.
¹⁵ et doctrinis . . . conscientiam] *supplied in margin*

resistitur, approbatur, nec caret scrupulo societatis occulte qui manifesto facinori desinit obviare. Ergo, si matrimonium malum esset, cum Dominus presens esset, et non illi malo resisteret cum resistere posset, nec illud redargueret, cum doctor veritatis existeret, dum non impediebat malum, approbat. Sed hoc est impossibilissimum. Ergo, et primum: matrimonium scilicet esse malum.

14. Item Apostolus, Ro. 1 (32), loquens de peccatis, sic in fine concludit quod 'non solum facientes, sed qui consentiunt facientibus digni sunt morte.' Sed consentire est tacere cum possis arguere. Sed si matrimonium malum erat, et Dominus redarguere poterat, et non redarguebat, ergo consentiebat, ergo peccabat, ergo filius mortis erat. Sed hoc impossibilissimum erat. Ergo matrimonium non est malum.

15. Tertio probatur hoc ipsum per sanctorum exempla. Nam constat dominam nostram matrimonio Joseph fuisse coniunctam. Unde dicitur, Mt. [16]1 (20): 'Ioseph fili David, noli timere accipere Mariam coniugem tuam'. Sed nulli matrimonialiter iuncta fuisset, si matrimonium malum esset. Ergo matrimonium bonum est.

16. Item, si dicas matrimonium ratione carnalis copule, non in se, esse malum, quare domina nostra potuit matrimonialiter Ioseph iungi, sed non ab eo cognosci, contra dicitur Luc. 1 (6–7) quod Zacharias et uxor illius erant ambo iusti ante deum incedentes in omnibus mandatis Domini sine querela: et addiditur ibi quod sterilis erat Elysabeth. Sed sterilem se esse nescivisset nisi vir suus *eam cognovisset. Ergo non peccat eam cognoscens, quia si peccasset, iustus non fuisset.

17. Item ibidem (13) dicitur: 'Ne timeas', inquit angelus, 'Zacharia, quoniam exaudita est deprecatio [*fo. 97[vb]*] tua, et Elysabeth uxor tua pariet tibi filium', etc. Sed filium non pareret nisi eam cognosceret; nec ad eam ipse accederet, nec angelus ei hoc diceret, si hoc esset peccatum. Ergo uxorem cognoscere causa prolis habende [17]et ad cultum dei [18]nutriende non est peccatum, sed potius magnum bonum.

18. Item dicitur in Mt. (8: 14) quod Dominus intravit domum ubi socrus Petri tenebatur magnis febribus. Sed si socrus Petri erat, ergo eius filiam in uxorem Petrus habebat, nec eam ob Christi discipulatum dimiserat, quia Christus contrarium docebat. Non est ergo malum, sed bonum.

19. In verbo premisso ostenduntur nuptie honorabiles: primo ex parte invitantium, secundo [19]vero ex parte convivantium. Nam ad nuptias invitantes fuerunt sancti et Domini consobrini. Sed ad nuptias convivantes fuerunt sanctissimi, quia mater Domini, Christus et eius discipuli. Primum notatur cum dicitur (Io. 2: 1): 'Nuptie facte sunt',

[16] 1] 2 *ms.*
[17] et] *d'Avray: om. ms.*
[18] nutriende] *d'Avray:* nutriendum *ms.*
[19] vero] *supplied in margin*

supple, a consobrinis. Secundum notatur cum additur (ibid.) 'et erat
mater Iesu ibi' tunc.

20. Ut ergo de carnalibus nuptiis nichil ultra dicamus, quia habun|danter
[*fo. 98ra*] iam diximus quantum ipse Dominus donare est dignatus, notandum est breviter quod Dominus noster triplices nuptias fecit. Nam
primas nuptias celebravit in utero virginis per nostre nature assump-
tionem. Secundas nuptias celebravit in crucis patibulo per ecclesie sibi
copulationem. Tertias nuptias fecit in celo per eternam refectionem.

21. Dico quod primas nuptias Dominus fecit in virginis utero, dum nostram naturam assumpsit et sibi eam perpetuo copulavit. O quales
nuptie fuerunt iste, quam humano generi pretiose, quam deliciose,
quam amande, quam venerande, quantisve laudibus extollende! In
quo rex noster nos magis potuit honorare, quam nostram naturam sibi
in unitate persone unire, ut non sit alius Dominus, alius hominis filius,
sed idem et unus simul homo et deus? O quanta gratia, quam ampla
misericordia, quam caritas immensa, quia non angelos apprehendit,
sed semen Abrae apprehendit. Et propterea ad [*fo. 98rb*] gaudendum
invitamur, Apoc. 19 (7): 'Gaudeamus', inquit, 'et exultemus, et demus
gloriam deo, quia venerunt nuptie agni', etc.

22. Et vere dicuntur facte in Chana Galilee, quia et zelo amoris maximi
factum est, ut 'a summo celo esset egressio eius' (Ps. 18: 7), et quia
'ipse tamquam sponsus esset procedens de thalamo suo' (Ps. 18: 6).

23. Secundas nuptias Christus fecit in ligno quando ecclesiam sanguine
suo mundavit et eam sibi perpetuo federe copulavit. Hee nuptie quamvis fuerint sponso valde amare, nobis facte sunt valde proficue, dum
nobis tradidit carnem in cibum, sanguinem in potum, et se totum in
pretium. Unde dicitur ad Eph. v (25) 'Sicut Christus dilexit ecclesiam',
etc. Et ideo de hiis nuptiis exponitur illud Mt. (22: 2) 'Simile factum
est regnum celorum homini regi qui fecit nuptias filio suo.' Tunc enim
deus pater nuptias filio suo fecit quando ei ecclesiam copulavit.

24. Tertias nuptias Dominus fecit et facit in celo, dum suos dilectos sibi
in gloria copulat. De [*fo. 98va*] torrente voluptatis sue satiat, et de vino
sue ubertatis inebriat: Ps. (35: 9–10) 'Inebriabuntur ab ubertate domus
tue, et torrente voluptatis tue potabis eos, quoniam apud te est fons
vite'. Et ideo ipse dicit in Luc. (14: 17) Ecce parata sunt omnia: venite
ad nuptias.[20]

25. O felices nuptie, ubi omnes *convivantes sunt reges, ubi ferculum
mense appositum est omne bonum et ubi ministrator est summum
bonum. Et propterea dicitur, Apoc. (19: 9) 'beati qui ad cenam agni
vocati sunt'.

26. Nonne illi vere beati sunt, [21]cui omnia optata succedunt, omnia bona

---

[20] Paraphrase more than direct quotation.
[21] cui] quibus *recte*

apposita sunt, et omnia mala absunt? Ad hanc igitur cenam nos Dominus introducat, cui soli cum patre et spiritu sancto est honor et gloria in secula seculorum, Amen.

1. 12. A sermon on marriage by Aldobrandino da Toscanella[1] (Schneyer no. 404)

This sermon and the next one both illustrate the same main argument that marriage symbolism goes together with a highly positive presentation of marriage on the literal and human level. The two texts belong to the 'model sermon' genre. Like Servasanto, Aldobrandino likes quoting Aristotle. He too lived in the midst of a sophisticated Florentine public and it is probably no accident that these two preachers include much more philosophy in their sermons than was usual in their time among preachers based elsewhere. A glance at the notes will show, furthermore, that Aldobrandino draws much more learning into his preaching than any of the other preachers transcribed here, including Servasanto.

MS Rome, Casanatense 4560 (= C)[2]

In C the sermon is written in a clear expert hand, in two columns, with paragraph marks, perhaps in the first half of the fourteenth century. The scholarly catalogue of the Casanatense manuscripts that is in progress has not progressed as far as this one.

Fos. 42va–45rb:

Dominica prima post octavas Epiphanie. De evangelio.

1. Nuptie facte sunt in Cana Galilee, Io. secundo (1) [*fo. 42vb*] Secundum quod vult beatus Ieronimus super Ioanne,[3] iste nuptie celebrantur pro Iohanne [4]evangelista sponso, quem Iesus vocavit de hiis nuptiis, volentem nubere sponse carnis, quam non nominat. Vocatus autem est ad perpetuam virginitatem, unitus sponso deo, qui requirit spirituale connubium. Unde ea que in *evangelio ponuntur ad congruitatem nuptiarum carnalium, accipienda sunt ad necessitatem spiritualium, que sunt tria. Et primum est circumstantia temporis, quia 'die tertio'.

---

[1] Schneyer, *Repertorium*, i, no. 404, p. 254.

[2] I use a siglum in the apparatus rather than '*ms*.' because in Document **1. 13** I use this manuscript together with others.

[3] Cf. ps.-Jerome, *Expositio quattuor evangeliorum*, at the words 'Discipulus, quem amabat Iesus' (Migne, *PL* 30. 588); cf. E. Dekkers *et al.*, *Clavis patrum Latinorum*, 3rd edn. (Turnhout, 1995), no. 631, p. 219; K. Froelich and M. T. Gibson (eds.), *Biblia Latina cum glossa ordinaria: Facsimile Reprint of the Editio Princeps, Adolph Rusch of Strassburg 1480/81* (4 vols.; Turnhout, 1992), iv, Prologue to John, p. 223 (thanks to Patrick Nold for the reference).

[4] evangelista] evangelica C

Secundum est congruentia loci, quia 'in Chana Galilee'. Tertium est presentia matris, quia 'erat ibi mater Iesu'.

2. Quo ad primum, attendendum quod ad spirituale connubium oportet attendere ternarium in 'die', et hoc quia anima maxime perficitur cum coniungitur suo principio, propter quod facta est, scilicet deo: sicut vestimentum est [5]perfectum cum induitur et equus cum equitatur.

Omnis autem perfectio consistit in quodam ternario:—sicut videmus perfectionem in divinis esse in ternario personarum patris et filii et spiritus sancti; in angelis, perfectionem in tribus ierarchiis et ter ternis ordinibus; in corporibus: longitudinem, latitu|dinem [*fo. 42*^{va}] et profunditatem; in naturalibus: substantiam, virtutem et operationem; in moralibus: scire, velle et delectabiliter operari; in peccatoribus: concupiscentia carnis, concupiscentia occulorum et superbia vite; in medicina peccati: [6]contritio, confessio, et satisfactio; in virtutibus: fidem, spem, et caritatem. Ergo, die tertio fit et perficitur connubium spirituale.

3. Primo namque die inchoat fides, per cognitionem; secundo spes, per extensionem; tertio vero die perficit caritas per amplexativum amorem, per quam dicit (Cant. 3: 4): 'Tenui eum nec dimittam'. Fides enim non potest cum deo perficere nuptias primo die, quia compatitur secum peccatum mortale, licet remaneat informis: nam 'demones credunt et contremiscunt' (Iacob. 2: 19). Item, secundo die non facit spes, quia etiam peccator potest habere eam. Sed tertio die facit caritas, quia qui adheret deo, unus spiritus est. Amor enim est virtus unitiva, et transformans amantem in amatum. Exemplum: sicut beatus Ignatius, desponsatus deo per amorem, non potuit a suo sponso nec tor|mentis [*fo. 43*^{rb}] nec morte separari ab eo, unde eum inter tormenta nominans occisus est, in cuius corde diviso inventum est nomen Iesu, unde Apostolus, Ro. 8 (38–9) 'certus sum quod nec mors, nec vita, nec angeli poterunt nos separare a caritate dei, que est in Christo Iesu'. Et sic patet primum, scilicet circumstantia temporis.

4. Secundo, oportet attendere quod sit congruentia loci, quia 'in Chana Galilee', quod interpretatur 'zelus[7] transmigrationis'.[8] Unde oportet nos per zelum et amorem de hoc mundo transmigrare ad consummandum istud spirituale matrimonium, quod bene per Ysaac [9]significatur, de quo adiuravit Habraam servum suum ne acciperet ei uxorem de filiabus terre in qua habitat, sed iret in Mesopotamiam Sirie, ut notatur Ge(n.) 24. Nam in mundo isto non potest fieri matrimonium.

[5] perfectum cum induitur] perfectivum cum induimur C
[6] contritio] contrititio C
[7] 'Chana "zelus" . . .' (MS BL Add. 31,830, fo. 447ra).
[8] 'Galilea "rota" vel "volubilis" sive "transmeans" aut "transmigratio mea"' (ibid., fo. 452ra).
[9] significatur] *om.* C

5. Primo, quia in mundo non est aliqua creatura que conveniat nostre nobilitati. Videmus enim quod deus unicuique creature dedit locum secundum suam nobilitatem: ut plantis terram; et quia pisces sunt nobiliores plantis, dedit eis nobiliorem locum, scilicet aquam; [*fo. 43va*] et quia aves sunt nobiliores piscibus, dedit eis nobiliorem locum, scilicet aerem; et illa que conveniunt in natura, conveniunt in locum, sicut plante ¹⁰omnes in terra, et omnes pisces in aqua, et omnes aves in aere. Homo autem habet similitudinem cum deo, quia ad eius similitudinem factus, ergo conveniens est quod conversetur cum deo in celo, propter suam nobilitatem, et ibi matrimonium faciat. Apostolus, Ph. 3 (20): 'Nostra conversatio in celis est', id est, esse debet. Videmus enim quod peregrinus nobilis non libenter contrahit matrimonium in terra peregrinationis sue, specialiter si terra illa sit ignobilis, sed revertitur ad locum nativitatis sue, per quem modum Apostolus, volens connubium facere conveniens sue nobilitati, quia non habebat hic manentem civitatem, ¹¹dixit (Philipp. 3: 13): posteriorum oblitus, 'ad anteriora me extendo'.¹²

6. Secundo, quia mundus iste non competit nostre quieti. Nullus enim in mundo isto est bene quietus, eo quod mundus est semper in motu. Videmus autem quod qui est in re mota semper movetur ipse, sicut qui est in navi fluctuanti, fluctuat et ipse. Unde Augustinus:¹³ 'Fecisti nos, Domine, [*fo. 43vb*] ad te, et inquietum est cor nostrum donec requiescat in te.' Unde Boetius dicit:¹⁴ 'Quis est tam composite felicitatis qui non ex aliqua parte cum status sui qualitate rixetur?' Et Gregorius:¹⁵ 'Qui labenti innititur, necesse est ut cum labente labatur.'

7. Tertio, quia mundus iste non convenit nostre sanitati. Videmus enim quod locus est conservativus locati: sicut rosa quamdiu est in spina virens conservatur, sed in manu pallescit; et piscis in mari vel in aqua vivit, extra aquam moritur. Ita, in mundo isto tristamur, exurimur, sitimus, dolemus, infirmamur. Unde Augustinus dicit:¹⁶ 'Quesivi in mente mea et non inveni locum anime mee, nisi te, deus, in quo colliguntur dispersa.' In mundo enim isto nullus est qui habeat omnia

---

¹⁰ omnes] *supplied in margin*
¹¹ dixit] .d. *C*
¹² Cf. Phil. 3: 13: 'Unum autem, quae quidem retro sunt obliviscens, ad ea vero quae sunt prior, extendens meipsum'.
¹³ Augustine, *Confessions*, 1. 1 (Migne, *PL* 32. 659).
¹⁴ Boethius, *Philosophiae consolatio*, 2. 4. 12 (*Anicii Manlii Severini Boethii Philosophiae consolatio*, ed. L. Bieler (Corpus Christianorum Series Latina 94; Turnhout, 1984), 24).
¹⁵ Not found under Gregory in the CD-ROM of Migne, *PL*, but see Peter of Blois, *De XII utilitatibus tribulationis* (Migne, *PL* 207. 994): 'et inde consequi nullum bonum imo malum finem, secundum Gregorium, dicentem "Qui labenti innititur, necesse est ut cum labente labatur"'.
¹⁶ Augustine, *Confessions*, 10. 40 (Migne, *PL* 32. 806).

bona sine aliquo malo. Aliqui enim sunt pulcri, et tamen pauperes; aliqui nobiles, sed mendici; aliqui divites et nobiles, sed infirmi; aliqui divites et nobiles et sani, sed sine liberis; aliqui autem, licet sint cum filiis, tamen habent eos insensatos, vel malos; et si sint boni, sunt brevis vite.[17] Et ideo Boetius dicit: 'Anxia est [*fo. 44ra*] conditio humanorum bonorum, que vel numquam tota proveniat, vel numquam perpetua subsistat':[18] sed in deo sunt omnia bona collecta sine aliquo malo'. Unde David (Ps. 16: 15): 'Satiabor cum apparuerit gloria tua'. Exemplum de filio cuiusdam regis, qui intravit religionem. Cum autem pater voluit eum extrahere, dixit filius: 'Libenter faciam, dum tamen faciatis quod in regno nostro non infirmentur ita nobiles sicut igno- biles', cui cum pater diceret se non posse: 'Et ideo volo properare ad illud regnum ubi nullus infirmatur.' Quod pater audiens compunctus corde adquievit. Et sic patet secundum.

8. Tertio, oportet quod sit presentia matris, scilicet Maria, que interpre- tatur 'maris amaritudo',[19] et significat penitentiam de peccatis. Nullus enim se potest de peccato excusare, quia sicut dicit Apostolus, Ro. 3 (23) 'Omnes peccaverunt et egent gratia dei'. Mare autem, sicut sapi- ens dicit,[20] in superficie est amarum et salsum, quia calor solis trahit partes subtiles aque, et grosse remanentes aduruntur, et fiunt amare; profundum vero, quia calor solis non potest attingere nec agere, partes eius rema|nent [*fo. 44rb*] dulces: sic penitentia in presenti quidem, sicut in superficie, est amara, sed in fundo, id est, in futuro, dulcis erit, quia recipiet fructum pacatissimum. Et ideo dicit Apostolus, Ad He(br.) xii (11) 'Omnis [21]pena in presenti quidem videtur non esse gaudii, sed meroris, sed in fine recipiet fructum pacatissimum'.

9. Et convenienter penitentia etiam in presenti debet esse dulcis de pec- cato, quia ipsum peccatum infert multum dampnum, penitentia vero restituit dampnum. Ro(m):[22] Peccatum enim tollit naturam. Nam homo est substantia *animata, sensibilis, rationalis.

10. Sed peccatum primo tollit substantiam. Substantia enim dicitur quasi per se stans. Sed peccatum non per se stat, sed est ipsum nichil. Nichil enim est illud quod non includit finem, sicut dicitur de pomo putrido, quia nichil valet quia non includit debitum finem, scilicet manduca- tionem. Ita peccatum dicitur nichil quia excludit a fine, scilicet a vita

[17] This echoes the sentiments though not the precise wording of Boethius, *Philo- sophiae consolatio,* 2. 4. 13–14, p. 24 Bieler.
[18] Boethius, *Philosophiae consolatio* 2. 4. 12, p. 24 Bieler.
[19] 'Maria . . . aut "mare amarum" . . .' (MS BL 31,830, fo. 458vb).
[20] Cf. *Aristotle's* Meteorology *in the Arabico-Latin Tradition: A Critical Editon of the Texts, with Introduction and Indices,* ed. P. L. Schoonheim (Leiden, 2000), tractatus secundus, 3, p. 72.
[21] pena] disciplina *in Vulgate*
[22] Not found: perhaps Aldobrandinus misremembered. A space is left in *C.*

eterna. Et ideo dicit Augustinus[23] quod peccatum nichil est, et nichil fiunt homines cum peccant; et propheta (Ps. 72: 22): 'Ad nichilum redactus sum et nescivi'; et propter exclusionem a fine dicebat (Ps. 68: 3): 'Infixus sum in limo profundi, et non [*fo. 44va*] est substantia'.

11. Item secundo tollit animatum. Nam anima magis est ubi amat quam ubi animat, sicut Augustinus dicit.[24] Sed omne peccatum causatur vel ex amore vel ex timore deordinato: sicut Augustinus dicit[25] super illum Psalmi (79/80: 17): 'Incensa igitur et suffosa', etc., quod omne peccatum provenit vel ex amore male inflammante, vel ex timore male humiliante. Sed avarus deordinate amat pecuniam, et ideo anima eius plus est in bursa quam in corpore, et ita etiam de concupiscentia, quia anima plus est in re quam concupiscit quam cum corpore proprio. Unde propheta Osee [26]7 (11) dicit in persona peccatoris: 'Effraym quasi columba non habens cor'.

12. Item, tertio, peccatum tollit sensum. Nam, ut dicit sapiens,[27] nichil est sensitivum sine calore. Videmus enim quod paraliticus et dormiens non sentiunt, et ratio huius est quia calor in eis recolligitur ad cor, et sic remanent membra stupida, sicut in mortuis. Hoc autem facit peccatum. Nam facit sicut venenum, quod statim ut sumitur vadit ad cor, quod est fons vite, et occidit. Ita peccatum vadit ad fontem vite [*fo. 44vb*] spiritualis et caloris, scilicet ad ipsam caritatem, et occidit animam, quia accipit ab ea virtutem sensitivam. Unde in Cant.[28] anima peccatrix, insensibilis facta, dicit: 'Traxerunt me et non dolui, vulneraverunt me et non sensi'.

13. Item, quarto, peccatum tollit rationem. Nam peccatum est contra rationem facere, sicut dicit Dam(ascenus).[29] Videmus autem quod unum

---

[23] Augustine, *In Joannis evangelium tractatus CXXIV*, 13, on John 1: 3 (Migne, *PL* 35. 1385).
[24] Not found in Augustine, but see Bernard of Clairvaux, *De praecepto et dispensatione*, 60 in *Œuvres complètes*, xxi. *Le Précepte et la dispense. La Conversion*, ed. F. Callerot, J. Miethke, and C. Jaquinod (Sources chrétiennes, 457; Paris, 2000), 276 (the tag is much quoted with various attributions).
[25] Augustine, *Ennarationes in Psalmos*, at Ps. 79 (80): 17 (*Sancti Aurelii Augustini Ennarationes in Psalmos LI–C*, ed. D. E. Dekkers and I. Fraipont (Corpus Christianorum Series Latina, 39, Aurelii Augustini Opera, 10/2; Turnhout, 1956), para. 13, pp. 1117–18), possibly via Peter Lombard, *Sentences*, 2. 42. 4 (262) (*Magistri Petri Lombardi Parisiensis Episcopi Sententiae in IV libris distinctae*, 3rd edn., ed. Patres Collegii S. Bonaventurae ad Claras Aquas [I. Brady] (2 vols.; Spicilegium Bonaventurianum, 4–5; Grottaferrata, 1971–81), i/2. *Liber I et II*, 569).
[26] 7] *between lines*
[27] Aristotle, *De anima*, 425^{a}6, in William of Moerbeke's translation, 2. 25, p. 172 Gauthier; *Aristotle's* De Anima *in the Versions of William of Moerbeke and the Commentary of Thomas Aquinas*, ed. Foster *et al.*, p. 348.
[28] The quotation is a mixture of Prov. 23: 35 and Song of Songs 5: 7.
[29] Possibly an erroneous reference from memory to ps.-Dionysius, *De divinis nominibus*, 4. 32, perhaps via Thomas Aquinas, *Summa theologica*, 1–2 q. 71 a. 6:

contrarium destruit aliud, sicut egritudo destruit sanitatem, et fri-
giditas caliditatem: sic peccatum, quia est contra rationem, destruit
eam. Ablata vero ratione, homo remanet bestia, quia nulla est dif-
ferentia inter hominem et bestiam nisi per rationem, sicut sapiens
dicit.[30] Et ideo in octavo Methaphysice[31] dicit quod ita se habent dif-
ferentie in speciebus, sicut unitates in numeris. Videmus enim quod
unitate remota a quinario constituit aliam speciem, scilicet quater-
narium; addita autem, constituit aliam, scilicet senarium. Ita est in
speciebus, quia quedam sunt que habent esse tantum sicut unitatem,
ut lapides; quedam autem habent dualitatem, scilicet esse et vivere, ut
plante; quedam habent trinitatem, scilicet esse, vivere, et sentire, ut
animalia; quedam [*fo. 45ra*] autem habent quaternitatem, scilicet esse,
vivere, sentire, et intelligere vel ratiocinari, sicut homo. Sed peccatum,
ut dictum est, aufert rationem ab homine, et ita aufert a quaternario
unitatem, et ita reponitur in alia specie, scilicet in ternario, qui com-
petebat bestiis. Unde propheta dicit de peccatore (Ps. 48: 13 & 21):
'Homo cum in honore esset non intellexit. *Comparatus est iumentis
insipientibus', etc.

14. Item tollit peccatum potentiam. Omnis enim potentia dicit ordina-
tionem ad actum, sicut posse videre ordinatur ad videre et non ad
cecari vel cecum esse; et posse ambulare ordinatur ad ambulare et non
ad claudicare, quia claudicare est defectus potentie. Cum ergo potentia
hominis ordinetur ad aliquid perfectum, quia egreditur a perfecto sicut
ab ipso homine, peccare autem tollat perfectionem, ergo tollit potentiam, quia fornicari non est posse, sed defectus potentie, quia est vinci
a passione concupiscentie, et decipi non est potentia sed impotentia.
In omni enim peccato est victoria alicuius virtutis vel potentie a vitio,
sicut in avaro vincitur liberalitas, et vincit avaritia, et in guloso vincitur
temperantia, et vincit gula. Et propterea [*fo. 45rb*] dicebat propheta, tali
potentia destitutum se videns, 'Miserere mei, quoniam infirmus sum';
et alibi (Ps. 30: 11): 'infirmata est virtus mea'.

15. Item, peccatum tollit vitam, quod super omnia diligitur, quod patet

---

'Sed *malum hominis est contra rationem esse*, ut Dionysius dicit, 4 cap. *De div. nom.*
Ergo potius debuit dici quod peccatum sit contra rationem, quam quod peccatum sit
contra legem eternam.' For a roughly similar thought, but not in the same wording,
in Burgundio of Pisa's translation of St John Damascene, *De fide orthodoxa*, 95, see
Saint John Damascene, *De fide orthodoxa: Versions of Burgundio and Cerbanus*, ed.
E. M. Buytaert (Franciscan Institute Publications, Text Series, 8; St Bonaventure,
NY, etc., 1955), 359–60. I may have missed a closer match at some less obvious place
in the text.

[30] Possibly a reference to the discussion of Aristotle's views in Thomas Aquinas,
Summa theologica, 1, q. 85, a. 3.

[31] Cf. *Aristoteles Latinus*, xxv/3.2. *Metaphysica Lib. I–XIV*, ed. Gudrun Vuillemin-Diem (Leiden etc., 1995), 173–4 (*Metaph.* 1043^{b}35 and 1044^{a}10).

quia omnis operatio hominis ordinatur ad vite conservationem, sicut
agricultura et molendinus et panificatura propter cibum, qui conservat
vitam; lanificium, texture ars et sutoria propter vestitum qui defendit
a frigore, quod tollit vitam; hedificativa et medicina et pigmentaria
propter potionem qua elongatur vita. Et ideo ingeniavit natura quod
loca illa ubi est vita sint bene munita, quia cerebrum munivit for-
tissimo osse, venas abscondit in occultissimo loco, cor vallavit mul-
tis costis. Sed peccatum frangit caput, quia abicit Christum. Caput
enim viri Christus. Item, inficit venas: Ps. (13: 1): 'Corrupti sunt et
³²abhominabiles facti sunt in studiis suis'. Item, occidit cor. Rogemus (etc.).

**1. 13. A sermon on marriage by Aldobrandino da Tosca-
nella¹ (Schneyer no. 48)**

See comments on Document 1. 12.

MS Rome, Casanatense 4560 = C

Fos. 45ʳᵇ–47ʳᵃ:

1. 'Nuptie facte sunt', etc., Io. secundo. In serie presentis evangelii no-
tantur quat*t*uor. Et primum est iucunditas coniugii: ibi: 'Nuptie'. Secundum est pietas subsidii: [*fo. 45ᵛᵃ*] ibi: 'dixit mater Iesu ad eum'.
Tertium est sublimitas miraculi, ibi: 'implete ydrias aqua'. Quartum
est utilitas collegii, ibi: 'et crediderunt in eum discipuli eius'.

2. Primo quidem evangelium loquitur de iocunditate coniugii, quia
'Nuptie facte sunt'. Matrimonium quidem est res magne iocunditatis,
et ideo in nuptiis consueverunt ostendi signa magne letitie, ad hoc ut
sponsus et sponsa mutuo se diligant, qui in tanto gaudio et letitia coniunguntur. Et vere est materia *magne iocunditatis, quia: conservat
naturam, sanat plagam, adquirit gratiam, conservat amicitiam:—que
omnia sunt iocunda. Et ideo, primo, matrimonium est in officium
nature, in remedium concupiscentie, in sacramentum ecclesie, in consortium amicitie.

3. Primo est in officium nature et conservat eam. Sed res naturales sunt
iocunde, quod sic patet: Quelibet res est delectabilis in suo tempore,
sicut vinum dulce in hyeme, acerbum in estate. Et quia ars imitatur
naturam, videmus quod artes diversa artificiata secundum diversa
tempora faciunt. Matrimonium autem est nature opus. Unde legitur in primo ²Distinctionum quod ius naturale est maris et femine

---

³² abhominabiles] abhominabilis *C*

¹ Schneyer, *Repertorium*, i, no. 48, p. 226.

² Distinctionum quod ius naturale] *supplied from MS Troyes, Bibliothèque Municipale 1263, fo. 44ʳ*: quamvis naturale *C*

[*fo. 45vb*] coniunctio,[3] quam nos vocamus matrimonium. Quod etiam patet sic. Natura etiam intendit esse perpetuum et divinum, et ideo in rebus incorruptibilibus, in quibus salvatur per unum individuum, non dedit generationem. Unde non sunt plures soles, nec lune, nec plures stelle unius speciei, sed quelibet facit speciem. Inferioribus autem et [4]corruptibilibus, quia individua corrumpuntur, fecit multitudinem individuorum, et ideo dicit Philosophus, in secundo de Anima,[5] quod data est vis generativa in rebus ut quod non potest salvari in se, salvetur in suo simili, propter esse divinum, et sic conservat naturam: quod est primum.

4. Item, secundo, sanat plagam matrimonium. Unde institutum est in remedium concupiscentie, si legittime teneatur. Unde facit quod concupiscentia carnalis, que alias esset peccatum mortale, si recte teneatur, fit sine [6]peccato.

5. Item, tertio, in matrimonio confertur gratia. In quantum fide Christi contrahitur, habet ut conferat gratiam adiuvantem ad illa operanda que in matrimonio requiruntur. Et huius exemplum videmus in naturalibus, quia cuicumque datur aliqua facultas, dantur etiam auxilia quibus ad illa perveniri possit. Unde cum in matri|monio [*fo. 46ra*] detur homini ex divina institutione facultas utendi uxore sua ad prolis procreationem, datur etiam gratia sine qua id convenienter facere non posset: sicut deus, vel natura, que dedit virtutem gressivam animali, dedit ei instrumenta, scilicet pedes, per quos gradi posset.

6. Item, quarto, matrimonium conservat amicitiam, facit societatem communicativam, et institutum est in consortium, propter mutuum obsequium. Nam quedam sunt que naturaliter viris competunt, scilicet, fodere, scribere, hedificare; quedam autem mulieribus, sicut panificare, et nere, et huiusmodi, que [7]videntur naturam consequi mulieris, quia ab ipsa pueritia panificant de luto, nent lanam, que opera muliebria sunt. E converso pueri lignum equitant, gladio se precingunt, que opera virilia sunt, sicut Plato dicit.[8] Unde bene dicitur, Gen. ii (18): 'faciamus ei adiutorium simile sibi'.

7. Sequitur secundum, scilicet pietas patrocinii, quia 'dixit mater Iesu ad eum'. Mater pietatis semper in necessitate succurrit, quod quidem competit sibi quadruplici ratione. Et primo propter convenientiam

---

[3] Gratian, *Decretum*, Pars I, D. 1 c. 7.
[4] corruptibilibus] *corrected from* incorruptibilibus *in C*
[5] Perhaps Aristotle, *De anima*, 415^{a–b}, in William of Moerbeke's translation, 2. 7, p. 95 Gauthier; *Aristotle's De anima in the Versions of William of Moerbeke and the Commentary of Thomas Aquinas*, ed. Foster *et al.*, p. 210.
[6] peccato] *C adds and deletes* mortali
[7] videntur] videtur (vi^{ur}) *C*
[8] Direct Latin source not found.

240 Documents: 1. 13

vocabuli. Secundo propter congruentiam principii. Tertio propter
habundantiam beneficii. Quarto propter excellentiam preconii.
8. Primo propter con|venientiam [fo. 46ʳᵇ] vocabuli. Dicitur enim Maria
'stella maris',⁹ id est, peccatoris amari, quia cor peccatoris quasi mare
fervens. Videmus autem quod stella, quanto plus influit de luce, non
minus habet. Et ratio huius est quia spiritualia, quanto plus commu-
nicantur, non minuuntur, sicut scientia, quanto plus communicatur,
magis augetur, et candele lumen quotcumque candelis communicetur,
non minuitur.¹⁰ Corporalia vero communicata diminuuntur: sicut pa-
nis, si a pluribus videatur, non diminuitur, quia color quid spirituale
est in recipiente, scilicet in organo; si vero a pluribus gustetur, consumitur, quia sapor materialiter et naturaliter percipitur. Quia igitur
beata virgo est ditissima in donis sive bonis spiritualibus, absque sui
diminutione ea communicat. Unde ipsa invitat, dicens (Eccli. 24: 26):
'Transite ad me, omnes qui concupiscitis me, et a generationibus meis
implemini'.
9. Secundo propter congruentiam principii. Videmus enim in natura
quod ea que habent rationem principii, quicquid virtutis habent influ-
unt, sicut cor influit spiritus vitales omnibus membris, sicut cerebrum
influit sensum et motum in totum corpus, [fo. 46ᵛᵃ] sicut radix influit
humorem in omnibus ramis, sicut sol influit lumen omnibus stellis, sicut mare influit humorem omnibus humidis, sicut ignis influit calorem
omnibus calidis, et sicut celum influit motum omnibus elementis. Et
ideo Bernardus dicit:¹¹ 'Intuemini quanto dilectionis affectu eam a nobis voluit honorari, qui totius boni plenitudinem posuit in Maria, ut si
quid nobis boni est et virtutis et gratie, ab ea in nos noverimus redun-
dare que est ortus plenus deliciarum quem perflavit auster ille divinus,
ut undique fluant et refluant aromata eius et carismata gratiarum'.
10. Tertio, propter habundantiam beneficii. Ipsa enim est aqueductus, qui
quantum recipit, tantum influit, et se omnibus communiter exhibet:
sic beata Maria omnibus sinum sue pietatis et gratie ¹²aperit, ut de
plenitudine eius accipiant universi, sicut Bernardus dicit.¹³
11. Quarto, propter excellentiam ¹⁴patrocinii. Sic enim dicit quidam ad
beatam virginem: 'Si non essent peccatores, mater [fo. 46ᵛᵇ] dei num-

⁹ 'Maria . . ."stella maris" . . .' (MS BL Add. 31,830, fo. 458ᵛᵇ).
¹⁰ The sense of this is made clearer by the free variant in MS Troyes, Bibliothèque
Municipale 1263, fo. 45ʳ: 'Sicut patet in candela, quia licet ad unam candelam
centum accendantur, non minuitur lumen prime'.
¹¹ Bernard of Clairvaux, Sermo in dominica infra octauam assumptionis, 2, in Sancti
Bernardi opera, v. Sermones II, ed. J. Leclercq and H. Rochais (Rome, 1968), 263.
¹² aperit] apperit C
¹³ Bernard of Clairvaux, Sermo in nativitate beatae Virginis, 6, pp. 278–9 Leclercq
and Rochais.
¹⁴ patrocinii] preconii C

quam fores, et si non essent redimendi, nulla tibi [15]pariendi fuisset necessitas'. Quia ergo propter peccatores et miseros facta est mater dei, rependit peccatoribus vicem, [16]admittendo eis et eis impetrando gratiam adiutricem. Et sic patet secundum.

12. Tertio ponitur sublimitas miraculi, ibi: 'Implete ydrias aqua'. Circa quod quattuor includuntur, scilicet:

13. Transmutatio humoris, quia convertit aquam in vinum. Mutavit enim qualitatem, sed servavit quantitatem.

14. Secundo perfectio saporis, quia optimum vinum fecit. In omnibus enim que deus fecit, hoc servavit: quod melius fecit quam natura posset, sicut primum hominem pulcriorem omnibus hominibus qui post naturaliter generantur, et primam feminam pulcherimam, preter Christum et beatam virginem. Et cum illuminavit cecos, dedit eis pulcherimos oculos. Et cum sanavit febricitantes, ut socrum Symonis, reddidit eam subito perfectissime sanitati, sine langore et aliqua debilitate, quod non potest facere natura. Cum autem aquam transmutavit in vinum, fe|cit [*fo. 47ra*] melius quam grecum vel vernacinum, et melius quam natura facere posset.

15. Tertio, ostensio [17]vigoris, quia, sicut dicit Crisostomus,[18] istud fuit primum miraculum quod Christus fecit, per quod eliditur Liber de Infantia Salvatoris,[19] qui dicit eum multa miracula fecisse, quod non fuisset conveniens, quia potuisset credi fantasma, et eius miracula fantastica. Unde filius dei, verus homo, servavit tempus humane [20]operationis conveniens, scilicet xxx annorum, ne phantasma reputaretur.

16. Quarto ponitur assecutio honoris, quia manifestavit gloriam suam, quam prius puerilis etas obtexerat. Rogemus [etc.].

[15] pariendi] patiendi *C*
[16] admittendo eis] *MS Vatican City, BAV Chigi C. IV. 99, fo. 271vb*: admittendo *C*
[17] vigoris] viroris *C* (*a possible reading*)
[18] For John Chrysostom's homilies on the Gospel of St John see F. Liotta, 'Burgundione', in *Dizionario biografico degli Italiani*, xv (Rome, 1972), 423–8 at 425; he gives references to incunable editions (Hain, *Repertorium*, nos. *5036 and *5037), but in the absence of a critical edition I have used MS Merton College Oxford 30: the passage arguing that Jesus had not worked miracles before the Cana wedding is on fo. 155^{rb–va}.
[19] Cf. M. R. James, *The Apocryphal New Testament* (Oxford, 1924), 58–65, 70–9.
[20] operationis] *MS Vatican City, BAV Chigi C. IV. 99, fo. 272^m*: generationis *C*

Documents Relating to Chapter 2: Indissolubility

2. 1. Proof in 'forbidden degrees' cases: Hostiensis attacks laxity

This relates to the discussion in Chapter 2 about the efficacy of the Fourth
Lateran Council's measures to reduce the number of annulments. It comes
from Hostiensis's *Lectura* on the Decretals at X. 2. 20. 47, 'De testibus et
attestationibus', c. *Licet ex quadam.* Hostiensis or Henry of Susa (Henricus
de Segusio, Henricus de Bartholomaeis) was with Innocent IV probably
the greatest and most influential canonist of the Decretalist period (1234–
1917). He wrote in the established genre of commentary on the Decretals of
Gregory IX. Here he attacks judges who ignored the Lateran IV rules. This
passage seems to suggest that the council did not achieve its objective with
respect to annulments, but the inference may be false, because Document
2. 2 gives reason to think that Hostiensis set the bar of legally valid proof
exceptionally high.

MS Oxford, New College 205 (=*O*), using MS BL Arundel 485
(=*A2*)[1] to illustrate the second edition of the *Lectura*

O^2

A parchment manuscript, 400×280 mm. Script is second half of the
thirteenth century (I concur with Pennington's dating). One might even
narrow it down further. The Decretals text is written below the top
ruled line, a sign that the manuscript is after 1250, but there are two-
compartment 'a's where the top compartment is not closed, so it may
not be after about 1280. The main text is in two columns, the gloss
spreading over the margins, left and right, head and foot. 'The format of the Decretals of Gregory IX in the manuscript was obviously
designed to accommodate a much larger apparatus than usual' (Pennington). Both main text and gloss are written in expert hands, both
of which look Italian. The glossing hand has the distinctive superscript
'r', as in 'Ma^{u}tinus', which seems peculiar to Italian scribes. Pennington
describes the glossing hand as 'small, but careful and clear', but in places

---

[1] I choose this siglum because later on I use *A1* for BL Arundel 471. Arundel 485
contains books 1–2 and Arundel 471 books 3–5. This is why I do not stick to the same
manuscript of the later version of the commentary. Both the Arundel manuscripts
seem to be *pecia* manuscripts, representing a text or texts probably widely available.

[2] Description based on K. Pennington, 'An Earlier Recension of Hostiensis's
Lectura on the Decretals' (1987), repr. in id., *Popes, Canonists and Texts, 1150–1550*
(Aldershot etc., 1993), no. XVII (retaining the original pagination: 77–90) at 77, and
on personal inspection of the manuscript.

it is faded and consequently a little difficult. There are initials in red and blue, in both the main script and the glossing script.

On fo. 1 there are tables of contents in later medieval hands. The Decretals and Hostiensis's apparatus on them in the form of a gloss take up fos. 2^r–241^r. 'The back flyleaf (fol. 242) is the text of a commentary on X. 1. 3. 32–1. 3. 37. Several glosses are signed Johannes Andreae' (Pennington).

$A2$[3]

A parchment manuscript, 440×285 mm., 2 columns, the final folio numbered 320, initials and paragraph marks in red and blue.

Writing is below the top line. The script or scripts (see below) could be Italian to judge from the 'u'-shaped superscript 'r/'re', but otherwise it would be hard to say whether the scribe was Italian and he may not have been. It is a *pecia* manuscript, produced by the university stationers. See e.g. 'finitur hic li' in the margin on fo. 253vb, alongside what looks like a change of handwriting.

The manuscript is taken up with Hostiensis's *Lectura* on the first two books of the Decretals of Gregory IX.

The discoveries of Kenneth Pennington have shown that it is desirable to compare manuscripts of the two authorial 'editions' of this commentary.[4] I use the early recension, transmitted in *O*. Pennington says of this manuscript that it 'will be an indispensable text for those who wish to study Hostiensis's ideas. . . . I have checked its readings in many passages, and they are most often as good or better than the best manuscripts we have of his second recension. With it we will be better able to understand his thought and trace its development' (86). It was apparently completed between 1254 and 1265 (ibid. 81); the *terminus post quem* may be pushed a little later, to 1262.[5]

To compare the passages in question in this manuscript with the second edition, which was the version most people would have known, I have given variants from MS BL Arundel 485 in the apparatus (ignoring orthographic variants, transpositions, a few silly errors, and other trivia). As noted above, it is a *pecia* manuscript—a further reason for using it, since it was probably representative of an important proportion of the transmission of the text.

The early printed editions of Hostiensis's *Lectura on the Decretals* are

---

[3] Description based on personal inspection.

[4] Pennington, 'An Earlier Recension', 82, 85.

[5] K. Pennington, 'Henry de Segusio (Hostiensis)' (1993), repr. in id., *Popes, Canonists and Texts*, no. XVI (paginated 1–12) at 8. For the dates of the other great synthesis of Hostiensis, see ibid. 5–6. Note that the information about the dating of the two syntheses in J. Brundage, *Medieval Canon Law* (London etc., 1995), 214, does not correspond to Pennington's findings and may be mistaken.

not necessarily reliable: see Pennington, 'An Earlier Recension', 85. I did consult the Paris 1512 edition (British Library call number C.104.l.10), and in fact it does not give a substantially different text from that of *A2*. Still, the text of a *pecia* manuscript from around 1300 is clearly better for our comparative purpose: it takes us directly to what was widely available in the second half of the thirteenth century.

O, fo. 91ra, left-hand gloss, and *A2*, fo. 238vb:

1. *'quia tamen*, verbo *exemplis*—puta Raymundi Barelli, habitatoris castri de Pilia Niciensis diocesis, qui hac occasione omnia matrimonia separabat. Erat enim antiquus homo et statim adinveniebat parentelam et ipsam computabat, dicens [6]se quasi omnes vidisse. Et hoc asserebat coram x vel xii. Postea dividebat illos per partes tres vel quatuor, et sic tres ex illis coram aliis x hoc [7]idem asserebant simul, dicentes quod ita audierant a maioribus suis; et illos secundos inducebat postea ad probandam consanguinitatem. *Experimentis*: experto crede magistro. Et de hoc [8]nota supra, eodem, *Preterea*, ad finem.[9]

O, fo. 91rb, right-hand gloss, and *A2*, fo. 239rb–va:

2. . . . Primum est quod considerari oportet utrum testis sit gravis vel levis. Secundum utrum ante litem motam testificata didicerit. Tertium, utrum ab antiquioribus suis hoc audierit. Quartum, utrum ad minus a duobus hoc [10]audierit. Quintum, utrum illi duo essent suspecti vel infames vel fidedigni et omni exceptione maiores. Sextum, utrum unus tantum hoc audierit a pluribus, quamvis bone fame, vel plures infames ab hominibus etiam bone fame. Septimum, esto quod plures [11]sunt bone fame, qui a pluribus bone fame hoc audierunt, utrum odio, amore, timore vel commodo ad hoc procedant. [12]Octavum utrum propriis nominibus vel saltem sufficientibus circumloqutionibus personas graduum [13]duxerint exprimendas. Nonum, utrum singulos gradus ab utroque latere clara computatione distinguant. Decimum, utrum concludant in suo iuramento quod secundum quod deponunt a suis maioribus acceperunt. Undecimum, utrum [14]credant ita esse. Duode-

[6] se] *om. A2*
[7] idem] *om. A2*
[8] nota] no. *O, A2*: notatur *is possible*
[9] 'Etenim circumspectus judex atque discretus motum animi sui ex argumentis et testimoniis, quae rei aptiora esse compererit, confirmabit' (X. 2. 20. 27 =E. Friedberg, *Corpus iuris canonici* (2 vols.; Leipzig, 1879–81; repr. Graz, 1955), ii. 324, omitting the words in italic, since these were not in the Decretals as 'published' in the Middle Ages: Friedberg restored them from the sources of the Decretals).
[10] audierit] audiverit *A2*
[11] sunt] sint *A2*
[12] Octavum] Octavo *A2*
[13] duxerint] dixerint *A2 (evident error)*
[14] credant] credan *then space then erasure in A2*

cimum, utrum viderint aliquas de personis graduum quos computant pro consanguineis se habere.

3. Hec sunt xii, per ordinem supra specificata, que sunt omnino consideranda, et super maiori parte querendo a testibus examinatio facienda, quorum si unum deficiat, testimonium insufficiens reputatur, ut patet in hoc verbo in principio.

   Et hec duodecim interrogatoria circa causam matrimonialem, quando ob causam consanguinitatis seu affinitatis ad divortium agitur, debet habere iudex in memoria, et super ipsis sive maiori parte ipsorum testem quemlibet interrogare, ita quod nec unum dimittat, imo ad unguem examinet, etsi partes etiam contradicant. Argumentum infra 'De eo qui cognovit consanguineam uxoris sue', *Super eo;*[15] . . .

4. Hec tamen male servaverunt actenus iudices nostri temporis, de talibus parum aut nichil curantes. Unde contra deum et iustitiam, hac forma canonica spreta, multas sententias divortii, non sine animarum suarum et multarum aliarum periculis, protulerunt:—que obsecramus de cetero non negligant, sed advertant.

5. Diceret quis: quare sic artatur hic probationis facultas, cum alias subveniatur probationibus: supra, eodem, *Significavit,*[16] et c. *Albricus.*[17] Respondeo: quia plurimis exemplis, etc., ut supra, eodem, rubrica i, verbo *Quia tamen plurimis;*[18] et quia *quartum gradum hec prohibitio non excedit:* supra, eodem, §i, in principio.[19]

6. Diceret alius: si hec forma servetur, ob causam consanguinitatis vel affinitatis dabitur divortii sententia vix aut numquam: [20]numquid tutius esset hanc formam omittere et sententiam divortii ferre, et si [21]omittantur aliqua de predictis? Respondeo: Non! Imo melius [22]est, nisi ad unguem probentur omnia, pro matrimonio iudicare. Et sic continuatur sequens verbum [23]*tolerabilius*, etc.

7. *tolerabilius*, verbo *hominum.* Ergo loquitur quando queritur de secundo vel saltem tertio vel quarto gradu, quos non prohibet lex divina, ut patet in eo quod legitur et notatur infra 'De divortiis', *Gaudemus*[24]

[15] X. 4. 13. 5.
[16] X. 2. 20. 41.
[17] X. 2. 20. 43. The two decretals just cited both tend to maximize the amount of evidence legally admissible.
[18] The part of the decretal which deals with the dangers of hearsay evidence, and where Hostiensis's commentary discusses the scam of Raymundus Barellus.
[19] That is, after the forbidden degrees had been reduced from seven to four, it was no longer necessary to reconstruct the distant genealogical past, and it was possible to insist on rigorous evidence for the relatively recent genealogies required.
[20] numquid] numquid igitur *A2*
[21] omittantur] omittatur *A2*
[22] est] *om. A2*
[23] *tolerabilius*, etc. *tolerabilius*, verbo] *tolerabilius* verbo *A2* (*error by eyeskip*)
[24] X. 4. 19. 8.

[25]rubrica i. Primus enim [26]et secundus pro maiori parte [27]reputantur notorii. Unde in illis non [28]requireretur accusator vel testis, ut patet infra, 'De divortiis', *Porro*,[29] § *Praeterea*.

8. *Dimittere copulatos.* Hic enim nullum periculum est, ex quo is qui impedimentum induxit dicit quod *tolerabilius est*, cum et ipse videatur tacite [30]dispensare. Et ex hoc, in dubio debeant coniuges ad sui prelati consilium suam conscientiam informare: infra, 'De sententia excommunicationis' *Inquisitioni*.[31]

9. Et ex hoc [32]nota quod quandocumque agitur de impedimento canonico semper est in dubio pro matrimonio iudicandum, ut hic, et infra, 'De [Sententia et] re iudicata',[33] circa finem. Et appello 'dubium' ex quo deficit testis in uno de xii superius numeratis. Et est istud contra magistros qui consueverunt glosare contra matrimonia et pro divortiis iudicare, ut patet [34]supra, eodem §, verbo *et ab utroque*, super verbo *singulos gradus*.[35]

10. Non dicat ergo se ubi dubitandum est [36]certum iudex; supra, 'De rescriptis', *Cum contingat*,[37] § penult. *Domini separare,* sive coniungere: [38]hic enim semper periculum est, quia nec papa potest in talibus dispensare, ut legitur et notatur supra, 'De [39]restitutione spoliatorum' *Litteras*.[40]

2. 2. Proof in 'forbidden degrees' cases: the rigorism of Hostiensis

The following passage from the same commentary of Hostiensis dilutes the force of the preceding passages: it suggests that he was a hard-liner on the calculation of degrees, and that the canonists he accuses of laxity may

[25] rubrica] responsio *or* respondeo *A2*
[26] et] vel *A2*
[27] reputantur] ruputantur *A2*
[28] requireretur] requiretur *A2*
[29] X. 4. 19. 3.
[30] dispensare] dispensare. Et super hoc ius istud promulgatur: licet ad quodlibet preceptum iudicis non intendat dispensare, ut legitur et notatur supra, 'De restitutione spolii', *Litteras*, § Opinioni (X. 2. 12. 13) *A2*
[31] X. 5. 39. 44.
[32] nota] no *A2* (*could be extended as* notatur)
[33] X. 2. 27.
[34] supra, eodem §, verbo *et*] om. *A2*
[35] These references are to phrases within the decretal which is the subject of the whole analysis, X. 2. 20. 47.
[36] certum] *A2*: certus *O, in error*
[37] X. 1. 3. 24.
[38] hic] hoc *A2*
[39] restitutione] rescriptis *A2*
[40] X. 2. 13. 13.

have been within the limits of honest interpretation of the law. In fact, he seems to be addressing his polemic against a particular canonist, Johannes Teutonicus, who wrote a commentary on the decrees of the Fourth Lateran Council. The passage printed here in heavy type and between brackets from '*singulos gradus*' to 'improbari, ut supra, eodem, *Series*' is a close paraphrase of the earlier writer.[1] Hostiensis is quoting him in full before refuting him. It is not the historian's place to pass judgement on the dispute between canonists, but it does not look as though Johannes Teutonicus is deliberately playing fast and loose with the law and with indissolubility.

That alters the picture significantly. Hostiensis may be right in thinking that some people were cutting corners to obtain fake annulments, but he may exaggerate the problem and his fellow canonists may have been less complicitous in subverting the law than might at first appear.

The transcription is based on the same manuscripts as Document **2. 1**, q.v. for sigla and descriptions.

O, fo. 91ʳᵇ, **gloss at foot of the page, and** *A2,* fo. 239ʳᵃ⁻ᵇ:

1. *Et ab utroque* verbo: et est hoc tertium quod requiritur quo ad dictum **singulos gradus.** {Sed numquid tenetur probare de stipite? Non, quia non reperitur cautum. Imo sufficit incipere a germanis, infra 'De consanguinitate', *Tua;*[2] supra, eodem, *Series,*[3] dummodo gradus ex utroque latere distinguantur, ut hic, et ibi, et supra, eodem, *Cum in tua*[4] Rubrica i;[5] xxxv q.v. c.i etc., *Parentele.*[6] Sed quid si quidam testes probant de uno latere tantum et alii de alio tantum? Numquid [7]erat probata consanguinitas? Quidam dicunt quod non, quia nec isti probant consanguinitatem nec illi. Sed certe qui hoc dicunt ceci sunt, quia si probatur de Martino quod sit filius Iohannis, per consequens probatur quod Iohannes est pater Martini. Item si aliqui alii testes probant quod Berta est filia Iohannis, per consequens probatum est quod Iohannes est pater Berte. Cum ergo constet iudici quod Iohannes est pater Martini, item constet ei quod est pater Berte, ergo constat ei quod Martinus et Berta sunt frater et soror, et ita probata est consanguinitas—quod concedo. Etiam sic non semper requiritur quod testes ex utroque latere notam habeant

---

[1] For the passage in question, see *Constitutiones Concilii Quarti Lateranensis una cum commentariis glossatorum,* ed. A. García y García (Monumenta Iuris Canonici, Series A: Corpus Glossatorum, 2; Vatican City, 1981), 261.

[2] X. 4. 14. 7.

[3] X. 2. 20. 26.

[4] X. 2. 20. 44.

[5] Rubrica] *Probably a reference to the first section of Hostiensis's own commentary on this decretal*

[6] Decretum, Pars II, C. 35, q. 5, c. 1: especially c. 4.

[7] erat] erit *A2*

consanguinitatem. [8]Item, si volo improbare consanguinitatem, non est necesse quod omnes gradus improbentur, sed sufficit unum gradum improbari, ut supra, eodem, Series.[9]}—Secundum Io(hannem Teutonicum).

2. Sed, salva pace sua, magis cecus est qui non videt: nam hic aperte dicitur [10]contrarium, scilicet quod non sufficit computatio unius lateris: imo necesse est quod utrumque latus computent iidem testes, . . . Nec obstat exemplum Iohannis, cum alius Iohannes posset esse pater Martini, et alius Iohannes [11]pater Berte.

3. Etsi etiam constaret quod utrique testes de eodem Iohanne intelligerent, ad hoc ut vera probatio esset non sufficeret testimonium de auditu: imo multa alia requirerentur ad hoc ut filiatio probaretur, quia nec facilis, imo valde difficilis est probatio, ut patet in eo quod notatur supra, 'De filiis presbiterorum', *Michael.*[12] In casu autem isto sufficit testimonium de auditu pro maiori parte, et ideo non admittitur nisi consanguinitas ex utroque latere computetur. Et est ratio quare sub hac forma restringitur, quia [13]*plurimis exemplis*, etc, ut supra, eadem Rubrica, verbo *quia tamen*; et quia *tolerabilius est*, etc., ut infra, eodem capitulo, ante finem.

4. Cecus est ergo qui per glosam capitaneam conatur textum maxime tot [14]virium contra rationem et in periculum animarum subvertere et hanc destruere formam scriptam quam omnino servari oportet. Argumentum supra, 'De electione', *Quia propter*;[15] supra, 'De rescriptis', '*Cum dilecta*';[16] § fi(ne), *clara.*[17] Non ergo ab uno latere tantum, alioquin computatio reputari debet obscura que nec gradus hinc inde distinguit.

5. *Et in suo*, verbum: quasi dicat: adhuc non sufficit quod [18]testes [19]computent clare distinguendo gradus ex utroque latere, quicquid scribat Iohannes. Imo adhuc requiritur quod in suo nichilominus etc. Et est hoc quartum quod requiritur quo ad dictum. *Quod deponunt*: dictam scilicet claram computationem ex utroque latere. *Et credere*: [20]et hoc est quintum quod requiritur. *Sed nec tales*, verbum: adhuc addit sextum,

[8]   Item . . . consanguinitatem] *om. A2*
[9]   X. 2. 20. 26: García y García, *Constitutiones*, 261 n. 17, gives the reference X. 2. 20. 30, which does not seem to fit.
[10] contrarium] contrarius *A2*
[11] pater] esse pater *A2*
[12] X. 1. 17. 13.
[13] plurimis] pluribus *A2*
[14] virium contra] fultum viribus et contra *A2*
[15] X. 1. 6. 42.
[16] X. 1. 3. 22.
[17] '§ fi(ne), *clara*' is almost certainly a reference to the words 'clara computatione' towards the end of the decretal *Licet ex quadam* (X. 2. 20. 47) which is the subject of this whole part of the commentary.
[18] testes computent] testis computet *A2*
[19] computent] computet *O*
[20] et hoc] verb*um*: et hoc *A2*

ad maiorem confusionem Iohannis, quod si deficiat *quantumcumque testis ex utroque latere gradus computet, testimonium non valebit. Et hoc est *Sed nec tales sufficiant* etc. *vidisse.* Sic nec sufficit testimonium de auditu per omnia.

Documents Relating to Chapter 3: Bigamy

3. 1. Johannes de Deo, *De dispensationibus*, on bigamy

This passage shows symbolism providing the principles for a casuistry of the applications of the bigamy rules to concrete cases: illustrating the important point that where symbolism provides a criterion for settling tricky specific cases it is more than just a traditional survival without causal importance. The work from which the passage comes belongs to the genre of canon-law treatises on special topics.

MS London, BL Royal 5 A 1[1]

Parchment manuscript, originally belonged to Rochester Priory, 170 × 130 mm., 206 folios, thirteenth century, 'in several different hands', paragraph marks and initials in red; the section from which this passage comes is in one column. The contents are a varied selection of theological, moral, and canon legal writings, fully listed in the admirable Royal catalogue.

Fo. 157[r–v]:

Dicturi de bigamia, distinguendum est que sit causa quare dispensatur in una bigamia et non in altera, et debes tenere quod non possit cum vero bigamo dispensare quia non est in eo [2]signatum nec consignatum. Signatum est coniunctio vel unio inter Christum et ecclesiam, quod signatur per illam unionem maris et femine [*fo. 157[v]*] in commixtione carnis. § Item consignatum est, scilicet unio deitatis ad carnem Christi, que unio numquam fuit [3]divisa. Tres enim sunt uniones, scilicet: deitatis ad carnem Christi: hec numquam separata fuit. § Item unio deitatis ad animam. Similiter hec numquam divisa fuit. § Item unio anime ad carnem: hec in morte Christi fuit separata. § Est etiam unio anime iuste ad deum per fidem et caritatem. Hec quandoque propter peccatum mortale separatur. Sic ergo propter defectum non dispensatur in bigamo vero, quia esset contra Apostolum. Ut

---

[1] Description based on personal inspection and on G. F. Warner and J. P. Gilson, *Catalogue of Western Manuscripts in the Old Royal and King's Collections* (4 vols.; London, 1921), i. 93–4.

[2] signatum] sig^{a}tum, *which can also be extended as* significatum. *Here and in subsequent cases I have chosen the more probable alternative*

[3] divisa] diversa *ms.?*

ergo sciat quis sit vere bigamus, et quis presumptivus, sic distinguimus. § Verus bigamus est qui duas uxores successive habuit. § Item bigamus est qui contraxit cum vidua vel repudiata ab alio et cognita. § Item bigamus est iuris interpretatione qui cum prima contraxit de iure et cum secunda de facto. Credo tamen quod papa possit cum tali dispensare, quia non deficit in illo sacramentum. Item bigamus est qui post ordinem sacramentum contraxit cum corrupta, scilicet *iuris interpretatione. Si tamen contraheretur cum virgine, possit post longam penitentiam ab episcopo dispensari. § Item bigamus dicitur monachus si contraxit matrimonium, cum in talibus possit dispensari, quia [4]non verum fuit matrimonium. § Item qui similiter contrahit cum duabus vel de facto contraxit successive cum duabus. Queritur utrum possit esse uxor, et tum presumptive vel interpretative dicitur bigamus, et possit cum talibus dispensare. Hii sunt modi bigamie. Unde versus: Bigamus est factus hic si transibis ad actus.

3. 2. Innocent IV (Sinibaldo dei Fieschi) on Decretals of Gregory IX, X. 5. 9. 1: bigamy and loss of clerical status

In the following passage Innocent IV anticipates the ruling of the Second Council of Lyons that clerics in minor orders lost their status and privileges if they did something 'altogether contrary to [their] order, such as marrying a second wife or a woman who was not a virgin': a strict definition of the 'irregularity' of bigamy and one that would be applied in secular courts. I put the most significant passages in heavy type.

Printed edition, BL L. 23. f. 3. (1): *Apparatus . . . Innocentii pape . . . super V libris decretalium* (Lyons, 1525)

Fo. cxciiii[rb]:

Item no. H.[1] dixit quod nedum alii sed etiam psalmista et lector semper gaudebunt privilegio clericali, et ulterius non possunt vivere seculariter nec fieri milites. xx.[2] q. iii. *Eos.*[3] Sed alii contradicunt, cum quibus et nos sentimus, distinguentes: si sumpsit **aliquid penitus contrarium ordini, ut si accepit secundam uxorem vel corruptam** vel fecit se militem et seva exercuerit: tunc privatur omni privilegio clericali. lxxxiiii. di. *Quisquis.*[4] **Si vero non fecit penitus aliquid contrarium ordini, scilicet ducendo virginem,** vel fiendo miles, dummodo non exerceat seva, potest vivere

----

[4] non] autem *ms., making no sense*
[1] Hostiensis?
[2] xx] xxi *in edition*
[3] Gratian, Pars II, C. 20, q. 3, c. 3.
[4] Gratian, Pars I, D. 84, c. 5.

clericaliter, et privilegio clericali gaudere. xxxii. di. *Seriatim,*[5] *Si qui vero.*[6]
Sed si velit vivere seculariter, negotiando, tabernam tenendo, vel tonsuram
dimittendo, tunc nullo gaudebit privilegio.

3. 3. Innocent IV (Sinibaldo dei Fieschi) on Decretals of Gregory IX, X. 1. 21. 5: the symbolic understanding of bigamy

This passage shows that Innocent IV explained 'bigamy' in symbolic
terms.
In the analysis in Chapter 3 I do not discuss the last part of this extract.
This is because I believe that at this point in his argument the symbolism
may be simply rationalizing a position that he and others held for other
reasons (whereas in the rest of the extract the symbolism is an active
ingredient in his thought, so to speak). Innocent seems to make his own
the strong line on bigamy, viz., that the wife the candidate for the priesthood
has lost must have been a virgin when they married. It must not only have
been her first marriage: she must not have had any other sexual partner
before. This raised for him and others the following tricky question. If the
wife had to have been a virgin when they married, why did it not matter
for strict legal purposes if the candidate had slept with a concubine since
his wife's death?

I suspect the real reason was that too many men would have been barred
from the priesthood if there had been a rule that candidates be virgins
or even a rule that they had not slept with a woman since their wife had
died. The rule that if a candidate had been married before it must have
been once only and to a virgin would not eliminate so many. Who was
going to test whether the deceased wife was a virgin? In any case it was
more likely that a respectable woman would be a virgin before marriage
than a man of the same social status. In other words, there is a gender
asymmetry here explicable from the simple fact that it was a man's world,
rather than from symbolism. Symbolism explains why the deceased wife
had to be a virgin, or the living wife, in the case of clerics in minor orders,
but not why the priest or cleric did not have to be a virgin too: there
a degree of pragmatic indulgence is a more probable explanation than
symbolism. Some symbolic justification or other had to be found, but it
could have been simply epiphenomenal, a cloak for the real reason, even if
contemporaries would not have seen that clearly. If I thought that this was
the case with symbolic reasoning generally, the thesis of this book would be
much weaker; however, it does seem to be true in the case of this particular
gender asymmetry.

[5] Gratian, Pars I, D. 32, c. 14.
[6] Gratian, Pars I, D. 32, c. 3.

Even so, the symbolic reasons, or rationalizations, discussed by Innocent IV are quite interesting. He alludes to an explanation offered by
Huguccio (perhaps the most famous of commentators on the *Decretum* of
Gratian, though his great work has never been printed). According to this
reading of the symbolism, the husband is the Church, and the Church
often commits adultery by straying from the faith. This view sounds controversial, if Huguccio did indeed say that. It seems to suggest that the
Church as a whole regularly errs. The line of thought deserves investigation from the manuscripts, though it is tangential here. Also interesting
is the reversal of the gender roles, so that the wife represents Christ, who
never sent the Church away. Again, this is a motif worthy of investigation.

Innocent IV in any case gives a different symbolic account. For him, the
husband is Christ. He married first the Synagogue and then the Church.
Thus it does no harm if the husband's flesh is divided. But the Church, in
the wife's role, remains always a virgin, at least in mind. Here he quotes
1 Corinthians 11: 2: 'For I have espoused you to one husband, that I
may present you as a chaste virgin to Christ'. Thus the *sacramentum*, the
representation, is defective in the wife if she should divide her flesh.

Transcription is from the early printed edition used for Document **3. 2**,
q.v. Note that here I use square brackets where elsewhere I would use round
parentheses. This is because this early printed edition, unlike medieval
manuscripts, uses round brackets, which I have retained.

Fo. xlv^rb–va:

Debitum. . . . § (*Iuxta quod*) id est ad ostendendum quod carnalis copula est
sacramentum incarnationis Christi, et quod tantum inter duos coniuges
est sacramentum illud quod in matrimonio signatur, id est, una ecclesia
uni viro Christo subdita; non est autem sacramentum hic ubi alter coniugum carnem suam in plures divisit. . . . [*fo. xlv^va*] . . . § Sed queres
quomodo ex hac auctoritate sumitur hoc sacramentum. ¹Respon*deo*: ex eo
quod in singulari numero posuit [Gen: 2: 23; Eph. 5: 30] 'os' 'caro' 'carne'
'uxori', et ex verbo ultimo [Gen. 2: 24; Eph. 5: 31]: 'erunt duo in carne
una', quasi non divident carnes suas in plures. (*Sacramenti*): illius scilicet quia matrimonium inter duos tantum signat unam ecclesiam uni viro
Christo subditam: in secundo autem coniugio non est hoc sacramentum,
nec esse potest: immo potius posset significare plures ecclesias uni viro
subditas. Ministerium autem incarnationis bene potest ²signare in secundo
matrimonio. . . . (§ Carnem): sed quare magis exigitur in uxore quam in
viro? Nam maritus corrupte promoveri non potest, xxxiiii. di. *Curandum,*³
*Precipimus,*⁴ sicut si vir. Ille autem qui post uxorem habuit concubinam

---

¹ Rn'] *can also be extended as* Responsio
² signare] *read* signari?
³ Gratian, Pars I, D. 34, c. 9.
⁴ Gratian, Pars I, D. 34, c. 10.

promoveri potest, xxxiiii. di. *Fraternitatis.*[5] Ugo[6] dicit quod vir significat ecclesiam que sepe adulteratur exorbitando a fide, et ita non deest significatio sacramenti, licet vir adulteretur. Uxor autem significat Christum qui numquam ecclesiam dimisit. Ipse enim est fons vivus cui non communicat alienus. Ego credo quod vir significat Christum qui sibi copulavit sinagogam et post ecclesiam, et ideo non nocet si vir dividit carnem suam in plures. Uxor autem ecclesiam que semper virgo permansit, saltem mente: unde 'Despondi enim vos uni viro', etc. [2. Cor. 11: 2]: C. xxvii. questio. i. *Nuptiarum.*[7] Unde si uxor in plures carnem suam dividat, deficit in ea sacramentum.

3. 4. Bull of Pope Alexander IV to the prelates of France

Unlike the bulls that follow, this has been printed, and in a modern edition, but it is useful to publish it afresh here as background to the others. For the existing edition see Archives Nationales, *Layettes du trésor des chartes*, ed. J. B. A. T. Teulet *et al.* (5 vols.; Paris, 1863–1909), iii, ed. J. de Laborde (1875), no. 4580, p. 504.

For description see *Les Actes pontificaux originaux des Archives Nationales de Paris*, ed. B. Barbiche (3 vols.; Vatican City, 1975–82), i. *1198–1261* (1975), no. 1037, p. 400.

Bulls like this would not normally result from an unprompted papal initiative. The words 'bigami et viduarum mariti et alii etiam clerici uxorati' (lines /2/–/3/) probably reflect the phraseology of the letter to which the pope is responding. The hypothesis is that the French king had begun by mentioning 'bigamous' clergy to weaken any instinct to back the clergy's privileges in any circumstances. Papal bulls were more often than not a response to a request from someone else rather than an independent initiative. The form of the bull is quite normal.

Paris, Archives Nationales J 709 no. 296

31 Jan. 1260 (Anagni):

Alexander episcopus servus servorum dei. Venerabilibus fratribus archiepiscopis et episcopis et dilectis filiis aliis ecclesiarum /1/ prelatis per regnum Francie constitutis salutem et apostolicam benedictionem. Ex parte carissimi in Christo filii nostri .. regis /2/ Francorum illustris fuit propositum coram nobis quod nonnulli clerici bigami et viduarum mariti et alii etiam /3/ clerici uxorati regni sui diversa maleficia committere non verentur que oculos divine maiestatis offendunt /4/ et homines scandalizant. Quocirca universitati vestre per apostolica scripta mandamus quatinus non

---

[5] Gratian, Pars I, D. 34, c. 7.
[6] i.e. Huguccio (I have not traced the passage).
[7] Gratian, Pars II, C. 27, q. 1, c. 41.

impediatis /5/ quominus idem rex comites et barones ipsius regni sub quorum iurisdictione malefactores ipsi consistunt /6/ ipsos in enormibus dumtaxat criminibus deprehensos que sanguinis penam requirunt eis primitus /7/ clericali gradu previa ratione privatis puniant secundum quod iustitia suadebit, consuetudine contraria /8/ non obstante. Datum Anagnie ii kal. Februar' /9/ pontificatus nostri anno sexto. /10/

3. 5. Bull of Pope Gregory X to King Philip III of France

For the source genre see Document **3. 4.** For description see *Les Actes pontificaux originaux des Archives Nationales de Paris*, ii. *1261–1304*, ed. B. Barbiche (Vatican City, 1978), no. 1511, p. 189.

The words 'consuetas iustitias et debita servitia' (lines /4/–/5/) suggest that clerical status exempted a man from more than just secular jurisdiction. This helps establish the social impact of the denial of clerical status to 'bigamous' clerics in minor orders by the Second Council of Lyons.

Paris, Archives Nationales J 709, no. 296 (2)

31 March 1273 (Orvieto):

Gregorius episcopus servus servorum dei. carissimo in Christo filio .. regi Francorum illustri salutem et apostolicam /1/ benedictionem. Ex parte tua fuit propositum coram nobis quod nonnulli clerici coniugati, tam bigami quam mo|nogami, /2/ terre tue habitu et tonsura clericali reiectis civitatum et aliorum locorum efficiuntur maiores, pares, /3/ et scabini, et principum ballivi, vicomites seu prepositi seculares, et, per exigentiam officiorum taliter as|sumptorum, /4/ sanguinis vindictam exercent, clericis interdictam, et tamen sub pretextu clericatus tibi consuetas /5/ iustitias et debita servitia subtrahere non verentur. Cum igitur reddenda sint que sunt Cesaris Cesari, et /6/ que sunt dei deo, equanimiter duximus tolerandum si a talibus iustitias debitas velut ab aliis uxo|ratis /7/ exigas et servitia consueta. Datum apud Urbemveterem ii kal. aprilis /8/ pontificatus nostri anno secundo. /9/

3. 6. Bull of Pope John XXII to King Philip V of France

The interest of the phrase 'consuetas iustitias et debita servitia' is explained in the introduction to Document **3. 5.** Philip V became king in this year and presumably wanted the privilege renewed, suggesting that the issue was still alive. For the source genre see Document **3. 4.** For description see *Les Actes pontificaux originaux des Archives Nationales de Paris*, iii. *1305–1415*, ed. B. Barbiche (Vatican City, 1982), no. 2547, p. 129; see too *Jean XXII (1316–1334): Lettres communes*, ed. G. Mollat (16 vols.; Bibliothèque des Écoles françaises d'Athènes et de Rome; Paris, 1904–47), no. 4740, i. 436.

Paris, Archives Nationales J 709, no. 298 (10)

13 Aug. 1317 (Avignon):

Johannes episcopus servus servorum dei, carissimo in Christo filio .. regi Francie et Navarre illustri, salutem et apostolicam benedictionem. Ex parte /1/ tua fuit propositum coram nobis quod nonnulli clerici coniugati, tam bigami quam monogami, terre tue, habitu et tonsura cleri|cali /2/ reiectis, civitatum et aliorum locorum efficiuntur maiores, pares, et scabini, et principum ballivi, vicomites seu /3/ prepositi seculares, et, per exigentiam officiorum taliter assumptorum, sanguinis vindictam exercent, clericis interdictam, et /4/ tamen, sub pretextu clericatus, tibi consuetas iustitias et debita servitia subtrahere non verentur. Cum igitur redden|da /5/ sint que sunt Cesaris Cesari, et que sunt dei deo, felicis recordationis Gregorii papae X predecessoris nostri, /6/ qui super hoc litteras apostolicas clare memorie .. regi Francie, proprio nomine non expresso, concessit, vestigia immittantes /7/ equanimiter duximus tolerandum si a talibus iustitias debitas velut ab aliis uxoratis exigas et servitia consueta. /8/ Datum Avinion' idus augusti pontificatus nostri anno primo. /9/

3. 7. Bull of Pope John XXII to King Charles IV of France

The interest of the phrase 'consuetas iustitias et debita servitia' is explained in the introduction to the Document **3. 5.** Charles IV became king in this year and presumably wanted the privilege renewed. For the genre see above, Document **3. 4.** For description, see *Les Actes pontificaux originaux des Archives Nationales de Paris*, iii. *1305–1415*, ed. B. Barbiche, no. 2646, p. 169; cf. *Jean XXII (1316–1334): lettres communes*, ed. Mollat, no. 15725, iv. 122.

Paris, Archives Nationales J 709, no. 298 (12)

3 July 1322 (Avignon):

Iohannes episcopus servus servorum dei carissimo in Christo filio .. regi Francie et Navarre illustri, salutem et apostolicam /1/ benedictionem. Ex parte tua fuit propositum coram nobis quod nonnulli clerici coniugati, tam bigami quam monogami , /2/ terre tue, habitu et tonsura clericali reiectis, civitatum et aliorum locorum efficiuntur maiores, pares, et scabini /3/ et principum ballivi, vicomites seu prepositi seculares, et per exigentiam officiorum taliter assumptorum, sanguinis /4/ vindictam exercent, clericis interdictam, et tamen, sub pretextu clericatus, tibi consuetas iustitias et debita servitia subtra|here /5/ non verentur. Cum igitur reddenda sint que sunt Cesaris Cesari et que sunt dei deo, felicis recordatio|nis /6/ Gregorii pape X predecessoris nostri, qui super hoc litteras apostolicas clare memorie regi Francie, proprio nomi|ne /7/ non expresso, concessit, vestigia immitantes, equanimiter duximus tolerandum, si a talibus iustitias debitas velut /8/ ab aliis uxoratis exigas et servitia consueta. Datum Avinione v non. Iulii pontificatus nostri anno sexto. /9/

3. 8. Questions on marriage in MS London, BL Royal 11. A. XIV

The following question on second marriages is relevant in the context of 'Bigamy', especially for the light it sheds on marriage liturgy and its meaning.

MS London, BL Royal 11. A. XIV[1]

> Parchment manuscript, 215 × 160 mm., last parchment folio numbered 312, initials and paragraph marks in red and blue. Ian Doyle[2] dates it to the early to mid-fifteenth century.

Fos. 184ᵛ–187ʳ:

1. Sic igitur expeditum est de hiis que querebantur de matrimonii fundamento et de eius complemento. [3]Consequenter querebatur de eiusdem ornamento, ad quod pertinet solempnis benedictio.

2. Circa quam querebuntur duo, quarum prima est [4]Cum benedictio in secundis nuptiis simpliciter prohibeatur, *Extra* 'De secundis nuptiis', *Capellanum*[5] et in solempnizatione nuptiarum plures fiunt benedictiones, querebatur utrum illa prohibitio se extendat ad omnes illas benedictiones vel ad unam tantum illarum, et, si ad unam, quero: Ad quam? Quod autem ad omnes videtur, quia decretalis nullam excipit.

3. In oppositum est communis consuetudo que solam illam benedictionem que sit circa *Agnus dei* in secundis nuptiis dimittit. Hec questio est michi multum dubia: tum quia qui nichil excipit totum includere videtur, nunc autem decretalis predicta prohibens benedictionem in secundis nuptiis nullam excipit; tum quia sola consuetudo est in contrarium. Scribitur[6] enim *Extra*, 'De secundis nuptiis', *Capellanum*:[7] 'Capellanum, quem benedictionem cum secunda constiterit celebrasse ab officio beneficioque suspensum cum litterarum tuarum testimonio ad sedem apostolicam nullatenus destinare postponas.'[8]

---

[1] Description based on Warner and Gilson, *Catalogue of Western Manuscripts*, i. 341–2, and on personal inspection.

[2] To whom I showed the manuscript.

[3] Consequenter] Convenienter *could be read*

[4] Questio trigesima tertia *added in margin in ms.*

[5] X. 4. 21. 1.

[6] Scribitur] Scibitur *ms.*

[7] X. 4. 21. 1.

[8] Capellanum . . . postponas] *underlined in red*

4. Dicunt autem hic quidam, sicut patet in quodam apparatu super Rey-
mundum libro tertio, t(itulo) 'De sacramentis iterandis vel non et
consecratione ecclesiarum',[9] quod predicta decretalis potest intelligi
de illo qui, sciens maritum alicuius vivere, benedixerit uxorem eius
cum alio; vel secundum consuetudinem illarum ecclesiarum in quibus
non adhibetur benedictio secundis nuptiis.

5. Nescio unde istud dictum autoritatem habeat. Nam infra, e(odem)
t(itulo), scilicet 'De secundis nuptiis', *Vir autem*,[10] simpliciter inter-
dicitur benedictio supradicta hoc modo: 'Vir autem aut mulier ad
bigamiam transiens non debet a presbitero benedici, quia, cum alia
vice benedicti sint, eorum benedictio [*fo. 185ʳ*] iterari non debet.' Hic
autem dicit [11]Rymundus ubi supra quod *hoc intelligendum est ubi de
consuetudine alicuius ecclesie [12]aliud obtineret; tunc enim possent sine
periculo iterari: 'De penitentia', D(istinctio) tertia [Gratian, Pars II,
D. 3 de pen. c. 33], § *ex persona*.[13] Videtur tamen aliis, ut Hostiensi,[14]
quod nulla consuetudo [15]hoc operatur. Sed quicquid sit de hoc, hic
in primis est sciendum, quod secunde nuptie dicuntur quecumque se-
cuntur primas, etiam si millesime sint, ut patet § 'De secundis nuptiis',
Si quis, § *Talem*;[16] licet vulgo 'secundum' dici consueverit quod statim
post primum sequitur.

6. Secundo est sciendum quod in illo capitulo *Vir autem aut mulier ad*

---

[9] Gloss by Guillelmus Redonensis on Raymond of Peñaforte's *Summa* for con-
fessors: '*Capellanum*. Ibi precipitur quod capellanus qui benedictione cum secunda
celebraverat ab officio et beneficio suspensus mittatur ad curiam: sed istud potest
intelligi de illo qui, sciens maritum alicuius vivere, benedixit uxorem eius cum alio;
vel intelligitur vel [vel . . . vel *sic ms.: read* vel . . . secundum?] consuetudinem
illarum ecclesiarum in quibus non adhibetur benedictio secundis nuptiis, nec debet
nisi ubi est consuetudo quod iteretur. Ambr(osius) De Penitentia di. i. iii *Reperi-
untur* [=Gratian, D. 1 de pen. c. 3]. Licite ibi vero notavit H. quod Lazarus post
suscitationem suam non posset repetere uxorem suam vel e converso, et quod si
vellet eam [*fo. 148ʳ, right-hand gloss*] iterum [interim *ms.*] habere uxorem, oporteret
contrahere de novo. Non tamen esset bigamus quia [*corr. from* qui] non divideret
carnem suam propter hoc in duas' (MS BL Royal 8. A. II, fos. 147ᵛ–148ʳ, gloss).
Incidentally, this manuscript has an extraordinary layout, in which the main text
and gloss are laid out in a varied series of geometric patterns.
[10] X. 4. 21. 3.   [11] Rymundus] *sic ms.*   [12] aliud] aᵗ *ms.*
[13] i.e. Gratian speaking in his own person rather than quoting an authority.
[14] Cf. Hostiensis, *Lectura*, on X. 4. 21. 3: *Vir autem* (MS BL Arundel 471, fo. 193ʳᵇ,
lines 24 ff.).
[15] hoc] hic *could be read*
[16] *Corpus Iuris Civilis*, code 5. 9. 8. 2, quoted by Hostiensis (Henricus de Segusio,
Summa aurea (Lyons, 1548 edn.), fo. 225ᵛᵇ), probably in the light of the ordinary
gloss on 'secundo toro', which reads: 'id est, tertio. omne enim matrimonium potest
dici secundum, quod primum sequitur. Vel forte respectu secundi quod est primum
post secundum. et sic de aliis' (*Corpus iuris civilis*, ed. I. Fehi, iv (Lyons, 1627;
repr. Osnabrück, 1966), col. 1174). (Many thanks to Martin Brett, Gero Dolezalek,
Charles Donahue, and Anders Winroth for finding these sources for me after an
appeal to a canon lawyers' e-mail list.)

bigamiam transiens,[17] per bigamiam intelliguntur secunda vota, hoc est, matrimonia secundo contracta, ut sit sensus *ad bigamiam transiens,* id est, ad secunda vota, vel matrimonia secundo contracta, supra eodem titulo, capitulo illo—Quod ideo fit quia per secunda vota sepius contrahitur bigamia.

7. Quantum autem ad questionem in se, nullam penitus invenio autoritatem qua possumus informari de qua benedictione intelligi debeat decretalis, et ideo in proposito sola consuetudo locum tenet, et summe valet autoritas illa que scribitur *Extra* 'De consuetudine' *Cum dilectus,*[18] quod consuetudo approbata est optima legum interpres, nam Decretorum Distinctio prima *Consuetudo* dicitur sic: 'Consuetudo [19]autem est ius *quoddam moribus institutum quod pro lege suscipitur dum defficit lex,[20] ubi Glossa dicit sic, quod tunc demum recurrendum est ad consuetudinem cum lex deficit.[21] Sed planum est quod hic deficit nobis lex quantum ad expressionem supradicte benedictionis. Unde quantum est ex parte legis scripte, non magis est omittenda vel danda tanquam prohibita una benedictio in secundis nuptiis quam alia.

8. Nunc autem communis ecclesie consuetudo est quod ista benedictio que datur post *Agnus dei,* et ante osculum pacis datum, in secundis nuptiis est omittenda seu non danda: [22]ergo pro prohibita est habenda: et quod ista consuetudo tamquam rationabilis sit *approbanda declaro sic. Nam, cum quattuor dentur benedictiones in primis nuptiis, una in ostio ecclesie, alia in principio misse, tertia ante pacis osculum et quarta ad lectum: inter istas tertia benedictio principalitatem tenet, quia maxime respicit totius matrimonii perfectionem et consummationem. Nunc autem benedictio potissime respicit matrimonii consummationem, et hoc attestatur quod scribitur Gen. 2: 'Masculum et feminam creavit eos, benedixitque illis deus, et ait: Crescite et multiplicamini et replete terram'. Unde beatus Augustinus *De Civitate Dei* Libro [23]decimo quarto capitulo [24]vicesimo secundo dicit sic:[25] 'Nos autem nullo modo dubitamus secundum benedictionem dei "Crescite et multiplicamini et implete terram" donum esse nuptiarum, quas deus ante peccatum hominis ab initio constituit, creando masculum et feminam, qui sexus utique in carne est'; hec Augustinus, et infra [*fo. 185ᵛ*], dicit quod cum 'evidentissime appareat in diversi sexus corporibus,

[17] X. 4. 21. 3. [18] X. 1. 4. 8. [19] autem] pro *ms.*
[20] Gratian, Pars I, D. 1, c. 5.
[21] '**is lacking**—Here it seems recourse is made to custom only when ordinance is lacking' (Gratian, *The Treatise on Laws* (*Decretum DD. 1–20*) *with the Ordinary Gloss,* ed. and trans. A. Thompson, J. Gordley, and K. Christensen (Studies in Medieval and Modern Canon Law, 2; Washington, 1993), 5.
[22] ergo] igitur *could be read*
[23] decimo quarto] 14° *ms.*
[24] vicesimo secundo] 22.a *ms.*
[25] Augustine, *De civitate Dei,* 14. 22 (Migne, *PL* 41. 429).

masculum et feminam, ita creatos, ut prolem generando crescerent, et multiplicarentur, et impleant terram, magne [26]surditatis est reluctari', dicendo scilicet predictam benedictionem non [27]referri ad prolis multiplicationem. Hec ergo multiplicatio est principalis effectus predicte benedictionis. Sed hec in sola tertia [28]benedictione imprecatur: ibi enim dicitur: 'Sit fecunda in sobole',[29] et nusquam alibi in tota sollempnitate nuptiali.

9. Nam loquendo de prima benedictione que fit in ostio ecclesie ibi dicuntur tres orationes, in quarum prima pro sponsis petitur longevitas secure conversationis, in secunda sagacitas superne cognitionis, in tertia, condignitas divine acceptationis.

10. Prima oratio incipit: 'Respice Domine de celo', etc. Secunda incipit: 'Deus Abraham, deus Ysaac', etc. Tertia: 'Benedicat vos omnipotens deus', etc.[30]

11. De benedictione vero anuli nichil ad propositum nostrum.

12. In secunda vero benedictione que fit ante inchoationem misse tres dicuntur orationes in quarum prima pro sponsis petitur benignitas paternalis remissionis; in secunda iocunditas filialis consolationis; in tertia stabilitas visceralis copulationis. Prima oratio incipit sic: 'Benedicat vos deus pater' etc.[31] Secunda sic: 'Respice Domine propitius super hunc famulum tuum et hanc famulam tuam', etc.[32] Tertia sic: 'Omnipotens deus, qui primos parentes' etc.[33]

13. In tertia vero benedictione, que fit post *Agnus dei* et ante osculum pacis, dicuntur due tantum orationes: una brevis, in qua pro sponsis petitur celestis auxilii assistentia, et alia bene prolixa, in qua petitur finalis matrimonii efficacia. Prima incipit: *Propitiare Domine* etc.[34] Secunda incipit: *Deus qui potestate virtutis tue*, etc.[35]

14. In ista vero ultima oratione, in qua petitur finalis matrimonii efficacia

---

[26] surditatis] absurditatis *Augustine*

[27] referri] referi *ms.*   [28] benedictione] benedictio ne *ms.*

[29] Cf. *Manuale ad usum percelebris Ecclesie Sarisburiensis: From the Edition Printed at Rouen in 1543 . . .*, ed. A. J. Collins (Henry Bradshaw Society, 91; London, 1960), 54.

[30] I have not found this exact pattern of blessings, but cf. J.-B. Molin and P. Mutembe, *Le Rituel du mariage en France du XIIe au XVIe siècle* (Théologie historique, 26; Paris, 1974), 288, 305.

[31] Cf. *Manuale*, ed. Collins, 49 (where this blessing is placed before the rubric 'Hic intrent ecclesiam usque ad gradum altaris'); *Missale Romanum Mediolani, 1474*, facsimile ed. R. Lippe (2 vols.; Henry Bradshaw Society, 33; London, 1899–1907), ii. 320.   [32] Cf. *Manuale*, ed. Collins, 50.

[33] Cf. ibid. (which adds 'sempiterne' after 'Omnipotens').

[34] Ibid. 53; *The Gregorian Sacramentary under Charles the Great*, ed. H. A. Wilson (Henry Bradshaw Society, 49; London, 1915), 121; *Missale Romanum*, ed. Lippe, ii. 321

[35] *Manuale*, ed. Collins, 53; *Gregorian Sacramentary*, ed. Wilson, 121; *Missale Romanum*, ed. Lippe, ii. 321. For this prayer see MS BL Add. 41174, fo. 264^{va–b}.

cum suis annexis, ad inclinandam clementiam et benivolentiam autoris matrimonii, qui deus est, allegantur in principio eiusdem orationis tria bona matrimonii tamquam propterea matrimonium instituerit.

15. Primo [36]igitur pro bono prolis allegatur fecunditas propagationis, et hoc est quod in primis dicitur: *Deus qui potestate virtutis tue de nichilo cuncta fecisti, qui dispositis universitatis exordiis homini ad ymaginem dei facto, ideo inseparabile mulieris adiutorium condidisti, ut femineo corpori de virili carne dares* [*fo. 186ʳ*] *principium docens quod ex uno placuisset institui numquam liceret disiungi.*

16. Secundo pro bono sacramenti allegatur significationis congruitas, et hic est quod convenienter in eadem oratione dicitur: *Deus qui tam excellenti misterio coniugalem copulam consecrasti ut Christi et ecclesie sacramentum presignares in federe nuptiarum.*

17. Tertio pro bono fidei, quod etiam in prima parte tactum est, allegatur coniunctionis inseparabilitas, et hoc est quod continue dicitur in predicta oratione: *Deus per quem mulier iungitur viro et societas principaliter ordinata, ea benedictione donatur que sola nec per originalis penam peccati nec per diluvii est ablata sententiam, respice propitius super hanc famulam tuam,* etc. Et versus finem orationis dicitur: *sit fecunda in sobole,* etc.

18. Ex quibus omnibus patet quod ista benedictio est principalis, tamquam ad quam cetere precedentes ordinantur, et pro cuius effectus conservatione fit sequens benedictio, scilicet ad lectum, sicut patet intuentibus.

19. Ad hoc etiam poterit esse congruitas bona, nam, secundum beatum Augustinum, in illa oratione *Summe sacerdos,* in communione corporis et sanguinis Christi yma *summis coniunguntur, scilicet mens humana corpori Christi, immo ipsi deo. Quia ergo copulatio maritalis istam coniunctionem significat, immo et ipsam unionem qua personaliter ipsa deitas humanitati in Christo unitur, qui verissime in sacramento predicto continetur, ordinatissime institutum est quod illa benedictio qui principalitatem in matrimonio tenet ante communionem seu perceptionem eiusdem corporis benedicti solempniter conferatur tamquam signum ante signatum.

20. Propterea due ponuntur rationes quare benedictio in secundis nuptiis non est danda. Una est sacramenti attestatio, in signum enim quod hec benedictio que datur in primis nuptiis est quasi sacramentalis, ideo iterari non debet. Prima q. prima *Quod quidam*[37] et trigesima secunda q. septima **Quemadmodum,*[38] et De Consecratione Distinctio quarta, *Ostenditur;*[39] et hec ratio implicatur in decretali supradicta *Vir autem.*[40]

[36] igitur] ergo *could be read*
[37] Gratian, *Decretum,* Pars II, C. 1, q. 1, c. 97.
[38] Gratian, *Decretum,* Pars II, C. 32, q. 7, c. 10.
[39] Gratian, *Decretum,* Pars III, D. 4 de cons., c. 32.   [40] X. 4. 21. 3.

21. Alia ratio est secundarum nuptiarum detestatio, quia quantum ad istam benedictionem iterandam secunde nuptie fornicatio dicuntur: trigesima prima q. prima: *Hac ratione.*[41] Ibi enim sic scribitur: 'Hac ratione Apostolus [42]precepit secundas nuptias adire propter incontinentiam hominum. Nam secundam quidem accipere secundum preceptum Apostoli licitum est, secundum autem [43]veritatis rationem vere fornicatio est': quasi dicat, secundum Hostiensem, titulo 'De secundis nuptiis' super primum capitulum: Sicut nec fornicatores benedicendi sunt, sic nec secundo contrahentes, quia alias benedicti fuerunt.[44]

22. Illa igitur benedictio inter ceteras principalitatem tenet in qua maxime exprimitur ipsum matrimonii sacramentum quantum ad eius bona et eis annexa quo ad primam [*fo. 186ᵛ*] rationem, et in qua maxime imprecatur castitatis et honestatis munditia quo ad secundam rationem. Sed hec est illa tertia benedictio, que datur post *Agnus dei*. In ipsa enim maxime exprimitur ipsum sacramentum et eius triplex bonum, ut patuit ex predictis.

23. In ipsa etiam maxime castitas et honestas petitur seu imprecatur. Ibi enim dicitur: [45]*Fidelis et casta nubat in Christo, imitatrixque sanctarum permaneat feminarum*, et infra, *Uni thoro iuncta contactus illicitos fugiat*, et infra, *Sit verecundia gravis, pudore venerabilis doctrinis celestibus erudita.*[46]

24. Predictam igitur consuetudinem tamquam rationalem approbando, dico pro questione quod prohibitio papalis expressa in decretali supradicta se [47]extendit vel ad illam solam tertiam benedictionem que datur post *Agnus dei*; vel ad omnes adeo quod quicumque sacerdos illam dederit in secundis nuptiis, etiam ceteris omissis, penam superius taxatam a iure eo facto incurrit, si vero eam non dederit, nulla ceterarum benedictionum omissa, credo quod ratione predicte consuetudinis predicte pene subiacere non debet.

25. Nec obstant communes rubrice que ponuntur in oratione ad sponsalia facienda, quia quamvis in prima benedictione, que fit in ostio, et in secunda, que fit in principio misse, tituli seu rubrice sint 'benedictiones', in tertia vero benedictione, que fit post *Agnus dei*, titulus seu rubrica sit 'orationes', ille tamen orationes verius et realius sint benedictio quam prime, ut prius ostensum est.

26. Hoc iterum patet. Nam prime due benedictiones non sunt nisi divine

[41] Gratian, *Decretum*, Pars II, C. 31, q. 1, c. 9.
[42] Apostolus precepit] apostoli preceperunt *Friedberg edn.*
[43] veritatis] *unclear in ms.*
[44] Hostiensis, *Lectura*, at X. 4. 21. 1 (MS BL Arundel 471, fo. 193ʳᵃ, from line 15 up).
[45] *Fidelis*] *ffidelis* ms.
[46] Cf. *Manuale*, ed. Collins, 54.
[47] extendit] extentit *ms.*

benedictionis imprecationes, et hoc quo ad quedam que tam sponsis quam aliis sunt communia, sicut intuentibus patet. Tertia vero benedictio est divine benedictionis imprecatio, non solum pro vite sanctitate et honestate et aliis huiusmodi, sed etiam pro propagationis fecunditate, et non solum est divine benedictionis imprecatio, immo eius domini benedictionis tamquam collate rite contrahentibus explicatio. *Deus*, inquit, per quem mulier iungitur viro et societas principaliter ordinata ea benedictione donatur, etc.[48]

27. Ad argumentum in oppositum cum dicitur quod decretalis illa nullam benedictionem excipit, igitur ad omnes se extendit, dicendum quod aliud est nichil excipere, et totum exprimere. Nam sequitur: qui totum exprimit vel dicit, nichil excipit, non tamen e converso: quia et si in aliqua lege vel iure nichil expresse excipiatur, poterit tamen aliquid excipi, vel per consuetudinem, vel per aliquam aliam legem: et sic est in proposito.

28. Non enim prohibet expresse predicta decretalis omnem benedictionem dari nec precipit nullam benedictionem dari, sed absolute interdicit benedictionem dari [*fo. 187ʳ*] cum quo stare potest quod alique dentur et alia tanquam principalis non detur.

3. 9. Passage on bigamy in the *Pupilla oculi* of Johannes de Burgo

This passage shows the impact of the rule against blessing second marriages. The penalty for blessing them clearly caused so much worry that someone took the trouble of forging a decretal diminishing the consequences. Pope John XXII was the alleged author of this decretal, which allowed the local bishop to absolve priests who blessed second marriages. Note that the symbolic rationale of the rule against blessing second marriages comes out clearly.

The work comes within the genre of pastoral manuals. It was probably intended primarily for ecclesiastical administrators with an academic training behind them,[1] and it was popular, to judge from the surviving manuscript diffusion. For the author see R. Sharpe, *A Handlist of the Latin Writers of Great Britain and Ireland before 1540* (Publications of the *Journal of Medieval Latin*, 1; [Turnhout], 1997), no. 626, p. 222.

The passage comes in part 8, ch. 18, of the *Pupilla oculi*.

[48] Cf. *Manuale*, ed. Collins, 54.
[1] This is convincingly argued by R. M. Ball, 'The Education of the English Parish Clergy in the Later Middle Ages with Particular Reference to the Manuals of Instruction' (unpublished Ph.D. dissertation, Cambridge University, 1976), 70–1.

MS London, BL Royal 11. B. X²

Parchment manuscript, 265 × 170 mm. 'iii + 188 folios', possibly late fourteenth century, initials blue with red decoration, paragraph marks in red (but blue in some passages written in red). In addition to the *Pupilla oculi*, it includes pastoral materials, a defence of religious images by Walter Hilton, the 'Vision of St Paul', and an 'Apocryphal epistle of Christ to St Peter': full details in the scholarly catalogue. It is the sort of combination of texts that an educated parish priest in late medieval England might be expected to enjoy and find useful.

Fos. 146ᵛᵃ–147ʳᵃ:

1. Capitulum ³decimum octavum. De secundis nuptiis et quomodo uxor est tractanda.
2. Infra tempus luctus, id est, infra annum post mortem mariti sui, mulier, sine aliqua legalis infamie iactura seu alia pena, nubendi alteri liberam habeat facultatem: Extra de secundis nuptiis, capitulo ult.⁴
3. Nullus ad secundas nuptias migrare presumat donec ei constet quod ab hac vita migravit coniux eius. Si autem alter coniugum non certificatus de morte sui coniugis alteri ⁵nupserit, debitum tenetur reddere, sed non potest exigere, et si de prioris coniugis vita postmodum constiterit, relictis adulterinis amplexibus ad priorem coniugem revertatur. Extra, eodem titulo, capitulo 2.⁶ De hac materia vide supra, capitulo 12.s.⁷
4. Item vir vel mulier ad bigamiam transiens non debet iterum a presbitero benedici. Extra ⁸eodem titulo *Vir autem.*⁹ Hoc intelligunt B(ernardus)¹⁰ et Go(ffredus):¹¹ nisi consuetudo alicuius ecclesie aliter obtineret. Tunc enim possent sine periculo benedici.¹² *De Penitentia* Di. 3 § *ex per-*

---

² Description based on Warner and Gilson, *Catalogue of Western Manuscripts*, i. 348, and on personal inspection.
³ decimum octavum] 18ᵐ *ms.*
⁴ X. 4. 21. 5.
⁵ nupserit] nupterit *or* nupcerit *ms.?*
⁶ X. 4. 21. 2.
⁷ The 's' refers to a subdivision of ch. 12. In this manuscript at least marginal letters mark sections of the text of chapters.
⁸ eodem] c. *ms.?*
⁹ X. 4. 21. 3.
¹⁰ I initially read the 'B' in ms. as a 'W', and it is not like the 'B' a few lines later (see below at n. 15), but both cases must refer to Bernard of Parma, *Glossa ordinaria* on X. 4. 21. 3: 'Et benedictio ista cum aliquis secundam ducit virginem iteratur secundum consuetudinem quorumdam locorum; et hoc si papa sciat talem consuetudinem: alias non licet' (MS BL Royal 9. C. I, fo. 152ᵛᵃ, left-hand gloss).
¹¹ This must be Goffredus de Trano but I have not identified the passages with certainty. Goffredus de Trano, *Summa super titulis decretalium* at X. 4. 21 (I have used MS BL Arundel 431, fo. 80ᵛᵃ)—a dense mass of cross-references—might be one of them but the wording does not seem very close.
¹² De benedictionibus in secundis nuptiis *in margin*

sona.[13] Et quod dicitur de secundis nuptiis non benedicendis intelligi debet quando tam ex parte viri quam ex parte mulieris sunt secunde, vel saltem ex parte mulieris. Si autem virgo contrahat cum illo qui prius habuit uxorem aliam, nichilominus nuptie benedicentur, secundum Tho(mam), Di. 43.[14] Et concordat Ber(nardus) super capitulo *Vir autem.*[15]

5. Dicit Hostiensis: persone nubentes non benedicuntur in secundis nuptiis: cuius ratio est quia per carnem a|lias [*fo. 146vb*] benedictam caro non benedicta cum qua iungitur benedicitur. In commixtione enim corporum, per quam efficiuntur una caro vir et mulier, caro benedicta trahit ad se non benedictam, sicut oleum sanctum trahit ad se oleum mixtum, non sanctum: et sic totum fit sanctum, secundum Hostiensem in Glosa super capitulo *Vir autem.*[16] Hic videtur Hostiensis innuere quod nulle secunde nuptie sint benedicende. Cuius contrarium dicit Tho(mas), sed huic antique concertationi finem ponit quedam constitutio que creditur fuisse Io(hannis) 22, ubi dicitur quod si forsan alter eorum vel ambo ad secundas nuptias transeuntium in primis benedicti non fuerint, danda est benedictio in secundis nuptiis:[17] quod sic intelligo: quod si maritus vidue mortue, qui non fuit benedictus in secundis nuptiis illius vidue, contraxit cum relicta vidua, que non fuit benedicta in secundis nuptiis mariti sui, debent nuptie eorum secunde benedici, quia neuter eorum prius in nuptiis fuerat benedictus.

6. Consimiliter, si ille qui prius contraxit cum vidua, et non fuit in secundis nuptiis eius benedictus, contrahat cum virgine, seu e converso, benedicende sunt nuptie eorum. Sic intelligo illam constitutionem que incipit *Concertationi antique.*[18]

7. Item, de iure antiquo capellanus benedicens secundas nuptias suspensus erat ab officio et beneficio, et mittendus fuerat ad sedem apostolicam pro absolutione obtinenda, ut *Extra,* eodem titulo, capitulo 1.[19] Sed iste rigor hodie temperatur, ita quod presbiteri qui secundas nuptias benedixerint, etiam scienter, ex hoc ad sedem apostolicam venire minime teneantur, sed a pena suspensionis in hoc casu a iure inducta per suos possunt diocesanos absolvi. Hec habentur in dicta constitutione *Concertationi antique,* que dicitur fuisse Johannis 22.

8. Sed quia in nuptiis plures dantur benedictiones, videlicet super nu-

[13] Gratian, Pars II, D. 3, de pen., c. 21.
[14] For '43' read '42': see *S. Tommaso d'Aquino: Commento alle Sentenze di Pietro Lombardo e testo integrale di Pietro Lombardo. Libro quarto. Distinzioni 24–42. L'Ordine, il Matrimonio,* trans. and ed. 'Redazione delle Edizioni Studio Domenicano' (Bologna, 2001), dist. 42, q. 3, a. 2, solutio, p. 890.
[15] Bernard of Parma, passage cited above (n. 10).
[16] Hostiensis, *Lectura,* on X. 4. 21. 3 (MS BL Arundel 471, fo. 193rb).
[17] See above, p. 155, on this probably fake bull.
[18] See above, p. 155.
[19] X. 4. 21. 1.

bentes introitu ecclesie, super pallium post missam, et super thorum in sero, ideo notandum quod omnes benedictiones sive orationes benedictionales que dicuntur in primis nuptiis, dicuntur etiam in secundis, etiam ubi uterque coniugum vel alter prius fuerat benedictus, preter illam que incipit *Deus qui tam* [*fo. 147ra*] *excellenti misterio coniugalem copulam consecrasti* [20]etc., usque *Deus per quem mulier*, in qua agitur de unitate Christi et ecclesie que figuratur in primis nuptiis non in secundis, ut *Extra, De Bigamis*, capitulo *Debitum*.[21] Ideo in secundis nuptiis illa oratio penitus omittenda est, ubi videlicet alter nubentium est bigamus prius benedictus vel vidua prius benedicta.

9. Si vir et mulier contrahant in facie ecclesie et [22]benedicantur, [23]et postea [24]divortietur inter eos ante carnalem copulam propter aliquod impedimentum legitimum, neutrius secunde nuptie benedicentur si convolent ad secunda vota, quia benedictio spiritualis tante efficacie est quod semper operatur nisi recipiens fuerit contrarie voluntatis, et benedictio semel accepta non potest amitti: quod enim factum est, nequit non fieri, secundum Hostiensem in Summa, rubrica 'De secundis nuptiis'.[25]

3. 10. A 'bigamy' case from the gaol delivery rolls (6 June 1320)

This document shows how the rules about 'bigamy' could be a matter of life and death. The Second Council of Lyons ruled that clerics in minor orders who married widows or were otherwise 'bigamous' lost their clerical status, and hence their immunity from secular justice. This was rapidly adopted in England. Because he was married to a widow, John of Worcester was unable to plead his clergy and escape hanging for his very considerable felonies.

For a brief mention of this case see J. Röhrkasten, *Die englische Kronzeugen 1130–1330* (Berliner historische Studien, 16; Berlin, 1990), 345 and n. 837.[1] For gaol delivery rolls as a genre of source see ibid. 44–58.

The National Archives, JUST 3. 41/1

The manuscript consists of long strips sewn together, varying in length but very approximately 700×220 mm., with cases recorded on both sides. The following summary is attached to the document on a modern

[20] etc.] c. *ms.*
[21] X. 1. 21. 5.
[22] benedicantur] benedicuntur *ms.*
[23] et] *om. ms.*
[24] divortietur] divortiatur *ms., with a mark over the* a
[25] Hostiensis (Henricus de Segusio), *Summa aurea* (Lyons, 1548 edn.), fo. 225vb.
[1] I owe this reference to Dr Susanne Jenks.

typed sheet: 'Newgate gaol deliveries by Henry Spigurnel and fellows, 10–14 Edward II (1316–1320). Plea Roll.'

Membrane xxxviii d:

Iohannes de Wyrcestre captus ad sectam Iohannis de Weston' militis pro quadam roberia ei facta apud Novum|Castrum /1/ super Tynam de quindecim libris sterlingorum in denariis numeratis, anulis, et firmaculis au|reis /2/ et Ciphis argenteis et aliis iocalibus et bonis et catellis ad valentiam centum librarum. Et pro burga|ria /3/ domus Roberti de Kestevene in Distaflane² in Warda de Bredstrete London' et quadam /4/ roberia ibidem noctanter felonice facta de bonis et catallis .. Bathonensis et Wellensis Episcopi ad valentiam /5/ centum librarum etc. Et etiam pro burgaria domus Hervici de Staunton' Cancellarii de Scaccario domini Regis /6/ infra Aldredesgate, et roberia eidem Hervico ibidem felonice facta de bonis et catallis ad valentiam quadra|ginta /7/ librarum. Unde re*t*tatus est, etc. Venit et quesitus qualiter se velit de feloniis predictis acquietare, /8/ dicit quod clericus est, etc., et non potest hic inde respondere, etc. Et super hoc obiectum est eidem Iohanni /9/ quod privilegio clericali gaudere non debet, eo quod bigamus est, eo quod duxit in uxorem quamdam viduam /10/ nomine Aliciam, que prius fuerat uxor cuiusdam Willelmi de ³Thurston', qui obiit in prisona domini Regis /11/ in Turri ⁴London' etc. Et predictus Iohannes dicit quod ipse non est bigamus, et quod numquam aliquam /12/ habuit uxorem, etc. Ideo inquiratur per patriam, etc. Et super hoc Robertus de Ware, Iohannes de Waleden', /13/ Willelmus le Maderman, Gilbertus le Sherman, Willelmus le Skynnere, Johannes de Kent, deyere, Simon /14/ de Tournham, Henricus de Somerset, Willelmus le Hastere, Thomas atte Ramme, Simon le Taillour, /15/ et Willelmus de Nottele, iurati Warde Castri Baynardi et de visneto kaii⁵ Sancti Pauli, ubi predicti Iohannes et predicta /16/ Alicia fecerunt moram iam per quinquennium, dicunt super sacramentum suum quod predictus Iohannes de Wyrecestre, post mor|tem /17/ cuiusdam Willelmi de ⁶Thurston' primi viri predicte Alicie, qui obiit in prisona in Turri ⁷London', duxit /18/ eamdem Aliciam viduam in uxorem, et in eorum visneto ipsam tenuit pro uxore sua. Unde dicunt precise quod predictus /19/ Iohannes bigamus est, etc. Ideo idem Iohannes respondit de feloniis predictis. Et quesitus qualiter se velit de roberiis, /20/ burgariis, et feloniis predictis acquietare, precise refutat se ponere inde super aliquam patriam, etc. Ideo, tamquam /21/ refutans communem legem, committitur gaole ad penam, etc. Postea, coram eisdem

---

² i.e. Distaff Lane.
³ Thurston'] *or* Thurstoun
⁴ London'] *or* Londoun
⁵ i.e. St Paul's wharf or quay.
⁶ Thurston'] *or* Thurstoun
⁷ London'] *or* Londoun

iustitiariis et coram Iohanne de /22/ Shirbourn', tenente locum Stephani de [8]Abyndon', coron(atoris) domini Regis Civitatis [9]London', predictus Iohannes de Wy|recestre /23/ cognovit roberias, burgarias, et felonias ei impositas, et se esse latronem, et devenit probator, etc. Et fecit /24/ appellum, etc. Postea coram eisdem iustitiariis, die sabbati proxima post festum translationis sancti Thome Martiris anno /25/ Regis nunc quartodecimo, idem Iohannes probator recusavit se de appello suo predicto. Ideo ipse suspensus, etc. /26/

At head of recto folio:

Adhuc de Deliberatione Gaole de Neugate Die Veneris proxima post Octabas sancte Trinitatis Anno regni regis E. filii regis E. tertiodecimo.

—Spigurnel.

In margins:

by line 1: Northumbr'
by line 2: Lond'
by line 4: Bredstr'
by line 6: Aldredesg'
by line 22: pena
by line 24–5: probator
by line 26: suspensus

3. 11. The case of Five-Wife Francis, from the archive of the Apostolic Penitentiary

This document suggests that the privileges of clerics in minor orders did not stop with 'privilege of clergy' (subjection to church courts rather than secular courts). These privileges were forfeited through 'bigamy' (unless the cleric could obtain a dispensation, as here). Thus the loss of a range of real privileges can be traced back causally to marriage symbolism, another example of its practical impact on society.

The document comes in a register of decisions by the Apostolic Penitentiary.[1]

Archivio Segreto Vaticano Penitenzieria ap. 75[2]

Paper manuscript, 295 × 215 mm.; the last modern folio number is 478.

According to the Prospettivo (a very brief unprinted conspectus of Penitentiary registers), vol. 75 is Clem VII, 1526. The volume identifies itself throughout as 'Anno 4° Clementis papa VII'.

---

[8] Abyndon'] *or* Abindoun
[9] London'] *or* Londoun
[1] See above, p. 165 n. 88, for bibliography on the Penitentiary.
[2] Description based on personal inspection.

Fo. 298ʳ, new foliation:

At head of page Anno 4° Clementis Pape vii
Heading, left-hand margin: Bigamia
Heading, centre: Cordellas. Taxatio xiii½³
Halfway down entry, left-hand margin: iiii Idus Aprilis
Halfway down entry, right-hand margin: Gerundensis

Franciscus Scola clericus Gerundensis exponit quod /1/ ipse ex magno
devotionis fervore desiderat suo cleri|cali /2/ caractere, quo alias rite in-
signitus fuit, et illius /3/ privilegiis uti et gaudere. Sed quia postmodum
cum /4/ tribus virginibus et duabus viduis ⁴mulieribus /5/ successive matrimonium contraxit et consumavit, bigamiam /6/ incurrendo, desiderium
suum in hac parte adimplere /7/ posse dubitat inconsulta ⁵desuper apostolica sede. Quare /8/ ipse asserens se cum prima muliere matrimonium
/9/ forsan consumasse et similiter, antequam ultimo contraheret, /10/ ut
clericali caractere et privilegiis clericalibus uti vale|ret /11/ a sede apostolica
indultum forsan fuisse,⁶ supplicatur, etc. /12/ sibi ut dicto suo clericali ca-
ractere ac omnibus et singulis /13/ privilegiis, gratiis, concessionibus et
indultis quibus clerici /14/ cum unica et virgine coniugati utuntur, potiun-
tur, et /15/ gaudent, seu uti, potiri et gaudere poterunt quomodolibet,
/16/ in futurum uti, potiri et gaudere libere et licite /17/ valeat in omnibus
et per omnia, citra tamen ascensum /18/ ad superiores ordines, perinde
ac si bigamiam huiusmodi /19/ ⁷F. nullatenus incurrisset, veris, etc., con-
cedere et in|dulgere, /20/ non obstantibus premissis et apostolicis ac in
provin|cialibus /21/ et sinodalibus conciliis editis generalibus vel /22/ spe-
cialibus constitutionibus et ordinationibus, necnon impe|rialibus /23/ ac
regiis, regnique legibus et ⁸practmaticis /24/ sanctionibus, statutisque mu-
nicipalibus privilegiisquoque in|dultis /25/ et literis apostolicis etiam feli-
cis recordationis dominorum Innocentii viii, Alexandri vi, /26/ et aliorum
Romanorum pontificum etiam super observantia dictarum sanctionum et
certi /27 habitus delatione concessis ceterisque contrariis quibuscumque
dignemini /28/ de gratia speciali.
Fiat de speciali M. R(egens).

---

³ ½] looks like a division sign.
⁴ mulieribus] *ms. adds and deletes* viduis
⁵ desuper] de super *ms.*
⁶ The implication is that this previous dispensation had been meant to take care of
past marriages but not to allow him to marry again and yet keep his clerical status.
⁷ F.] *deleted? I am also not quite certain that this is an* F
⁸ Practmaticis] *sic ms.*

3. 12. The case of Petrus Martorel, from the archive of the Apostolic Penitentiary

This reinforces the points made on the basis of Document 3. 11.

Archivio Segreto Vaticano, Penitenzieria ap. 75

See Document 3. 11.

Fo. 473ᵛ, new foliation:

At head of page: Roma apud S.P. [=Sanctum Petrum]
Head of facing page: Anno 4° Clementis pape vii
Heading, left-hand margin: Bigamia cum assistentia.
Heading, centre: Villa Nova, tax. xviiii$\frac{1}{2}$
Halfway down entry, left-hand margin: xi kl. decembr.
Halfway down entry, right-hand margin: Barchinonen(sis)

Petrus Martorel Clericus coniugatus Barchinonesis /1/ exponit quod ipse ex magno devotionis fervore cupit /2/ clericali caractere quo alias rite insignitus fuit uti, sed /3/ quia postmodum matrimonium per verba de presenti cum una, /4/ virgine, et, illa de medio sublata, cum alia, vidua, mulie|ribus /5/, contraxit, illudque carnali copula consumavit, /6/ bigamiam incurrendo, desiderium suum in hac parte adim|plere /7/ posse non sperat, sede apostolica 'de super inconsulta. /8/ Supplicat igitur humiliter S(anctitati) V(estre) idem orator quatenus sibi ut /9/ dicto suo clericali caractere, illiusque omnibus et singulis privi|legiis, /10/ immunitatibus, exemptionibus, gratiis, favoribus /11/ concessionibus, preeminentiis, libertatibus et indultis /12/ quibus alii clerici, cum unica et virgine coniugati, utuntur, /13/ potiuntur, et gaudent, seu uti, potiri, et gaudere pote|runt /14/ quomodolibet, in futurum uti, potiri et gaudere libere /15/ et licite possit et valeat, citra tamen ascensum ad /16/ superiores ordines, indulgere ac secum misericorditer dispensare, /17/ non obstantibus premissis necnon constitutionibus et ordinationibus /18/ apostolicis ac tam provincialibus quam sinodalibus etiam Barchinonensis /19/ ecclesie iuramento confirmatione apostolica vel quavis /20/ firmitate alia roboratis statutis et consuetudinibus /21/ privilegiisquoque, indultis et litteris apostolicis ac legibus /22/ imperialibus et regalibus ac pragmaticis sanctionibus /23/ quibus omnibus illorum omnium tenores ac si de verbo ad /24/ verbum insererentur presentibus pro sufficienter expressis /25/ habendis, illis alias in suo robore permansuris, hac vice /26/ dumtaxat specialiter et expresse placeat derogare /27/ ceterisque contrariis quibuscumque dignemini de /28/ gratia speciali. /29/ Fiat de speciali L. Gomez Regens /30/

Cum assistentia que committatur discretis /31/ viris priori monasterii

¹ desuper] de super *ms.*

sancti Dominici Barchinonensis /32/ et Iacobo Zaragossa Canonico Barchinonensi et /33/ eorum cuilibet.
Fiat L

Documents Relating to Chapter 4: Consummation

4. 1. Consummation and its consequences in a canon-law commentary: a link to late medieval papal dissolutions of *ratum non consummatum* marriages

This text shows how closely marriage symbolism is bound up with the question of the dissolution (not annulment) of a non-consummated (but valid) marriage in the thought of one of the most influential medieval canonists. It sets the background to the late medieval and early modern developments analysed in Chapter 4. It is from Hostiensis's *Lectura* on Decretals of Gregory IX, X. 3. 32. 7, 'De conversione coniugatorum', *Ex publico instrumento*. For a good analysis based on the 1581 Venice edition see T. Rincón, *El matrimonio, mistero y signo: siglos IX al XIII* (Pamplona, 1971), 397–402.

For the reasons for using two manuscripts rather than the edition see above, introduction to Document **2. 1.** As noted there, Kenneth Pennington's discovery of the early version in MS Oxford, New College 205 opened up the whole question of the manuscript tradition of the *Lectura*.[1] The Oxford manuscript represents an edition probably completed between 1262 and 1265.

To see the early and late versions of this passage together is extremely interesting: one can see how Hostiensis's thought developed. The long additions in the later version show how much his mind had continued to work on the topic.

The case deals with a woman who had not yet consummated her marriage and who wanted to enter a religious order instead of doing so. The bishop of Verona had ordered her to return to her husband or face excommunication. Innocent had reversed this: she had two months to enter a religious order or return to her husband. If she entered the order, the marriage was dissolved.

MS Oxford, New College 205 (=O), using MS London, BL Arundel 471 (=*A1*)[2] to illustrate the second edition of the *Lectura*

For the base manuscript, see above at Document **2. 1.** It will be remembered that MS Oxford, New College 205 (fo. 151rb, right-hand gloss)

[1] Pennington, 'An Earlier Recension of Hostiensis's *Lectura* on the Decretals'.
[2] To distinguish it from *A2*, MS BL Arundel 485, used above at Documents **2. 1–2.**

($=O$) is the earlier edition of Hostiensis's *Lectura*. As at Document **2**. 1 (and **2**. 2), the later edition's readings are shown in the apparatus criticus, though from a different manuscript since the manuscript used for **2**. 1 and **2**. 2 does not cover this part of the *Lectura*.

For the later edition I have chosen MS London, BL Arundel 471 (fo. 95ra) ($=A_1$). This is a parchment manuscript, 440 mm.×280 mm.; the last folio number is 308. There are initials and paragraph marks in red and blue. It contains the commentary by Hostiensis on the last three books of the Decretals of Gregory IX, and is a *pecia* copy: see below. The script seems to be Italian: at least, it has the 'u'-shaped superscript, which is a fairly good indication of Italian origin when it replaces 'r' or 'er'. Thus it may have been produced by the *pecia* system at Bologna, though further research (e.g. into the number of *peciae*) would be needed to establish this with certainty. It could be late thirteenth century. It is thus a good manuscript of the later recension to compare with O, the carrier of the early version.

A section of the passage edited below is also irreproachably edited by Pennington in the article discussed above. He was illustrating the difference between the two recensions. The passage he edited begins 'Hac etiam ratione . . .' and ends '. . . melius commutavit, infra de vot. Scripture' (see p. 83 of Pennington). I have marked the passage clearly in my edition, and duplicated Pennington's work in order to help the reader by keeping the passage as a whole. I retain my own slightly different editorial style and I have clearly marked the point where I continue without Pennington's guidance.

The small duplication of effort is useful for another reason than the reader's convenience. It suggests that the version in the 1581 edition used by Pennington for Hostiensis's 'second edition' is fairly close to the manuscript I used, which is representative of a family almost certainly widely available, because it is a *pecia* manuscript, diffused by the university system of multiple copying. In A_1 the *pecia* evidence is clear: e.g. fo. 95va, four lines up: 'fi. xlvii.pe.'. To show how a *pecia* text compares with the first recension, I have recorded all significant readings, including errors: it is useful to be reminded how poor *pecia* texts can be. Note, however, that though the scribe has a habit of writing 'coniuc-' for 'coniunc-', I have not recorded these cases.

O, fo. 151rb, right-hand gloss; A_1, fo. 95ra:

1. Hac etiam ratione considerata possent sponsi de presenti ante carnis copulam auctoritate pape se adinvicem absolvere, sicut legitur in ³sponsalibus 'De Sponsalibus' c. ii,⁴ quia contrarius actus congruus intervenire potest. Argumentum infra, 'De regulis iuris', *Omnis res:*⁵ licet

---

³ sponsalibus 'De Sponsalibus' c. ii, quia] sponsalibus de futuro. Infra de spon-
[*See p.* 272 *for n.* 3 *cont. and nn.* 4 *and* 5.

altero invito [6]hoc non posset. . . . Sed post [7]carnis copulam non posset hoc fieri, quia nec actus [8]congruus intervenire posset. . . .

2. Hoc autem intelligo de potestate absoluta, non de potestate [9]ordinaria, nisi alia causa subesset. Non enim fit quod hic statuitur sine [10]causa.

3. Potuit ergo papa circa non consumatum matrimonium hanc constitutionem facere etiam de potestate ordinata: et est ratio quia, cum per tale matrimonium caritas, que consistit in spiritu inter deum et iustam animam, tantum representetur, supra, 'De bigamis', *Debitum*[11] nichil absurdum [12]sequi si talis possit religionem intrare, quia non dissolvitur sed potius augetur [13]hoc vinculum caritatis, nec videtur voti violator qui hoc in melius commutavit, [14]infra 'De voto', [15]*Scripture*.[16]

---

salibus c. ii. Et posset reddi ratio quia ante carnis copulam utroque consentiente in dissensu *A1*

[4] X. 4. 1. 2.   [5] X. 5. 41. 1.   [6] hoc non] hoc vero *A1*
[7] carnis] carnalis *A1*   [8] congruus] contrarius congruus *A1*
[9] ordinaria] ordinata *A1*
[10] causa] causa. Sed et probabiliter dici potest quod cum ecclesia circa impedimenta matrimonii restringenda vel laxanda potestatem habeat, ut patet in eo quod legitur et notatur infra 'De consanguinitate', *Non debet* (X. 4. 14. 8), statuere vero [*corrected from* non?] potuit et hoc: quod coniunx ante carnis copulam etiam invito consorte posset religionem intrare, et alius in seculo remanens cum alia contrahere, impedimento hoc non obstante. Et hanc rationem reddidit [*corrected from* reddit] michi Dominus Matheus Sancte Marie in Portic. Dyaconus Cardinalis. Et si queras unde procedit tanta potestas ecclesie, vide quod legitur et notatur supra, 'De translatione *episcopi' c. i R(ubrica) i et c. ii et iii (X. 1. 7. 1–3). *A1*
[11] X. 1. 21. 5.
[12] sequi] sequitur *A1*   [13] hoc] per hoc *A1*   [14] infra] vel infra *A1*
[15] *Scripture*. Verum] *Scripture*. [**Extract edited by Pennington ends here.**] Ad quod etiam designandum gloriosa domina nostra [*interlined*] beatissima virgo Maria, quamvis vera sponsa Ioseph, hoc tamen non obstante vero deo matrimonialiter iuncta fuit. xxvii q. ii, *Beata Maria* et § *Cum ergo* (Gratian, *Decretum*, Pars II, C. 27, q. 2, c. 3 and c. 2). Unde et circa matrimonium non consummatum potest ecclesia interpretari et statuere quicquid placet, dum tamen iusta causa subsit, ut notatur infra, eodem, *Ex parte* ii §i, verbo *Etiam et si unus* (X. 3. 32. 14). Et hoc est [cum *ms.?*] quod hic evidenter voluit ostendere quando dixit: *Sane quod Dominus*, etc. [=*Sane, quod Dominus in Evangelio dicit, non licere viro, nisi ob causam fornicationis, uxorem suam dimittere: intelligendum est, secundum interpretationem sacri eloquii, de hiis quorum matrimonium carnali copula est consummatum, sine qua consummari non potest*], quasi dicat: 'Nec obstat si [sed *ms?*] opponas: quando interpretamur vel statuimus per quod videatur solvi matrimonium coniugale videmur facere contra deum, qui dixit: 'Quos deus coniunxit', etc. (Matt. 19: 6; Mark 10: 9); et per consequens videmur errare, cum nichil possumus statuere contra deum, ut patet in eo quod notatur supra 'De restitutione spolii', *Litteras*, § *Opinioni*. Vere dico: Non obstat talis oppositio, quia illa auctoritas intelligenda de coniunctis non tantum animo sed et corpore. Ubi ergo deest coniunctio corporum, nichil facimus contra deum, et ideo circa tale matrimonium possimus [posimus *ms.*] statuere quicquid placet de potestate nostra absoluta, id est de plenitudine potestatis. Quod et verum est: sed non expedit quod in hoc nimis laxet habenas, nec etiam tutum est. . . . Verum *A1*
[16] X. 3. 24. 4.

[**Extract edited by Pennington ends here.**]

4. Verum, ex quo matrimonium [17]consumatum est, hoc nequit fieri, [18]quia cum per ipsum representetur conformitas que consistit in carne inter Christum et ecclesiam, ut supra, 'De bigamis', *Debitum*,[19] hec nullatenus rumpi potest. Ideo si quis diceret quod postea posset vir vel uxor ad religionem migrare, unionis dicte [20]conformitatis violator esset, et innueret quod expectaret adhuc aliam fidem et aliam ecclesiam [21]quam Christus sibi uniret, et iterum desponsaret, quod falsissimum et hereticum esset . . .

4. 2. Ricardus de Mediavilla: marriage and entry into a religious order before consummation[1]

In this text a thirteenth-century theologian gives a symbolic rationale for the law or principle that a non-consummated marriage, though real and valid, could be dissolved by one partner's entry into a religious order. The author is rather an obscure figure but the work from which this comes was very widespread and influential. It is a commentary on the *Sentences* of Peter Lombard, the most common genre for high-level theological synthesis in the last three medieval centuries.

I have used the 1499 Venice edition *Ricardus de Media Villa super quarto Sententiarum* (BL call number IA 23001). A comparison with MS Oxford, Bodl. 744 leads me to think that the edition gives a reliable text.

Fos. 189vb–190ra:

[Distinctio XXVII, Articulus II, Questio II]

1. Secundo queritur utrum matrimonium non consumatum possit dissolvi per religionis ingressum: et videtur quod non, quia, matrimonio contracto, statim alter coniugum tenetur alteri petenti reddere debitum, quia, sicut dicitur ff. 'De regulis iuris', *In omnibus*: 'In omnibus obligationibus in quibus dies non ponitur presenti die debetur.'[2] Sed hoc non esset verum si matrimonium non consumatum solvi posset per religionis ingressum, quia coniunx exactus obiicere posset petenti se velle religionem intrare. Ergo non solvitur tale matrimonium per religionis ingressum.

2. Item altero intrante religionem, aut alter statim potest contrahere aut non. Si non, non est solutum matrimonium. Si sic, cum ille qui intravit

[17] consumatum est] consumatum *A1*
[18] quia] quod *A1*
[19] X. 1. 21. 5.
[20] conformitatis] conformitas *A1*
[21] quam] qua *A1*
[1] Cf. Aquinas, *Summa theologica*, 3, q. 29, a. 2.
[2] 'ff' = Justinian, *Dig.* 50. 17. 14.

religionem possit ante suam professionem redire ad seculum, contingere posset quod una esset sponsa duorum simul in seculo remanentium, quod falsum est.

3. Item, aut ille qui remansit in seculo potest contrahere matrimonium ante alterius professionem, aut non. Si sic, tunc solveretur matrimonium, nulla interveniente morte, nec corporali, nec spirituali, quia intrans religionem non moritur spiritualiter seculo usque ad suam professionem. Si non, tunc ille qui religionem intravit posset parum ante suam professionem aliam religionem intrare, et postea aliam, et sic remanens in seculo sine culpa sua defraudaretur multo tempore suo iure, quod est inconueniens.

4. Contra, Magister, huius Di[stinctionis] c. 6, et est 27 q. 2, *Desponsatam*[3] 'Desponsatam puellam non licet parentibus alii viro tradere, tamen licet monasterium sibi eligere': quod verum non esset nisi illa obligatio solvi posset per religionis ingressum.

5. Item, Extra 'De conversione coniugatorum', *Verum*:[4] 'Post consensum legitimum de presenti, licitum est alteri, altero etiam repugnante, eligere monasterium'. Et parum post: 'dummodo carnalis commixtio non intervenerit inter eos, et alteri remanenti, si commonitus continentiam [*fo. 139*[va]] servare [5]noluerit, licitum est ad secunda vota transire.'

6. Respondeo: quod in matrimonio non consumato adhuc non est nisi coniunctio spiritualis, et ideo per mortem qua homo spiritualiter seculo moritur potest solvi: qua morte moritur per hoc quod in religione profitetur. Et hec ratio tangitur Extra, 'De conversione coniugatorum', *Verum*,[6] ubi dicitur quod 'cum non fuissent una caro simul effecti, satis potest unus ad deum transire, et alter in seculo remanere.' Huic concordat significatio predicti matrimonii, quo non significatur unio humane nature ad personam filii dei, que est indissolubilis, sed significat dissolubilem unionem que est inter deum et animam per charitatem vie; nec illud verbum salvatoris scriptum, Matth. 19—Non licet viro nisi ob causam fornicationis uxorem suam dimittere—intelligendum est: nisi de his quorum matrimonium carnali est copula consumatum: Extra, 'De conversione conjugatorum', *Ex publico*.[7]

7. Ad primum in oppositum dicendum quod in illa obligatione, si alter coniugum proponat se velle religionem intrare, est indulta a iure dilatio duorum mensium ad reddendum debitum: Extra, 'De conversione

---

[3] See Peter Lombard, *Sentences*, 4. 27. 6, ii. 425 Brady. Brady, the anonymous editor, notes that the Decree beginning 'Desponsatam puellam . . .', attributed here by the Lombard to Eusebius papa, is spurious.

[4] X. 3. 32. 2.

[5] noluerit] voluerit *1499 edition*

[6] X. 3. 32. 2.

[7] X. 3. 32. 7.

coniugatorum', *Ex publico.*[8] In casu tamen committitur arbitrio iudicis utrum plus vel minus tempus indulgeat ad profitendum, ut dicit Gl(ossa) ibidem.[9]

8. Ad secundum dicendum quod remanens in seculo non potest contrahere matrimonium ante professionem alterius in religione, quia tunc primo ille qui est in religione moritur spiritualiter mundo, et ideo tunc primo vinculum matrimonii solvitur.

9. Ad tertium dicendum quod ille qui remanet in seculo non potest matrimonium contrahere ante professionem illius qui religionem intravit: et si de facto contraheret, et alius ante suam professionem de religione exiret, ei esset restituendus. Ad subveniendum tamen remanenti in seculo, ne suo iure fraudulenter privetur, iudex illi qui intravit religionem prefigere debet terminum peremptorium infra quem profiteatur, aut consumet matrimonium: alioquin ipsum excommunicet: ut habetur in predicta decretali[10] in gl(ossa),[11] et supra, titulo proximo, capitulo *Statuimus,*[12] in glo(ssa).[13]

4. 3. Ricardus de Mediavilla on the marriage of Mary and Joseph

See introduction to Document 4. 2.

Fo. 202[rb–va]:

[Distinctio 30, Articulus 2, Questio 2]

1. Secundo queritur utrum inter Mariam et Ioseph fuerit perfectum matrimonium. Et videtur *quod non. . . . Item, ad perfectum matrimonium requiritur consensus in carnalem copulam, quia ad hoc requiritur obligatio ad reddendum debitum cum ab altero coniuge exigitur. Sed beata virgo in carnalem copulam non consensit, quia, ut habitum est in questione precedenti, voverat virginitatem: et constat quod votum suum

---

[8] Ibid.

[9] Bernard of Parma, *Glossa ordinaria,* X. 3. 32. 7: 'Licet dicatur de duobus mensibus, credo quod istud committeretur arbitrio iudicis utrum plus vel minus tempus indulgeat ad profitendum dicenti se velle intrare religionem, et currit a tempore illo quo iudex statuit terminum' (MS BL Royal 9. C. 1, fo. 123[vb], right-hand gloss).

[10] X. 3. 32. 7.

[11] For the gloss of Bernard of Parma see above, n. 9.

[12] X. 3. 31. 23.

[13] The following passage fits well enough. Bernard of Parma starts with the case of a church left vacant while the prospective monk is trying his vocation, then moves on to the case of a married man: 'Idem credo servandum si alter sponsus intret religionem quod infra certum tempus profiteatur, alioquin compellitur redire ad sponsam, quia et ibi periculum imminet fornicationis' (MS BL Royal 9. C. 1, fo. 123 [rb], right-hand gloss).

non violavit. Ergo inter ipsam et Ioseph perfectum matrimonium non fuit. . . .

2. Respondeo quod perfectio rei duplex est: quedam in esse primo, quedam in esse secundo. Prima in hoc consistit quod res habet omnia que pertinent ad eius essentiam. Secunda consistit in quibusdam perfectionibus non pertinentibus ad essentiam.

3. Primo modo fuit perfectum matrimonium inter Mariam et Joseph, non secundo: quia non ita perfecte significavit *indivisibilem unionem Christi et ecclesie et humane nature cum divina persona sicut matrimonium consumatum. Unde dicit Magister huius distinctionis c. 3[1] quod fuit perfectum: non in significatione, quia, ut infra dicitur, eodem,[2] matrimonium consumatum perfectius unionem Christi et ecclesie figurat [*fo. 202*[va]] . . . Ad tertium dicendum quod ad primam matrimonii perfectionem non requiritur consensus in carnalem copulam, nisi implicite et sub conditione, scilicet, si alter coniunx eam exegerit, et si deus debitum reddendi non relaxaverit: et sic beata virgo in carnalem copulam consensit. Nec in hoc periculo se exposuit, nec suo voto in aliquo derogavit, quia divina inspiratione certificata fuit quod Ioseph ab ea numquam exigeret carnalem copulam, et quod si Joseph exigeret, deus eam a debito absolveret reddendi. Et sic intelligitur auctoritas allegata secundo ad secundam partem, quod patet, quia postquam dictum est: 'consensit in carnalem copulam', statim subiungitur: 'non illam appetendo, sed divine inspirationi in utroque obediendo.'

4. 4. A consummation case in the papal registers (John XXII)

These passages show that the practical social and political implications of the symbolic theology and canon law of non-consummated marriages are more far-reaching than is at first apparent. They are from Archivio Segreto Vaticano, Vatican Register 115, which has not been calendared except for entries connected with France.[1] This is a register deriving from

---

[1] Peter Lombard, *Sentences*, 4. 30. 2. 3, ii. 440 Brady (note: chapter 2, not chapter 3).

[2] Ibid. 4. 30. 2. 5, ii. 440–1 Brady.

[1] The following note in the calendar for France is worth quoting as a warning about the numbering of the folios: 'Les lettres secrètes des années XIII et XIV du pontificat de Jean XXII (5 septembre 1328–4 septembre 1330) sont conservées dans le registre Vatican 115. Chacun des feuillets de celui-ci porte une double numérotation, la première en chiffres romains dans la marge supérieure du recto, l'autre, en chiffres arabes, dans le coin supérieur droit de la même page. Ces deux numérotations ne coïncident pas car, d'une part, le premier numérorateur n'a pas tenu compte des feuillets contenant l'Index placé en tête du registre, et d'autre part, pour les lettres de l'année XIV, il a recommencé la numérotation au fol. 1, qui correspond ainsi au folio 205 de la numérotation en chiffres arabes, alors que celle-ci est continue du premier au dernier feuillet du registre' (*Lettres secrètes et curiales du*

the Camera Apostolica (as opposed to the Cancellaria Apostolica): see M. Giusti, *Studi sui Registri di bolle papali* (Collectanea Archivi Vaticani, 1; Vatican City, 1979), 27–8, 130, 139.
On the Vatican Registers of this period see K. A. Fink, *Das vatikanische Archiv: Einführing in die Bestände und ihre Erforschung,* 2nd enlarged edn. (Rome, 1951), 36–7, one good guide among several.

The background to these extracts from the uncalendared papal register is elucidated by documents printed in *Vatikanische Akten zur deutschen Geschichte in der Zeit Kaiser Ludwigs des Bayern, auf Veranlassung seiner Majestät des Königs von Bayern herausgegeben durch die historische Commission bei der königlichen Akademie der Wissenschaften,* ed. S. von Riezler (Innsbruck, 1891): no. 785, p. 311; no. 864, p. 331; no. 890, p. 338; no. 911, p. 347; no. 943a, p. 357; no. 1000, p. 374.

Pope John XXII was in the middle of a struggle *à l'outrance* with Ludwig of Bavaria. John refused to recognize Ludwig as Holy Roman Emperor elect. Ludwig countered by leading an army into Italy, allying with the papacy's Ghibelline opponents, capturing Rome, installing an antipope, and declaring John a heretic and no pope.[2] Ludwig controlled Rome from 7 January to 4 August 1328. Historians have perhaps tended to underestimate the degree of danger to John XXII as pope. At any rate, it would have taken a clairvoyant to be sure in 1327 that Ludwig was certain to lose.

Stefano da Colonna was on the papal side—more or less. In fact, John XXII seems to have been far from confident of his loyalty. In January 1327 John wrote to Stefano about news that the latter had received rebels against the Roman Church, 'which we can scarcely believe';[3] on 16 June of the same year he provided Jacopo son of Stefano with a canonry at the Lateran church, presumably to keep him sweet;[4] on 28 November 1327 he wrote to tell Stefano of his trust in him despite the rumours, but exhorted him to think of his good name;[5] in a letter of 24 September to the legate of Tuscany John expresses what sounds like genuine confidence in Stefano;[6] on 17 April 1328 he expresses surprise at Stefano's apparent

pape Jean XXII (1316–1334) relatives à la France, publiées ou analysées d'après les registres du Vatican, ed. A. Coulon and S. Clémencet, fasc. 8 (Paris, 1965), 3 n. 1).

[2] For a convenient summary of these events and their context see H. Thomas, *Deutsche Geschichte des Mittelalters 1250–1500* (Stuttgart etc., 1983), 177–80, or the old but good G. Mollat, *Les Papes d'Avignon 1305–1378* (Paris, 1949), 330–46.
[3] *Vatikanische Akten,* no. 785, p. 311.
[4] Ibid, no. 864, pp. 331–2.
[5] Ibid., no. 943a, p. 357.
[6] 'Et ut melius et utilius procedere valeas ad premissa, datis in oblivionem preteritis, que tuis possent in hac parte processibus multipliciter obviare, te cum dilecto filio, nobili viro, Stephano de Columpna, quem circa ea, que honorem ecclesie ac regium respiciunt, promptum reperies, (ut) credimus, et devotum, amicabiliter habeas et . . . favorabiliter prosequaris' (ibid., no. 911, p. 347).

inactivity in the cause.[7] However, it appears that Stefano came through in the end, spearheading with one other man the papal come-back in Rome after Ludwig had left the city.[8]

Thus John XXII owed much to Stefano da Colonna. Against this background, the documents printed below fall into place. The count of Anguillaria had married Colonna's daughter by consent but had not yet consummated the union. That put the woman in a very difficult position. An unconsummated marriage could be dissolved, but only through entry into a religious order. In all probability, she did not want to do this, which would have allowed the count to marry another woman and add insult to injury. She herself could not marry anyone else, since the count evidently had no plans to become a monk. John XXII helped out by putting pressure on the count to consummate the marriage and make it indissoluble.

Vatican Register 115

Fo. 1ʳᵃ, from the table of contents to the volume:

Episcopo Mothon' et duobus collegis scribitur quod cogant comitem Anguillarie resilientem a consumatione matrimonii cum Agnete de Columpna, quam desponsaverat, ad consummandum matrimonium cum eadem.

Eiusdem super eodem quod summarie et de plano eundum Comitem compellant.

Eidem comiti quod adimpleat promissum matrimonii contrahendi.

Eidem comiti conceditur quod dictum matrimonium solempnizare possit temporibus prohibitis a iure.

Johanni sancti *Theodori diacono cardinali legato scribitur quod nedum desistat ab impedimento dicti matrimonii, ymmo inducat dictum comitem ad consumandum. . . .

---

[7] 'Miramur, quod de aliis devotis ipsarum partium in imminentibus negociis ibi ecclesie audivimus devocionem, quam operose curant ostendere, de te autem nichil, quod in faciendo consistat, ab aliquo nunciatur. Rogamus igitur discretionem tuam et hortamur attente, ut te promptius quam abhactenus habeas in agendis, unde tibi laudis premium non immerito redimas et uberiorem benivolenciam consequaris ecclesie, sicut optas, non omittens carissimi in Christo filii nostri R. Regis Sicilie illustris te in premissis voluntati et placito coaptare' (ibid., no. 1000, p. 374).

[8] In a letter of 28 August 1328 John XXII reported thus to the king of France: 'die 4. presentis mensis Augusti Ludovico. . . . Urbem cum ignominia et dispendiis plurimis exeunte dilecti filii, nobiles viri, Stephanus de Columpna miles et Bertuldus de Filiis Ursi Urbem intraverunt eandem, per quorum solertem industriam Romanus populus se peccasse considerans et cognoscens, pacificatus et humiliatus extitit et eosdem nobiles pro nobis et st. Dei ecclesia constituit senatores' (ibid., no. 1075, p. 396).

Fos. 29^(ra)–30^(ra), from the letters as registered:

Episcopo Mothonensi et Laurentio Capocie Lateranensi ac Nicolao de
Fuscis de Berta Tiburtinensi ecclesiarum canonicis.

Significavit nobis dilectus filius nobilis vir Stephanus de Columpna quod
dilectus filius nobilis vir Ursus comes Anguillarie tractatu prehibito de
matrimonio inter ipsum Ursum et dilectam in Christo filiam nobilem
mulierem Agnetem eiusdem Stephani filiam contrahendo sponsalia primo
cum eadem Agnete tunc etatis nubilis existente per procuratorem ad id
sufficiens mandatum habentem contraxit et de huiusmodi sponsalibus non
violandis sed ad effectum deducendis prestitit sacramentum per procuratorem eumdem; et deinde, non multo tempore post, Ursus prefatus ad contrahendum matrimonium per verba de presenti cum Agnete prefata certum
constituit solemniter et legittime procuratorem et nuncium specialem, dans
etiam in mandatis eidem quod iuraret ad sancta dei evangelia in animam
ipsius comitis quod idem comes quando ipse procurator et nuntius esset
in presentia dicte Agnetis ex tempore ipsius mandati pro tempore eiusdem
presentie et ex tempore ipsius presentie pro tempore eiusdem mandati in
eamdem Agnetem velut in suam veram et legittimam uxorem per ipsum
procuratorem et nuntium consenserat et eam ab ipsa vel illa hora in antea [*fo. 29^(rb)*] in suam veram et legittimam uxorem haberet, et ea vivente,
aliam non reciperet temporibus vite sue, ac ipsam Agnetem ad domum
suam traduceret et cum eadem matrimonium carnali copula consummaret
ac potestatem liberam omnia alia faciendi que in premissis forent opor-
tuna etiam si mandatum exigerent speciale, promisit tuncque idem comes
se gratum et ratum habiturum perpetuo quicquid in premissis et circa
premissa procuraret et ageret procurator et nuntius antedictus, et quoquo-
modo vel causa non contra faceret vel veniret, hecque omnia et singula ipse
comes iuravit ad sancta dei evangelia semper grata et rata habere et tenere
et contra ea quovis tempore quomodolibet non facere vel venire. Procurator itaque et nuntius sepedictus huiusmodi mandato suscepto ad dicte
Agnetis accedens presentiam cum ipsa vice et nomine dicti Ursi comitis, et
pro ipso, matrimonium per verba de presenti rite contraxit et ipsam anulo
subarravit. Ad maiorem huiusmodi rei firmitatem ad sancta dei evangelia
in animam dicti comitis ipsi Agneti iuravit vice et nomine quibus supra hoc
matrimonium perpetuo tenere, et nullo umquam tempore quomodolibet
contrafacere vel venire; ac nichilominus nomine dotis a Stephano supra-
dicto certam recepit pecunie quantitatem. Et insuper, ut fertur, prefatus
comes Agnetem predictam post premissa suam nominavit uxorem. Cum
autem idem comes, ut dicitur, seductus, supradictum matrimonium distu-
lerit atque differat plus debito ac etiam recusaverit et recuset solemnizare
et consumare ac sepedictam Agnem traducere in uxorem, eamque maritali
affectione tractare, pretendens supradictum mandatum ad dictum matrimonium contrahendum priusquam idem matrimonium contraheretur se

revocasse, post tamen sponsalia predicta, ut premittitur, iurata, et penitus ignorante sepedicta Agnete, fuit nobis pro parte dicti Stephani suppliciter postulatum ut providere super hoc de oportuno remedio digneremur. Nos itaque, huiusmodi supplicationibus inclinati, mandamus quatenus vos, vel alter vestrum, si summarie, de plano, sine strepitu et figura iudicii premissis vel alicui ex ipsis quod sufficiet veritatem reperitis suffragari, prefatum comi|tem [*fo. 29ᵛᵃ*] ad observandum et implendum promissiones et iuramenta predicta dictumque matrimonium solemnizandum et prefatam Agnetem in suam uxorem traducendam, eamque maritali affectione tractandum, per censuram ecclesiasticam ratione previa compellatis. Datum Avinione X. kal. januarii anno tertiodecimo [23 December 1328].

Eisdem

Significavit nobis, etc., ut in precedenti usque ad illum locum 'et penitus ignorante sepedicta Agnete', super hoc per dictum Stephanum provisionis nostre remedio suppliciter implorato. Nos suis in hac parte supplicationibus inclinati committimus et mandamus quatenus, vocatis qui fuerint evocandi, faciatis super premissis simpliciter summarie et de plano, sine strepitu et figura iudicii iustitie complementum, facientes quod inde decreveritis per censuram ecclesiasticam firmiter observari, contradictores, etc., nonobstant' si eis, etc. Quod si non omnes hiis exequendis potueritis interesse, tu, frater episcope, una cum eorum altero, ea nichilominus exequaris. Datum Avinione X kal. martii anno tertiodecimo [20 February 1329].

Urso Comiti Anguillarie

Attendentes impedimenta varia que morosa dilatatio coniugalem consumandi copulam matrimoniis interdum ingerere consuevit, cupientesque eisdem quantum cum deo possumus obviare, ut matrimonium, quod inter te et dilectam in Christo filiam nobilem mulierem Agnetem natam nobilis viri Stephani de Columpna contractum asseritur, vel, si illud contrahi contigerit, postquam contractum, alias tamen canonice, fuerit, possitis temporibus a iure vel consuetudine seu statuto prohibitis in facie solemnizare ecclesie impune devotioni vestre tenore presentium indulgemus. Nulli ergo, etc. Datum Avinione XVII kalendas maii anno tertiodecimo [15 April 1329].

In eumdem modum dilecte in Christo filie nobili mulieri Agneti nate dilecti filii nobilis viri Stephani de Columpna verbis competenter mutatis. Datum ut supra.

. . .

[*fo. 29ᵛᵇ*]

. . .

Urso comiti Anguillarie

Alias tibi, fili, post nostre salutationis eloquium per nostras litteras scrip-
simus in hac forma: Scias, fili, ex quorumdam relatione fideli ad nostram
pervenisse notitiam quod dilectam in Christo filiam nobilem mulierem
Agnetem natam dilecti filii nobilis viri Stephani de Columpna in uxorem
tuam desponsasti per verba matrimonium exprimentia de presenti. Sane,
quia, ut intelleximus, quorumdam seductus consilio a contracto intendis
et niteris resilire, nos, attendentes quod hoc tibi non licet nec posses,
nisi de facto dumtaxat, [9]perficere sine dei offensa, tue periculo anime, ac
scandalo plurimorum, nobilitatem tuam rogamus et hortamur attente, tibi
nichilominus paterno ac sano consilio suadentes, quatenus prudenter tue
in hac parte saluti providens et honori sine deffectu adimpleas quod lau-
dabiliter actore Domino promisisti. Verentes autem quod propter viarum
discrimina non sic cito ut cupimus ad te littere ipse perveniant, et habentes
cordi predictum negotium pro partis bono et commodo utriusque, predic-
tas litteras paterna solicitudine duximus iterandas. Datum V kal. januarii
anno tertiodecimo [28 December 1328].

Johanni Sancti Theodori diacono cardinali apostolice sedis legato

Quorumdam relatione fideli ad nostram noveris notitiam pervenisse quod
quamvis dilectus filius nobilis vir Ursus Comes Anguillarie dilectam in
Christo nobilem mulierem Agnetem natam dilecti filii nobilis viri Stephani
de Columpna desponsaverit in uxorem suam per verba matrimonium exprimentia de presenti, impedimentum, quod [*fo. 30ra*] vix credere possumus, per te tamen ingeritur, quominus ipsum matrimonium consum-
metur. Sane, attendentes quod ab hoc eidem comiti resilire non licet nec
posset nisi de facto dumtaxat aliud perficere sine dei offensa, sue periculo
anime, ac scandalo plurimorum, discretionem tuam rogamus et hortamur
attente, tibi nichilominus, fili, salubriter suadentes ut, premissis attentis,
nedum a predicto impedimento desistas, sed quantum in te alias fuerit et a
Domino tibi conceditur illius complemento efficacem prebeas operam, et
diligenter obstacula quecumque removeas, si per alios ingerantur. Datum
II non. Novembris anno tertiodecimo [4 November 1328].

In eumdem modum, mutatis mutandis, nobili viro Neapoleoni de Filiis
Ursi de Urbe

In eumdem modum nobili viro Bertoldo de Filiis Ursi de Urbe.

In eumdem modum mutatis mutandis nobili mulieri Constantie matri dicti
Ursi relicte quondam Francisci Comitis Anguillarie.

[9] perficere] ⟨aliud⟩ perficere?

4. 5. Consummation and indissolubility in the *Oculus sacerdotis* of William of Pagula

This document shows that diffusion to a wider audience of the symbolic rationale of the rule that entry into a religious order by one partner in an unconsummated marriage left the other partner free to remarry. Pastoral manuals like this were designed for ordinary priests to help them look after their lay parishioners better. The Latin is simple and clear. The *Oculus sacerdotis* is an exellent example of the genre, especially well developed in England, apparently. For the author see Sharpe, *Handlist*, no. 2141 ('William of Paull'), p. 799, with further references, especially to work by Leonard Boyle. The passage is from *Oculus sacerdotis*, 3. 14.

London, BL MS Royal 6. E. I[1]

Parchment manuscript, 390 mm. × 270 mm., 121 folios; paragraph marks in red and blue, initial letters mostly or all in blue but with red decoration. The manuscript looks late fourteenth century, according to Warner and Gilson. In addition to the *Oculus sacerdotis*, it contains the *Sacramentale*, 'a treatise, mainly theological, on the sacraments, by the canonist W[illelmus] de Monte Hauduno . . . d. *circ*. 1343'. There is more pastoral material at the extremities of the manuscript.

Fo. 68[va]:

Matrimonium solvi potest ante consummationem matrimonii, puta per ingressum religionis, et non post matrimonium consummatum. Ratio est quia in coniugio sunt duo, videlicet consensus animorum, et commixtio corporum. Consensus *animorum [2]significat caritatem, que consistit in spiritu inter deum et iustam animam—et anima separari a deo potest per peccatum: sic matrimonium *solvi potest per ingressum religionis, sed commixtio corporum [3]significat conformitatem que consistit in carne inter Christum et ecclesiam, et illa coniunctio Christi ad ecclesiam designatur per unionem qua iuncta est divinitas carni humane in utero virginali. Unde quia humana caro nunquam a deitate separata est, ideo propter talem coniunctionem nunquam dissolvitur matrimonium. Vel potest dici quod facilius potest una anima separari a deo quam tota ecclesia: Extra 'De Bigamis' c(apitulo). *Debitum*,[4] et xxvii q. ii. c(apitulo) *Qua propter*[5] in Glosa[6] et Extra '[De] Conver. Coniugatorum' c(apitulo) *Ex publico*[7] in Glosa ult.[8]

[1] Description based on Warner and Gilson, *Catalogue of Western Manuscripts*, i. 150, and on personal inspection.
[2] significat] *or* signat
[3] significat] *or* signat
[4] X. 1. 21. 5.
[5] Pars II, C. 27, q. 2, c. 37.
[6] '*Qua propter. perficiunt.*—Non quo ad sui essentiam, sed ad significatio-
[*See p.* 283 *for n.* 6 *cont. and nn.* 7 *and* 8.

Documents: 4. 6   283

4. 6. Johannes de Burgo on the marriage of Mary and Joseph

This text is from the *Pupilla oculi* (8. 1–2). The work is another pastoral manual. It was in fact based on the *Oculus sacerdotis* of William of Pagula, though it was probably aimed at a somewhat different readership: academically trained ecclesiastical administrators as opposed to ordinary parish priests (see discussion in the introduction to Document **3. 9**). It puts over in a practical genre the view that the marriage of Mary and Joseph was in a sense lacking in perfection because it had not been consummated. Johannes agrees that in another sense it is perfect, but the passage shows how far the importance of consummation had penetrated into the world of religious administration and high-level pastoral government.

Johannes de Burgo was learned and cites interesting authorities. The ideas of Duns Scotus to which he alludes are interesting in their own right and deserve close study, which the references below in n. 2 aim to facilitate.

nem. Non tamen sequitur quod ante non fuerit perfectum, quia perfectum amplius potest perfici: xi. q. iii *Quod predecessor* (Pars II, C. 11, q. 3, c. 105), perficitur autem matrimonium per coitum quo ad sui significationem, quia tunc utramque habet significationem, scilicet, coniunctionem anime fidelis ad deum, et Christi ad ecclesiam, ut Extra 'De bygamis' in c. *Debitum* (X. 1. 21. 5). Sed quare separatur matrimonium causa religionis post coniunctionem anime fidelis ad deum et non post coniunctionem Christi ad ecclesiam? Ratio est quia anima separatur a deo per peccatum. Unde non est mirum si post talem *coniunctionem matrimonium sepa-retur. Sed illa coniunctio Christi ad ecclesiam designatur per unionem qua unita est divinitas carni humane in utero virginali, unde quia humana caro numquam a deitate separata [separatur *ms.*] est ideo per talem coniunctionem numquam dissolvitur matrimonium; vel potest dici quod facilius est quod una anima separetur a deo quam tota ecclesia, immo impossibile est quod tota ecclesia separetur a deo, quia ecclesia non potest nulla esse' (MS BL Royal 9. C. III, fo. 225rb, right-hand gloss).

⁷ X. 3. 32. 7.
⁸ The following passage from Bernard of Parma's *Glossa ordinaria* to the Decretals could be meant ('Duplex' is supplied in the margin in a different hand before initial 'Est'): 'Est consummatio que sit quo ad matrimonii essentiam que fuit facta in paradiso ab ipso Domino per coniunctionem animorum que designat conformitatem fidelis anime ad Christum, ut ibi; et est consummatio quo ad sacramentum Christi ad ecclesiam per incarnationem verbi dei in utero virginali quod designatur per illud matrimonium quod est carnali copula consummatum, ut hic, et supra, "De Bigamis", *Debitum* (X. 1. 21. 5); xxvii. q. ii, *In omni*, R(ubrica) (Pars II, C. 27, q. 2, c. 36); vel saltem quo ad hoc quod impedire possit propositum religionis: Lau(rentius). Notavit hic Alanus quod matrimonium non consummatum sortitur naturam ex constitutione ecclesie, et ideo circa illud latissime patet pape potestas. Vin(centius) dixit quod papa per dispensationem posset dissolvere tale matrimonium, posset etiam statuere quod secundum matrimonium rumperetur; secus de consummato, quod ab ipso Domino rationem suam [sortitur], et ideo sola interpretatio circa illud pertinet ad papam, non dispensatio vel contraria constituendo [*read* constitutio?]. Contra tamen infra "De sponsa duorum", c. ult.' (MS Royal 9. C. 1, fo. 123vb, right-hand gloss).

MS London, BL Royal 11. B. X

For a brief description of the manuscript see Document **3. 9.**

Fo. 124^{ra-b}:

Item ad verum matrimonium requiritur intentio specialis vel generalis, ut scilicet vir intendat tradere mulieri perpetuam potestatem corporis sui, et e converso, ipsa corporis sui potestatem viro suo quo ad carnalem copulam, saltem sub conditione implicita, videlicet si petatur. Unde inter beatam Virginem et Ioseph fuit perfectum matrimonium perfectione quam facit consensus per verba de presenti expressus, sed non perfectione quam facit carnalis copula, que est actus proprius matrimonii, in quem numquam consensit explicite, sed implicite solum, ut dicit Tho. Di. 30:[1] id est, sub conditione implicita, si peteretur. Et hoc in nullo preiudica|vit [*fo. 124rb*] voto suo de virginitate servanda, quia sufficienter certificata fuit a deo quod actus huiusmodi matrimonialis numquam a suo coniuge peteretur. Transtulit ergo in virum suum potestatem sui corporis, sed non usum, secundum Scotum Di. 30. q. 2.[2] [3]Hec dicit Ber. in Glossa,[4] quod quamvis alter coniugum vel uterque intendat numquam reddere debitum alteri, quin etiam negare petitum, tenet matrimonium, ut creditur, dum tamen illud non deducatur in pactum.

---

[1] Cf. Aquinas, *Commento alle Sentenze di Pietro Lombardo*, trans. and ed. 'Redazione delle Edizioni Studio Domenicano', dist. 30, q. 2, a. 1, solutio II, p. 346.

[2] The critical edition of John Duns Scotus has not reached book 4 of either his Oxford or his Paris commentary on the Lombard's *Sentences*. Sharpe, *Handlist*, no. 674, p. 239, comments with respect to the *Opus Oxoniense* that the 'text printed by Wadding and reprinted . . . is not pure'. He does not make the same comment of the pre-critical edition of the *Opus Parisiense*, but it has seemed simpler and safer to use manuscripts. The relevant passage from the Oxford *Sentence* commentary is in a question inc. 'Secundo quero utrum inter Mariam et Iosep fuerit verum matrimonium' (MS Oxford, Merton College 66, fos. 214vb–215rb, a manuscript contemporary with the author, to judge from the script, and designated one of the 'codices constanter adhibiti' in the introductory volume to the critical edition which is in progress: see *Ioannis Duns Scoti opera omnia*, ed. C. Balic *et al.*, i (Vatican City, 1950), 32*–34*). Note especially the passage beginning 'Respondeo [*or* Responsio]: In contractu matrimonii [matrimonium *ms. here and below?*] mutua est datio corporum ad copulam carnalem nonnisi sub conditione implicita, scilicet: si petatur' and ending 'propter honestam causam aliquam' (ibid., fo. 215^{ra-b}). The pertinent passage in the Paris *Sentence* commentary of Scotus is also in a question 'Utrum inter Mariam et Ioseph fuerat [*sic*] verum matrimonium' (MS Oxford, Merton College 63, fos. 63^r–64^r). Note especially the passage beginning 'Ideo dico quod absolute vovit castitatem' and ending 'Ergo potest esse dominium corporis sine usu perpetuo' (ibid., fos. 63^v–64^r).

[3] Hec] *sic ms.*

[4] Not found (but presumably a gloss of Bernardus of Parma).

4. 7. A case from the archive of the Apostolic Penitentiary: Constance of Padilla

The case, discussed in detail in Chapter 4, illustrates the way in which high-level ideas about consummation could affect real-life situations.

Penitenzieria Apostolica Register, vol. 48

Paper manuscript, 285×215 mm. The last folio in the volume is numbered 989.[1] Line numbers refer to the main body of the entry only.

Fo. 634ʳ⁻ᵛ:

Head of the page: Anno octavo domini Alexandri pape vi[2]
Above the entry: Octobr' 1499[3]
Halfway down the entry, left-hand margin: Rome iiii Non. Septembris
Halfway down the entry, right-hand margin: Segobien [=Segubien(sis)]

Constantia de Padilla, mulier Segoviensis, exponit /1/ quod alias, postquam ipsa matrimonium per verba legitima /2/ de presenti cum quodam viro nullo iure sibi prohi|bito /3/ coniuncta contraxerat, carnali copula minime /4/ subsecuta, ⁴ipsam per vim et metum cuiusdam nobilis /5/ Bonadille Marchisie Modie Conchensis[5] diocesis, cui /6/ tunc ipsa exponens inserviebat et forsan certarum /7/ aliarum personarum ⁶*compulsi monasterium Sancti Petri /8/ de Las Ducuans ordinis ⁷*Conceptionis[8] sub regula Sancte Clare /9/ Toletan' ingressa fuit et professionem ⁹pro ¹⁰moniales /10/ dicti monasterii emitti solitam *emisit; et deinde dictus /11/ eius vir matrimonium seu potius contubernium pro¹¹ simi|lia /12/ verba de presenti cum quadam alia muliere nullo /13/ etiam sibi iure prohibita contraxit, illudque carnali /14/ copula consumavit. Postmodum vero dicta exponens /15/ dictum monasterium illicentiata exivit et ad civitatem /16/ Abulen-

---

[1] I ignore all foliations apart from the modern stamped foliation.
[2] At the head of fos. 633ᵛ and 634ᵛ: 'Rome apud sanctum Petrum'.
[3] But this may not relate to this particular case.
[4] ipsam] ipsa *recte*
[5] i.e. of Cuenca
[6] *compulsi] compulsa *recte. The scribe may have been unsure how to extend the abbreviation: he had written* ipsam *above, as if for an accusative and infinitive construction, but then goes on to write* ingressa fuit *below*
[7] *Conceptionis] *ms. very unclear: looks like* Conceptianum
[8] This may be the same as the house listed as 'Toledo, *Sancta Maria Immaculada*' in the brief article by T. Morel in *Diccionario de historia eclesiastica de España* (5 vols. so far; 1972–87, the last being suppl. 1), iii (Madrid, 1973), 1684. According to Morel, it was only long afterwards that the community joined the Benedictine Order. He makes no mention of the Franciscan rule, but the 'Immaculate' (an allusion to the Immaculate Conception) fits the description in our case.
[9] pro] per *recte*
[10] moniales] m'ˡᵉˢ *ms.*
[11] pro] per *recte*

sem[12] se transtulit, in qua est de presenti. Cum autem, /17/ Pater Sancte, dicta exponens *antequam *dictum monasterium /18/ ingrederetur, matrimonium per verba de presenti cum /19/ dicto viro nullo sibi *iure prohibito consueta ut /20/ premittitur contraxit et pro vi et metum[13] ingressa /21/ et in eo cum animi sui quiete manere non valens /22/ ut premissum est exivit, cupiatque in seculo cum dicto /23/ suo viro remanere, et mater effici liberum,[14] a nonnullis /24/ [15]tamen simplicibus et iurisignarus[16] ac ipsius ex|ponentis /25/ forsan emulis asseritur ipsam propter premissa /26/ dicto ordini astrictam esse et propterea in seculo /27/ cum dicto suo viro[17] /28/ licite remanere non posse, ad ora igitur talium et /29/ aliorum sibi super hiis obloqui volentium emulorum obstruenda, /30/ [*fo. 634ᵛ*] quare, etc., quatenus ipsam ab excessibus hiusmodi absolvi /31/ necnon in seculo cum dicto suo viro postquam a dicta /32/ secunda muliere in iudicio ecclesie separatus fuerit rema|nere /33/ possit libere et licite, alio tamen canonico /34/ non obstante, prolem suscipiendam exinde legitimam decer|nere /35/ declarari mandare dignemini: ut in forma. /36/

Et committatur vicario generali ordinis /37/ sancte Clare provincie Hispanie /38/ et archdiacono de Sepulveda in /39/ ecclesia Segobiensi. Fiat Iul.[18]

Videat eam D. Do. De Iacobatiis Iul. /40/

[19]Committatur eisdem ut vocatis vocandis | constito de assertis et quod | per metum quod caderet in | constantem professionem emi|serit nec postea expresse | vel tacite ratificaverit | declaret ut petitur.

4. 8. Another non-consummation case from the archive of the Apostolic Penitentiary

In this case Juan from the diocese of Burgos claims that he married Catherine daughter of Juan Gómez, who committed adultery with another man before the marriage had been consummated; she then repented and entered a religious order. Juan subsequently became engaged to Maria and asks permission to marry her. It is a classic 'ratum non consummatum' case and illustrates the same point as Document 4. 7.

---

[12] i.e. Avila.
[13] pro vi et metum] *sic ms.*
[14] liberum] liberorum *recte*
[15] tamen] tamen et *could be read*
[16] iurisignarus] iurisignaris *recte*
[17] viro] remanere et mater effici liberum (*sic*) *added and deleted in ms.*
[18] Presumably a Penitentiary official.
[19] *The following passage is indented and behind a bracket; I discontinue the line numbering*

Penitenzieria Apostolica Register vol. 60

Paper manuscript, 285 × 205 mm. The last folio in the volume is numbered 468. Line numbers refer to the main body of the entry only.

Fos. 21ᵛ–22ʳ:

Head of fo. 21ᵛ: Rome apud s. P.
Head of fo. 22ʳ: Anno quarto Leonis pape X
Above the entry: Contreras taxatio iiii ÷ 3
Heading, left-hand margin: Declaratio matrimonialis
Halfway down the left-hand margin: iiii Id. Aprilis[1]
Halfway down the right-hand margin: Burgen.[2]

Iohannes Sams[3] de Rochas laicus Burgensis diocesis /1/ exponit quod postquam ipse alias matrimonium per verba /2/ de presenti cum Catherina filia Iohannis Gomez /3/ muliere loci de Rochas dicte diocesis contraxerat, non /4/ tamen cognoverat, eademque Catherina post commissum /5/ cum alio viro adulterium, penitentia ducta seu alias, habitum /6/ ordinis sancte Trinitatis per manus ministri monasterii eiusdem /7/ sancte Trinitatis probe et extra muros Burgen. /8/ [*fo. 22ʳ*] assumpserat, et professionem per moniales dicti ordinis /9/ emitti solitam, absque tamen ingressu alicuius monasterii earumdem /10/ monialium, in manibus dicti ministri emiserat regularem, /11/ prefatus orator sponsalia per verba de futuro cum quadam /12/ Maria filia Gundisalvi Martieres de Quexiquata,[4] /13/ muliere dicte diocesis, contraxit. Cuperet idem orator cum eadem /14/ Maria matrimonium contrahere et in eo postquam contractum /15/ foret licite remanere, ab aliquibus tamen simplicibus /16/ et iurisignaris etc. Ad igitur talium et aliorum sibi /17/ in futurum obloqui volentium ora obstruenda, supplicatur etc. /18/ quatenus, si vocatis vocandis constiterit de assertis, oratorem /19/ ipsum premissis non obstantibus, matrimonium cum prefata /20/ Maria contrahere, et in eo postquam contractum fuerit /21/ remanere, licite posse declarari, prolem exinde suscipiendam /22/ etc. man(dare) dignemini in forma. FIAT IN FORMA M. R(egens)

[1] This is repeated halfway down the left-hand margin of the continuation of the entry on fo. 22ʳ.
[2] This is repeated halfway down the right-hand margin of the continuation of the entry on fo. 22ʳ.
[3] Sams] Sa *followed by three minims and an* s *in ms., so could also be* Savis *or* Sains *or* Sanis
[4] Quexiquata] *I transcribe this tentatively as I have not been able to find the name*

Bibliography

XIV homélies du IXe siècle de l'Italie du Nord, ed. P. Mercier (Sources chrétiennes, 161; Paris, 1970).

ABELARD: *The Letters of Abelard and Heloise*, trans. B. Radice (Harmondsworth etc., 1974; rev. edn. by M. Clanchy: Harmondsworth, 2003).

Les Actes pontificaux originaux des Archives Nationales de Paris, i. *1198–1261*; ii. *1261–1304*; iii. *1305–1415*, ed. B. Barbiche (Vatican City, 1975–82).

ÆLFRIC: *Ælfric's Catholic Homilies: Introduction, Commentary and Glossary*, ed. M. Godden (Early English Text Society, SS 18; Oxford, 2000).

AMOS, T. L., 'The Origin and Nature of the Carolingian Sermon' (unpublished Ph.D. dissertation, Michigan State University, 1983).

—— 'Preaching and the Sermon in the Carolingian World', in T. L. Amos, E. A. Green, and B. M. Kienzle (eds.), *De ore Domini: Preacher and Word in the Middle Ages* (Kalamazoo, 1989), 41–60.

Analecta reginensia: extraits des manuscrits latins de la Reine Christine conservés au Vatican, ed. A. Wilmart (Studi e testi, 59; Vatican City, 1933).

The Anglo-Saxon Missionaries in Germany, Being the Lives of SS. Willibrord, Boniface, Sturm, Leoba and Lebuin, together with the Hodoeporicon *of St. Willibald and a Selection from the Correspondence of St. Boniface*, ed. and trans. C. H. Talbot (London etc., 1954).

[Anon.], 'Aquinas', supplement to *Summa theologica*, in *Sancti Thomae Aquinatis . . . opera omnia, iussu . . . Leonis XIII P.M. edita*, xii (Rome, 1906).

AQUINAS, THOMAS: *S. Tommaso d'Aquino: Commento alle Sentenze di Pietro Lombardo e testo integrale di Pietro Lombardo. Libro quarto. Distinzioni 24–42. L'Ordine, il Matrimonio* , trans. and ed. by 'Redazione delle Edizioni Studio Domenicano' (Bologna, 2001).

—— *Sentencia libri de anima*, ed. [R.-A. Gauthier], in *Sancti Thoma Aquinatis . . . opera omnia, iussu Leonis XIII P.M. edita*, xlv/1 (Rome, 1984) [includes critical edn. of William of Moerbeke's translation of Aristotle].

—— See also Anon.; Aristotle.

ARISTOTLE: *Aristotle's* De Anima *in the Version of William of Moerbeke and the Commentary of St. Thomas Aquinas*, ed. and trans. K. Foster, S. Humphries, and I. Thomas (London, 1951).

—— *Metaphysics: Aristoteles Latinus*, xxv/3.2. *Metaphysica Lib. I–XIV*, ed. Gudrun Vuillemin-Diem (Leiden etc., 1995).

—— *Aristotle's* Meteorology *in the Arabico-Latin Tradition: A Critical Edition of the Texts, with Introduction and Indices*, ed. P. L. Schoonheim (Leiden, 2000).

AUGUSTINE, *De bono coniugali*, in *Augustine:* De bono coniugali; De sancta virginitate, ed. and trans. P. G. Walsh (Oxford, 2001).

—— *Aurelii Augustini Opera*, x/2. *Sancti Aurelii Augustini Ennarationes in Psalmos LI–C*, ed. D. E. Dekkers and I. Fraipoint (Corpus Christianorum Series Latina, 39, Aurelii Augustini Opera, 10/2; Turnhout, 1956).

AURELLE, M., *Les Noces du comté: mariage et pouvoir en Catalogne (753–1213)* (Paris, 1995).

AVAGIANOU, A., *Sacred Marriage in the Rituals of Greek Religion* (Europäische Hochschulschriften, ser. 15, 54; Berne etc., 1991).

BACON, ROGER, *Opus tertium*, in *Fr. Rogeri Bacon opera quaedam hactenus inedita*, ed. J. S. Brewer, i (Rolls Series; London, 1859).

BAKKER, E. J., DE JONG, I. J. F., and VAN WEES, H. (eds.), *Brill's Companion to Herodotus* (Leiden etc., 2002).

BALDWIN, J. W., *Masters, Princes, and Merchants: The Social Views of Peter the Chanter and his Circle* (2 vols.; Princeton, 1970).

—— *The Government of Philip Augustus: Foundations of French Royal Power in the Middle Ages* (Berkeley etc., 1986).

BALL, R. M., 'The Education of the English Parish Clergy in the Later Middle Ages with Particular Reference to the Manuals of Instruction' (unpublished Ph.D. dissertation, Cambridge University, 1976).

BARRÉ, H., *Les Homéliaires carolingiens de l'école d'Auxerre: authenticité, inventaire, tableaux comparatifs, initia* (Studi e testi, 225; Vatican City, 1962).

BARROW, J., 'Hereford Bishops and Married Clergy c.1130–1240', *Historical Research* [formerly *Bulletin of the Institute of Historical Research*], 60 (1987), 1–8.

BARTLETT, R., *England under the Norman and Angevin Kings 1075–1225* (Oxford, 2000).

BATAILLON, L.-J., 'Approaches to the Study of Medieval Sermons', *Leeds Studies in English*, NS 11 (1980), 19–35; repr. in id., *La Prédication au XIIIᵉ siècle en France et Italie: études et documents* (Aldershot, 1993), no. 1.

—— 'Les conditions de travail des maîtres de l'université de Paris au XIIIᵉ siècle', *Revue des sciences philosophiques et théologiques*, 67 (1983), 417–32.

BEDE: *Bedae Venerabilis opera, pars III: opera homiletica, pars IV: opera rhythmica*, ed. D. Hurst (Corpus Christianorum Series Latina, 122; Turnhout, 1955).

BELLAMY, J. G., *The Criminal Trial in Later Medieval England: Felony before the Courts from Edward I to the Sixteenth Century* (Stroud, 1998).

BENSON, R. L., *The Bishop Elect: A Study in Medieval Ecclesiastical Office* (Princeton, 1968).

BÉRIOU, N., *L'Avènement des maîtres de la Parole: la prédication à Paris au XIIIᵉ siècle* (2 vols.; Collection des études augustiniennes, Série Moyen Âge et temps modernes, 31; Paris, 1998).

—— 'Les prologues de recueils de sermons latins du XIIᵉ au XVᵉ siècle', in J. Hamesse (ed.), *Les Prologues médiévaux: actes du colloque international organisé par l'Academia Belgica et l'École Française de Rome avec le concours de la F.I.D.E.M. (Rome, 26–28 mars 1998)* (Textes et études du Moyen Âge, 15; Turnhout, 2000), 395–426.

—— 'Les sermons latins après 1200', in B. M. Kienzle (ed.), *The Sermon* (Typologie des sources du Moyen Âge occidental, 81–3; Turnhout, 2000), 363–447.

—— and D'AVRAY, D. L., 'The Image of the Ideal Husband in Thirteenth Century France' (1990), in Bériou and d'Avray, *Modern Questions about Medieval Sermons*, 31–61.

———— 'Henry of Provins, O.P.'s Comparison of the Dominican and Franciscan Orders with the "Order" of Matrimony', in Bériou and d'Avray, *Modern Questions about Medieval Sermons*, 71–5.

—— —— (with P. COLE, J. RILEY-SMITH, and M. TAUSCHE), *Modern Questions about Medieval Sermons: Essays on Marriage, Death, History and Sanctity* (Spoleto etc., 1994).

BERNARD DE CLAIRVAUX, *Œuvres complètes*, xxi. *Le Précepte et la dispense. La Conversion*, ed. F. Callerot, J. Miethke, and C. Jaquinod (Sources chrétiennes, 457; Paris, 2000).

—— *Sancti Bernardi opera*, ed. J. Leclercq and H. Rochais, v. *Sermones II* (Rome, 1968); vii. *Epistolae, I: corpus epistolarum 1–180* (Rome, 1974).

BIBLIOTHÈQUE NATIONALE, *Catalogue général des manuscrits latins*, vi. (*Nᵒˢ 3536 à 3775ᴮ*) (Paris, 1975); vii. (*Nᵒˢ 3776 à 3835*): *Homéliaires* (Paris, 1988).

BILLER, P., *The Measure of Multitude: Population in Medieval Thought* (Oxford, 2000).

BINDER, B., *Geschichte des feierlichen Ehesegen von der Entstehung der Ritualien bis zur Gegenwart, mit Berücksichtigung damit zusammenhängender Riten, Sitten und Bräuche: Eine liturgiegeschichtliche Untersuchung* (Metten, 1938).

BLACKBURN, B., and HOLFORD-STREVENS, L., *The Oxford Companion to the Year* (Oxford, 1999).

BLAIR, J., and SHARPE, R. (eds.), *Pastoral Care before the Parish* (Leicester etc., 1992).

The Blickling Homilies of the Tenth Century, from the Marquis of Lothian's Unique MS. A.D. 971, ed. R. Morris (London, 1880).

BOETHIUS: *Anicii Manlii Severini Boethii Philosophiae Consolatio*, ed. L. Bieler (Corpus Christianorum Series Latina, 94; Turnhout, 1984).

BOLLÉ, K. W., 'Hieros Gamos', in M. Eliade (ed.), *The Encyclopedia of Religion*, vi (New York etc., 1987), 317–21.

BONIFACE, Saint: see *The Anglo-Saxon Missionaries in Germany*.

BORGOLTE, M., 'Kulturelle Einheit und religiöse Differenz: Zur Verbreitung der Polygynie im mittelalterlichen Europa', *Zeitschrift für historische Forschung*, 31 (2004), 1–36.

BOUCHARD, C. B., 'Eleanor's Divorce from Louis VII: The Uses of Consanguinity', in B. Wheeler and J. C. Parsons (eds.), *Eleanor of Aquitaine: Lord and Lady* (New York and Basingstoke, 2002), 223–35.

BOUHOT, J.-P., 'Un sermonnaire carolingien', *Revue d'histoire des textes*, 4 (1974), 181–223.

BOUTRUCHE, R., *Seigneurie et féodalité: l'apogée (XIᵉ–XIIIᵉ siècles)* (Paris, 1970), 228–30.

BOWKER, J. (ed.), *The Oxford Dictionary of World Religion* (Oxford, 1997).

BOYLE, L. E., 'A Study of the Works Attributed to William of Pagula: With Special Reference to the *Oculus sacerdotis* and *Summa summarum*' (unpublished D.Phil. thesis, Oxford University, 1956).

BRANDL, L., *Die Sexualethik des heiligen Albertus Magnus: Eine moralgeschichtliche Untersuchung* (Studien zur Geschichte der katholischen Moraltheologie, 2; Regensburg, 1955).

BROOKE, C. N. L., *Europe in the Central Middle Ages, 962–1154* (London, 1964; 3rd edn. Harlow, 2000).

—— *The Medieval Idea of Marriage* (Oxford, 1989).

BROWN, R. E., FITZMYER, J. A., and MURPHY, R. E. (eds.), *The Jerome Biblical Commentary*, i (London, 1968).

BRUGUIÈRE, M.-B., 'Le mariage de Philippe-Auguste et d'Isambour de Danemark: aspects canoniques et politiques', in Université des Sciences Sociales de Toulouse, *Mélanges offerts à Jean Dauvillier* (Toulouse, 1979), 135–56.

—— 'Canon Law and Royal Weddings, Theory and Practice: The French Example, 987–1215', in S. Chodorow (ed.), *Proceedings of the Eighth International Congress of Medieval Canon Law* (Monumenta Iuris Canonici, Series C, Subsidia, 9; Vatican City, 1992), 473–96.

BRUNDAGE, J. A., *Law, Sex, and Christian Society in Medieval Europe* (Chicago etc., 1987).

—— *Medieval Canon Law* (London etc., 1995).

—— 'The Merry Widow's Serious Sister: Remarriage in Classical Canon Law', in R. R. Edwards and V. Ziegler (eds.), *Matrons and Marginal Women in Medieval Society* (Woodbridge, 1995), 33–48.

BURCH, S. L., 'A Study of Some Aspects of Marriage as Presented in Selected Octosyllabic French Romances of the 12th and 13th Centuries' (unpublished Ph.D. thesis, University College London, 1982).

BURGUNDIO: *De fide orthodoxa: Versions of Burgundio and Cerbanus*, ed. E. M. Buytaert (Franciscan Institute Publications, Text Series, 8; St Bonaventure, NY, etc., 1955).

BURR, D., *The Persecution of Peter Olivi* (Transactions of the American Philosophical Society, NS 66, pt. 5; Philadelphia, 1976).

BYNUM, C. W., *Fragmentation and Redemption: Essays on Gender and the Human Body in Medieval Religion* (New York, 1991).

CAESARIUS, bishop of Arles: *Sancti Caesarii Arelatensis sermones*, pt. 2, ed. G. Morin (Corpus Christianorum Series Latina, 104; Turnhout, 1953).

CARTLIDGE, N., *Medieval Marriage: Literary Approaches, 1100–1300* (Cambridge etc., 1997).

CERBANUS: see Burgundio.

CHARLIER, C., 'Une œuvre inconnue de Florus de Lyon: la collection "de fide" de Montpellier', *Traditio*, 8 (1952), 81–109.

CHÉLINI, J., *L'Aube du Moyen Âge: naissance de la chrétienté occidentale. La vie religieuse des laïcs dans l'Europe carolingienne (750–900)* (Paris, 1991).

CHENEY, C. R., and JONES, M., *A Handbook of Dates for Students of British History* (Royal Historical Society Guides and Handbooks, 4; Cambridge, 2000).

CHOJNACKI, S., 'Il divorzio di Cateruzza: rappresentazione femminile ed esito processuale (Venezia 1465)', in Menchi and Quaglioni, *Coniugi nemici*, 371–416.

CLANCHY, M. T., *Abelard: A Medieval Life* (Oxford, 1997).

——— see Abelard.

CLAYTON, M., *The Cult of the Virgin Mary in Anglo-Saxon England* (Cambridge, 1990).

Concilia aevi Karolini, ed. A. Werminghoff (2 vols.; Monumenta Germaniae Historica, Legum Sectio III, Concilia, 2. 1–2; Hanover, 1906–8).

Conciliorum oecumenicorum decreta, ed. J. Alberigo et al., 3rd edn. (Bologna, 1973).

Constitutiones Concilii Quarti Lateranensis una cum commentariis glossatorum, ed. A. García y García (Monumenta Iuris Canonici, Series A: Corpus Glossatorum, 2; Vatican City, 1981).

CONTRENI, J. J., *The Cathedral School of Laon from 850 to 930: Its Manuscripts and Masters* (Munich, 1978).

COXE, H. O., *Catalogus codicum mss. qui in collegiis aulisque Oxoniensibus hodie adservantur* (2 pts.; Oxford, 1852).

CROSS, F. L., and LIVINGSTONE, E. A. (eds.), *The Oxford Dictionary of the Christian Church* (Oxford, 1997).

CROUZEL, H., 'Les pères de l'Église ont-ils permis le remariage après séparation?', in id., *Mariage et divorce, célibat et caractère sacerdotaux dans l'église ancienne: études diverses* (Études d'histoire du culte et des institutions chrétiennes, 11; Turin, 1982), 3–43.

CUNNINGHAM, M. P., 'Contents of the Newberry Library Homiliarium', *Sacris erudiri*, 7 (1955), 267–301.

DAUDET, P., *Études sur l'histoire de la juridiction matrimoniale: les origines carolingiennes de la compétence exclusive de l'église — France et Germanie* (Paris, 1933).

—— *L'Établissement de la compétence de l'église en matière de divorce & de consanguinité (France — Xème–XIIème siècles)* (Études sur l'histoire de la juridiction matrimoniale; Paris, 1941).

DAUVILLIER, J., *Le Mariage dans le droit classique de l'église depuis le Décret de Gratien (1140) jusqu'à la mort de Clément V (1314)* (Paris, 1933).

DAVID, P., 'Un recueil de conférences monastiques du VIIIe siècle: notes sur le manuscrit du chapitre de Cracovie', *Revue bénédictine*, 49 (1937), 62–89.

DAVIDSOHN, R., *Philipp II. August von Frankreich und Ingeborg* (Stuttgart, 1888).

DAVIES, W., *Small Worlds: The Village Community in Early Medieval Brittany* (London, 1988).

DAVIS, I., MÜLLER, M., and REES JONES, S., *Love, Marriage, and Family Ties in the Later Middle Ages* (International Medieval Research, 11; Turnhout, 2003).

D'AVRAY, D. L., *The Preaching of the Friars: Sermons Diffused from Paris before 1300* (Oxford, 1985).

—— 'Peter Damian, Consanguinity and Church Property', in L. Smith and B. Ward (eds.), *Intellectual Life in the Middle Ages: Essays Presented to Margaret Gibson* (London, 1992), 71–80.

—— *Death and the Prince: Memorial Preaching before 1350* (Oxford, 1994).

—— 'The Gospel of the Marriage Feast of Cana and Marriage Preaching in France', in Bériou and d'Avray, *Modern Questions about Medieval Sermons*, 135–53.

—— 'Christendom: Medieval Christianity', in P. Byrne and L. Houlden (eds.), *Companion Encyclopedia of Theology* (London etc., 1995), 206–29.

—— 'Philosophy in Preaching: The Case of a Franciscan Based in Thirteenth-Century Florence (Servasanto da Faenza)', in R. G. Newhauser and J. A. Alford (eds.), *Literature and Religion in the Later Middle Ages: Philological Studies in Honor of Siegfried Wenzel* (Binghampton, NY, 1995), 263–73.

—— 'Marriage Ceremonies and the Church in Italy after 1215', in T. Dean and K. J. P. Lowe (eds.), *Marriage in Italy 1300–1650* (Cambridge, 1998), 107–15.

—— *Medieval Marriage Sermons: Mass Communication in a Culture without Print* (Oxford, 2001).

—— 'Lay Kinship, Solidarity and Papal Law', in P. Stafford, J. L. Nelson, and J. Martindale (eds.), *Law, Laity and Solidarities: Essays in Honour of Susan Reynolds* (Manchester, 2001), 188–99.

—— 'Symbolism and Medieval Religious Thought', in P. Linehan and J. L. Nelson (eds.), *The Medieval World* (London etc., 2003), 267–78.

—— 'Printing, Mass Communication and Religious Reformation: The Middle Ages and After', in J. Crick and A. Walsham (eds.), *The Uses of Script and Print, 1300–1700* (Cambridge, 2004), 50–70.

—— 'Authentication of Marital Status: A Thirteenth Century English Royal Annulment Process and Later Medieval Cases from the Papal Penitentiary', *English Historical Review*, forthcoming.

—— (with A. C. DE LA MARE), 'Portable *Vademecum* Books Containing Franciscan and Dominican Texts', in A. C. de la Mare and B. C. Barker-Benfield (eds.), *Manuscripts at Oxford: An Exhibition in Memory of Richard William Hunt . . . on Themes Selected and Described by Some of his Friends* (Exhibition catalogue, Bodleian Library; Oxford, 1980), 60–4.

—— and TAUSCHE, M., 'Marriage Sermons in *ad status* Collections of the Central Middle Ages' (1980), in Bériou and d'Avray, *Modern Questions about Medieval Sermons*, 77–134.

DE BARTHOLOMAEIS, HENRICUS: see Hostiensis.

DE GIORGIO, M., and KLAPISCH-ZUBER, C. (eds.), *Storia del matrimonio* (Rome etc., 1996).

DEKKERS, E., *et al.*, *Clavis patrum Latinorum*, 3rd edn. (Turnhout, 1995).

DE LABRIOLLE, P., 'Le "mariage spirituel" dans l'antiquité chrétienne', *Revue historique*, 137 (1921), 204–25.

DELEEUW, P. A., 'Gregory the Great's "Homilies on the Gospels" in the Early Middle Ages', *Studi medievali*, 3rd ser., 26 (1985), 855–69.

DELPINI, F., *Indissolubilità matrimoniale e divorzio dal I al XII secolo* (Archivio ambrosiano, 37; Milan, 1979).

DENZLER, G., *Das Papsttum und der Amtszölibat*, i. *Die Zeit bis zur Reformation* (Päpste und Papsttum, 5.1; Stuttgart, 1973).

DE REU, M., *La Parole du Seigneur: moines et chanoines médiévaux prêchant l'Ascension et le Royaume des Cieux* (Brussels etc., 1996).

DESTREZ, J., *La Pecia dans les manuscrits universitaires du XIIIe et du XIVe siècle* (Paris, 1935).

DINAPOLI, R., *An Index of Theme and Image to the Homilies of the Anglo-Saxon Church, Comprising the Homilies of Ælfric, Wulfstan, and the Blickling and Vercelli Codices* (Hockwold cum Wilton, 1995).

Documenti capitolari del secolo XIII (1265–66, 1285–88, 1291, 1296–98), 'a cura di Pietro Dacquino', ed. A. M. Cotto Meluccio (Asti, 1987).

DONAHUE, C., Jr., 'The Policy of Alexander the Third's Consent Theory of Marriage', in S. Kuttner (ed.), *Proceedings of the Fourth International Congress of Medieval Canon Law, Toronto, 21–25 August 1972* (Monumenta Iuris Canonici, Series C, Subsidia, 5; Vatican City, 1976), 251–79.
—— 'The Monastic Judge: Social Practice, Formal Rule, and the Medieval Canon Law of Incest', in P. Landau, with M. Petzolt (eds.), *De iure canonico medii aevi: Festschrift für Rudolf Weigand* (Studia Gratiana, 27; Rome, 1996), 49–69.
—— (with NORMA ADAMS), *Select Cases from the Ecclesiastical Courts of the Province of Canterbury, c. 1200–1301* (Selden Society, 95; London, 1981).
DOUGLAS, M., 'Raisonnements circulaires: retour nostalgique à Lévy-Bruhl', *Gradhiva*, 30–1 (2001–2), 1–14.
—— *A Feeling for Hierarchy* (Dayton, Oh., 2002).
—— *Purity and Danger: An Analysis of Concept[s] of Pollution and Taboo*, with a new preface by the author (London etc., 2002).
DUBY, G., *Medieval Marriage: Two Models from Twelfth-Century France*, trans. E. Foster (Baltimore etc., 1978).
—— *Le Chevalier, la femme et le prêtre: le mariage dans la France féodale* (Paris, 1981).
DUCHESNE, L., *Christian Worship, its Origin and Evolution: A Study of the Latin Liturgy up to the Time of Charlemagne*, trans. M. L. McClure, 5th edn. (London, 1919).
DUNS SCOTUS: *Ioannis Duns Scoti opera omnia*, ed. C. Balic *et al.*, i (Vatican City, 1950).
DYE, J. M., 'The Virgin as *Sponsa c.*1100–*c.*1400' (unpublished Ph.D. dissertation, University College London, 2001).
DYER, C., *Standards of Living in the Later Middle Ages: Social Change in England c. 1200–1520* (Cambridge, 1989).
ELLIOTT, D., *Spiritual Marriage: Sexual Abstinence in Medieval Wedlock* (Princeton, 1993).
English Historical Documents c. 500–1042, ed. D. Whitelock (London, 1955).
ERDÖ, P., *Storia della scienza del diritto canonico: una introduzione* (Rome, 1999).
ESMEIN, A., *Le Mariage en droit canonique*, 2nd edn., rev. R. Génestal and J. Dauvillier (2 vols.; Paris, 1929–35).
ESMYOL, A., *Geliebte oder Ehefrau: Konkubinen im frühen Mittelalter* (Beihefte zum Archiv für Kulturgeschichte, 52; Cologne etc., 2002).
ÉTAIX, R., 'Sermon pour l'Épiphanie tiré d'un homiliaire en Écriture de Luxeuil', *Revue bénédictine*, 81 (1971), 7–13.
FAHRNER, I., *Geschichte der Ehescheidung im kanonischen Recht*, i. *Geschichte*

des Unauflöslichkeitsprinzips und der vollkommenen Scheidung der Ehe (Freiburg i.Br., 1903).

FEDELE, P., 'Vedovanza e seconde nozze', in *Il matrimonio nella società altomedievale* (Settimane di Studio del Centro Italiano di Studi sull'alto Medioevo, 24; 2 vols.; Spoleto, 1977), ii. 820–43.

FINK, K. A., *Das vatikanische Archiv: Einführung in die Bestände und ihre Erforschung*, 2nd enlarged edn. (Rome, 1951).

——— 'Frühe urkundliche Belege für die Auflösung des matrimonium ratum consumatum durch päpstliche Dispensation', *Zeitschrift der Savigny-Stiftung für Rechtsgeschichte*, 77 [*Zeitschrift für Rechtsgeschichte*, 90], kanonistische Abteilung, 46 (1960), 434–42.

FOLLIET, G., 'Deux nouveaux témoins du sermonnaire carolingien récemment reconstitué', *Revue des études augustiniennes*, 23 (1977), 155–98.

FRANSEN, G., 'La rupture du mariage', in Centro italiano di studi sull'alto medioevo, *Il matrimonio nella società altomedievale* (2 vols.; Settimane di studio del centro italiano di studi sull'alto medioevo, 24; Spoleto, 1977), ii. 603–30.

FREDEGAR: *The Fourth Book of the Chronicle of Fredegar, with its Continuations*, ed. J. M. Wallace-Hadrill (London etc., 1960).

FREED, J. B., *Noble Bondsmen: Ministerial Marriages in the Archdiocese of Salzburg, 1100–1343* (Ithaca, NY, etc., 1995).

FRIEDBERG, E., *Verlobung und Trauung, zugleich als Kritik von Sohm: Das Recht der Eheschließung* (Leipzig, 1876).

——— *Corpus iuris canonici* (2 vols.; Leipzig, 1879–81; repr. Graz, 1955).

FROELICH, K., and GIBSON, M. T. (eds.), *Biblia Latina cum glossa ordinaria: Facsimile Reprint of the Editio Princeps, Adolph Rusch of Strassburg 1480/81* (4 vols.; Turnhout, 1992).

FUHRMANN, H., *Einfluß und Verbreitung der pseudoisidorischen Fälschungen: Von ihrem Auftauchen bis in die neuere Zeit* (3 vols.; Schriften der Monumenta Germaniae Historica, 24. 1–3; Stuttgart, 1972–4).

FULLER, C. J., 'The Divine Couple's Relationship in a South Indian Temple: Minaksi and Sundaresvara at Madurai', *History of Religions*, 19 (1980), 321–48.

GABEL, L. C., *Benefit of Clergy in England in the Later Middle Ages* (Smith College Studies in History, 14. 1–4; New York, 1969).

GANSWEIDT, B., 'Haimo. 1. Haimo v. Auxerre', in *Lexikon des Mittelalters*, iv (Munich etc., 1989) 1863.

GAUDEMET, J., 'Recherche sur les origines historiques de la faculté de rompre le mariage non consommé', in S. Kuttner and K. Pennington (eds.), *Proceedings of the Fifth International Congress of Medieval Canon Law* (Monumenta Iuris Canonici, Series C, Subsidia, 6; Vatican City, 1980), 309–31.

——— *Le Mariage en Occident: les mœurs et le droit* (Paris, 1987).

—— 'Le symbolisme du mariage entre l'évêque et son église et ses consé-
quences juridiques' (1985); repr. in id., *Droit de l'Église et vie sociale au
Moyen Âge*, no. IX, 110–23.

—— 'Le dossier canonique sur mariage de Philippe Auguste et d'Ingeburge de Danemark (1193–1213)', *Revue historique de droit français et
étranger*, 62 (1984), 15–29; repr. in id., *Droit de l'Église*, no. XIV.

—— *Droit de l'Église et vie sociale au Moyen Âge* (Northampton, 1989).

GAUNT, S., *Gender and Genre in Medieval French Literature* (Cambridge,
1995).

GAUTIER D'ARRAS, *Ille et Galeron*, ed. and trans. P. Eley (King's College
London Medieval Studies, 13; London, 1996).

GEERTZ, C., 'Thick Description: Toward an Interpretive Theory of Culture', in id., *The Interpretation of Cultures: Selected Essays* (London etc.,
1973; repr. 1993), 3–30.

GÉNESTAL, R., *Le Privilegium fori en France du décret de Gratien à la fin du
XIVᵉ siècle* (2 vols.; Bibliothèque de l'École des hautes études, Sciences
religieuses, 35, 39; Paris, 1921–4).

GIEYSZTOR, A., '*Pauper sum et peregrinus*: la légende de saint Alexis en
Occident. Un idéal de pauvreté', in M. Mollat (ed.), *Études sur l'histoire
de la pauvreté* (Publications de la Sorbonne, série 'Etudes', 8; Paris,
1974), 125–39.

GILLINGHAM, J., 'Love, Marriage and Politics in the Twelfth Century'
(1989); repr. in id., *Richard Cœur de Lion: Kingship, Chivalry and War
in the Twelfth Century* (London etc., 1994), 243–55.

GIUSTI, M., *Studi sui Registri di bolle papali* (Collectanea Archivi Vaticani,
1; Vatican City, 1979).

GLORIEUX, P., 'Le Quodlibet de Pierre de Tarentaise', *Recherches de théologie anciennne et médiévale*, 9 (1937), 237–80.

GOLD, P. S., 'The Marriage of Mary and Joseph in the Twelfth-Century
Ideology of Marriage', in V. L. Bullough and J. A. Brundage (eds.),
Sexual Practices and the Medieval Church (1982; repr. Amherst, NY,
1994), 102–17 and 249–51.

GOODY, J., *The Development of the Family and Marriage in Europe* (Cambridge, 1983).

GOSWAMI, S., 'Radha: The Play; and Perfection of *Rasa*', in Hawley and
Wulff, *The Divine Consort*, 72–86.

GRATIAN, *The Treatise on Laws* (*Decretum DD. 1–20*) *with the Ordinary
Gloss*, ed. A. Thompson, J. Gordley, and K. Christensen (Studies in
Medieval and Early Modern Canon Law, 2; Washington, 1993).

GRÉGOIRE, R., *Bruno de Segni, exégète médiévale et théologien monastique*
(Centro italiano di studi sull'alto medioevo, 3; Spoleto, 1965).

—— *Les Homéliaires du Moyen Âge: inventaire et analyse des manuscrits*
(Rerum Ecclesiasticarum Documenta, series maior, 6; Rome, 1966).

—— 'La collection homilétique du Ms. Wolfenbüttel 4096', *Studi medievali*, ser. 3, 14 (1973), 259–86.

The Gregorian Sacramentary under Charles the Great, ed. H. A. Wilson (Henry Bradshaw Society, 49; London, 1915).

GREGORY IX (pope): *Les Registres de Grégoire IX*, ed. L. Auvray, i (Paris, 1896).

GUGLIELMO CASSINESE: *Guglielmo Cassinese (1190–1192)*, ed. M. W. Hall, H. C. Krueger, and R. L. Reynolds (2 vols.; Notai liguri del sec. XII, 2; Documenti e studi per la storia del commercio e del diritto commerziale italiano, 12–13; Turin, 1938).

GULLICK, M., 'From Parchmenter to Scribe: Some Observations on the Manufacture and Preparation of Medieval Parchment Based upon a Review of the Literary Evidence', in P. Rück, *Pergament: Geschichte, Struktur, Restaurierung, Herstellung* (Historische Hilfswissenschaften, 2; Sigmaringen, 1991), 145–57.

HALL, E., *The Arnolfini Betrothal: Medieval Marriage and the Enigma of Van Eyck's Double Portrait* (Berkeley etc., 1994).

HALLAM, E. M., *Capetian France 987–1328* (London etc., 1980).

—— 'Berengaria', in H. C. G. Matthew and B. Harrison (eds.), *The Oxford Dictionary of National Biography* (60 vols.; Oxford, 2004), v. 321–2.

HALM, C. F., *et al.*, *Catalogus codicum Latinorum Bibliothecae Regiae Monacensis (secundum Andreae Schmelleri indices)*, 2nd rev. edn. (2 vols.; Munich, 1892–4).

HASLETT, A., 'A Critic at Large', *New Yorker* (31 May 2004), 76–80.

HAWLEY, J. S., 'A Vernacular Portrait: Radha in the *Sur Sagar*', in Hawley and Wulff, *The Divine Consort*, 42–56; see also Hein, below.

—— and WULFF, D. M. (eds.), *The Divine Consort: Radha and the Goddesses of India* (Berkeley, 1982).

—— —— (eds.), *Devi: Goddesses of India* (Berkeley etc., 1996).

HAYMO OF AUXERRE, *Homilia XVIII: Dominica II post Epiphaniam*, in Migne, *PL* 118. 126–37.

HEANEY, S. P., *The Development of the Sacramentality of Marriage from Anselm of Laon to Thomas Aquinas* (The Catholic University of America Studies in Sacred Theology, Second Series, 134; Washington, 1963).

HEIN, N., 'Comments: Radha and Erotic Community', in Hawley and Wulff, *The Divine Consort*, 116–24 [commenting on Hawley, 'A Vernacular Portrait'].

HEIRIC OF AUXERRE: *Heirici Autissiodorensis homiliae per circulum anni*, ed. R. Quadri (Corpus Christianorum Continuatio Mediaevalis, 116; Turnhout, 1992).

HELMHOLZ, R. H., *Marriage Litigation in Medieval England* (Cambridge, 1974).

HENRICUS DE BARTHOLOMAEIS/SEGUSIO (Henry of Susa): see Hostiensis.

HERDE, P., *Audientia litterarum contradictarum: Untersuchungen über die päpstlichen Justizbriefe und die päpstliche Delegationsgerichtsbarkeit vom 13. bis zum Beginn des 16. Jahrhunderts* (2 vols.; Bibliothek des Deutschen historischen Instituts in Rom, 31–2; Tübingen, 1970).

HERLIHY, D., *Medieval Households* (Cambridge, Mass., etc., 1985).

HINCMAR OF REIMS, *De divortio Lotharii regis et Theutbergae reginae*, ed. L. Böhringer (Monumenta Germaniae Historica, Concilia, 4, Subsidia, 1; Hanover, 1992).

HINNEBUSCH, W. A., *The Early English Friars Preachers* (Institutum Historicum FF. Praedicatorum, Dissertationes Historicae, 14; Rome, 1951).

HOLLYWOOD, A., *The Soul as Virgin Wife: Mechtild of Magdeburg, Marguerite Porete, and Meister Eckhart* (Studies in Spirituality and Theology, 1; Notre Dame etc., 1995).

HONORIUS (pope): *Regesta Honorii Papae III*, ed. P. Pressuti, i (Rome, 1888; repr. Hildesheim etc., 1978).

HOSTIENSIS (Henricus de Bartholomaeis/Segusio, Henry of Susa), *Summa aurea* (Lyons, 1548).

HUBALDUS OF PISA: *Das Imbreviaturbuch des Erzbischoflichen Gerichtsnotars Hubaldus aus Pisa (Mai bis August 1230)*, ed. G. Dolezalek (Forschungen zur neueren Privatrechtsgeschichte, 13; Cologne etc., 1969).

HUGHES, D. O., 'Il matrimonio nell'Italia medievale', in De Giorgio and Klapisch-Zuber, *Storia del matrimonio*, 5–61.

HUMPHREYS, K. W., *The Book Provisions of the Mediaeval Friars 1215–1400* (Amsterdam, 1964).

—— *The Library of the Franciscans of the Convent of St. Antony, Padua, at the Beginning of the Fifteenth Century* (Studies in the History of Libraries and Librarianship, 3, Safaho-Monografien, 4; Amsterdam, 1966).

—— *The Friars' Libraries* (Corpus of British Medieval Library Catalogues; London, 1990).

HURTER, H., *Nomenclator literarius theologiae Catholicae theologos exhibens aetate, natione, disciplinis distinctos*, 3rd edn. (5 vols.; Innsbruck, 1903–13; repr. New York, n.d.).

IMKAMP, W., *Das Kirchenbild Innocenz' III. (1198–1216)* (Päpste und Papsttum, 22; Stuttgart, 1983).

INGRAM, M., 'Spousals Litigation in the English Ecclesiastical Courts c.1350–c.1640', in R. B. Outhwaite (ed.), *Marriage and Society: Studies in the Social History of Marriage* (London, 1981), 35–57.

INNOCENT V (pope): *Innocentii Quinti Pontificis Maximi . . . In IV. librum Sententiarum commentaria*, iv (Toulouse, 1651).

JAFFÉ, P.: see *Regesta*.

JAMES, M. R., *The Western Manuscripts in the Library of Trinity College, Cambridge* (4 vols.; Cambridge, 1900–4).

—— *The Apocryphal New Testament* (Oxford, 1924).

JOHN XXII (pope): _Jean XXII (1316–1334): lettres communes_, ed. G. Mollat (16 vols.; Bibliothèque des Écoles françaises d'Athènes et de Rome; Paris, 1904–47).

—— _Lettres secrètes et curiales du pape Jean XXII (1316–1334) relatives à la France, publiées ou analysées d'après les registres du Vatican_, ed. A. Coulon and S. Clémencet, fasc. 8 (Paris, 1965).

JOHN DAMASCENE, _De fide orthodoxa_: see Burgundio.

JOHN OF SALISBURY: _The Letters of John of Salisbury_, i. _The Early Letters (1153–1161)_, ed. W. J. Millor, SJ, H. E. Butler, and C. N. L. Brooke (Oxford, 1986).

JOYCE, G. H., _Christian Marriage: An Historical and Doctrinal Study_ (London etc., 1933).

JUSSEN, B., _Der Name der Witwe: Erkundungen zur Semantik der mittelalterlichen Bußkultur_ (Veröffentlichungen des Max-Planck-Instituts für Geschichte, 158; Göttingen, 2000).

KAY, R., 'Innocent III as Canonist and Theologian: The Case of Spiritual Matrimony', in J. C. Moore (ed.), _Pope Innocent III and his World_ (Aldershot etc., 1999), 35–49.

KELLER, H. E., _My Secret is Mine: Studies on Religion and Eros in the German Middle Ages_ (Leuven, 2000).

KELLY, H. A., _Love and Marriage in the Age of Chaucer_ (Ithaca, NY, 1975).

KELLY, W., _Pope Gregory II on Divorce and Remarriage_ (Analecta Gregoriana, 203, Series Facultatis Iuris Canonici, Sectio B, 37; Rome, 1976).

KER, N. R., _Medieval Libraries of Great Britain: A List of Surviving Books_, 2nd edn. (London, 1964). See also Watson.

—— _Fragments of Medieval Manuscripts Used as Pastedowns in Oxford Bindings, with a Survey of Oxford Binding c. 1515–1620_ (Oxford Bibliographical Society Publications, NS 5; Oxford, 1954).

KIENZLE, B. M. (ed.), _The Sermon_ (Typologie des sources du Moyen Âge Occidental, 81–3; Turnhout, 2000).

KNOWLES, D., _The Religious Orders in Engand_, ii. _The End of the Middle Ages_ (1955; repr. Cambridge, 1961).

The Koran: Commonly Called the Alkoran of Mohammed, ed. and trans. G. Sale (London etc., 1887).

KOTTJE, R., 'Kirchliches Recht und päpstlicher Autoritätsanspruch: Zu den Auseinandersetzungen über die Ehe Lothars II.', in H. Mordek (ed.), _Aus Kirche und Reich: Studien zu Theologie, Politik und Recht im Mittelalter. Festschrift für Friedrich Kempf zu seinem fünfundsiebzigsten Geburtstag und fünfzigjährigen Doktorjubiläum_ (Sigmaringen, 1983), 97–103.

KRAMER, S. N., _The Sacred Marriage Rite: Aspects of Faith, Myth, and Ritual in Ancient Sumer_ (Bloomington, Ind., etc., 1969).

KRUEGER, R. L., 'Questions of Gender in Old French Romance', in ead. (ed.), *The Cambridge Companion to Medieval Romance*, 132–49.

—— (ed.), *The Cambridge Companion to Medieval Romance* (Cambridge, 2000).

KUHRT, A., 'Babylon', in E. J. Bakker, I. J. F. De Jong, and H. van Wees (eds.), *Brill's Companion to Herodotus* (Leiden etc., 2002), 475–96.

KUITERS, R., 'Saint Augustin et l'indissolubilité du mariage', *Augustiniana*, 9 (1959), 5–11.

KUTTNER, S., 'Pope Lucius III and the Bigamous Archbishop of Palermo' (1961); repr. in id., *The History of Ideas and Doctrines of Canon Law in the Middle Ages* (London, 1980), no. VII, pp. 409–53.

—— *Repertorium der Kanonistik (1140–1234): Prodromos Corporis glossarum*, i (Studi e testi, 71; Vatican City, 1937).

LABRIOLLE: see de Labriolle.

LANDAU, P., with PETZOLT, M. (eds.), *De iure canonico medii aevi: Festschrift für Rudolf Weigand* (Studia Gratiana, 27; Rome, 1996).

LAWRENCE, R. J., *The Sacramental Interpretation of Ephesians 5: 32 from Peter Lombard to the Council of Trent* (The Catholic University of America Studies in Sacred Theology, Second Series, 145; Washington, 1963).

LEA, H. C., *History of Sacerdotal Celibacy in the Christian Church*, 3rd rev. edn. (2 vols.; London, 1907).

LE BRAS, G., 'Mariage. III. La doctrine du mariage chez les théologiens et canonistes depuis l'an mille', in *Dictionnaire de théologie catholique* (15 vols. excluding indexes; Paris, 1899–1950), ix (1926), 2123–223.

LEBUIN, Saint: see *The Anglo-Saxon Missionaries in Germany*.

LECLERCQ, J., 'Préface' to R. Grégoire, *Les Homéliaires du Moyen Âge: inventaire et analyse des manuscrits* (Rerum Ecclesiasticarum Documenta, series maior, 6; Rome, 1966).

—— *Monks and Love in Twelfth-Century France: Psycho-Historical Essays* (Oxford, 1979).

—— *Le Mariage vu par les moines au XIIᵉ siècle* (Paris, 1983).

LEICK, G., *Sex and Eroticism in Mesopotamian Literature* (London etc., 1994).

LE JAN, R., *Famille et pouvoir dans le monde franc (VIIᵉ–Xᵉ siècle): essai d'anthropologie sociale* (Paris, 1995).

LEOBA, Saint: see *The Anglo-Saxon Missionaries in Germany*.

LERNER, R., review of d'Avray, *Medieval Marriage Sermons*, in *Speculum*, 79 (2004), 163–5.

LEVISON, W., 'Eine Predigt des Lupus von Ferrieres', in id., *Aus rheinischer und fränkischer Frühzeit* (Düsseldorf, 1947), 561–4 [not seen, but the sermon is in MS BL Royal 8. B. XIV, fos. 131ᵛ–133ᵛ].

LEYSER, H., *Medieval Women: A Social History of Women in England 450–1500* (London, 1995).

LIOTTA, F., 'Burgundione', in *Dizionario biografico degli italiani*, xv (Rome, 1972), 423–8.

LOMBARDI, D., *Matrimoni di antico regime* (Annali dell'Istituto storico italo-germanico in Trento, Monografie, 34; Bologna, 2001).

LUSCOMBE, D., 'From Paris to the Paraclete: The Correspondence of Abelard and Heloise', *Proceedings of the British Academy*, 74 (1988), 247–83.

LUTTERBACH, H., *Sexualität im Mittelalter: Eine Kulturstudie anhand von Bußbüchern des 6. bis 12. Jahrhunderts* (Cologne etc., 1999).

MABILLE, M., 'Les manuscrits de Jean d'Essomes conservés à la Bibliothèque Nationale de Paris', *Bibliothèque de l'École des Chartes*, 130 (1972), 231–4.

MACCARRONE, M., 'Sacramentalità e indissolubilità del matrimonio nella dottrina di Innocenzo III', *Lateranum*, 44 (1978), 449–514.

MACFARLANE, A., *Marriage and Love in England, 1300–1840: Modes of Reproduction* (Oxford, 1986).

MCLAUGHLIN, R. E., 'The Word Eclipsed: Preaching in the Early Middle Ages', *Traditio*, 46 (1991), 77–122.

MCNAMARA, J.-A., and WEMPLE, S. F., 'Marriage and Divorce in the Frankish Kingdom', in S. M. Stuard (ed.), *Women in Medieval Society* (Philadelphia, 1976), 96–124.

Manuale ad usum percelebris Ecclesie Sarisburiensis: From the Edition Printed at Rouen in 1543 . . ., ed. A. J. Collins (Henry Bradshaw Society, 91; London, 1960).

MARCULF, St: *Marculfi formularum libri duo*, ed. A. Uddholm (Collectio Scriptorum Veterum Uppsaliensis; Uppsala, 1962).

MARGLIN, F. A., 'Types of Sexual Union and their Implicit Meanings', in Hawley and Wulff, *The Divine Consort*, 298–315.

Il matrimonio nella società altomedievale (Settimane di Studio del Centro Italiano di Studi sull'alto Medioevo, 24; 2 vols.; Spoleto, 1977).

MATTER, E. A., *The Voice of my Beloved: The Song of Songs in Western Medieval Christianity* (Philadelphia, c.1990).

MECHTILD OF MAGDEBURG, *The Flowing Light of the Godhead*, trans. and intro. F. Tobin (New York etc., 1998).

MEEK, C., '"Simone ha aderito alla fede di Maometto": la "fornicazione spirituale" come causa di separazione (Lucca 1424)', in Menchi and Quaglioni, *Coniugi nemici*, 121–39.

MENCHI, S. S., and QUAGLIONI, D., *Coniugi nemici: i processi matrimoniali. La separazione in Italia dal XII al XVIII secolo* (I processi matrimoniali degli archivi ecclesiastici italiani, 1; Annali dell'Istituto storico italogermanico in Trento, Quaderni, 53; Bologna, 2000).

MERCIER, P.: see *XIV homélies*.

MINISTÈRE DE L'ÉDUCATION NATIONALE, *Catalogue général des manuscrits des bibliothèques publiques des départements* (7 vols.; Paris, 1849–85), ii. *Troyes* (1855).

MIRBT, C., *Quellen zur Geschichte des Papsttums und des römischen Katholizismus*, 5th edn. (Tübingen, 1934).

Missale Romanum Mediolani, 1474, facsimile ed. R. Lippe (2 vols.; Henry Bradshaw Society, 33; London, 1899–1907).

MOLHO, A., *Marriage Alliance in Late Medieval Florence* (Cambridge, Mass., etc., 1994).

MOLIN, J.-B., and MUTEMBE, P., *Le Rituel du mariage en France du XIIᵉ au XVIᵉ siècle* (Théologie historique, 26; Paris, 1974).

MOLLAT, G., *Les Papes d'Avignon 1305–1378* (Paris, 1949).

MOORE, J. C. (ed.), *Pope Innocent III and his World* (Aldershot etc., 1988).

MOREL, T., 'Toledo, *Sancta María Immaculada*', in *Diccionario de historia eclesiástica de España* (5 vols. so far; Madrid, 1972–87), iii (1973), 1684.

MORIN, D. G., 'Textes inédits relatifs au symbole et à la vie chrétienne', *Revue bénédictine*, 22 (1905), 505–24.

MUESSIG, C. (ed.), *Preacher, Sermon and Audience in the Middle Ages* (Leiden etc., 2002).

MULCHAHEY, M., 'More Notes on the Education of the *Fratres communes* in the Dominican Order: Elias de Ferreriis of Salagnac's *Libellus de doctrina fratrum*', in J. Brown and W. P. Stoneman (eds.), *A Distinct Voice: Medieval Studies in Honor of Leonard E. Boyle, O.P.* (Notre Dame, Ind., 1997), 328–69.

MÜLLER, M., *Die Lehre des hl. Augustinus von der Paradiesesehe und ihre Auswirkung in der Sexualethik des 12. und 13. Jahrhunderts bis Thomas von Aquin: Eine moralgeschichtliche Untersuchung* (Studien zur Geschichte der katholischen Moraltheologie, 1; Regensburg, 1954).

MURPHY, R. E., 'Canticle of Canticles', in Brown *et al.*, *The Jerome Biblical Commentary*, i. 506–10.

NEDDERMEYER, U., *Von der Handschrift zum gedruckten Buch: Schriftlichkeit und Leseinteresse im Mittelalter und in der frühen Neuzeit. Quantitative und qualitative Aspekte* (2 vols.; Buchwissenschaftliche Beiträge aus dem Deutschen Bucharchiv München, 61; Wiesbaden, 1998).

NELSON, J. L., *Charles the Bald* (London etc., 1992).

NEWHAUSER, R. G., and ALFORD, JOHN A. (eds.), *Literature and Religion in the Later Middle Ages: Philological Studies in Honor of Siegfried Wenzel* (Binghampton, NY, 1995).

NEWMAN, B., *From Virile Woman to WomanChrist. Studies in Medieval Religion and Literature* (Philadelphia, 1995).

NOBLE, T. F. X., 'The Place in Papal History of the Roman Synod of 826', *Church History*, 45 (1976), 434–54.

NOONAN, J. T., 'Power to Choose', *Viator*, 4 (1973), 419–34.

O'FLAHERTY, W. D., 'The Shifting Balance of Power in the Marriage of Siva and Parvati', in Hawley and Wulff, *The Divine Consort*, 129–43.

ORTONY, A. (ed.), *Metaphor and Thought* (Cambridge, 1979).

PACAUT, M., 'Sur quelques données du droit matrimonial dans la seconde moitié du XIIᵉ siècle', in *Histoire et société: mélanges offerts à Georges Duby. Textes réunis par les médiévistes de l'Université de Provence* (2 vols.; Aix-en-Provence, 1992), i. 31–41.

PALMER, N. F., *Zisterzienser und ihre Bücher: Die mittelalterliche Bibliotheksgeschichte von Kloster Eberbach im Rheingau unter besonderer Berücksichtigung der in Oxford und London aufbewahrten Handschriften* (Regensburg, 1998).

PANTIN, W. A., *The English Church in the Fourteenth Century*, 2nd edn. (1962; repr. Toronto etc., 1980).

PAPAL BULLS: Archives Nationales, *Layettes du trésor des chartes*, ed. J. B. A. T. Teulet *et al.* (5 vols.; Paris, 1863–1909), iii, ed. J. de Laborde (1875).

—— see also *Les Actes pontificaux*.

PAYER, P. J., *The Bridling of Desire: Views of Sex in the Later Middle Ages* (Toronto etc., 1993).

PEDERSEN, F., *Marriage Disputes in Medieval England* (London etc., 2000).

PEGG, M. G., *The Corruption of Angels: The Great Inquisition of 1245–1246* (Princeton etc., 2001).

PENNINGTON, K., 'An Earlier Recension of Hostiensis's *Lectura* on the Decretals' (1987); repr. in id., *Popes, Canonists and Texts, 1150–1550*, no. XVII.

—— 'Henry de Segusio (Hostiensis)' (1993); repr. in id., *Popes, Canonists and Texts*, no. XVI.

—— *Popes, Canonists and Texts, 1150–1550* (Aldershot etc., 1993).

PERSSON, I., *Ehe und Zeichen: Studien zu Eheschließung und Ehepraxis anhand der frühmittelhochdeutschen religiösen Lehrdichtungen 'Vom Rechte', 'Hochzeit' und 'Schopf von dem lône'* (Göppinger Arbeiten zur Germanistik, 617; Göppingen, 1995).

PETER DAMIAN: *Die Briefe des Petrus Damiani*, ed. K. Reindel, i (Monumenta Germaniae Historica: Die Briefe der deutschen Kaiserzeit, 4; Munich, 1983).

PETER LOMBARD: *Magistri Petri Lombardi Parisiensis Episcopi Sententiae in IV libris distinctae*, 3rd edn., ed. Patres Collegii S. Bonaventurae ad Claras Aquas [I. Brady] (2 vols.; Spicilegium Bonaventurianum, 4–5; Grottaferrata, 1971–81).

—— See also Aquinas.

PETERS, C., 'Gender, Sacrament and Ritual: The Making and Meaning of Marriage in Late Medieval and Early Modern England', *Past and Present*, 169 (2000), 63–96.

PFAFF, V., 'Das kirchliche Eherecht am Ende des zwölften Jahrhunderts', *Zeitschrift der Savigny-Stiftung für Rechtsgeschichte*, 94 [*Zeitschrift für Rechtsgeschichte*, 107], kanonistische Abteilung, 63 (1977), 73–117.

PIERRE DE TARANTAISE, commentary on Peter Lombard, *Sentences: Innocentii Quinti Pontifici Maximi . . . in IV. librum Sententiarum commentaria*, iv (Toulouse, 1651).

PIGNATELLI, J., *Consultationes canonicae*, i (Venice, 1736).

POLLOCK, F., and MAITLAND, F. W., *The History of English Law before the Time of Edward I*, ed. S. F. C. Milsom (Cambridge, 1968).

POTTHAST, A.: see *Regesta*.

POWICKE, F. M., *Stephen Langton* (Oxford, 1928).

—— *King Henry III and the Lord Edward: The Community of the Realm in the Thirteenth Century* (2 vols.; Oxford, 1947).

POWITZ, G., '*Libri inutiles* in mittelalterlichen Bibliotheken: Bemerkungen über Alienatio, Palimpsestierung und Makulierung', *Scriptorium*, 50 (1996), 288–304.

QUAGLIONI, D., ' "Divortium a diversitate mentium": la separazione personale dei coniugi nelle dottrine di diritto comune (appunti per una discussione)', in Menchi and Quaglioni, *Coniugi nemici*, 95–118.

REDDY, M. J., 'The Conduit Metaphor: A Case of Frame Conflict in our Language about Language', in Ortony, *Metaphor and Thought*, 284–324.

Regesta pontificum Romanorum inde ab a. post Christum natum 1198 ad a. 1304, i, ed. A. Potthast (Berlin, 1874).

Regesta pontificum Romanorum ab condita Ecclesia ad annum post Christum natum MCXCVIII, ed. P. Jaffé, W. Wattenbach, *et al.*, 2nd edn. (2 vols.; Leipzig, 1885–8).

REYNOLDS, P. L., *Marriage in the Western Church: The Christianization of Marriage during the Patristic and Early Medieval Periods* (Leiden etc., 1994).

REYNOLDS, R. E., 'The Pseudo-Augustinian "Sermo de Conscientia" and the Related Canonical "Dicta sancti Gregorii papae" ', *Revue bénédictine*, 81 (1971), 310–17.

RICARDUS DE MEDIA VILLA, *Super quarto sententiarum* (Venice, 1499) [BL call no. IA. 23001].

RINCÓN, T., *El matrimonio, misterio y signo: siglos IX al XIII* (Pamplona, 1971).

—— *El matrimonio cristiano: sacramento de la Creación y de la Redención. Claves de un debate teológico-canónico* (Estudios canónicos, 1; Pamplona, 1997).

RITZER, K., *Formen, Riten und religiöses Brauchtum der Eheschließung in den christlichen Kirchen des ersten Jahrtausends*, 2nd edn., ed. U. Hermann and W. Heckenbach (Liturgiewissenschaftliche Quellen und Forschungen; Münster, 1981).

Robb, F., 'Intellectual Tradition and Misunderstanding: The Development of Academic Theology on the Trinity in the Twelfth and Thirteenth Centuries' (unpublished Ph.D. thesis, University College London, 1993).

Roberg, B., *Das zweite Konzil von Lyon [1274]* (Paderborn etc., 1990).

Röhrkasten, J., *Die englischen Kronzeugen, 1130–1330* (Berliner historische Studien, 16; Berlin, 1990).

—— 'Mendikantische Armut in der Praxis: Das Beispiel London', in G. Melville and A. Kehnel (eds.), *In proposito paupertatis: Studien zum Armutsverständnis bei den mittelalterlichen Bettelorden* (Vita regularis: Ordnungen und Deutungen religiösen Lebens im Mittelalter, 13; Münster, 2001), 135–67.

The Roll and Writ File of the Berkshire Eyre of 1248, ed. M. T. Clanchy (London, 1973).

Rouse, R. H., and Rouse, M. A., *Preachers, Florilegia and Sermons: Studies on the* Manipulus florum *of Thomas of Ireland* (Studies and Texts, Pontifical Institute of Mediaeval Studies, 47; Toronto, 1979).

—————— and Mynors, R. A. B., *Registrum Anglie de libris doctorum et auctorum veterum* (Corpus of Medieval Library Catalogues; London, 1991).

Salonen, K., *The Penitentiary as a Well of Grace in the Late Middle Ages: The Example of the Province of Uppsala 1448–1527* (Annales Academiae Scientiarum Fennicae, 313; Helsinki, 2001).

Saurwein, E., *Der Ursprung des Rechtsinstituts der päpstlichen Dispens von der nicht vollzogenen Ehe: Eine Interpretation der Dekretalen Alexanders III. und Urbans III.* (Analecta Gregoriana, 125, Series Facultatis Iuris Canonici, Sectio B, 43; Rome, 1980).

Schadt, H., 'Die Arbores bigamiae als heilsgeschichtliche Schemata: Zum Verhältnis von Kanonistik und Kunstgeschichte', in W. Busch (ed.), *Kunst als Bedeutungsträger: Gedenkschrift für Günter Bandmann* (Berlin, 1978), 129–47.

Schmugge, L., Hersperger, P., and Wiggenhauser, B., *Die Supplikenregister der päpstlichen Pönitentiarie aus der Zeit Pius' II. (1458–1464)* (Tübingen, 1996).

Schnell, R., *Sexualität und Emotionalität in der vormodernen Ehe* (Cologne etc., 2002).

Schneyer, J. B., *Repertorium der lateinischen Sermones des Mittelalters für die Zeit von 1150–1350* (11 vols.; Münster, 1969–90).

Schön, D. A., 'Generative Metaphor: A Perspective on Problem-Setting in Social Policy', in Ortony, *Metaphor and Thought*, 254–83.

Schulte, J. F. von, *Die Geschichte der Quellen und Literatur des canonischen Rechts*, ii (Stuttgart, 1877; repr. Graz, 1956).

Schumacher, M., *Die Auffassung der Ehe in den Dichtungen Wolframs von Eschenbach* (Germanische Bibliothek, Abt. 2, Untersuchungen und Texte, 3. Reihe, Untersuchungen und Einzeldarstellungen; Heidelberg, 1967).

SHARPE, R., *A Handlist of the Latin Writers of Great Britain and Ireland before 1540* (Publications of the *Journal of Medieval Latin*, 1; [Turnhout], 1997).

SHEEHAN, M. M., 'The Formation and Stability of Marriage in Fourteenth-Century England: Evidence of an Ely Register' (1971), in id., *Marriage, Family, and Law in Medieval Europe: Collected Studies*, ed. J. K. Farge (Cardiff, 1996), 38–76.

SMALLEY, B., *English Friars and Antiquity in the Early Fourteenth Century* (Oxford, 1960).

SMETANA, C. L., 'Paul the Deacon's Patristic Anthology', in P. E. Szarmach and B. F. Huppé (eds.), *The Old English Homily and its Backgrounds* (Albany, NY, 1978), 75–97.

SOHM, R., *Das Recht der Eheschließung aus dem deutschen und kanonischen Recht geschichtlich entwickelt: Eine Antwort auf die Frage nach dem Verhältniss der kirchlichen Trauung zur Civilehe* (Weimar, 1875).

SOUTHERN, R., *Western Society and the Church in the Middle Ages* (Harmondsworth, 1970).

SPUFFORD, P. (with the assistance of W. WILKINSON and S. TOLLEY), *Handbook of Medieval Exchange* (Royal Historical Society Guides and Handbooks, 13; London, 1986).

STAFFORD, P., *Queens, Concubines and Dowagers: The King's Wife in the Early Middle Ages* (London, 1983; repr. London etc., 1998).

STEGMÜLLER, F., *Repertorium commentariorum in Sententias Petri Lombardi* (2 vols.; Würzburg, 1947).

STEVENSON, K., *Nuptial Blessing: A Study of Christian Marriage Rites* (Alcuin Club Collections, 64; London, 1982).

STUHLMUELLER, C., 'Deutero-Isaiah', in Brown *et al.*, *The Jerome Biblical Commentary*, i. 366–86.

STURM, Saint: see *The Anglo-Saxon Missionaries in Germany*.

SUTTON, OLIVER: *The Rolls and Register of Bishop Oliver Sutton, 1280–1299*, ed. R. M. T. Hill, vi. *Memoranda, May 19, 1297–September 12, 1299* (Lincoln, 1969).

SZARMACH, P. E., and HUPPÉ, B. F. (eds.), *The Old English Homily and its Backgrounds* (Albany, NY, 1978).

TANNER, N., *Heresy Trials in the Diocese of Norwich 1428–31* (Camden Fourth Series, 20; London, 1977).

TENBROCK, R. H., *Eherecht und Ehepolitik bei Innocenz III.* (doctoral dissertation for the University of Münster; Dortmund-Hörde, [1933?]).

THOMAS, H., *Deutsche Geschichte des Mittelalters 1250–1500* (Stuttgart etc., 1983).

THOMAS AQUINAS: see Aquinas.

TOXÉ, P., 'La *copula carnalis* chez les canonistes médiévaux', in M. Rouche (ed.), *Mariage et sexualité au Moyen Âge: accord ou crise?* (Cultures et civilisations médiévales, 21; Paris, 2000).

Die Urkunden der burgundischen Rudolfinger, ed. T. Schieffer with H. E. Mayer (Monumenta Germaniae Historica Regum Burgundiae e Stirpe Rudolfina, Diplomata et Acta; Munich, 1977).

VAN DER WALT, A. G. P., 'The Homiliary of the Venerable Bede and Early Medieval Preaching' (unpublished thesis, University of London, 1981).

VASOLI, R. H., *What God Has Joined Together: The Annulment Crisis in American Catholicism* (New York and Oxford, 1998).

Vatikanische Akten zur deutschen Geschichte in der Zeit Kaiser Ludwigs des Bayern, auf Veranlassung seiner Majestät des Königs von Bayern herausgegeben durch die historische Commission bei der königlichen Akademie der Wissenschaften, ed. S. von Riezler (Innsbruck, 1891).

VERGIER-BOIMOND, J., 'Bigamie (l'irrégularité de)', in R. Naz (ed.), *Dictionnaire de droit canonique*, ii (Paris, 1937), 853–88.

VLEESCHOUWERS-VAN MELKEBEEK, M., 'Incestuous Marriages: Formal Rules and Social Practice in the Southern Burgundian Netherlands', in Davis, Müller, and Rees Jones, *Love, Marriage, and Family Ties in the Later Middle Ages*, 77–95.

VODOLA, E., *Excommunication in the Middle Ages* (Berkeley, 1986).

VOLFING, A., *John the Evangelist and Medieval German Writing: Imitating the Inimitable* (Oxford, 2001).

VON RIEZLER, S.: see *Vatikanische Akten*.

WAKEFIELD, W. L., and EVANS, A. P., *Heresies of the High Middle Ages* (New York etc., 1969).

WALLACE-HADRILL, J. M., *The Long-Haired Kings* (Toronto etc., 1982).

—— *The Frankish Church* (Oxford, 1983).

WARNER, G. F., and GILSON, J. P., *Catalogue of Western Manuscripts in the Old Royal and King's Collections* (4 vols.; London, 1921).

WATSON, A.: N. Ker, *Medieval Libraries of Great Britain: A List of Surviving Books. Supplement to the Second Edition* (London, 1987).

WAUGH, S. L., *The Lordship of England: Royal Wardships and Marriages in English Society and Politics 1217–1327* (Princeton etc., 1988).

WEBER, I., ' "Consensus facit nuptias!": Überlegungen zum ehelichen Konsens in normativen Texten des Frühmittelalters', *Zeitschrift der Savigny-Stiftung für Rechtsgeschichte*, 118, kanonistiche Abteilung, 87 (2001), 31–66.

WEBER, M., *Wirtschaft und Gesellschaft: Grundriß der verstehenden Soziologie*, ed. J. Winckelmann, 5th rev. edn. (3 vols.; Tübingen, 1976).

—— *Die Wirtschaftsethik der Weltreligionen: Hinduismus und Buddhismus*

(1916–20); repr. in *Gesammelte Aufsätze zur Religionssoziologie*, ii. *Hinduismus und Buddhismus* (Tübingen, 1988).

WEIGAND, R., 'Zur mittelalterlichen kirchlichen Ehegerichtsbarkeit: Rechtsvergleichende Untersuchung' (1981); repr. in id., *Liebe und Ehe im Mittelalter* (Bibliotheca Eruditorum, 7; Goldbach, 1993), new pagination at foot pp. 307*–341*.

WEISHEIPL, J., *Friar Thomas d'Aquino: His Life, Thought, and Works* (Oxford, 1974).

WHITELOCK, D. (ed.), *English Historical Documents c. 500–1042* (London, 1955).

WILLIAM OF MOERBEKE: see Aquinas; Aristotle.

WILLIBALD, Saint: see *The Anglo-Saxon Missionaries in Germany*.

WINCH, P., *The Idea of a Social Science and its Relation to Philosophy* (London etc., 1958).

WINROTH, A., *The Making of Gratian's* Decretum (Cambridge, 2000).

WRIGHT, C. D., 'Vercelli Homilies XI–XIII and the Anglo-Saxon Benedictine Reform: Tailored Sources and Implied Audiences', in C. Muessig (ed.), *Preacher, Sermon and Audience in the Middle Ages* (Leiden etc., 2002), 203–27.

WULFF, D. M., 'Radha: Consort and Conqueror of Krishna', in Hawley and Wulff, *Devi*, 109–34.

ZARRI, G., *Recinti: donne, clausura e matrimonio nella prima età moderna* ([Bologna], 2000).

ZIEGLER, J. G., *Die Ehelehre der Pönitentialsummen von 1200–1350: Eine Untersuchung zur Geschichte der Moral- und Pastoraltheologie* (Regensburg, 1956).

Index of Manuscripts

I include only manuscripts I have personally used at least on microfilm. Manuscripts discussed at second hand are included in the main index.

London, BL Add. 33956: 120 n. 126
London, BL Add. 18347: 122 n. 132
London, BL Add. 31830: Documents
  1. 9–13 notes *passim* (I use this
  manuscript as a source for inter-
  pretations of Hebrew names)
London, BL Arundel 132: Document
  1. 9
London, BL Arundel 431: 263 n. 11
London, BL Arundel 471: 257 n. 14,
  261 n. 44, 264 n. 16, Document
  4. 1
London, BL Arundel 485: Documents
  2. 1–2, 270 n. 2
London, BL Cotton Cleopatra E. 1:
  182 n. 41, 183 n. 42
London, BL Cotton Domitian XV: 90
  n. 59
London, BL Harley 2385: 120 n. 126
London, BL Harley Charter 45. F. 11:
  184 n. 47
London, BL Lansdowne 397: 122 n.
  130
London, BL Royal 5. A. I: Document
  3. 1
London, BL Royal 6. E. I: Document
  4. 5
London, BL Royal 8. A. II: 257 n. 9
London, BL Royal 8. B. XV: p. 117
  nn. 121–2
London, BL Royal 9. C. I: 263 n. 10,
  275 nn. 9 & 13, 283 n. 8 (from
  282)
London, BL Royal 9. C. III: 282–3 n.
  6
London, BL Royal 11. A. XIV: 145,
  151–2, Document 3. 8
London, BL Royal 11. B. X: p. 118 n.
  123, Document 3. 9
London, BL Royal 11. B. X: Documents 3. 9, 4. 6

London, The National Archives,
  JUST 3. 41/1: Document 3. 10

Munich, Staatsbibliothek Clm 2946:
  Document 1. 10
Munich, Staatsbibliothek Clm 3833:
  Documents 1. 1–2

Oxford, Merton College 30: 241 n. 18
Oxford, Merton College 63: 284 n. 2
Oxford, Merton College 66: 284 n. 2
Oxford, New College 205: Documents
  2. 1–2, 4. 1

Paris, Archives Nationales J 709 no.
  296 [*sic*]: 158, Document 3. 4
Paris, Archives Nationales J 709 no.
  296 (2): Document 3. 5
Paris, Archives Nationales J 709 no.
  298 (10): Document 3. 6
Paris, Archives Nationales J 709 no.
  298 (12): Document 3. 7
Paris, BN lat 3742: Document 1. 10
Paris, BN lat. 3794: Document 1. 3

Rome, Casanatense 4560: Documents
  1. 12–13

Troyes, Bibliothèque Municipale
  1263: 238 n. 2, 240 n. 10
Troyes, Bibliothèque Municipale
  1440: Document 1. 11

Vatican City, Archivio Segreto Vaticano Penitenzieria ap. 48: Document 4. 7
Vatican City, Archivio Segreto Vaticano Penitenzieria ap. 60: Document 4. 8
Vatican City, Archivio Segreto Vaticano Penitenzieria ap. 75: Documents 3. 11–12

Vatican City, Biblioteca Apostolica Vaticana Chigi C. IV. 99: 241 nn. 16, 20

Vatican City, Biblioteca Apostolica Vaticana Vat. Lat. 3994: 165–6 n. 90

General Index

Though I have not attempted to index all the scholars whose works are cited in the notes, I have included some where I thought this would help readers. The line is rather arbitrary and there is a bias towards more recent writers. I include also manuscripts which are mentioned as studied by other scholars but which I have not consulted personally (conversely, I have not included these in the Index of Manuscripts). When indexing the Documents, I have not included names and themes if the appropriate forward references are already provided in the main text; nor do I index the sources identified in the notes. Thus the index is highly selective so far as the Documents are concerned.

Abbo of St-Germain 30
Abelard 98–9
Adelaide, wife of Louis the Stam-
    merer 83
Adelaïde, wife of Louis V of France
    92
adultery 82, 123
    creatures and Document **1. 11. 6**
Ælfric 34, 36
affectio maritalis: *see* marital affection
affinity 14, 175
    see also forbidden degrees
Agde, Council of (506) 79
age of first marriage 182, 191
ages of history 32, 33
Agobard of Lyons 29
Ahasuerus 60
Aldobrandino da Toscanella 63–4,
    Documents **1. 12–13**
Alexander III, Pope 126–7, 143–5,
    171, ch. 4 *passim*, 201, 203
Alexander IV, Pope 142, 158
allegory 61
Alpaida, wife of Pippin of Herstal 80
Altmünster, Bridgettine nunnery 223
Amandola, partner of Rozelin 90
Amos, T. 21–31 *passim*
Angers, Council of (453) 79
Anglo-Saxon England:
    divorce in 79–80
    preaching in 33–4
    see also Bede
Anguillaria, Count of 180–1, 182,
    Document **4. 4**

annulments ch. 2 *passim*
Ansgard 83
Anstey case 183–4
anthropology 17
Antibes 110
Antoninus of Florence, St 195
Aquinas 8, 9, 145–8, 150
Archon Basileus 4
Aris, Marc-Aeilko 42 n. 79
Aristotle, 226, 232
    see also marriage, Aristotle and
Assuerus 60 n. 146
Asti 115, 123
asymmetry, gender 251
Atto of Vercelli 29
attrition of manuscripts ch. 1 (c)
    passim
Audientia litterarum contradictarum
    122 n. 130, 124, 185–6
Augsburg, ninth-century homily com-
    posed for church of Documents **1.
    1–2**
Augustine of Hippo 30, 75–8, 81, 88,
    129–30, 202
    and 'bigamy' 133
Augustinian Hermits 57
Aurelle, M. 101
Auxerre, School of, audience of homi-
    lies from 25–7

Baldwin, J. W. 14, 94 n. 73, 100 n. 87,
    102 n. 94, 104 nn. 97–8
Ball, R. M. 262 n. 1
banns 65

Barellus, Raymund 109–10, 119
Barré, H. 25–6, 208 n. 1
Barrow, J. 91 n. 62
Bartlett, Robert 1 n. 3, 116, 181 n. 38
Basilinna 4
Bataillon, L.-J. 37 n. 69, 55, 56 n. 122
'Bavarian Homiliary' 30, 31, 32,
      Documents **1. 1–2**
'Beaune Homiliary' 32–3, Document
      1. 3
Becket, Thomas 158
Bede 24–5
    Pseudo-Bede 28
Bellamy, J. G. 163 n. 84
Benedict XII, Pope 148 n. 46, 155 n.
      66
Benedictine libraries 41, 46
benedictio sacramentalis 118 n. 124,
      153–5
benefit of clergy, and 'bigamous'
      clerics 159–65
Bériou, N. 37 n. 69, 226 n. 1
Berkshire Eyre, 184–5
Bernard of Clairvaux, St 3, 5, 7, 9,
      10–11, 20
Bernard of Parma 144
Bernard of Pavia, 118 n. 124, 148
Bertram, Martin 54 n. 117
Bertrand de la Tour 45
betrothal 60
    see also initiation
Bhakti 4
bigamy, irregularity of 111, ch. 3
      passim, 168–9, 171, 199
    Tree of 137–9
Biller, P. 144 n. 37
Binder, B. 150 n. 53
binding, and book destruction 42–4
bishop, marriage to his church 16, 87,
      138–9
Blair, J. 35 nn. 61–2, 36 n. 64
blessings, at weddings ch. 3 (b) *passim*,
      200
Blickling Homilies 34
Böhringer, L. 85–6 nn. 41–2
Bonaventure 39, 118 n. 124
Boniface, St 25
    homilies attributed to 28
'book massacre' 42–4
Book of Two Principles 66
books:
    borrowing of 44, 47–8
    cost of 55–7

history of the book ch. 1 (c) *passim*
    production by friar scribes 53–7
    sale of by friars 49
    unattached to libraries 46–8
    utilitarian attitude to 41
    see also manuscript books; printed
      books; small manuscripts
Borgolte, M. 15, 92 n. 63
Borst, A. 66 n. 165
Bouchard, C. B. 92 n. 66, 94 n. 72
'Bouhot–Folliet' sermon collection 28
Boyle, L. E. 196 n. 69
Brandl, L. 12, 170 n. 6
Brautmystik 5, 6
Brescia, bishop of 173–4
bridegroom, qualities of 63
Brooke, C. N. L. 14, 90 n. 57, 91 n.
      61, 93 n. 69, 95–6, 126–7 n. 144,
      175 n. 22, 181 n. 38, 184 n. 46,
      201
Brown, Peter 78
Bruguière, M.-B. 104 n. 97
Brundage, J. 13, 118 n. 124, 126 n.
      142, 131 n. 1, 183, 197 n. 71
Bruno of Segni 37
'Büchersterben' 43
Burgos 187
Burk, Kathy 125 n. 139
Bynum, Caroline Walker 11 n. 36

Caesarius of Arles 23–4
Cana, marriage feast of ch. 1 *passim*
canon law 10, chs. 2–4 *passim*
    German Protestant scholars and
      11–12
canon-law manuscripts, lack of impro-
      visation in 54
Canticle of Canticles: *see* Song of
      Songs
Capetian dynasty, marriage policy of
      96
Carmelites 57
Carolingian period 22, 25–33, 72, 73,
      82–8
    see also Hincmar of Reims
Cartlidge, N. 13, 181 n. 36
casuistry, as index of symbolism's
      force 140–1
'Catéchèses celtiques' 27
Cathars 21, 65–7, 226
Catherine Gomez 187, Document **4. 8**
causation 74, 88
    'neutralizing' causation 74

reciprocity of substructure and
  superstructure 205–7
time lag in 129
celibacy of the clergy 88–91, 129
Charlemagne 82, 83
Charles Martel 80
chastity, marital, according to Jean
  Halgrin Document **1. 9. 3**
Chaucer 167
childlessness:
  and indissolubility 76
  as affliction 63, Document **1. 12. 7**
child psychology, in the Supplement
  to the *Summa theologica* 106 n.
  102
China, classical, marriage in 75
chivalry 63
Chrétien de Troyes 63, 99
Christ, represented by the wife 252
Christina of Markyate 181–2
Christmas, meaning of 149–50
Chrysostom, John, homilies on John
  241 n. 18
Cistercian libraries 41, 46
Clanchy, M. T. 98 nn. 81–2, 185 n. 48
clandestine marriages 65 n. 164, 68,
  105
Clarke, Peter 165 n. 89
Clayton, M. 34 n. 55
clergy, and celibacy 74, 88–91, 204–5
  minor orders 133 and ch. 3 (c)
    passim, 200
  marriage of clerics in major orders
    invalid (from 1139) 140
  marriage without sex 133, 178
  see also celibacy of the clergy; minor
    orders, clerics in
Cligès, of Chrétien de Troyes 99
Clm. 12612: 29
coercion, marriage voided by 124–9
Collins, A. J. 152–6 notes *passim*,
  259–62 notes *passim*
Colonna, Agnes 180, Document **4. 4**
Colonna, Stefano da 180, 182, 277–8
'commensurable household units' 78
Common Law, English, and 'bigamy'
  162–3
Compiègne, Council of (757) 83
Conceptionists 186
Congregation of the Council [of
  Trent] 191–2
consanguinity 14, 92–3
  see also forbidden degrees

consent to marriage, free 75, 124–9
Constance of Padilla 186–7, Document **4. 7**
consummation and indissolubility
  59–60, ch. 4 *passim*
consummation of marriage 58, 60, 61,
  86, 97, 111, ch. 4 *passim*, 201, 205
  and decretal *Debitum* 136, 198
  and John XXII 155 n. 66
Contreni, J. 30
Council of Lyons, Second (1274)
  159–64
councils 79, 82
courts, ecclesiastical 73, 74, 94–5,
  107–16, 123–4, 127–8
  and clerical privilege ch. 3 (c) *pas-
    sim*
  fallibility of 190
criminous clercs ch. 3 (c) *passim*
Crouzel, H. 77 n. 7
custom Document **3. 8. 7**

Dante 197
Daudet, P. 92 nn. 64–5, 93 n. 68, 94
  n. 74, 96 n. 77
David, P. 28
Davidsohn, R. 103 n. 97
Davies, W. 35
Dean, T. 115 n. 117
Decretals of Gregory IX 107, 143–
  4 nn. 34–5, 156, 164, 173–4,
  Documents **2. 1–2, 3. 2–3, 4. 1**,
  source references beginning 'X.'
  passim
de Jong, Mayke 92–3 n. 67
Delcorno, Carlo 226 n. 1
Denmark 102
Denzler, G. 90 nn. 56 & 58
Desiderius 82
desponsata, meaning of 174 n. 19
Destrez, Jean 50–52
Devil, 'marriage' to 58
Dionysius Exiguus, 141, 151, 152
Dionysus (Greek god) 4
dispensations:
  and 'bigamy' 139–40
  to dissolve unconsummated mar-
    riage 192–5, 204
distinction collections 39
divorce, 14, 84, 88, 92, 99, 191–4
  formularies and 81
  in modern sense 78
  in world religions 75

Dolezalek, G. 127 n. 147
Dominicans 20
  as preachers ch 1 (d) *passim*
  as scribes 53–7
Donahue, C. 12, 114–16, 126 nn. 141
  & 143, 127 n. 145
Douglas, M. 132, 205–6
Doyle, Ian 256
Duby, G. 1 n. 3, 14–15, 93 n. 69, 103
  n. 96
Duns Scotus 118 n. 124, 283–4
Dyer, C. 56 n. 126

Eberbach, Cistercian monastery of 219
ecclesiastical courts: *see* courts
economic infrastructure, weak in
  Carolingian period 73
economics and monogamy 75
Edward I of England 162
Edward II of England 163
Egbert, Archbishop of York 25, 35
Eliduc 96, 99
Eligius, homilies attributed to 28
Elizabeth de Lezano 191–2
Elliott, D. 15
Emery, Kent 54, 116
endogamy 14
ends–means calculation 132, 192–5
enforcement of indissolubility 121–2
England, marriage ritual in 155 and
  ch. 3 (b) *passim*, 204
  cases of delayed consummation
    from 183–5
Ephesians 5: 32: 176, 194
Erec and Eneide, of Chrétien de
  Troyes 99
Esmein, A. 131 n. 2, 142, 144 nn.
  38–9, 145 nn. 40–1, 148 n. 45
Esther 6, 60–1
  as Church 61
Étaix, R. 29
Eucharist 60, 145
Eugenius II, Pope 84
Eugenius IV, Pope 195
excommunication for deserting spouse
  74, 122
exempla 39
ex officio prosecutions in ecclesiastical
  courts 114, 116
exogamy 14

fallibility of the Church, according to
  a canonist 252

False Decretals 87–8, 129
fasting, homily on 29
Fedele, P. 131 n. 1
Fink, K. A. 195–6, 277
Florence, intellectual milieu 226, 232
Florus of Lyons 29
Folliet: *see* 'Bouhot–Folliet' sermon
  collection
forbidden degrees 14, 92–4, 104–16,
  175, 182
  pope's power to dispense 197–8
forged bull 148 n. 46, 155
forms of life 88, 91
formularies 81, 122 n. 132, 185–6
  and divorce, 81
Fouracre, Paul 80 n. 19
Fourth Lateran Council 14, 65, 104–8
  commentary on by Johannes Teu-
    tonicus 247
France:
  bulls to kings of 158–9, Documents
    3. 5–7
  *c.*1200, power of 102
Franciscans, 20
  as preachers ch. 1 (c) and (d) *passim*
  as scribes 53–7
Franciscus Sola 166
friars 20
  'honorary', educated secular clergy
    as 49
  as preachers ch. 1 (d) *passim*
  as scribes ch. 1 (c) *passim*
Fuhrmann, H. 87 n. 49
Fulbert of Chartres 96

Gabel, L. C. 162–3 nn. 82–3
García de Vargas 191–2
Gaudemet, J. 12, 16–17 n. 69, 81 n.
  24, 82 n. 27, 83–7 notes *passim*,
  102 n. 93, 104 n. 98, 176–9
Gaunt, S. 89–90 n. 54
Gautier d'Arras 96–8, 99
Geertz, C. 17, 149
gender 10–11 n. 36, 89–90, 201–2,
  204–5, 251–2
Génestal, R. 163–4, 168–9
Gérard de Mailly ch. 1 (d) *passim*, 171
Gervase of Mont Saint-Éloi 49
gifts, books as 53
Gillingham, J. 93 n. 69, 170
Goethe 181
Goffredus of Trani 144–5
Gold, P. S. 172 n. 12

Gomer 59
Goody, J. 12
gopis 4–5
Grand coutumier 169 n. 3
Gratian 93, 125–6, 142–4, 176, 179, 202, 252
Greece, classical, marriage symbolism in 4
Gregorian Reform 88, 90–1
Gregory II, Pope 84
Gregory the Great 22, 30, 66–7
Gregory VII, Pope 75, 90, 134
Gregory IX 120
  see also Decretals of Gregory IX
Guglielmo Cassinese 115 n. 116
Guibert de Tournai ch. 1 (d) *passim*, 171
Guido Faba 42
Guillelmus Redonensis 257 n. 9
Gullick, M. 55 n. 121, 56 n. 125

Haistulf of Metz 28
Hallam, E. 56 n. 124, 164 n. 87
Haymo of Auxerre 20–1, 25–6, 67
heaven, 'marriage' of soul to God located in 63–4
Hebrew names, interpretation of 59
Heiric of Auxerre 25–6
Helmholz, R. H. 12, 105 n. 101, 112, 114
Héloïse 98–9
Henricus de Bartholomaeis: *see* Hostiensis
Henry III of England 182–3
Henry of Susa: *see* Hostiensis
Herde, P. 122 n. 130, 185–6 nn. 50–3
Hereford Cathedral, canons at 91
Hereford rite 153 n. 62
Herlihy, D. 78, 182 n. 39
Hildebrand: *see* Gregory VII, Pope
Hildegard, and Charlemagne 82
Himiltrud, and Charlemagne 82
Hincmar of Reims, 85–7, 178–9, 195, 200–1, 202
Hindu marriage 142
  and indissolubility 7, 89, 170
  and marriage symbolism 3, 4–8, 200
  and polygamy/polygyny 5–6, 88–9, 170
history, six ages of 32, 33
holy orders, and non-consummation 188–9
homiliaries 20–37 *passim*, Documents

1. 1–3
homilies transmitted in vernacular 33–4
'honorary friars', educated secular clergy as 49
Honorius III, Pope 164
Hosea 59
Hostiensis 74, 107–12, 148 n. 46, 183, 197–9, 205, Documents 2. 1–2, 4. 1
  and Tree of Bigamy 137–9, 203
Hughes, D. O. 127 n. 147
Huguccio 252
Hugues de Saint-Cher 60 n. 142, 67 n. 170, 68 n. 175, 69 n. 180
humanism 63
  Christian Document 1. 12. 5
Humphreys, K. W. 44, 46 n. 90, 47–8

ideal type, as explanation 91–5
Ille et Galeron 96–8, 99
ill health, 63 Document 1. 12. 7
Imbert, cleric 168
Imkamp, W. 100 n. 87, 101 n. 89
impotence 175, 189–94
incarnation as marriage 59, Document 1. 2. 2
indissolubility 14, 73, 59–61, ch. 2 *passim*, 176, 199
individuals, influence of on social history 74
Ingeborg of Denmark 102–4, 171
Ingram, M. 112–13
initiation of marriage 58, 60, 61
initiation–ratification–consummation 58, 61, 171
Innocent II, Pope 184 n. 46
Innocent III, Pope 73, 74, 75, 85, 91–2, 203, 205
  advice on sex and marriage to Philip Augustus 170
  analytical abilities of 190
  and a case from Auxerre 189–91
  changes law to make annulments hard to get 104–8 119, 121
  decretal *Debitum* 136–7, 155, 156, 161–2, 168, 198
  influenced by marriage symbolism 99–102
  refuses annulments to rulers 101–4, 171
Innocent IV, Pope 160–2, 203 Documents 3. 2–3

instrumental rationality 132, 192–5
intellectual property 40
Islam, marriage in 75, 89
Israel, people of, as bride of God 7–8, 75, 200

Jacques de Lausanne 42
Jean d'Essômes 49
Jean de la Rochelle 171
Jean Halgrin ch. 1 (d) *passim*, Document **1. 9**
Jenks, Susanne 265 n. 1
jesters (*hystriones*), at marriage celebrations Document **1. 9. 4**
Jewish people: *see* Israel
Joan of Ponthieu 182–3
Johannes de Burgo 117–18, 148 n. 46, 156–7, 172, 175, Documents **3. 9, 4. 6**
Johannes de Deo 139–40, Document **3. 1**
Johannes Teutonicus 247
John, King of England 102
John XXII, Pope 148 n. 46, 155 n. 66, 180–1, 188, Document **4. 4**
John Chrysostom, St 62 n. 149
homilies on John 241 n. 18
John the Evangelist, marriage of 11 n. 36, 58 n. 130, 189 n. 54
John of Naples 188
John of Worcester 163
Joseph, marriage to the Virgin Mary 171–3, 175, Document **4. 3**
Joyce, G. H. 12, 83, 175 n. 21, 195, 197 nn. 70 & 72
Juan Sams (?) 187, Document **4. 8**
Judaism, marriage in 75, 89
judges delegate, papal 185–7
Judocus, St, sermon on 29
Jussen, B. 131 n. 1

Kay, R. 101 n. 91
Kelly, W. 83–4 n. 35, 84 n. 39
Ker, N. 44–5
knight, image of 63
Knowles, D. 57 n. 129
Konrad Holtnicker ch. 1 (d) *passim*, Document **1. 10**
Koran 89 n. 53
Kottje, R. 85 n. 41
Krishna 3, 4, 5
Kuhrt, Amelie 3–4 n. 12
Kuiters, R. 76–7

Kuttner, S. 16 n. 69, 131 n. 2, 133 n. 7, 144 n. 36

Lakshmi 3
Langton, Stephen 176
Lantperhtus of St Michael 30
Laon, School of 30
Lateran IV: see Fourth Lateran Council
Latin, parish priests' knowledge of 22, 26, 34–6, 72
law as social force chs. 2–4 *passim*
Le Bras, G. 12, 118 n. 124
Leclercq, Jean 12–13, 15, 26
legal separation of spouses 74–5, 123–4
Legifer, sermon collection called 50, 51
Le Jan, R. 80 n. 20, 81 n. 22
Leo I, Pope 177–9, 194
Lerner, Robert 39 n. 72, 41 n. 78, 52 n. 109, 55 n. 119, 57 n. 127
Le Roi Ladurie 66 n. 165
Le Saulchoir 51
Leyser, H. 80 n. 16
libri inutiles 42–6
logic, formal 226
Lombardi, D. 114, 175 n. 23
London, Dominican and Franciscan convents 45
loss rate: see manuscript books
Lothar II, king of the Middle Kingdom 82, 85
Louis V of France 92
Louis IX of France 158
Louis the Pious 82
Louis the Stammerer 83
love:
    transforms lover into loved one Document **1. 12. 3**
    see also marriage, love and
Lucius III, Pope 142
Ludwig of Bavaria 180, 277–8
Lupus of Ferrières 29
Luscombe, D. 98 n. 83
Lutterbach, H. 13, 92–3 n. 67

Maccarrone, M. 101 n. 88
McNamara, J. A. 79 nn. 11 & 15, 80, 82 n. 25
Maitland, F. W. 162–3 n. 82
'Makulierung' 42–4, 46
manuscript books, loss rate of 20, ch.

1 (c) *passim*
see also small manuscripts
Marculf, formulary of 81
Maria de Montpellier 101
Marie de France 96, 99
marital affection 122, 125, 174
marriage:
  Aristotle and 71–2
  Cathar view of 65–6
  church wedding not always required
    by Church 65, 105, 150
  controlled by lord 1, 126
  to create family alliances 1, 2
  of Christ and Church *passim*
  of Christ and human nature 59
  and Christ's passion 9, 59
  of Christ and soul *passim*
  consent enough for sacramentality
    117–19
  free consent to, 1–2, 75, 124–9
  goodness of 21, 64–72
  goodness of sex in 72, 146, 169–70
  and grace 70–1
  heretics condemn 21
  layers of meaning in sacrament of 8
  love and 2, 9, 69, 127; *see also*
    marital affection
  marriage debt 21
  'marriage' to the Devil 58
  married woman can be better than
    proud virgin 31
  medieval model unique in world
    history 2
  preaching and sacralization of 65,
    200
  remarriage legitimate 142
  second marriages ch. 3 (b) *passim*
  sex before 31, 68
  'spiritual marriage', meaning of
    phrase 15
  symbolic marriages 16–17
  topoi about, 68–70
  see also clandestine marriages
marriage feast of Cana ch. 1 *passim*
Martin V, Pope 195–7, 204
Mary the Virgin, marriage to Joseph
  171–3, 175, Document **4. 3**
mass communication ch. 1 *passim*, 200
  effects, 19, 39, 58
Matthew, Book of:
  19: 5: 176
  19: 6: 194
meaning: *see* social meaning

Mechtild of Magdeburg 5
Mercier, P., homilies edited by 22, 28
Merton College, books lost 44
Mesopotamia, marriage symbolism in
  3
metaphor 17
Mikat, Paul 92–3 n. 67
Minaksi 3 n. 9
minor orders, clerics in 133
minster system 35
missionaries, English, to the Continent
  25
model sermons 37–8 and ch. 1 *passim*
Modena 183
Molin, J.-B. 150 n. 53, 155 n. 68, 259
  n. 30
monastic libraries 46
'Mondsee Homiliary' 30
monogamy 14
  see also polygyny and polygamy
Morin, D. G. 29
'mother churches' 35
MS Cambridge, Trinity College 347:
  347–8
MS Cracow, Capitular Library 43: 28
MS Laon, Bibliothèque Municipale
  265: 30
MS London, BL Royal 4. D. iv: 45 n.
  93
MS Montpellier H308: 29
MS Oxford, Bodleian Library, Bodl.
  429: 45
MS Oxford, Bodleian Library,
  Bodleian Lat. bib. d. 9: 45
MS Oxford, Bodleian Library, Douce
  239: 45
MS Oxford, Merton College 132: 45
MS Paris, BN lat. 16499: 49
MS Vatican Library Reg. Lat. 49: 27
MS Verdun 64: 29
MS Wolfenbüttel 4096: 30–1 n. 50
Mulchahey, M. 53 n. 112
Müller, M. 12, 69 n. 176, 170 n. 5
Munich 195–6
Mutembe, P. 150 n. 53, 155 n. 68, 259
  n. 30
Mynors, R. A. B. 44
mysticism, bridal 4–5

narrative history, the book's argument
  rearranged as 202–4
nature and marriage 71–2
Neddermeyer, U. 41 n. 78, 52 n. 110

Nelson, J. L. 82 n. 27, 83 n. 28, 85 n. 41, 86 n. 45
Neocaesarea, Council of 141, 151, 152
'Newberry Library Homiliary' 28
Newman, B. 5 n. 18, 10 n. 36
newspapers, impact of on opinion 39
Nice, diocese of, annulments in 109
Nicholas I, Pope 85
nobility 63
 and indissolubility 14 n. 65
 of man Document **1. 12. 5**
Noble, T. F. X. 84 nn. 37-8 & 40
Nold, Patrick 180 n. 35, 183 n. 45, 189 n. 54, 232 n. 3
Noonan, J. T. 125–6, 127, 128
norms and social behaviour 75
Nuptiae factae sunt sermons, ch. 1 *passim*
nuptial blessing 118, ch. 3 (b) *passim*

Oliver Sutton, bishop of Lincoln 122
oral events 52, 61
Orange, bishop of, scandalous behaviour of 120–1
Order of the Holy Trinity 187, Document **4. 8**
Origen 8
originality in preaching 40, 49, 62
original sin 69
Osee 59
Oxford Medieval Texts 14

Pacaut, M. 16
Padua, Franciscan Library at 46
Palmer, N. F. 219 n. 2
Pantin, W. A. 156 n. 69, 175 n. 24
papacy, compliant attitude towards kings 160
papal registers, evidence of 120–1, 127–8, Document **4. 4**
Paradise:
 marriage instituted in 68, 69 n. 176
 pleasure of sex in 170
parchment, cost of 55–6
Paris, Council of (829) 83
parish priests, knowledge of Latin 22, 26, 34–6, 72
parish system 20, 35
Parvati 3, 6,
Parzifal, of Wolfram von Eschenbach 99
Passion, Christ's, and marriage 9
pastedowns 42–6

Patareni (i.e. Cathars) 226, Document **1. 11. 11**
patriarchal societies, and indissolubility of marriage 88–9
Patrologia Latina, contains few sermons on text *Nuptiae factae sunt* 36–7
Paul, St 31
Payer, J. 170 n. 6
peasant girl, social condition of 62
pecia transmission 50–2, 54, 243, 271
Pedersen, F. 103 n. 95, 104 n. 97, 113
Pedro Martorel 166
Pegg, M. G. 65 n. 163
Penitentiary: see next entry
Penitenzieria Apostolica 165–7, 186–7, 204, Documents **3. 11–12, 4. 7–8**
Pennington, K. 107 n. 103, 242–4, 270–1
perfection, triple in character Document **1. 12. 2**
Perrin, cleric 168–9
Persson, I. 173 n. 16
Peter I of Aragon 101
Peter the Chanter 94, 119
Peter Damian 119, 134–5
Peter Lombard 8–9 n. 29, 99–100, 142–6, 172–3, 202
Peter of Poitiers 100
Peters, Christine 118–19 n. 124
Pfaff, V. 93 n. 71
Philip III of France 159
Philip Augustus, king of France 85, 102–4, 170, 171
Pierre de Reims 42, 51 n. 108, ch. 1 (d) *passim*
Pierre de Saint-Benoît ch. 1 (d) *passim*, 171
Pierre de Tarentaise 8–9 n. 29, 32
Pignatelli, Jacob 191–5
pilgrimage, life as 63, Document **1. 12. 5**
Pippin, first Carolingian king 83
Pippin of Herstal 80
'plagiarism' 40, 49
Plectrudis, wife of Pippin of Herstal 80
pocket books for preachers 38
polygyny and polygamy 5, 6, 15, 75, 78, 88–9, 91, 92
power, absolute and ordained 197–8
Powicke, Sir Maurice 176
Powitz, G. 42–4

preaching, popular ch. 1 *passim*
'pre-contract' cases 74, 115 n. 117,
  116–20
priests:
  knowledge of Latin 22, 26, 34–6
  as scribes 53
printed books, survival rate of 52
'print revolution', relativized 41, ch. 1
  (c) *passim*
Prisoner's Dilemma 95
privilegium fori: see benefit of clergy
proof in annulment cases 105–12
proxy marriages 182–3
Pseudo-Isidorian Decretals: *see* False
  Decretals
Pupilla oculi: see Johannes de Burgo

quaterni 37, 41, 48–9, 50–2, 57
quires: *see preceding entry*

Radha 3, 4, 5
Rama 3
ratification of marriage 58, 60, 61, 180
rational-choice theory 95–6
rationality 95–6
Raymund Barellus 109–10, 119
reason, destroyed by sin Document **1.**
  12. 13
reception, reconstruction of 62–3
recycling of manuscripts 42–4, 46
Remigius of Auxerre 25 n. 18
Reynolds, R. E. 28
Reynolds, R. L. 77–8, 79, 86 n. 45
Rhabanus Maurus 28
Ricardus de Mediavilla 171–3, Docu-
  ments **4. 2–3**
Rincón, T. 9 n. 32, 10, 100, 102 n. 92,
  270
Ritzer, K. 141 n. 19, 150 n. 53
Robb, Fiona 100 n. 86
Rochester Priory 249
Roger Bacon 48–9
Röhrkasten, J. 45 n. 88, 265
Roman synod of 826: 84–5
Rome, classical, marriage in 75
Rouse, R. H. and M. A. 44, 45
royal annulments 121 n. 129
  see also Innocent III
Rozelin, and his partner Amandola 90
rulers, sexual power of 80, 82, 88
Rusticus, Bishop 177

sacrament 8

sacramentality:
  of marriage without a wedding
  117–19
  of second marriages 146–8
St Alexis, legend of 181
St Paul's Cathedral, canons at 91
'Saint Père de Chartres' homiliary 28
saints' lives, as preaching aids 39
Salerno, bishop of 173–4
Salonen, K. 113 n. 112, 165 nn. 88–9
salvation history 61
Salzburg, ninth-century homily composed for church of Documents **1.**
  1–2
Sanmark, Alexandra 104 n. 97
Sarum manual 118 n. 124, 152–5
Schadt, H. 131 n. 2, 137–9
Schmugge, L. 113 n. 112, 165 nn.
  88–9
Schnell, R. 13
Schneyer, J. B. 38
scholastic method, rare in thirteenth-
  century preaching 226
scribal variation 41 n. 78, Documents
  1. 4–8
scribes, friars as 53–8
  commercial 53
script, German features 219
script, indications of date 219, 227,
  242–3
script, Italian features 226–7, 242–3,
  271
scriptoria, monastic 53
second marriages ch. 3 (b) *passim*
secular clergy, educated, as 'honorary
  friars' 49
Segor 66–7
senses 31, Documents **1. 1. 2–4, 1. 10.**
  10
separation, legal 123–4
sermo de conscientia 28
Servasanto da Faenza 60 n. 142, 69–
  70, 71–2, Document **1. 11**
servile status 62
sex: *see* marriage
Sharpe, R. 262, 282
Sheehan, M. M. 112, 114
Sinibaldo dei Fieschi: *see* Innocent IV
Sita 3
Siva 3, 6
slavery 78, 177–8
  wrong to look lustfully at *servus* or
  ancilla Document **1. 1. 3**

small manuscripts, disproportionately
  low survival rate of 52
Smaragdus of St Mihiel 27
Smetana, C. L. 26
social meaning 75, 148–50, 154, 157,
  169
Sodom 67
Song of Songs 3
soul, as bride 5–6
Southern, R. W. 38, 57 n. 128
Spain, clerical status in 167
Spigurnel, Henry 266
Stafford, P. 79 n. 13, 80 n. 17, 82 n.
  25, 83 nn. 28 & 31, 92 n. 64
stationers, university: *see pecia* trans-
  mission
Statute on Bigamists 162–3
Stephen II, Pope 84
Stephen Langton 176
Stephen of Auvergne 86, 178–9
Stevenson, K. 150 n. 53, 153 n. 62
Stone, Lawrence 1
subdeacons 133, 157, 178
substructure, 205–6
Summa theologica, Supplement to 106,
  129
Sundareśvara, 3 n. 9
superstructure 205–6
Sutton, Oliver, bishop of Lincoln 122
symbolism, literal foundation of 64–5

Tarentaise, Pierre de 8–9 n. 29
teleological thinking 71
Tenbrock, R. H. 103–4 n. 97
Theodore of Tarsus 79, 83
Theutberga, wife of Lothar II 85
Thomas Aquinas, St: *see* Aquinas
Thomas Becket 158
threes, and perfection Document 1.
  12. 2
timing, explanation of 204–5
tithes, homily on 29
tonsure 164
topoi about marriage 68–70
Toxé, P. 169 n. 4
Tree of Bigamy 137–9
Trent, Council of 191

universe, structured 63, Document 1.
  12. 5
university stationers: *see pecia* transmission
Urban III, Pope 144–5, 154

urbanization 201

vade-mecum books 38
value rationality 132
Vanderbilt heiress 125
Van der Walt, Andries 24
Vannes, Council of (465) 79
variants, textual, implications of 53–5
Vashti, 6, 61
  as synagogue 61
vernacular 33–4, 38
  vernacular romances and marriage
    96–7, 99
violence, husband's against wife 124,
  193
virginity 31
  loss of 168
virgins, wise and foolish Document 1.
  1
Vishnu 3
Vleeschouwers-Van Melkebeek, M.
  116 n. 119
Vodola, E. 159 n. 77
Volfing, A. 11. n. 36, 58 n. 130
von Riezler, S. 277
von Schulte, J. F. 161 n. 79, 162 n. 81

Waldensian movement 181
Wallace-Hadrill, J. M. 80, 83 n. 31
Weber, I. 125 n. 138
Weber, Max 4–5 n. 16, 132, 149, 167,
  170 n. 8, 192–3
wedding ritual ch.3 (b) *passim*
Weigand, R. 113, 115 n. 117
Wemple, S. F. 79 nn. 11 & 13, 80, 82
  nn. 25–6
Wertrationalität 132, 194–5
Wickham, Chris 115 n. 116
wife, represents Christ 252
Wife of Bath, Chaucer's 167
William of Pagula 117, 156, 196–7,
  Document 4. 5
Wilmart, A. 27
Winch, P. 149
Winroth, A. 93 n. 70
Wolfram von Eschenbach, 99
world, unsatisfactoriness of 63–4
writs, in England 185 n. 49

'X.': *see* Decretals of Gregory IX
Xerxes 60 n. 146

York rite 153 n. 62

Yvain, of Chrétien de Troyes 99

Zachary, Pope 83

Zarri, G. 17
Zweckrationalität 132, 192–5